NINE
SCORPIONS
IN A BOTTLE

NINE SCORPIONS IN A BOTTLE

GREAT JUDGES AND CASES OF THE SUPREME COURT

MAX LERNER

Edited by Richard Cummings

ARCADE PUBLISHING • NEW YORK

FIRST EDITION

Library of Congress Cataloging-in-Publication Data
Lerner, Max, 1902–1992
    Nine scorpions in a bottle: great judges and cases of the Supreme Court / by Max Lerner ; introduction by Richard Cummings. — 1st ed.
      p.   cm.
    ISBN 1-55970-168-4
    1. United States. Supreme Court.　2. Judges — United States.　3. Judicial review — United States.　I. Title.
    KF8742.L47　1994
    347.73'26 — dc20
    [347.30735]　　　　　　　　　　　　　　　　　　　　　　　　　　93-24463

Published in the United States by Arcade Publishing, Inc., New York
Distributed by Little, Brown and Company

10 9 8 7 6 5 4 3 2 1

BP

Designed by GDS / Jeffrey L. Ward

PRINTED IN THE UNITED STATES OF AMERICA

To the newest generation of constitutional students

And drunk delight of battle with my peers,
Far on the ringing plains of windy Troy.

ALFRED, LORD TENNYSON, *Ulysses*

CONTENTS

FOREWORD

I OFFER THIS BOOK AS A COLLECTION OF MY WRITINGS ON A THEME
that has run through almost six decades of my commentaries on
America: the United States Supreme Court in its role as interpreter of
the Constitution. It focuses on the battles that have raged over and
among the Court's formative members, the opinions they wrote, the
constitutional doctrines they employed and the guiding philosophy and
universe of values behind those doctrines, and the cultural and political context in which justice, doctrines, and values are embedded.

Every book, like every judicial opinion, is a record of a journey,
however well hidden. As a Supreme Court watcher through most of
my writing years, I have tried to get at the constitutional journey
implicit in its decisions. When the justices differed, it was because
the paths of their journeys diverged: they had started from different
sources and were led to different interpretations. From the clash of
my judicial philosophy with theirs, I mapped out a constitutional
journey of my own.

What has concerned me as much as the analysis of a decision is
the path each justice took to arrive at it. Behind every decision is a
narrative, giving it at once content and context, and within every
narrative is a dialectical tension between deep-rooted conflict and the
need for resolution. Hence my persistent use of the metaphors of
struggle and war, of confrontation and crisis.

I have always experienced sheer joy in the doctrinal struggles in
which I have been involved. I am drawn to power, but know that the
ideas behind power struggles count for more, since they reach to the
foundations of the national experience. Presidents come and go,

ideologies change, and today's headlines are tomorrow's footnotes. But Oliver Wendell Holmes's dissent in the *Abrams* free speech case, and the constitutional journey that led to the "clear and present danger" doctrine, touch the very foundations of our civilization. So does Chief Justice Earl Warren's opinion for a unanimous Court in *Brown v. Board of Education.*

I care deeply about how judges interpret the Constitution, technically and professionally. But I care even more about the effect that interpretation has on America, and whether it has helped hold it together or led to its divisions. For me, that is the enduring question.

My own strong preference is to stay clear of doctrinal absolutism, to give those who most count — the judges themselves — room to grow. Judicial creativity defies doctrines and formulas. The proof of a judgment rests on the actual judging — on the quality of the opinions a judge writes and whatever in his life prepared him for them.

My vision is of a Court of independent thinkers clashing with each other and wrestling with their great predecessors, reaching decisions that engage deeply whatever problems of interpretation they touch. I should prefer such a Court even to a benchful of earnest, hardworking but undistinguished justices (as was the case during the later Warren years) who operated by a philosophy I happened to share. Depth of insight counts for more than the correctness of the formulas they use.

While I have always accepted *judicial review* (the power of the Court to declare an act of government unconstitutional) as being integral to our system, I still believe that judicial *supremacy* as an absolute is not healthy, whether asserted by a "conservative" or "liberal" political culture. Judges must set limits on translating their own social vision into constitutional imperatives. Their impact on the future is greatest when they refrain from playing God with their power.

To a considerable extent the American people have turned the Constitution as covenant (with the justices as its keepers) into the stuff of myth. A crisis arises when this myth, which holds not only that America is the unique guarantor of equal justice under the text of the law but also that it can resolve its grand social conflicts by offering new perspectives on an old covenant, is put into question. This crisis is our occasion to reexamine the very foundations of our national identity.

M.L.

ACKNOWLEDGMENTS

I OWE A DEBT TO THE FRIENDSHIP AND INSIGHTS OF TWO JUSTICES, Felix Frankfurter and Hugo L. Black, whose work and conversations with me have had a considerable impact on my own thinking. Among constitutional scholars, I salute the memory of two greats — Walton H. Hamilton of the Brookings Graduate School and Yale Law School, and Thomas Reed Powell of Harvard Law School. Hamilton tried to teach me the breadth of constitutional thinking, and Powell always warned me of the rigors it demanded. I also owe much to my friend of almost forty years and my colleague at Brandeis University, Leonard Levy, formerly of the Claremont Graduate School, who likes my early essays but has tried fruitlessly to deal with my current departures from the "true" path.

My deepest obligation is to Ronald K. L. Collins of George Washington University School of Law in Washington, D.C. This book was his idea to start with. He rounded up many of the essays, steered me in their selection, and made an unlikely editorial task seem finally possible. For the past decade and more he has given me a chance to argue out the latest Supreme Court appointment or decisions with him and to test my thinking against his and his generation's. He has kept the constitutional tree green for me.

I owe a great debt also to Richard Cummings of Pace University School of Law, for undertaking to compile this volume and for writing his introduction. His insights and understanding have contributed substantially to converting these disparate insights into a coherent whole.

Like everything I have written, this book owes more to my wife,

Edna Albers Lerner, than she will acknowledge, and to our continuing dialogue on ideas and values. I am, as always, grateful to my friend and assistant Evelyn Irsay for her skill in guiding the unwieldy vessel of these papers through the currents of successive editings.

EDITOR'S INTRODUCTION

AMONG THE NONLAWYERS WHO HAVE CONTRIBUTED TO SUPREME Court scholarship over the years, Max Lerner stands out for his work on the Court as a *cultural* phenomenon, especially on the intellectual and symbolic underpinnings of its authority. Lerner approached the Court from a double angle of vision. One was the Court's effort to impose a spurious *judicial supremacy* on the economy and polity, in the guise of authentic *judicial review*. The other was an exploration of the deep sources of Constitution worship that led to the deification of both Constitution and Court. He saw it as the very human quest for an unchanging principle of authority in a largely secular society in constant flux.

Lerner's intellectual journey, as part of an immigrant family, was not out of pattern. After studying literature at Yale, with a brief taste of law school for a year, he spent two years at the liberal Robert Brookings Graduate School, working largely on constitutional law under Walton H. Hamilton. He then spent six critical years as managing editor of an ambitious new venture, the *Encyclopedia of the Social Sciences*. This led to his first long *Yale Law Journal* article, in 1931, entitled "The Social Thought of Mr. Justice Brandeis," followed by his most dramatic breakthrough piece, and the earliest piece in this volume, "The Supreme Court and American Capitalism," which branded him in constitutional circles as a radical.

In 1933 Lerner began teaching, first at Sarah Lawrence College, and then briefly at Harvard. Hungering for a more activist life, he resigned in 1936 to become political editor of the *Nation*, turning it into a spearhead of constitutional reform. His first book, *It Is Later*

Than You Think, was a plea for a more tough-minded "democratic collectivism," with Franklin D. Roosevelt as its consummate progressive leader in a time of crisis.

From that point on, Lerner led a double life as scholar and journalist — a combination more unfamiliar to the American academics than to those in the British tradition, as exemplified by his close friend, Harold J. Laski. He taught at Williams College, Brandeis University (for a quarter-century), Notre Dame, and finally at the United States International University (in San Diego).

It was a heady, adventurous life, with its energies doubtless too widely diffused in a long-running syndicated column. But the scholarly achievement is solid, not only in his magisterial *America as a Civilization* (1957; updated edition 1987) but also in his two volumes of essays on "the history and uses of ideas," in his massive introduction to Tocqueville's *Democracy in America,* and in the collection here presented.

Behind it all is perhaps the "cultural patriotism" of the immigrant tradition, and with it Lerner's undying passion not for any particular form of liberalism or conservatism, but for democracy itself — and for what could keep it viable.

Lerner joined in the search for doctrinal approaches that might permit democratic reform of the economy. When the Court struck down several key elements of Roosevelt's New Deal program, Lerner's role became pivotal. His scholarship and energy propelled him into the constitutional battlefield. As journalist, scholar, and lecturer, Lerner became a leading light of the constitutional revolution. Small in stature physically, with his large head, penetrating eyes, and resonant, commanding voice, Lerner captured the imagination of a generation as an enfant terrible through his stinging attacks on the anti-Roosevelt Supreme Court.

But he could also write in a belles lettres style that elevated his law review articles to an art form. Following the repressive *Schechter Poultry* (295 U.S. 495 [1935]) and *Carter Coal* (298 U.S. 238, 56 S.Ct. 855, 80 L.Ed. 1160 [1936]) cases, Lerner wrote his classic essay for the *Yale Law Journal,* "Constitution and Court as Symbols." Describing the Supreme Court as a form of "divine right" in America, his condemnation of the Court is eloquent. "It has, to be sure, walked along the evolutionary path, but only as Orpheus once walked along the pathway out of Hell, with head turned backward."

Like those of his poetic ideal, Walt Whitman, Lerner's writings are affirming and uplifting. But behind the affirmation is also great wrath, and the wrath of Max Lerner reads like that of the Old Testament God of Noah's flood. He sees in American group politics today a perversion of the passion for democracy that inspired him during the New Deal and after.

Lerner's work emphasizes judicial restraint, in which judicial review is exercised only when absolutely necessary. It is the refusal to exercise judicial power that Lerner admires, just as he respects the willingness to exercise political power. Now perceived as essentially conservative, the doctrine of judicial restraint was fashioned by Louis Brandeis as a rationale for persuading the Court not to overturn progressive legislation, whether passed by the states or the Congress. Lerner is eager to give the new, authentic democratic forces a chance to assert themselves. He hopes that judicial restraint will prevail in the current Court, so that these forces can assert themselves in the legislative and executive branches, as they did during the New Deal. This will turn the attention of the body politic away from the Supreme Court and toward the political and cultural process, where it belongs. But he also knows that the intellectual culture has been splintered, and that its custodians are still far removed from the true culture of the people.

Reaching out across time, Lerner dedicates his book "to the newest generation of constitutional students." Never has a thinker whose writings span so long a stretch remained so young in outlook, retaining a sense of stubborn daring in so conformist a time.

Lerner asks only one thing of the newest generation — to be read without preconceptions, as if for the first time.

RICHARD CUMMINGS

PART I

SEARCHING FOR THE
FOUNDATIONS

PREFACE

THE METAPHORS IN THIS FIRST BATCH OF ESSAYS ARE UNRESERVEDLY warlike. With their high stakes and vivid sense of the enemy, the days of the New Deal moved swiftly upon us and brought with them constitutional as well as political struggles. The themes unifying these essays are the dominance of both capitalist and judicial power in American society, and the dynamic linkage that existed between them, with each feeding and reinforcing the other.

The first essay, "The Supreme Court and American Capitalism," and the three that followed it (all were written between 1932 and 1938) sounded a call to radical thought and action. Written at a time when both capitalism and judicial power were at risk in America, and when the viability of both was being debated, they explored an area few constitutional scholars had entered.

While I picked up tools of economic interpretation from Marx's writings on history, which were coming on strong in the liberal culture, I drew even more heavily from Thorstein Veblen, Charles Beard, Vernon Parrington, and Louis Boudin. Yet these were scattered sources that I put to use in my own brand of historical thinking and constitutional interpretation.

At law schools, graduate schools of history and government, and among the young lawyers who invaded Washington with FDR, including Thomas Corcoran, Abe Fortas, Philip Graham, and Edward Prichard, these essays were perceived as a challenge from the intellectual Left. I was determined from the start, however, to go beyond the provincial and reductionist Marxist canon. Some of my colleagues from the *Encyclopedia of the Social Sciences* and academia were doctrinaire Marxists, and I didn't like the narrowing and rigidifying results I saw. I wanted to describe an arc that included thinkers from every school, every discipline. My work as a young editor at the *Encyclopedia,* under Alvin S. Johnson, like my graduate work with Walton H. Hamilton, taught me the necessity of cross-disciplinary thinking. I packed into these early essays everything I had been meditating on since my Brookings years.

It was in these essays — on American constitutional history and analysis, on the nature of the judicial process, on economic and power structures, on the sway of ideas and of contemporary symbols and myths — that I sought to build a base for what a group of us came later to call the "independent Left." By the end of the 1930s, deeply disillusioned with the decadence of Western European ruling groups in appeasing Hitler and with the corruptions of Soviet power, we would need to move beyond what the traditional New Deal canon offered.

There was a tiny group of constitutional warriors in Washington and New York and at the law schools, and among them were the "legal realists," who took on the entrenched legal and judicial establishment. I was on the fringes of the group. First we engaged the conservative Court majority on their use of an activist judicial power to repress Bill of Rights freedoms during World War I and the postwar hysteria and to strike down liberal state legislation in the pre–New Deal 1920s and early 1930s. Once the Roosevelt administration, with its crisis legislative agenda for Congress, started work in earnest, we had new ammunition to use against that majority (the "lawless majority," I dubbed it) when it struck down the federal laws and agencies that were the lifeblood of the New Deal.

I was happy to have two emplacements from which to engage the enemy. One was the law journals, run by young militant student editors whom I knew at Yale, Harvard, Columbia, and the University of Pennsylvania. The other was my new post as political editor of the *Nation,* from 1936 to 1938.

My *Nation* commentaries on judicial supremacy and "divine right" brought some flutters to that citadel of laissez-faire liberalism, especially since my predecessor, Oswald Garrison Villard, had used his position to attack Franklin Roosevelt and all his works and ways. I preferred an interventionist rather than passive brand of liberalism, in domestic as well as foreign policy. My call for a new constitutional jurisprudence went naturally with a call for new policies toward labor, joblessness, welfare, securities control, and the entire panoply of the economy, polity, and society.

The ruling philosophy of the legal realist school, to which these essays were more or less closely related, was its rejection of legal formulism and its insistence that law could not be ripped out of the total context of the polity and society. The difference between this view and the conservative Court majority's brand of activist intervention (in the form of judicial supremacy over the constitutional roles of legislatures) was that it recognized that intervention in the Constitution should not be gone into lightly. The message we were sending the justices was to change their votes on New Deal legislation — or else!

We left the "or else" vague because we hadn't yet figured out what sanctions to propose in reforming the Court. But when FDR sprang his surprise "court-packing" plan, he presented his own liberal supporters (as well as the judges) with a weapon few of us liked. The *Nation* saw the plan as a blow to the independence of the judiciary — which it was, in fact, although not in form. In form it was coy, indirect, and irrelevant to the major issue, which was not the age of the judges but their arrogating for themselves a policy-making function that belongs with the polity as a whole.

While FDR's plan was to "pack" the Court, it never came to that, and I suspect he knew it wouldn't. His intent was probably to scare the Court and thus dislodge it from its policy-making position. I was one of the few commentators to support him in 1937, and I lost my *Nation* editorship as a consequence. Many critics of the Court majority lashed out at FDR's court-packing plan as an instrument of dictatorship. Looking back, I believe FDR was a shrewder strategist than they. Had the bill passed, it would have given him new judges; in failing — as it did — it scared the sitting majority into changing their decisions. He would have won either way. He was lucky the legislation failed, since the storm it raised was soon over; had it succeeded, the damage to the nation — and to his reputation — would have been lasting.

The grand result was that FDR, once he began to get Court vacancies, ended up with a Roosevelt court. But how would I, as a member of the emerging liberal constitutional culture, find a way of reconciling my attack on "divine right" with my strong intellectual and moral support of the new Roosevelt court majority?

I was thus forced into a deeper engagement with the complexities of judicial power and had to walk a perilous line between its abuses in judicial supremacy and its legitimate functions in judicial review, by which it mediates between fluid social change and the rigors of the Constitution. This meant looking beyond the immediate fate of the New Deal programs.

From 1937 to 1947 I channeled my energies into the struggles over collective security, World War II, and the war's atomic aftermath. Thereafter I sought to examine American society as a whole and to place constitutional law within the context of the entire national culture. The essay "Keepers of the Covenant in Mythic America," a product of this effort, is excerpted both from the original 1957 edition of my book, *America as a Civilization,* and from the revised thirtieth-anniversary edition (1987) and provides my reflections on the judicial power at the midpoint of my constitutional journey, as it were, and at its end. The final essay may be read as the continuing juristic reflections of a civilization watcher.

It has been a long journey. I began by battling against judicial supremacy, which seeks to govern social change instead of mediating between it and the legislative process, and ended much as I began. The difference lies in the Court majorities of which I have been critical. First they were on the Right, then on the Left. A guiding vision of constitutional governance has sustained me throughout.

1

The Supreme Court and American Capitalism

Sometime in 1932 I had a letter from the student editor of the Yale Law Journal, *Abe Fortas (later Supreme Court Justice Fortas), asking if I had an essay on hand to send him or would write one. I wrote one. This essay should be read in the context of the Great Depression and Franklin Roosevelt's election, and within the frame of the one that follows it, "Constitution and Court as Symbols." The "Capitalism" essay had greater relevance for the 1930s and 1940s. The "Symbols" essay, which seemed to be validated by the Roosevelt court-packing defeat in 1937, the year it appeared, still has relevance for the judicial confirmation crises of our time.*

1

The American state has developed two of its institutions to a degree never before attained — the capitalist form of business enterprise and the judicial power. At first sight the combination seems paradoxical, joining in a single pattern an exploitative type of economic behavior with the objectivity of the judicial process. But those who have studied the building of the American state know that the paradox lies only on the surface. It is not historical accident but a matter of cultural logic that a Field should grow where a Morgan does; and a Brandeis is less organic a product of capitalist society than a Debs. If the gulf between the first pair and the second is precipitous, it is nonetheless contrast and not contradiction. Between our business enterprise and our judicial power there is the unity of an aggressive and cohesive cultural pattern. They seem of the same fiber; they have, both of them, the same toughness, richness, extravagant growth; they hold out at once portent and promise.

Capitalist business enterprise, while it has reached its most consummate form in the United States, is generic to the whole Western world. But judicial power — or, more exactly, judicial supremacy — is a uniquely American institution.[1] It could arise only in a federal state that attempts, as ours does, to drive a wedge of constitutional uniformity between heterogeneous sectional and economic groupings. The core of judicial supremacy is, of course, the power of judicial review over legislative acts and administrative decisions. And the exercise of that power by the United States Supreme Court has made it not only "the world's most powerful court"[2] but also the focal point of our bitterest political and constitutional polemics.

At the heart of these polemics is the recognition that the real meaning of the Court is to be found in the political rather than the legal realm, and that its concern is more significantly with power politics than with judicial technology. The Court itself of course disclaims any relation to the province of government or to the formation of public policy; it pictures itself as going about quietly applying permanent canons of interpretation to the settlement of individual disputes. If there is any truth in this position, the Court's quietness must be regarded as that of the quiet spot in the eye of a hurricane. However serene it may be or may pretend to be, the Court is the focal point of a set of dynamic forces that play havoc with the landmarks of the American state and determine the power configuration of the day. Private law restricts itself to the settlement of disputes and the channeling of conduct in society; public law in a constitutional state operates to shift or stabilize the balance of social power.

There has been a tendency in some quarters to regard the Court's power as the result of an imperialistic expansion by which the justices have pushed their way to a "place in the sun." We still think in the shadow of Montesquieu and view the political process as an equation in government powers. The growth of the Court's power has, by this conception, taken place at the expense of the legislative and executive departments, and the American state has become the slave of a judicial oligarchy. The literature in which this enslavement is traced and expounded is voluminous, polemical, and, even when very able, somewhat dull. It is dull with the dullness of a thin and mechanical leitmotiv — the theory of usurpation, of the deliberate annexation by the Court of powers never intended for it. This theory is part of the general philosophy of political equilibrium, which, originating with the eighteenth-century philosophes, was reinforced by nineteenth-century physics. It holds that the safety of the individual can be assured only by maintaining a balance between the departments of the state. Whatever may have been the validity of such a philosophy in a preindustrial age, it has become archaic in a period when government is itself dwarfed by the new economic forces. It is as if generals in a besieged city were to quarrel over precedence while the enemy was thundering at the gates.

There was, let it be admitted, a period in which the problem of judicial usurpation was a lively issue. Readers of Beveridge's volumes on Marshall[3] are struck by the bitter political tone of the early years of the Court, beginning even with its decision in *Chisholm v. Georgia*.[4] Charge and countercharge, invective and recrimination, were staples, and in the din of party conflict, it was no wonder that the still small voice of judicial objectivity was often completely drowned. In such an atmosphere, usurpation had meaning and utility. The polity was in its formative stage, and there was little about the constitutional structure that was irrevocably settled. The Revolution had hewn out a new world, but, as we who have been contemporaries of another revolution can well understand, the task of giving that world content and precision of outline still remained. In the jockeying for political position and the general scrambling for advantage, every argument counted, and much of the political theory of the day can be best understood in terms of this orientation toward the distribution of power. But what counted even more than theory was the fait accompli. Every new governmental step was decisive for later power configurations — and might some day be used as precedent. And the battles of the giants, Marshall's with Jefferson and Jackson, were battles of men who knew how to use the fait accompli.

The Court has, then, from the very beginning, been part of the power structure of the state, acting as an interested arbiter of disputes between the branches of the government and between the states and the federal government, and with an increasingly magisterial air distributing the governmental powers. But to a great extent the significant social struggles of the first half-century of the new state were waged outside the Court. Each period has its characteristic clashes of interests and its characteristic battlegrounds where those clashes occur. In the preindustrial period the party formations measured with a rough adequacy the vital sectional, economic, and class differences in the country. The party battles of the period had some meaning, and accumulated stresses could find release through changes of party power. The function of the Supreme Court in this scheme lay more in establishing the lines of the polity than in resolving disputes that could not be resolved outside. But when party formations grew increasingly blurred and issues such as slavery and industrialism arose to cut across party lines, an attempt was made, notably in the Dred Scott case, to draw the Supreme Court into the struggle over social policy. The attempt was of course disastrous, for the slavery issue reached too deeply into the economic and emotional foundations of the life of the day to be resolved by a counting of heads of more or less partisan judges. It is significant that the most direct effect of the Dred Scott decision was the ascendancy of a new political party, which sought to settle the basic question of public policy at the polls. The Civil War taught us that there were issues too basic to be settled within the constitutional framework.

The Industrial Revolution changed the orientation and function of the Court, as it cut across every other aspect of American life. By the middle of the century the doctrine of judicial review, whatever may have been its precedents and whatever the legalities of its growth, had become an integral part of the American political system. But it did not dominate the system, nor had it acquired the compelling incidence on public policy that it has today. Before that could happen, there had to be a shift in the nature of the state so powerful that the characteristic clashes of interest would be taken out of the sphere of democratic control. In short, only through the building of an extra-democratic structure could the judiciary be given real power or the Supreme Court attain the towering command over public policy it has today.

That transformation was effected by the maturing of capitalism, with its strange combination of individualism as a pattern of belief and the corporation as a pattern of control. Business enterprise furnished the framework within which the Court was to operate, and the framework revolutionized the meaning and function of judicial power. That power had always, when exercised, had far-reaching effects on the process of our national life; even when in abeyance it had been a force to be reckoned with. By expounding and applying the written Constitution, the Court had always helped determine the shape and direction of the real constitution — the operative controls of our society. But the real constitution under capitalism became merely the modus operandi of business enterprise. Between those controls on the one hand, and, on the other, the ideals of the American experiment and the phrases in which the eighteenth century had clothed those ideals was an ever-widening gulf: it became the function of the Supreme Court to bridge that gulf. Capitalist enterprise generated in America, as it had everywhere, forces in government and in society hostile to capitalist expansion and bent on curbing it: it became the function of the Court to check those forces and to lay down the lines of economic orthodoxy. Capitalist enterprise requires legal certainty amid the flux of modern life, legal uniformity amid the heterogeneous conditions and opinions of a vast, sprawling country, the legal vesting of interests amid the swift changes of a technological society. The task of the Supreme Court was to provide them. The Court had, of course, other functions, and may be regarded from other angles. But if we seek a single and consistent rationale for the growth of judicial power in the past half-century, we must look for it in the dynamics of American business enterprise.

2

The steady growth of judicial power and the increasing evidence of its economic affiliations have made the Court one of the great American ogres, part of the demonology of liberal and radical thought. It has served, in fact, as something of a testing ground for political attitudes of every complexion. The Marxist, making the whole of politics merely an addendum to capitalism, sees the Court as the tool and capitalism as the primary force. The contemporary Jeffersonian, fearful of all centralizing power and zealous for the liberties of the common man, fears Wall Street and the Supreme Court alternately, uncertain as to which is the shadow and which the substance. His cousin the liberal, if he is of a constructive turn, counts on using the machinery of the Court to control in a statesmanlike fashion a developing capitalism, which it is futile to turn back; or, if he has lost faith in the efficacy of tinkering with governmental machinery and has become an ethical liberal, he refuses to regard either Big Business or the Supreme Court as important in themselves, but looks to the quality of the American experience that flows through them both. The technological liberal, who thinks in terms of blueprints and plans for the state, regards the Court as the greatest technical obstruction that his plans will encounter, and racks his brain for ingenious ways of avoiding the encounter.

The contemporary indictment of the Court, which furnishes the point of departure for all these shades of opinion, is, in the large, well known. It holds that the Court's decisions can be better explained by economic bias than by judicial objectivity, and that its trend has been to bolster the status quo. This indictment is itself of course far from objective. It is the expression of an attitude. And that attitude can be best studied in relation to its genesis in the Progressive movement, which ran its brief course between the turn of the twentieth century and the American entrance into the war. The Marxists might of course claim this approach derives from their own "materialist" conception, diluted or vulgarized in the course of its transmission to our shores. But whatever the degree of logical identity with Marxist materialism, in its actual historical growth, the economic interpretation of the Supreme Court is a native product. It was out of characteristic social conflicts of the Progressive period that the economic approach to the Court emerged, and from the intellectual dilemmas of the period that it received its formulation. In fact, if one still detects in the attitude of liberal critics of the Court an equivocal and confused note, it may be found not wholly alien to the irresoluteness, the divided sense of hostility and acceptance, that lay at the heart of the Progressive movement.

The Progressive period was one of great ferment in thought and gallantry in action. A peculiar emotional intensity surrounded public life. From the western plains, the storm of agrarian Populism had already broken, in the form of state Granger legislation, an Interstate Commerce Act, and all manner of heterodox currency proposals. The trust-busting offensive, which had opened with the Sherman Act, had startled Wall Street. In the cities, muckrakers were canvassing the tie-in between political corruption and the "Interests," and the labor movement was closing up its phalanxes and pressing for social legislation. Intellectually there was a prevailing malaise. The confidence in the national destiny was slipping, as was the faith in the adequacy of the democratic structure. Not since the days of Emerson and John Brown had Americans been forced thus to search their hearts and inquire into the direction of the national drift. The answer of the activists was the liberal revolt in politics against the increasing entrenchment of the illiberal forces. To that revolt the political thinkers made a definite contribution. Probing the principles underlying the American venture, they dug beneath the political ideals to their economic basis. They emerged with the discovery that the tie-in with the economic interests applied not only to current politics but was also part of the very fabric of the state; that the august Supreme Court and the still more august Constitution that it expounded and guarded were not, as had been supposed, detached and self-contained; and that between them and the realities of the marketplace there was an unlovely traffic.

This discovery was made not through a journalistic foray into contemporary reality, but through vast historical research. The re-valuation of American democracy was pushed back to the founding fathers themselves, and with explosive results. To be sure, the dy-namite was already at hand, in the temper and intellectual equipment of the period. The "vague terror" that "went over the earth" when "the word socialism began to be heard"[5] at about this time had to some extent been felt as far away from German Marxism as the American centers of academic thought, and the class struggle, as well as the materialist interpretation of history, was not unheard of. Veblen in 1904 had shown in a chapter of his *Theory of Business Enterprise*[6] that the business influence extended to American law through a carry-over of the eighteenth-century natural-rights philosophy in the in-terests of Big Business. Even Frederick Jackson Turner's theory of a moving frontier, expounded as early as 1893, had suggested how important might be the economic base of political attitudes. But these stray leads in scholarship counted for less than the felt realities of the day. The air was filled with the clash of group and class economic interests: what easier than to project this clash back to the founding of the Republic?

The successive shifts of focus in American economic reality have done much to determine the large sweep of American constitutional law. They have done so in a threefold way: by setting the characteristic problems that have appeared for decision before the Supreme Court, by creating the conflicts and the clashes of interests that have made those problems important to the community, and by fashioning the ideologies that have to a large degree influenced the decisions. Put in another way, the impact of American capitalist development on the Court has been at once to pose the problems and to condition the answers.

The increasing push and thrust of economic problems on the business of the Supreme Court has been noted by Professors Frank-furter and Landis.[7] Within this larger trend, it is interesting to ana-lyze by what dynamics of the economic process the varied range of problems is brought into the area of decision. The ordinary group-ings, around legal subject matter, or the groupings around clauses in the Constitution or around devices in the Court procedure, are not entirely revealing. To know that a case is an injunction case, or that it came under a writ of certiorari, or that it appealed to the due process clause of the Fourteenth Amendment, conveys little of the emotions and beliefs that might give it meaning. The groupings might more realistically be built around those clashes of interests within the economic system or clashes of attitude about it, out of which the cases proceeded.

These clashes of interest are as varied, of course, as the economic life that they mirror. They are at once evidence of maladjustment and challenges to control. Some are concerned with the organizational aspects of capitalism, others with the incidence of its functioning, still others with the distribution of its flow of income. Thus one may find clashes of interest between workers and employers over wages or hours or working conditions or plans for social insurance; between groups of businessmen over trade practices (in the sphere of business mores) or the maintenance of competition (in the sphere of economic ideology); between consumers and other business groups over prices and standards; between ownership and control groups within the corporate structure over the division of profits; between agricultural and industrial groups, Big Business and Little Business groups, groups being taxed and the government as taxer; between all sorts of groups who would stand to gain from a particular government policy, such as a grant of direct relief or an issue of legal-tender paper, and those who would stand to lose; between the interests of autonomous busi-ness control and those of state-enforced competitive enterprise; be-tween the interests of individual enterprise and those of collective control; between those who have a property interest in the status quo and those who have a humanistic interest in changing it.

In short, capitalism pushes ultimately before the Court the clashes of interest that are attendant on the growth of any economic system, with the displacement in each successive phase of elements that had been useful in previous phases, with the antagonism it gen-erates among those who are bearing its burdens and the rivalry among those who are dividing its spoils, and with the inherent contradictions that the system may possess. If it be added to this that modern capitalism is perhaps the least organic system of economic organi-zation the world has seen — "often though not always, a mere con-geries of possessors and pursuers," J. M. Keynes has called it — and that the American social and political structure within which it operates is perhaps more sprawling and heterogeneous than that of any other major capitalist society, some notion may be had of the confusion of interests and purposes out of which it is the task of the Court to bring certainty and uniformity.

The dimensions of the task must, however, be qualified in several respects. Not every case that comes before the Court involves grave conflicts of interest or broad issues of public policy; it is only the exceptional cases that do. Moreover, the pressures and interests summarily analyzed above apply to the entire governmental process in a capitalist state, and not merely to the Court. In fact, the Court does not fight on the front lines but must be considered a reserve force. The brunt of the attack and the task of reconciling the conflicts are met by the legislatures and the administrative agencies, which are more amenable to democratic control than is a small tribunal holding office for life. It is only that which overcomes the legislative barriers and also the jurisdictional exclusions of the Court that comes finally to pose its issues. And even of this group, not every case involving an important conflict of interests will exact from the Court the intense absorption with its social values and implications that creates the nexus binding the judicial process to the economic system. Many a case that, if it had come either later or earlier in the country's development, might have been decided differently or might have constituted a leading case, fails at the time to call into play the entire concentration of the Court's social philosophy. For in any period, neither the Court nor the country can focus its energies on more than a few dominant issues. It is the area that includes these issues — let us call it the "area of vital conflict" — that determines the path of growth in the judicial process and fashions the outlines of constitutional law.

3

The nexus between the course of Supreme Court decisions and the realities of American capitalism poses some crucial problems as to the nature of the judicial process. It is on this broader question that all our current theoretical interests in American constitutional law converge, for it is here that one approaches the dynamics of growth in the law. Contemporary American thought on this question is in the transitional stage, attendant on having shattered the old absolutes without having yet arrived at new formulations. It has rejected the rhetoric and the traditional mumbo-jumboism with which the reverent generations had invested the fundamental law. It finds it no longer possible to regard the judicial utterances as Delphic and takes an almost irreverent delight in uncovering the bonds that link Supreme Court justices to other human beings. The myths have fallen away. But the absence of myths does not constitute theory — it is at best merely a preparation for it.

It will be well to distinguish two aspects of contemporary thought on the Supreme Court and its economic relations. One has to do with the function that the Court decisions perform, the other with the forces determining them. The prevailing view of the function of the Court is thoroughly realistic. It sees the Court as a definite participant in the formation of public policy, often on matters of far-reaching economic and social importance. Viewed thus, the Court, through its power to veto legislation, also has the power to channel economic activity. In this sense it has been often called a superlegislature, exercising powers tantamount to legislative power, but more dangerously, since it is not subject to the same popular control. The main contention here is sound, although the particular formulation it is given is often overstressed. Whether we shall call the Court a superlegislature or a superjudiciary has in reality only a propagandist relevance. But what is of great import is that, through its exercise of judicial power in the intricate context of contemporary capitalist society, the court has become a crucial agency of social control. As such it is part of our fabric of statesmanship and should be judged in terms of its effect on American life.

The second aspect of thought on the Court relates to an adequate theory of judicial decision. The contemporary trend is to regard each judge as acting on his own economic beliefs and his own preferences as to social policy, and as rationalizing or deliberately manipulating his legal views into conformity with his social views. This represents, of course, an extreme revulsion against the traditional view of the judge as objectively expounding a body of laws that has some superior truth-sanction. It looks toward a complete and perhaps unfruitful atomism: *tel juge, tel jugement.* It would hold that the course of judicial decision is the sum of personal choices and that the policy of the Court is determined at any time by the chance concatenation of nine arbitrary wills. Accompanying this is another trend toward a sort of environmentalism or economic determinism. While holding to the atomistic view of the judicial process, it emphasizes in each judge not the volitional and whimsical elements but the nonvolitional and determined. It examines his early life, education, economic affiliations, and property interests, and by a selective process with which every biographer is acquainted, it shows the inevitable flow of what he is from what he has been. Both these approaches stress the compelling reality of the judge's views of social policy over his adherence to legal rules in determining his decision. They mark a change from the tendency a decade or more ago to make the antithesis one between logic and experience, between a mechanical adherence to stare decisis and a realistic awareness of the changing needs of the day.

Such a theory of the judicial process obviously contains much that is sound and fruitful along with elements that tend to be merely impressionistic. Its atomism probably derives from influences similar to those that led Justice Cardozo to focus his analysis of the nature of the judicial process on the individual judge and the individual decision. Benjamin Cardozo's discussion of the various intellectual procedures open to the judge comes dangerously close to a new Benthamism, by which the isolated judge balances the compulsions of logic against the claims of philosophy, and balances both against the persuasions of sociology. By a similar Benthamism in the current atomistic view, the judge is made a lightning calculator not of competing intellectual methods but of his own desires and devices. Both views are helpful through their insistence that whatever the influences, the judicial decision must pass through the mind of the judge. But they do not take sufficient account of the fact that his mind is itself largely a social product, and that he is a judge within an economic system and an ideological milieu. Their influence is operative even when he is not applying the "method of sociology," or using law consciously as an instrument for social ends.

To understand the relation of capitalism to the Supreme Court, the construction of a theory of judicial decision is of crucial importance. If my historical analysis is valid, much in the development of American constitutional law is explainable in terms of a developing capitalism. Such an influence, to be effective, would have had to be operative somehow on the minds of the judges. But how? In what form and through what agencies have the effects of economic development been transmitted to the minds of the judges? The easiest answer, of course, would lie in a theory of pressures. But while this might be valid for some of the lower reaches of the American judiciary, it has no meaning at all for those who are placed, by their exalted and permanent positions, beyond the reach of corruption, as they are placed also beyond that of democratic control. A theory of interests is likely to be more valid. The judge is a member of an economic class, of a social grouping, of a geographical section. He shares their interests, and will, even if unconsciously, direct his policy-forming function to their advantage, but unless this theory is broadened to include general ideological influences as well as direct interests, it will suffer from the oversimplified and mechanical interpretation that has been applied to the framing of the Constitution.

An adequate theory of the judicial process in the Supreme Court would have to take account of a number of factors. Number one: the Court works first of all with a set of traditional and technical legal elements. It must stay within the framework of the Constitution, confine itself to the facts and issues of actual cases brought before it, observe and create for itself a body of procedure. It must maintain so much continuity with its own past decisions as to achieve the necessary minimum of legal certainty, and so much consistency with its own past reasoning as to make the body of constitutional law a somewhat orderly intellectual system. In the process, it creates concepts and develops doctrines, such as due process, liberty of contract, and police power, thereby giving them a directive force over its future decisions. There has been a tendency in recent thought to treat all these legal factors in the judicial process less as rules than as fairly flexible techniques, accordingly subservient to the more deeply rooted purposes of the judges.

Number two: the Court works within a cultural and institutional framework, which the justices share with their fellow citizens. They live in and are sworn to preserve a society that is the end product of a historical growth but is also changing under their very eyes. This society is dominated by its capitalist system of economic organization and is therefore best viewed as a capitalist society. Its institutions and modes of thought are partly incorporated in the Constitution, partly in the body of constitutional law, but they are mainly resident in the life of the society itself.

Number three: the Court works in a world of ideas that the justices share with their fellow men. These ideological elements — conceptions of human nature, human motive, social possibility, and ethical values — may be "preconceptions" and therefore submerged in consciousness, or they may be avowedly held and deliberately applied. Many of them, such as the competitive ideal and the right of property, proceed from the economic world; those that do not, such as human nature, individualism, and natural law, have nevertheless a definite bearing on economic problems; all of them are social products and are affected by changes in the social and economic structure.

Number four: there are personal and intellectual differences between the judges — differences of background, philosophy, social convictions, and sympathies.

Of these factors, those in the second and third groups — the world of social fact and the world of social idea — include and are conditioned by the nature of our economic life. The selection that any particular judge makes from them will constitute what Thomas Reed Powell has called the "logic" of his decision; the selection that he makes from the first group of factors — the legal tradition and technology — will constitute the "rhetoric" by which he supports and rationalizes his decision. For an explanation of the main trend of constitutional decision, we may therefore look to the institutional and ideological elements that exercise their compulsive force on the minds of the judges, and to the changes wrought in these elements, principally by economic development. For an explanation of the groupings within the Court, we may look to the variations in outlook and belief between the individual members.

This raises a question about the Court that is as important for social action as for juristic theory. What technique can be employed for shifting the trend of the Court's decisions? What are the chances, for example, that the Court will reverse the secular trend of its decisions during the past half-century and adopt an attitude toward private property that will tolerate experiments in the direction of a controlled and articulated economy? The contemporary emphasis on the judge's capacity to make his rhetoric march to the tune of his social beliefs has as corollary the view that the crucial concern, whether of liberals or conservatives, should be the selection of the right judges — a sort of eugenics program for the judicial process. It seems clear, however, that such a view is overoptimistic. It stops at the judge and does not push its analysis to what it is that determines his view of life. The judge's convictions and social preferences run in terms of the current ideologies of his day, and through those ideologies the operative economic forces and master trends of the period find their way into the Court's decisions. It has been said that a period deserves whatever Supreme Court it gets. A period in which capitalist enterprise is on the offensive and the individualistic ideal sweeps everything before it is not likely to read anything but an individualistic philosophy into its constitutional law. A period such as the present, in which the individualistic ideal has been undermined by worldwide economic collapse, is likely to be increasingly tolerant of departures from an absolute conception of liberty or property.

This does not involve, however, a rigorous determinism, either economic or ideological. The judicial process is not, as a too-mechanical view might hold, powerless in the clutch of capitalist circumstance. The institutions and thought of a period determine only the larger outlines that the constitutional law of the period is likely to take. Within them is room for a fairly wide selection and variation of emphasis. The Supreme Court effects a nexus between our fundamental law and our fundamental economic institutions. But by its very position as an agency of control, it is powerful enough to change the contours of those institutions. The same constitutional fabric that contains the absolute individualism of Justice Sutherland gives scope also to the humanistic individualism of Justice Holmes and the social constructivism of Justice Brandeis. The judicial process in the Supreme Court is no exception to the order of things everywhere. Within the limits set by its nature and function, it can be carried out with creativity and purpose, or it can become merely a form of submission to the current drift.

1933

2

Constitution and Court
as Symbols

Several years after this essay appeared, Kenneth Burke included in his Philosophy of Literary Form *(1941) a highly suggestive discussion of the extent to which a "ritual drama" pattern underlies its structure. The central theme of my essay, he wrote, is "the symbolic slaying of the sacrificial king" of judicial power. I am almost convinced. Burke says, however, that in "Act [section] 4" I move from the "dramatic" to the "naturalistic" in my discussion of hunger and fear as motives, and thus from social to biological coordinates. That may be true. Yet a fusion of the dramatic with the naturalistic — the social with the biological — would seem desirable in the analysis, even if it disrupts the ritual drama.*

In fact, whatever appeal this essay had lay in its willingness to cross disciplines and domains in pursuit of the relation between constitutional symbols and power. While I was not strongly conscious of being a "legal realist" when I wrote it, I now see that the school of Karl Llewellyn, Thurman Arnold, Jerome Frank, and my Brookings Graduate School teacher, Walton Hamilton, was held together by their attraction to the role of "folklore" and the "symbolic" in the American polity, and that, in a sense, I belonged with them.[1]

My only present difference with the essay turns on the ambivalence I felt about constitutional symbols, seeing them mainly as buttressing judicial power, even as I found myself drawn to their power. I later came to focus on myths as archetypal symbols, and to move beyond this ambivalence to a polar view of the mythic. Although I knew that the mythic may perpetuate class power, I also saw it as the most important element in the cohesion of the civilization.

We live by symbols.

JUSTICE HOLMES

SYMBOLS IN POLITICS

Man as a political animal lives in a world riddled with bugbears and taboos. Political thinkers as diverse as the English idealists and the classical Marxists have labored under a common fallacy: they have taken their own sense of the logical relation of things and read into it the way men behave. Actually, men behave in their political lives with a disheartening illogicality. They live in a jungle of fear, filled with phantoms of what they have heard and imagined and been told. Their world is the world of a child's nightmares — dark and brooding, crowded with dreads and anxieties, with the distortions of real objects, with the cruelest non sequiturs and anticlimaxes.

That is why men always find themselves forced to seek some symbol of divine right. Talk to the people on the street, the workers in the mines and factories and steel mills and real estate offices and filling stations, dig into their minds and even below the threshold of their consciousness, and you will in the main find that Constitution and Supreme Court are symbols of an ancient sureness and a comforting stability. If you watch the black-robed justices as they come filing in, if you listen to them read their opinions, you will be strong if you do not succumb to a sense of the Court's timelessness. Americans have been told that they are a people without a tradition, without a culture. And it does in truth seem surprising that the restless, unstable energies of the American people should have created anything that seems as deep-rooted and as eternal as the Supreme Court. Even today, in its new and imposing building, the Court still wears the ancient garments of divine right. The building has changed since the days of John Jay and John Marshall; the fashionables, the men in power, the plain men and women who come to visit the Court have changed; there is even that strange and modern creature, a "press contact man," to explain to correspondents the mysteries of a writ of certiorari and a dissenting opinion. But despite these concessions to the spirit of the times, the Court retains its tough historical fiber. It has, to be sure, walked along the evolutionary path, but only as Orpheus once walked along the pathway of Hell — with head turned backward.

What accounts for the extraordinary durability and viability of the Court? Why has it emerged relatively unscathed from its mortal combats with presidents and political reformers from Jefferson to Roosevelt II? The defenders of the Court answer that its survival indicates how futile are the attacks on it. The assumption seems to be that the Supreme Court has survived a medieval ordeal by fire, proving its innocence. But the successive crises of judicial power can no more be exorcised by this sort of mumbo jumbo than can the crises of the economic system. They cannot be explained away merely as "the same old story." The attacks on the Court's power have been real enough and dangerous enough. Its survival thus far shows that it has deep historical and psychological roots in American life; it has a clear relation to the development of the power of business enterprise; it has a strong symbolic hold over the American mind.

Most clearly and simply I should put it as follows: the nature and extent of the Supreme Court's power are best understood by seeing it as our basic instrument of sovereignty — an integral part of the American capitalist economic order. But the support of judicial power must be seen as the instrument of the few, although psychologically it is the symbol of the many. It is to the Supreme Court and the Constitution as symbols that we must first turn.[2]

Men have always used symbols in the struggle for power, but only lately have we grown aware generally of their importance. Realistic students of government today know that the state is not ruled, as the unwary reader of Plutarch might suppose, by copybook maxims and civic virtues. They know that one of the essential techniques of power groups is to manipulate the most effective symbols in such a way that they become instruments of mass persuasion. With its use of propaganda, the First World War brought that lesson home, and if it was not clear at the end of the war, it has become clear enough since through the European experience with fascist and Communist governments. People are notably more sensitive to images than to ideas, more responsive to stereotypes than to logic, to the concrete symbol than to the abstraction. Today we all recognize the power of the newest devices, such as the radio, the movies, and the press, to act as instruments of social cohesion and to line up an entire nation behind a single set of interests. The established weapon of dictators has become the microphone. But these techniques depend for their effectiveness on the symbols that they manipulate, and the symbols depend in turn on the entire range of association that they evoke.

Actually the whole of a culture is shot through with symbolism. Man is under the constant necessity, writes Thurman Arnold, of putting on ceremonial robes and watching himself go by. There are symbols like the flag and the national anthem that are clearly recognized as such — well-defined abbreviations of the national culture, sometimes called "referential symbols" because they refer directly to the things they symbolize. But the more important symbols, because their working is more obscure, are the "condensation symbols," which Edward Sapir defines as "a condensed form of substitute behavior for direct expression."[3] This is a symbolism to be found in neurotic behavior, in the life of primitive peoples, in the heavily charged symbolic atmosphere of religion and politics.

The Supreme Court as symbol goes hand-in-hand with the Constitution as symbol. Since the Supreme Court is popularly considered to be exercising guardianship over the Constitution, the result has been to invest the judges of the Court with the whole panoply of sanctity with which the Constitution has itself been invested. This has had an importance that can scarcely be overestimated for American history. Constitutions, like all creations of the human mind and the human will, have an existence in people's imagination and emotions quite apart from their actual use in ordering people's affairs. This function has been called "constitutionalism," which Walton Hamilton has defined as "the name given to the trust which men repose in the power of words engrossed on parchment to keep a government in order."[4] Edward S. Corwin, in his Harvard tercentenary address, has pointed out that the Constitution has two aspects: it is an *instrument* and a *symbol*. As an instrument it must be viewed hardheadedly and used flexibly to promote the people's welfare in the present and future. As a symbol it is part of the mass mind, capable of arousing intense popular hysteria, loaded with a terrible inertia, its face turned toward the past.

DIVINE RIGHT: AMERICAN PLAN

In a democracy in the twentieth century it may seem irreverent or whimsical or even merely literary to talk of divine right. Yet very little is clearer in the American scheme than the fact that the cult of the Supreme Court is the characteristic emotional cement by which American capitalism and American democracy are held together. The celebration of the Supreme Court in the capitalist America of the nineteenth and twentieth centuries performs the same social function as the celebration of kingship did in the mercantilist Europe of the sixteenth to eighteenth centuries. On the main highways of the development of the Western world, what used to be the divine right of kings has been replaced by the divine right of judges.

I mean this, of course, as a rough analogy, and yet I mean something beyond that, too. The feudal economic system exploited the panoply of idea and allegiance furnished by the universal Church. The mercantilist economic system that emerged in early modern times clothed itself in the vestments of a kingship that would have the strength to break down and override the princelings and local potentates who stood in the way of the expanding economic unit; but it had to contend with the spiritual authority of the Church, and it did not shrink finally from claiming for its kings the same divine right with which the Church had invested itself. In fact, the great ideological struggles of the sixteenth century were waged over the claims of the kingship to divine right, and the crux of this struggle was reached when the absolute monarchs in England evolved their *dispensing* power to challenge the power of the Church to grant *indulgences*. It seems to be a rule of the struggle for power that one species of appeal to divinity can be displaced only by another. The divine right of the Church had to yield to the divine right of kings that invested the absolute monarchy. In the course of the parliamentary struggles of the seventeenth century in England, and of the eighteenth- and nineteenth-century struggles that followed in their wake on the Continent, the Church had to give way to the divine right of parliaments; representative institutions were able to displace absolute monarchy by appealing to a "higher law": the "divinity [that] doth hedge a king" was transformed into the divine sanctions of some unchanging body of principles in terms of which the king's acts had to be measured and weighed.

But the logic of development did not stop there. America, which has carried capitalism to its highest peak, also needed a divine sanction of unusual potency with which to invest it. Because our parliamentary institutions — our Congress and presidents — are potentially too responsive to democratic impulses, the "higher law" was extended to them in the acts of the people's representatives themselves. That "higher law" was located in the Constitution. But being divine, it could not be contained even in the Constitution, so it overflowed and became a "brooding omnipresence in the sky,"[5] which could be brought to earth only when it was finally located in the minds of the men who took over the exclusive function of interpreting the Constitution. As Brooks Adams wrote in *Theory of Social Revolutions,* by the "rule of reason" in the Standard Oil cases of 1910, which exempted the oil trust from the operation of the Sherman Antitrust Act,[6] the Court was taking over the authority of the Church to "grant indulgences for reasonable causes."[7] From the medieval Church to American finance capitalism, the wheel has come a full turn.

There are three principal elements in the pattern of divine right as it may be found in the popular mind. One is the fetishism of the Constitution, the second is the claim of the Court to the exclusive guardianship of the Constitution, and the third is the tradition of judicial neutrality. In the past century the fortunes of the Constitution as symbol and the Supreme Court as symbol have to no small extent been linked. In the last analysis, what enabled the propertied groups to make use of judicial power was the strength and evocative force of the constitutional tradition.

But this tradition, seen as a cohesive force for the nation, had one great weakness. It left the gates wide open for divergent interpretations that, as shown by the quarter-century that furnished a swift runway to civil war, might grow in passion and intensity until they led to open conflict. The Civil War burned deep into the people the consciousness of the value of the constitutional symbol; it burned even deeper the danger of conflicting interpretations of the fundamental law. So long as the polity had to cope only with the oppositions of the party system, the constitutional symbol was broad enough to contain those oppositions and give them scope and play. But when the oppositions took on the fierceness of class and sectional conflicts, and when two well-knit economies, each with its emotional loyalties and intellectual rationalizations, met in a head-on collision, it was clear that something more was required than the constitutional symbol. That something more was judicial review. Space for endless debate and conflict had been left in the federal framework, based on the separation of powers and subject to a fundamental law, and it had to be closed up. Someone had to be empowered to decide finally how that fundamental law should be interpreted. The decision might, of course, have been left to Congress, but to the slavery interest and localist sentiment that would have been unthinkable before the Civil War; it was unthinkable after the Civil War to the capitalist interest, which above all else feared democracy. Something else had to be found. The fetishism of the Constitution, as a flexible instrument open to various constructions, was in itself inadequate. In short, a *faith* was not enough. It had to be a faith deposited in a *power*. That power was judicial. The function of interpreting the Constitution had to be concentrated in a single tribunal.

Thus arose the second element in the pattern of divine right: the exclusive claim of the Supreme Court to guardianship of the Constitution. John Marshall and Joseph Story urged it very early in our history, primarily from the viewpoint of safeguarding the Federalist interests. Daniel Webster's "Reply to Hayne" is principally important as a defense not so much of the Constitution as of judicial power. It is significant, as Charles Warren has pointed out, that it came at the end of the first fierce attack on judicial power since Jefferson's. Webster saw judicial power as a new bulwark against the propertied interests, adding to the bulwark of the Constitution — which could be used quite as much by John Calhoun and Thomas Hart Benton to their purposes as by Henry Clay and himself to their own. What Webster did not foresee was that even judicial power could be used by the enemy — if they captured the Court. It was one of the ironic twists of history that the arrow that Webster aimed at Hayne and the slavocracy he stood for was picked up by Chief Justice Roger Taney, another champion of the slavocracy, and aimed back at Webster and the capitalism of the North. The Dred Scott decision was the logical fulfillment of the "Reply to Hayne."

From Marshall through Taney, and increasingly after the Civil War, the Supreme Court offered to guard exclusively the charter of fundamental liberties. The justices offered to play the role of the Platonic guardians watching over the mythic Greek republic; they were ready to furnish at once wisdom and militancy. Part of John Marshall's genius lay in his skill at underplaying the power that the Court was gaining over economic policy, and emphasizing its guardianship role. Later justices have continued to do the same, and today it has become the official theory of the Court's power. To be sure, the fact that the role of guarding the Constitution involved also the power of deciding what the Constitution was did not by a whit diminish the ardor of the Court in offering its services. Like a jealous Cyclops, it wished to rule the domain that it guarded.

Because of the stress laid on their guardianship role, the justices have been associated in our minds with the function of protection rather than with the struggle for power. This has been of enormous importance. It has conscripted to the service of the judicial symbol all the accumulated Anglo Saxon tradition of the "rule of law" that America carried over from England. Under the form of "natural law," this tradition was itself a carryover from the Middle Ages. It had become domesticated in England — first in the subjection of King John to the Magna Charta of the barons at Runnymede; later by the rising English middle class, acting through Edward Coke, the stalwart lord chief justice who stubbornly fought royal prerogative in the cause of parliamentary liberties and wrote a magnificent commentary on Magna Charta that was more influential than was the instrument itself in building up the concept of the rule of law. The subjection of all public officials to a higher law that is "common" not only in the sense that it is available to all men but also in the sense that it exempts no one was carried over into the American colonies, and it took the form here of the concept of the Constitution as a "fundamental law." It cropped up timorously in some of the early cases that are now cited as forerunners of *Marbury v. Madison,* and in that case it took its first long step toward being converted into the doctrine of judicial review. It has been the principal ideological force bolstering judicial review as a necessary doctrine in "a government of laws and not of men." It is an influence that lingers today in the minds of those who have never heard of Coke, and who do not know the meaning — much less the "spirit" — of the common law.

Moving from Coke to Marshall, Story, and New York chancellor James Kent, to Charles Cooley on constitutional limitations, to the New Deal cases, represents a series of legal steps connected by the appeal to a higher law in the interests of the mercantile and industrial class. There is one paradox worth noting: in England Coke's doctrine has been maintained only so far as it called for a legal check on the monarch, but not so far as it applied to a legal check on Parliament; in America the check was placed on both the executive branch and the legislature. Identifying that check with the Constitution was only a step, and identifying it with the guardians and interpreters of the Constitution — and thus establishing judicial supremacy — was only another. The paradox resolves itself, however, when ideas are referred back to the interests they serve. It was no accident that the idea of the rule of law was among the reigning forces at our nativity as a nation. Historically, as well as psychologically, rule of law is linked with the development and power of the middle class in the Western world. It is part of the body of liberal doctrine that the middle class forged in the centuries during which it was clearing its way to power, and that the same class used as a rationalization and as an instrument for holding on to power. Useful to the rising capitalist class for removing the obstruction of monarchical and aristocratic interference, rule of law is useful now to the entrenched capitalist class for fighting off the threat of democratic and labor groups.

The emphasis has changed, but rule of law has kept its function and its psychological appeal and found favorable soil in America, where there has always been a dominant legalistic strain and an elaborate respect for the legal fabric of things. And it has been cherished by the most liberal tradition in American life, which has done little to orient itself to the new demands made on it by changing industrialism, and which is fighting all over again the battles of the Stuart period.

This brings us to the third element in the pattern of divine right: the tradition of judicial neutrality. The justices could not be proper guardians of the Constitution unless they approached it with detachment. We have somehow managed in our minds to place them above the fray. Despite every proof to the contrary, we have persisted in attributing to them the objectivity and infallibility that are ultimately attributes only of godhead. The tradition persists that they belong to no economic group or class; that they are not touched by economic interests; that their decisions proceed through some inspired way of arriving at the truth; that they sit in their robes like the haughty gods of Lucretius, high above the plains on which human beings swarm, unaffected by the preferences and prejudices that move common men.

There is a curious cult of judges that has grown up in America. President Taft, in the 1912 campaign, said with more than a trace of seriousness that he believed that heaven got its quality from the judicial character.[8] No German bourgeois ever surrendered himself more completely to the commanding dignity of a *Geheimrat*, no pre-Soviet peasant ever bowed lower to the czar's tax collector, than we bow before the judicial symbol. Office holding is, in a democratic state, a paradox at best: after election day we seek to invest with authority a man whom we have the day before impaled upon our invective as the blackest sort of scoundrel. In this sense, democratic government is a perpetual phoenix-renewal of the vigor and dignity of office that have only just before been consumed in the flames of party passion. Our experience with elected judges — with the state

courts and with the whole army of lesser judicial stalwarts and mercenaries — has certainly not been such as to add to the stature of
the judicial office they hold. For that reason the cult of judges and
the belief in their neutrality are all the greater a paradox.

The paradox is partly explained by our association of judges
with the rule of law. But even more it springs from our deep need
for some final authority. We are, in a sense, a barbaric people, only
several generations removed from the wilderness psychology. The
whole development of American life has been riddled with violence,
from the first extermination of the Indians, through the ruthless rifling
of a continent, to the use of spies and thugs against labor unions and
the mowing down of gangster "mobs" under the fire of submachine
guns. We live in fear of such violence, and both our exaggerated lip
service to "law and order" and our cult of judges are functions of
that fear. Most of us feel economically helpless in the midst of a
ruthless exploitative capitalism; we feel alone in a vast impersonal
urban civilization. We turn to "the law" as our final protection, and
we read into the judges our hopes for someone who will be above
the battle.

Most of us associate judges with the settlement of ordinary
litigation, where political bias seems irrelevant; or with criminal
trials, where the judge seems to sit as an avenging and impersonal
deity, expressing through his function the sense and conscience of
the community. What easier than to transfer this conception to the
Supreme Court? Especially since there are four elements that seem
to magnify the objectivity of the Supreme Court justices as compared
with judges in lower courts.

One element is that they are in a "supreme" court, and presumably are of some higher stature than ordinary mortals. The second
is that they are appointed, not elected, and thus escape the grueling
experience of a political campaign. The third is the greatness of the
judicial tradition of the Supreme Court: some of our judges have
actually been men of enormous ability. The fact that their ability has
not been conspicuously in the direction of detachment is not generally
known; what comes down to us is the almost Periclean devotion to
public trust shown by men like Marshall, Taney, and Holmes.[9] The
fourth factor, perhaps the most important, is that we transfer our
sense of the definitive and timeless character of the Constitution to
the justices who expound it. From our image of the Constitution as
the ultimate wisdom in government, it follows that the men versed
in its lore must reach their conclusions not by the paths of ordinary

men, but by some mysterious and inspired processes. The justices thus become not ordinary men, subject to ordinary passions, but discoverers of final truth, priests in the service of a godhead.

NEW SYMBOLS FOR OLD

The men who fashion America's symbols have, on the whole, wrought the Supreme Court symbol well. They have used every strategy at the command of minorities of privilege to protect their threatened dominance. They have controlled newspapers, dictated editorials, contrived slogans, selected textbooks, approved lectures, filled pulpits, guarded microphones, spoken with learning and authority through their proper oracles, the lawyers. They have perhaps benefited most from the ministrations of the lawyers, who, by the air of mystery in which they wrap themselves and by the impenetrable jargon they use, are adept at creating symbols. Moreover, as the expert technician in the refinements of corporate strategy, the lawyer becomes the lieutenant of Big Enterprise, its closest adjunct in the whole range of professional groups. Most important of all, being specialized in persuasion and hypnosis, the lawyer — even more than the preacher and the professor — manages finally to induce a sort of self-hypnosis that makes him forever after a servitor of the propertied groups. And he is aided in this function by his special type of mentality, which has its essence in its clinging to the symbols of authority.

The symbol makers have, I repeat, wrought well. But recently two sets of forces have been at work undermining the edifice they have been at pains to build. One set has operated through our economic institutions, and through the cross-purposes inherent in them. The other has operated through the nature of the judicial process itself.

Industrialism creates a climate in which a symbol has to be hardy to survive. There is a corrosive power in the machine process that makes men think increasingly in matter-of-fact terms and before which legends tend to crumble away. Thorstein Veblen has pointed out that the technicians and operatives of machines who spend their days in making, weighing, counting, measuring tangible things are apt finally to be skeptical of intangible — or what he called "honorific" — values. But the instability of capitalism as a system of economic order has proven even more corrosive to symbols than the machine process. The successive crises of American capitalism have left their mark on judicial power. And the history of the Supreme Court is a sequence of crises of judicial power that have been related to the crises of the economic system. It is no accident that the gravest constitutional crisis should have coincided with the gravest economic crisis in our history, and that the key figure in both should be the same president. Each crisis of the judicial power, each conflict with the democratic elements, weakens judicial power and paves the way for the next crisis.

This brings us to the second set of forces — those operating through judicial power itself. Historians in the future will probably count it not the least important result of the Great Depression that it made Americans "judge-conscious" to a degree they had never been before. The context of this new consciousness is to be found in the sharp contradiction between economic collapse and the "trained incapacity" of a political system hampered by judicial review to deal with it. The judges were faced with a fateful choice between the freezing of the vested interests and the survival of the capitalist system — and when they chose the latter and turned "liberal," they revealed, all too glaringly, a very human changeableness. However, they had also to respond to social pressures, to the threat posed by President Roosevelt's court-reorganization proposal, to the economic success of the steel and automobile drives, which left little choice in the Wagner Act decisions. And for judges who were accustomed to talking in absolutes, to act like any deliberative assembly, with its pressures and majorities, was to forfeit their godhead.

These were the forces at work; they came to a head during the judicial debate of 1937, which turned the eyes of the nation on judicial power. People began to translate what they learned in following the decisions into terms that had meaning in the debate over the reform of judicial power. The most enduring result of the conflict between the New Deal and the Supreme Court was educational. Americans had been politically naive about judicial power, and a set of forces converging on the New Deal decisions allowed them to realize that the judges were interested in social policy and capable of changing their minds. The Supreme Court became a schoolhouse, and Mr. Justice Owen Roberts proved an excellent schoolmaster, whether he stonily ignored the future, as in his decision in *United States v. Butler*,[10] or looked reluctantly at it, as in his vote in the Jones & Laughlin case.[11] Either way, Americans were no longer in complete innocence about the functioning of the judicial process. They began to see that judicial decisions were not babies brought by constitutional storks, but were born out of the travail of economic circumstance. They learned that judges were human, and that judicial power was no more sacred than any other power. They learned that, in America, real political sovereignty resides in the odd man on the court.[12] But they also learned that these isolated, self-contained individuals must respond, finally, in moments of intense economic and constitutional crisis, to the facts of the national life. Whatever happens, it is not likely that they will soon forget that experience. If only for a moment, they peered beyond the symbol of the divine right of judges to the realities of judicial power. They dared look upon the judicial Medusa-head, and lo! they were not turned to stone.

Education such as this comes hard and is hard paid for. It comes with crises, economic and constitutional. People are not moved to question their most deeply rooted and skillfully publicized symbols except under enormous pressure and great need. Only then does the erosive power of their reason begin to function and to turn to the future instead of the past. In the great need of economic crisis, the measures taken to relieve and temper that crisis were blocked by judicial power. The symbol of divine right began to crumble.

Thou wast not born for death, immortal Bird!

No hungry generations tread thee down.

Thus John Keats addressed the deathless symbol of the nightingale. But the Supreme Court is no deathless and unwavering symbol. If its evocative power declined during this period, as I believe it did, it was because it had stood between the hungry generations and the appeasement of their hunger, between Bill Jones and a decent standard of living.

I have spoken of hunger. There is fear also to consider.[13] The ultimate power of the Supreme Court and the Constitution does not derive wholly from vested interests, with all their external control over the molding of opinion. It comes from what is, in the last analysis, the strongest ally any institution or tradition can have — namely, fear. I do not mean fear of the Court, fear of judicial power, the fear one has of the whiplash of tyrants. I mean the fear of not having Court and Constitution to fall back on. I mean the terrible fear of change and the unknown, which to so many people is more powerful even than the felt needs and pressures of the day. Fear, not will, underlies a good part of our politics — the creeping fear of people who prefer to surrender their decisions to others.

This sort of womb-retreat is not unknown to social psychology.

It is a phenomenon common in every period of reaction, and familiar enough in fascism. It riddles the middle-class mentality especially, the mentality of those who have lost their secure economic roots in capitalism and not yet found roots in the emerging collectivism. We in America are just now beginning to explore and understand the length and breadth and depth of the middle-class mentality in our politics — fear-ridden, standardized, negativist, tenacious of symbols. The Court's ancient sureness is not something to be abandoned, lest we confront an uncharted future.

The propertied groups are not immune to fear, either. Their attitude toward constitutional law in the past has been, on the whole, coldly instrumental. "Every dominant class, as it has arisen," says Brooks Adams, "has done its best to use the machinery of justice for its own benefit."[14] The capitalists, as a dominant but minority group operating under democratic procedures, have used the Supreme Court so long and so blindly for their own purposes that they have finally succeeded in undermining its strength and prestige. The specter of a national symbol being twisted and turned to class interest has finally become viable through even the haze of rationalization. The capitalists find themselves thus faced with the prospect of losing their principal protection against the tyranny of the majority, and this they can ill afford to do. It is, says Nietzsche in one of his scorching passages, a sign of the weakening of ruling aristocracies that they hide behind constitutions, higher laws, humanitarian and judicial symbols.[15] The American capitalist elite is caught in a cruel dilemma. As a nonmilitary ruling class, it must depend for its protection on the Court and the fabric of legality that it can control; as a group specialized to pecuniary values and bent on maximizing profits and minimizing costs, it must twist the Court to its own purposes, openly defy laws when they are aimed at wresting a share of the national income from them, and thus tear the very fabric of legality on which they depend. Small wonder, then, that they are of a divided mind today; that the crumbling of the judicial symbol fills them with fear; that they do not contemplate with equanimity the prospects of either the gradual surrender of their economic power or the rise of fascism.[16]

Their fears, and the fears of the lower middle class, have as usual been felt by the intellectuals — even those liberated "liberals" who pride themselves on seeing through symbols. They too fear the tearing of the fabric of legality — a break that might result in either revolutionary upheaval or the heavy hand of fascism. We live, they feel, in a complicated and fragile civilization, where it is conceivable that a violent wrench might send the whole structure toppling. What separates us from anarchy is principally the accumulated strength of convention, otherwise known as "law." Like the Englishman in the jungle who clings desperately to the amenities of London life, they are jealous of any infraction of law, especially of property law and constitutional law, which form the fabric of the capitalist order. If they yield an inch, they surrender all. They, too, are caught in a cruel dilemma. Intellectuals have learned that revolutions and coups take place when a deadlock in the capitalist system makes democracy incapable of dealing with the continuing crisis of the capitalist system, and when democracies will the ends but do not will the means. The further Constitution and Court move from the realities of the common welfare, the more easily they could become symbols of barrenness and rallying points for movements seeking to suppress liberal democracy, impose fascism, and stamp out the intellectual groups. Thus intellectuals are divided, at once fearful of the crumbling of the American pattern of divine right and yet disturbed by the way it functions.

With the lower-income groups the case is somewhat different. Their role — the role of the common man in every culture — has always been at once symbol breaking and symbol making. In the past, these groups have seen the Constitution as a symbol of hope and authority, and the judiciary as a symbol of protection. These groups become the carriers of these symbols; in turn, these symbols appease them and lash down their allegiance to the existing order. In times of insecurity and hunger, however, the lower-income groups have turned increasingly toward their more direct representatives: to legislative remedies, to executive action — above all, to trade-union organization. The common man, from the California lettuce picker to the Pennsylvania steelworker, from the Minnesota truck driver to the Arkansas tenant farmer, has begun to scrutinize afresh the myths that stand between him and the satisfaction of his needs. Like the middle-class clerk, storekeeper, white-collar worker, farmer, intellectual, he is insecure, and insecurity is a breeding ground for myths and symbols. But he differs from them in one important respect; the path he is treading in his quest for economic security leads necessarily to new forms of social construction and therefore to the creation of new myths.

Thus the common man is again assuming his historical function of symbol breaker and symbol maker. Trade-union action and mass political action represent new collectivities. They are capable of building new myths and are well on the way to doing so. But like the constitutional myth in our early years, they promise to be myths rooted not in fear but in hope, not in negation but in affirmation, not in clinging to the old but in a collective will to build the new; and to be economically rooted not in the class power of a minority group but in an expanding economy for the majority groups. If these groups succeed in their efforts to make out of the Constitution once more, in Corwin's phrase, an "instrument" for the common interest, the constitutional symbol will be given renewed strength; but the path toward such a reshaping of the constitutional symbol means the common man will tread on the divine right of judges.

These are the forces at work. What pattern they will form one cannot prophesy. One can see, however, that what is going on in the American mind is at the core of every human society — the imperatives of hunger against the power of fear: fear clinging to the old symbols and looking toward the past; hunger looking toward new economic constructions, reshaping old symbols, shaping new ones.

1937

3

The Early Career of
Judicial Activism

*The question at the core of the pieces in this section was: Could the
Court reform itself in its decision-making process, or would reform
have to be imposed from without? What came to pass was a combination of both.*

*The essay "Judicial Supremacy as Fortress," excerpted from my
first book,* It Is Later Than You Think, *contains my response at the
time to the critics of FDR's court-packing plan — a position that
virtually isolated me. The critical problem I have with the plan today
is that it placed at peril the basic myth of the justices as independent
keepers of the covenant. But my quarrel with judicial (as against
presidential) activism is that it places the same myth equally at peril.
What strikes me as most ironic of all is that the activists for whom
FDR is still the paradigmatic president now regard as a minor ab-
erration a policy that was at the center of his being.*

1
THE LAWLESS SUPREME COURT
AND WALTER LIPPMANN

Nothing is clearer in Washington today than that the Supreme Court
justices are at sixes and threes. The personal tension among them is
no mere accident of individual temperament or will. One of the marks
of constitutional crisis is the sharpening of differences on the Court.

During the preliminary skirmishes on the New Deal legislation,

the Court seemed to fall into three loose groups. The most cohesive
was that of the four "die-hard" conservatives — Justice Van Devanter, Justice McReynolds, Justice Sutherland, Justice Butler. At the
opposite extreme were the three "liberals" — Justice Brandeis, Justice
Stone, and Justice Cardozo. That left a "balance-of-power" group
of two — Chief Justice Hughes and Justice Roberts. It was these two
who, by their vacillations, sent the judicial fever chart of the New
Deal careening from high to low. As the sense of economic panic
decreased and the political tension increased, the three groups became
two. The bitterness of the die-hard justices reached such a pitch that
they became completely indistinguishable from Liberty Leaguers. The
liberals suspended whatever differences of economic philosophy they
had, and even grew critical of the inherent abuses of the judicial
power itself. The balance-of-power pair, after a somewhat indecent
flirtation with the liberals in the Minnesota mortgage-moratorium
case and the *Nebbia* milk-control case, were finally forced to make
a definite choice. They could not continue to commute between two
worlds. Nor could they, when the heavens were falling, merely stand
aloof and murmur, "A plague on both your houses." Whatever may
have been their previous constitutional waverings, they threw in their
lot with the diehards and chose the side of the entrenched order. The
Supreme Court is now two armed camps confronting each other.

To the believers in judicial power, this is of course distressing.
It is not so much that the Court fails to present the serried ranks of
a united front. Since the days when John Marshall held the Court
under his hypnotic sway, no united front has been possible except
sporadically. What is distressing is that a persistent series of six-to-
three decisions will weaken the prestige of the Court. When justices
divide with monotonous uniformity, even the hardened believer in
divine right may feel that the Constitution is curiously unclear for
so compelling a document.

When the crisis was most desperate, it seemed for a time that
the Court might join the colors in the war against the Depression.
Among the brilliant young lawyers who flocked to Washington there
was an amazingly sanguine view that the New Deal would prove
constitutional. It seems surprising now that anyone should ever have
thought we could have a drastic dislocation of our economic life,
with all the desperate efforts at economic control that it entailed,
without having a constitutional dislocation as well. With the advantage of hindsight we glimpse today what the relation of the Supreme
Court is to capitalist crisis. At the period of greatest panic and despair,

the Court is likely to sanction heroic remedies. Enough liberals and balance-of-power judges can be mustered who have the wisdom to see that capitalist survival would be impossible without a summary use of the federal power. But it is only when the economic crisis itself has eased, and business enterprise has recovered from its mortal anguish, that the real constitutional crisis comes. The old taboos against government control are reasserted. The Court seeks to prevent the country from making the new measures of control permanent, and so therefore from paying too high a price for survival. The liberals on the Court find themselves isolated. The balance-of-power justices find it is no longer necessary to be liberal. The conservatives give every indication that in them is the grace confessed, if not the mercies multiplied.

To trace the career of the New Deal in the Court is to describe the rise and fall of a "felt need," to use Oliver Wendell Holmes's term. In 1933, before the New Deal legislation was passed, Chief Justice Hughes, speaking for the Court, took judicial notice of the Depression. That was in the Appalachian coal case.[1] In the Minnesota mortgage-moratorium case, in January 1934, Justice Hughes read a five-to-four decision upholding the government.[2] In March the same Court majority, speaking now through Justice Roberts in the *Nebbia* case, upheld price-fixing by the New York State milk-control board.[3] The Panama (hot-oil) case represented the first break. But that case turned on delegation of powers and administrative carelessness rather than on the substance of the legislation, and the next cases — the gold-clause cases — reassured those who had grown anxious. There, in unusually tortuous reasoning, Chief Justice Hughes seemed to go out of his way to save the financial stability of the government and uphold its contentions. This augured well, and Justice McReynolds's dramatic outburst in the courtroom, when he warned that the Constitution had been scrapped, seemed merely to be an elegy over an order that was dead. It was then that the really ominous decision came — the five-to-four opinion against the government in the railroad retirement case, read by Roberts. This opinion, when compared with Justice Roberts's earlier *Nebbia* opinion, measured the judicial crack-up of the New Deal. After that, of course, came the Schechter brothers, the Hoosac mills, the rice processors' case, and a brood that threatens to lengthen out into the future.

There is a measure of truth in the contention that if the crucial New Deal measures — the National Recovery Administration (NRA) and the Agricultural Adjustment Administration (AAA) — had come before the Court sooner, they might have fared differently. The timing was undoubtedly bad, and timing was at the heart of the matter. And yet the president had able lawyers among his advisers, some of whom may have felt, along with General Johnson, that the NRA should be given time to become an effectively functioning mechanism before it ran the gauntlet. Meanwhile, however, the crisis was passing. Had the cases been pushed earlier they might have been validated. If they had been declared unconstitutional early enough, President Roosevelt would have had behind him a vast force of opinion for any attack he might make on the judicial power.

Such reasoning, however, does not go far enough. When the economic tension has finally eased, the Court would find little difficulty in retracing its steps. The crux of the constitutional impasse today is that any permanent extension of the federal power would be regarded by concentrated wealth as a decisive threat to its dominance. The constitutional crisis might have been delayed; it could scarcely have been eliminated.

The overwhelming issue today is whether we shall have a power in the federal government that can meet and cope with the concentration of economic power in our society.

THIS QUESTION REALLY INVOLVES SOMETHING LIKE A THREE-RING circus. It involves, first, what we may call the *area of economic activity,* which has moved from independent farming and petty trade to the scale of the giant corporation. Second, it involves the *area of government control* of that economic activity. Finally, it involves the *area of judicial tolerance* — the extent to which the Supreme Court will allow the government control. While the first is part of the inevitable sweep of the machine process, and the second has responded to waves of democratic feeling, the last is unlimited except as it may limit itself. In the now-famous words of Justice Hughes, spoken while he was still governor of New York and therefore relatively irresponsible, "We are under a Constitution, but the Constitution is what the judges say it is."

WHAT HAS HAPPENED SINCE THE 1880s IS THAT GOVERNMENT CONTROL on the plane of state units has grown increasingly irrelevant. While through most of its history the Court has been intolerant of state control, and has fought it especially through the doctrine of due process of law, Justices Holmes and Brandeis succeeded in developing a persuasive philosophy of judicial toleration. Holmes was for allowing experiments in "the insulated chambers afforded by the several states." Brandeis was for giving the decisive weight to the legislative history of an act and the social context in which it was placed. But such philosophies are now less applicable. We have an economic system that can be run successfully or curbed effectively only on a national plane.

We must face the fact that the area of government control today must coincide with the area of economic activity. Since one is on a national scale, so must the other be. Industry is not contained within state lines. Mining, manufacturing, transportation, communication, labor, finance — all constitute an unbroken industrial chain flung out over a national market. Moreover, industry not only operates on a national scale, but in its magnitude and concentration, its power is also national. And when our economic system breaks down, it can be restored only by governmental action on a national scale. In fact, whether the economic system is functioning or threatening or in collapse, the states as the principal regulatory agencies are now anachronisms.

The New Dealers relied on three congressional grants of power in getting the courts to decide in their favor. One is the power of Congress to regulate commerce, the second is its taxing power, the third (closely related to the second) is its spending power.

The commerce power was the one most relied on for vaulting into the heaven of federal control. There was a strong tradition of liberal interpretation of the commerce power, and it did not need much stretching to make it adequate for industrial control. The tendency toward a broader construction, as Professor Corwin has shown, became marked under the influence of Holmes and Taft, starting with the *Swift* case in 1905. The Court had accepted the regulation of the meat-packing industry and the grain-futures exchanges as coming within the scope of the commerce clause. The only real stumbling block was *Hammer v. Dagenhart* (1918), the first child-labor case, which held invalid a federal act forbidding the shipment of the products of child labor in interstate commerce. In interpreting the term *commerce,* the Court has fluctuated between restricting it severely to physical transportation, and expanding it to mean anything essential to the functioning of the economic mechanism. In interpreting the term *regulate* it has at times restricted it to the Hamiltonian sense of fostering and aiding commerce, and at times ventured into the more militant sense of subjecting it to government restraint. Accordingly, when in the railroad-retirement case and again in the *Schechter* NRA case the Court adopted the narrow view of the commerce power, it was a deliberate choice of the less liberal among alternative lines of precedent.

When the commerce power had been blocked, a new white hope was the taxing power (under the general-welfare clause) and the power of making appropriations. Both were deeply entrenched in American constitutional history — in the history of legislative practice and in that of judicial interpretation. To have overturned those powers directly would have meant a judicial revolution. The only real precedent that the government had reason to fear was the child-labor tax case (the second child-labor case). After the Court had held an attempt to regulate child labor invalid under the commerce power in *Hammer v. Dagenhart,* Congress sought to accomplish the same regulation by imposing a tax on the products of child labor. As is well known, when confronted with the problem of the taxing and spending powers in the *Hoosac* case, the Court tried the flank attack. It studiously avoided ruling on the scope of the general-welfare clause or the spending power. It insisted that the purpose of the tax was the federal regulation of agriculture, which, according to the Tenth Amendment, was reserved to the states, and that Congress could not assume such a regulatory function under the guise of taxing the processors or making appropriations for the farmers.

I know that it is both a paradox and lèse-majesté to speak of the Supreme Court as lawless. And yet, if the meaning of the word *lawless* be properly understood, the conviction is overwhelming that the Supreme Court majority as constituted in 1936 represents the most lawless force in American life.

I can only list the counts in the most summary fashion. First, in economic terms, the present course of decision can only lead us to economic chaos. By denying the federal government the power to deal on a national plane with the problems of economic control, the Court is doing more to weaken the American economic structure than all the allegedly subversive radical parties in the country. But it is doing more than merely blocking the federal power in the name of states' rights. By a process familiar in our judicial history, which we may without loss of dignity call the "two-way stretch," it is also blocking the state power of economic control. The same session that saw the *Hoosac* decision saw the decision in the Vermont income-tax case and the North Dakota tax-commission case. The result is to cripple both state and federal control, leaving the public interest in a dark no-man's-land and leaving business enterprise itself at the mercy of the forces of collapse.

To economic chaos must be added administrative anarchy. Not only is the Supreme Court's animus against legislative control encouraging the lower federal courts to grant injunctions generously and to give free rein to their inherent conservatism. Something even more serious is presented in the Court's ruling in the rice millers' case.[4] With a reckless disregard for administrative consequences, the Court in effect placed a premium on the refusal to pay taxes. Those who do not pay but seek injunctive relief may have their taxes impounded in court and eventually returned to them. This would effectively sabotage any administrative setup, no matter how good.[5]

More strictly within the judicial realm are two other matters. One relates to the Court's cavalier treatment of established and fairly clear precedent. The other relates to the departure from the tradition of constitutional law that holds that if a case can be disposed of on narrow or procedural grounds, the larger issues ought not to be raised. If this tradition had been followed, much havoc might have been avoided in the interpretation of the commerce power. For some reason the Court seems anxious to look ahead and pass on the large and impeding constitutional issues. The result is a needlessly rapid and savage rate of legislative destruction.

Finally, there is a lawlessness involved in the Court's being a law to itself. In his brilliant *Hoosac* dissent, Justice Stone charged the majority with assuming an arbitrary and irresponsible power, subject to no restraint except for their own self-restraint. In a supposedly democratic state, based on the separation of powers, this is the height of lawlessness.

THE SIMPLEST WAY TO CURB THE COURT WOULD SEEM TO BE TO "pack" it. Congress has undisputed power to determine the size of the Court. In Jackson's administration the number of judges was increased from seven to nine to counterbalance the influence of the Marshall tradition. Under Lincoln, during the Civil War, the Court was conveniently increased to ten, to make it safe for the war powers of the president. There seems to be ample proof that Grant packed the Court to get a favorable decision on the legal tender cases. This is a technique that Mr. Roosevelt might have used if an unfavorable NRA decision had come down when the country was still under the spell of the New Deal, especially if the Court had been closely divided on the issue. Now such a procedure would be fruitless — and what is more, impossible with a campaign pending. Eventually, of course, an administration with enough temerity may do what the liberals did in England to the House of Lords — threaten to appoint so many new members that each individual would yield up some of his power.

The most frequent suggestion is to regulate not the number on the Court but the manner of their voting. It would provide that a majority of the justices is not enough to invalidate an act of Congress. Some number, such as seven or eight — or more than two-thirds of the Court — is usually suggested. Many argue that this would leave a decision about constitutionality in the hands of one or two justices. The reply to that argument is that just such an event is intended: since you can usually count on one or two justices to vote on the side of Congress, this leaves the decision on economic issues where it belongs — with Congress and the president. Another device, intended to have somewhat the same effect, would be to provide that unfavorable Court decisions could be overruled by a two-thirds vote of Congress. Still another would be to abolish entirely, by congressional action, the Court's right to invalidate acts of Congress; or to take certain types of cases or certain issues of legislation out of the jurisdiction of the Court. On the basis of precedent, a strong case could be made that Congress has the power to set the conditions under which the Supreme Court shall function, and that such a power would include the regulation of its number, voting, jurisdiction. The supreme irony of the whole situation is, of course, that whether or not Congress has such a power would have to be finally decided by the Court itself.

Another proposal for dealing with the Court's power is the amending process. The liberals and radicals want it, because it seems to them a fundamental attack on the whole problem. A constitutional amendment giving Congress the unimpeded right to legislate on all issues affecting agriculture, industry, labor, and finance on a national scale would meet the massed force of opposition from business enterprise. What lengths that opposition would go to is now difficult to say. But it is clear that such an amendment could only be carried as part of a larger movement to establish a controlled economy. Such a movement involves a greater degree of organization among productive groups than has yet been achieved, and a new political alignment. Into it the best democratic energies of the country will be poured. The Court and the country are both entering an "iron age." The struggles of that age will determine whether the promise of American life can be made constitutional.

Walter Lippmann, confronted by President Roosevelt's plan for reorganizing the Supreme Court, calls it dastardly, dishonest, reactionary, "audacious, ingenious, and at bottom stupid"; an act of "usurpation," a "bloodless coup d'état" that strikes at "the moral foundations of the republic."

It is possible to discuss the president's proposal on three planes: the plane of legality, the plane of morality, and the plane of the mechanics and dynamics of government. On the score of legality, Mr. Lippmann can have no quarrel with the president, except to say that it is only a cloak for dark motives and something morally sinister. On the score of morality I can have no quarrel with Mr. Lippmann: he is welcome to his own moral canon, provided he will let others have theirs. Mr. Lippmann should remember that the "moral foundations of the republic" is one of those stereotypes that he so admirably analyzed years ago in his book *Public Opinion,* and which is chiefly used as an emotional substitute for thought.

Let us stay on the plane of political analysis. Mr. Lippmann's chief fear is that the measure will destroy the independence of the judiciary. He sees the Court as being "packed" with "young henchmen" of the president, political hacks responsive to his desires. And then, by a parade of imaginary horribles, he converts a statute for retiring justices at seventy into a coup d'état.

What is not fantasy in this analysis is based on faulty history and naive political theory. The independence of the judiciary does not go beyond the constitutional safeguards. It does not extend to nonpartisanship. Every president "packs" the Court when he appoints a justice. Presidents have always wanted men of their own persuasion on the bench. Our greatest justices — Marshall and Taney, outstandingly — have been men of political and economic convictions, deeply embroiled in politics before their appointment. Surely Mr. Lippmann has read the letters between the earlier Roosevelt and Senator Lodge on the question of whether one O. W. Holmes, Jr., had the right sort of economic views. By accepting the myth of judicial neutrality, Mr. Lippmann misreads history. By charging the president with seeking to change the Constitution, he misreads judicial theory. The fact is that every important decision of the Court changes the Constitution. It was a pragmatic Tory lawyer who described the

Supreme Court as an "adjourned session of the constitutional convention." Under the new plan the "independent judiciary," which has never been independent of Big Enterprise, would merely continue its work within new limits on age and numbers legally set by Congress.

Mr. Lippmann admits that some of the Supreme Court decisions have distressed him. But he fears to limit the Court's power to render such decisions, and he fears also too extensive a grant of power to Congress. After whetting our appetite, Mr. Lippmann finally advances his own proposal. He favors a *specific amendment* each time a new specific power is needed by Congress and refused by the Court. But the amending process, he knows, is fearfully difficult. His answer is to amend the powers to amend, with respect to the commerce clause only (with a six-month limit for ratification), and to leave the rest alone.

Surely anyone with Mr. Lippmann's background does not need an education in the obvious. He does not have to be told that there is more in the heaven and earth of the Supreme Court than is dreamt of in the commerce power. *Hammer v. Dagenhart* (the child-labor case) is based not only on the commerce clause but also on the Tenth Amendment. The *Adair* case and the railroad-retirement pension case are based not only on the commerce clause but also on the due process clause. The briefs in the Wagner Act cases are built not only on the commerce power but on the First Amendment and the Fifth Amendment as well. For killing legislation, the justices have been equipped with a whole quiver of arrows, any of which they could draw as the occasion demanded.

Mr. Lippmann does not want to achieve real legislative flexibility. He thoroughly distrusts Congress, as he distrusts every organ of the people. He wants to entrench minority rule. He wants to consider the Constitution as a grant of *specific* powers, and he wants each additional specific power (that is, every important piece of new social legislation) to run the gauntlet of a two-thirds vote of Congress and a three-quarters vote of the states. This would be minority rule with a vengeance. And it is a tribute to Mr. Lippmann's intellectual athleticism that he can glorify minority rule in the name of democracy.

1937

2
THE JUDICIAL POWER AS FORTRESS

Government cannot be wholly based on the utilitarian majority calculus; neither can it allow minority rights to defeat the purposes that a society has set for itself. Majority rule tends to grow imperialistically until it makes the culture totalitarian, but minority rights tend to be fetishized into minority rule. If the answer to this problem were known, politics would not be a perilous and challenging art, but a methodical science.

Minority rights lend themselves readily as a screen for oligarchical rule. In America the Bill of Rights, embodying the experience of the Revolution and jammed into the Constitution by the common people to guard against the aristocracy of wealth and the insolence of power, has become increasingly the shield of those who cling to the power of wealth against the power of a democracy. The increasing need for regulating corporate enterprise has dashed itself against the wall that the courts have erected around property, which cannot be taken without "due process of law." The liberty to which we have built the biggest altar is "liberty of contract," which amounts in a capitalist context to the uninhibited liberty of exploiting labor. "Freedom of the press," which once meant something, has become in essence the freedom to fight union organization of newspaper employees. Civil liberties have come to mean in actuality not a body of tradition to set the boundaries of arbitrary power but a bag of tricks to defeat the purposes of majority rule.

The fault does not lie in the idea of civil liberties as such. It lies in the social context in which the idea has been developed. In a capitalist democracy the law stands in a complex and contradictory relation to the minority of economic power. On the one hand the main body of the law, especially the court-made and court-applied law — the body of precedent and procedure that we offer as "the rule of law" — is primarily a protection for property rights. To the extent that civil liberty is identified with this body of law, it is a minority concept. On the other hand, to the extent that it shifts in response to changing social needs, law is a majority instrument. Its safeguards, such as, for example, the National Labor Relations Act, are safeguards for majorities or potential majorities against the concentrated power of corporations either within their own factory walls or in the towns whose police and courts they control. Civil liberty in this sense — the right to organize and speak and vote and build new economic or party alignments — is a majority concept.

This is the sort of concept it was early in American history, when civil liberties meant the majority's Bill of Rights and had to be fought for as such by the majority. It is our failure to understand realistically the importance of civil liberties for the majorities of today that leads us to think of it as a minority concept. Ours is an age in which the majority is fighting the power of corporate capitalism, is seeking to regain control of the democratic machinery for purposes of socialization, and is determined to do so only through democratic procedures. This sets the meaning of civil liberties for us: the guarantee of legal procedures for the majority as well as minorities in this struggle.

Today in totalitarian states it is the minority groups who are oppressed and who most lack the protection of a code of civil liberties. But in capitalist democracies the real oppressions are against those to whose aid the law, taking the shape of capitalist power in the community, is not anxious to come — labor organizers who are beaten and shot, blacks who are lynched, sharecroppers who are flogged, teachers who are dismissed from their posts and preachers from their pulpits, liberals who are made the victims of Red hunts in their communities, radicals who are framed and deported, libertarians whose only sin is that they dare to challenge some local totalitarianism. These people and their sort are the people who in the past fought for the civil liberties. They are still being denied the civil liberties, but their quarrel does not lie in determining the exact limits of the province of government. For them there exists only the brutality of extragovernmental terrorism. The civil liberties of these people could be protected by a strong government. But that is not likely until that government has achieved economic order through an effective organization of the majority will, for vigilantism is an outgrowth of the basic unhealth of the political body.

We must, however, keep firmly in mind the fact that the strength of a government raises problems of liberty that are not solved merely by adding to its strength. To achieve economic order, legislative and executive supremacy is required, yet such supremacy must clearly allow for judicial guarantees and for administrative expertise.

The judicial guarantee of liberty does not, however, necessarily involve instituting judicial review. By making due process of law strictly a procedural concept instead of a substantive one, it would be possible to extend the protection of the courts to everyone without interfering with the province of the legislature and the executive branch. To be doubly sure, one could, in addition, adopt Justice Holmes's suggestion of limiting judicial review to acts of the state governments. There are two reasons for making this distinction. First, the economic system has become an interstate entity. Hence the crucial legislation for economic order must follow national rather than state lines and should not be put in the straitjacket of judicial review. Second, persistent infringements of civil liberties are likely to come from the states, where it is easier for corporate power to dominate the legislatures and local peace officers. Had due process been restored to its old meaning, and had judicial review of national legislation been abolished, President Roosevelt would not have had to resort to the elaborate circumventions of his court reorganization plan.

To this suggestion, as well as to the court-packing plan and the appointment of Hugo Black to the Court, the response has been the cry that the Court is being "politicized" and its role as the bulwark of civil liberties threatened. But that is to claim too much for it. The Court's record on civil liberties, as any critical historian will attest, has been equivocal. On issues that strike at the fabric of capitalist power, or in times of great stress, such as war, it has proved as susceptible as any Congress to the prevailing hysterias. No, to regard the Court or any governmental agency as the bulwark of civil liberties is to look through the wrong end of the telescope. Only the health of the economic organism can make civil liberties secure, and government agencies had best be viewed in relation to that health. From such a viewpoint the Supreme Court has much to answer for. Until the past few years, it has been a great anarchic force, causing social breakdown by obstructing the basic legislation intended to regulate the economic system. In an orderly economy, when the tensions that generate infringements of civil liberties have been calmed, the Court has a valid and indispensable function to make the Bill of Rights a reality in individual litigation and to enforce due process of law.

We may approach similarly the question of civil liberties and the executive branch. From England we inherit the belief that liberty must be jealously guarded against the executive power. Recently the fear that a fascist dictatorship will emerge from presidential encroachment on the other branches of government has been growing in America. But such a fear is far less warranted than the fear that it will emerge from a breakdown of executive power. The soil of fascism is found in economic collapse, political paralysis, psychological hysteria. Political efficiency is a function of the relations among the branches of government, the existence of a clear majority in the legislature, the working of the party system, and, above all, the organization and morale of the executive. The executive reorganization plan was one step toward the avoidance of political paralysis. It was ironic that it should have been defeated by the accusatory cry of dictatorship, for the defeat was not a victory for civil liberties. It was a victory only for those fighting governmental control of industry and eventual socialization.

Today, the vanguard of democratic advance is the administrative commission, whose intelligence and morale are decisive factors in determining whether we shall survive the transition toward a socialized economy. It is, therefore, not at all surprising that the reactionaries in America should have trained their heaviest guns on the administrative commissions, particularly the Labor Relations Board, the Securities and Exchange Commission, and the Tennessee Valley Authority.

These commissions are in the main carrying out their prescribed function with caution and tolerance, but they are accused of overstepping their administrative bounds and entering into the area of the legislature and judiciary, thus subjecting the individual to the unchecked power of a small group of men. Yet the combination of executive, legislative, and judicial functions is exactly what makes the commissions an effective new government form. They have investigatory and administrative tasks, in which they act in a quasi-judicial capacity; they have rule-making powers that have been delegated to them by Congress. It is notable in this connection that the Labor Board, which has been most vigorously attacked for combining the posts of judge and prosecutor and for violating the freedom of speech and press of the employers, has been upheld by a tolerably liberal Supreme Court in an overwhelming proportion of its test cases.

The real danger to civil liberties in capitalist democracies in the calculable future does not arise from the extensions of governmental power; it arises from the broad no-man's-land of industrial terrorism and fascist preparation into which the government has thus far been powerless to penetrate. The big question for us is not so much, How far can the majority go? — although that must not be neglected. It is, How far will the minority go? For in the transition toward socialization, the oligarchs will not be inactive. The great problem of civil liberties is whether freedom of speech, press, union organization, and political action can be preserved for a majority that wants to use it to socialize the economic structure and to achieve a democratic humanism.

We need civil liberties not for a minority but for all. The greatest tradition of liberty is that of an advancing majority fighting the absolute power of oligarchies and creating in the process new safeguards for the human spirit. Those safeguards must apply to rich and poor alike, and no code of liberty can afford to make any exceptions based on wealth or social status. But in the very nature of the struggle for democratic control, it is the powerful economic minority that represents the great obstacle in the path of achieving that control. Liberty has to cope with that obstacle without incurring the risk of arbitrary power and without corrupting the habit of tolerance.

The tradition, however, is concerned only with propagating an idea through verbal persuasion and through organization. It does not extend to political uniforms and drill and paramilitary organization. There is an urgent need for federal legislation banning the latter. There can be no toleration, even in the libertarian tradition, for the setting up of a state within a state. Democracy need not have a suicide urge as an imperative.

We cannot, as well, accept at its face value the contention of the industrialists that their civil liberties are threatened by the action of the administrative boards or congressional committees of inquiry. Doing so would sabotage administrative control of business and give the corporations a providential framework of rhetoric within which to hide from the advance of socialization.

Liberals once believed in the triumph of the idea. Democratic humanists still believe in it. But they know that a postponed triumph will be an empty one. And they know that the idea of civil liberties is more likely to triumph if its friends fight for the civil liberties of the many, instead of weeping unduly over the trumped-up infringements of the liberties of the few.

1938

4

Minority Rule and the Constitutional Tradition

The Constitution's Bicentennial in 1987 was a bland affair of self-congratulation compared with the sesquicentennial celebration of the Constitution in 1937. That year the meetings of the American Historical Association, which opened in Philadelphia on December 30, 1937, displayed a tumult of intellectual controversy.

Conyers Read and Caroline F. Ware, two historians who planned the celebration, requested that I give a paper.[1] I was at that time in the thick of battle at the Nation *over the Roosevelt court-packing plan, and I was also writing the last chapters of* It Is Later Than You Think, *which I had subtitled* The Need for a Militant Democracy. *At the heart of my argument in the essay was my contention that the true strength of America lay in democracy, not liberalism; that the Constitution — despite Charles Beard's "economic interpretation" — was an instrument for democracy that had been perverted from the majority will of democracy to the protection of the corporate-power minority, and that liberals were innocently allowing this to happen.*

Some forty years later the historian Page Smith, writing about the young iconoclasts at the sesquicentennial meeting in his narrative history, The Constitution (1978), *described me as "probably, at that time, the most radical of the essayists." He quoted my core theme — that judicial review was "the last barricade" of the antidemocratic forces, that "there, behind the safe networks of natural law, due process, minority rights, the judges can, in the plenitude of their virtue and sincerity, veto and outlaw the basic social program of the majority."*

52 /

Well enough. Yet it struck me as somewhat curious that he should regard another part of my thesis as radical — that there is "no antithesis between the Constitution as such and the democratic impulse," and that if you "scratch a fervent believer in judicial supremacy and like as not you will find someone with a bitterness about democracy. The two are as close as skin and skeleton." I should have thought that deep belief in majoritarian democracy in the face of judicial supremacy would not be transformed into a stigma proving "radicalism."

Rereading my essay in the light of the intervening half-century, I find it contains more than a foreshadowing hint of the use of the Constitution by later Courts to throw their mantle around vested minority interest groups — groups different in substance yet not in principle from the vested corporate groups I identified. I see the antimajoritarian bias continuing into the current constitutional culture.

1

"Law," Aaron Burr once remarked, "is that which is boldly asserted and plausibly maintained."[2] I prefer this insight, crude as it may seem, to much of the wisdom in the whole array of schools of legal philosophy. Burr must have had an uncanny prescience about the development of American constitutional law. Into the increasingly bold assertion of judicial supremacy — the history of the judicial power — I do not propose to enter here. It has been explored a good deal recently and is a matter of record in the annals of the Supreme Court. That record is one of tortuous maneuverings and daring faits accomplis in the field of governmental practice. The men who have guided the destinies of the judicial power, from Alexander Hamilton and John Marshall to Chief Justice Hughes in our own day, have been masters of the art of political manipulation and anything but novices in the technique of presenting the enemy with a decision.

I am not one of those who regard the assertion of judicial supremacy as an act of usurpation.[3] It is a truism, of course, that the power of judicial supremacy over the whole governmental process is nowhere to be found expressly granted in the constitutional document. It is a body of inferences, a system of "givens" and "therefores," an intellectual construction. But it has by this time become accepted as a living institution, and I have too much respect for any organic thing to think it can be exorcised out of existence by legalistic discussions. The judicial power has by this time written itself into the Constitution by Court interpretation and prescriptive right, just as much as if it were clearly granted in the document. In short, it is a colossal gloss, a gloss with which we must deal as we would with any political actuality.

It is time for American thinking on the Constitution to move away from the question of original intent, away from *whether* the men at the Constitutional Convention intended judicial review, to the question of *how* judicial supremacy has been built up and maintains itself. To move from the *whether* to the *how* is, perhaps, always a step forward — from what can be only subjectively guessed at to what can be objectively observed, from theology to science, from polemics to history. Although it will undoubtedly prove eternally interesting, what can be said of intent with respect to judicial review is actually rather little, and even that little is speculation. One may balance the warily expressed desires of the framers against the clear aversion of the people at the time and get nowhere.[4] What can be said of the logic behind the way judicial power has been built up is clearer: it is the natural outcome of the necessity of a capitalist minority to maintain rule in a democracy. Judicial review has not flowed merely from the will to power of individual justices; it has been the convenient channel through which the driving current of a developing business enterprise has found direction and achieved victory.

Let us, however, turn to the last half of Aaron Burr's definition. "Law is that which is boldly asserted *and plausibly maintained.*" "Bold assertion" takes place in the realm of political action and economic pressure. "Plausible maintenance" takes place in the realm of symbols, interest structures, and idea systems. The aggressions of judicial power cannot be understood unless we see them as part of the attempt to maintain the existing power structures in our peculiar form of capitalist democracy. But the defenses of judicial power are also formidable. Every institution seeks to build a triple line of defense. First, there is the area of *symbols,* or what Professor Charles Elliott calls "social myths" and Thurman Arnold sometimes calls "symbols" and other times "folklore."[5] The realm of symbols is most often an unconscious realm; when they have become too articulated their spell is broken. Second, there are *interest structures,* the pulls and thrusts of class relations that make various groups defend judicial power and make the Supreme Court defend those groups; those interest structures generally operate on the subconscious level, but in times of tension they become articulated. In between these two there is the third area, that of *formal apologetics* — the ideology by which judicial power has operated and been defended. Thus around judicial power, we have a triple defense-ring: symbolic structures, interest structures, and idea structures. It is with the relation of the last two that I am here principally concerned.

2

The Court's own apologia for its power — what may be called the "official" theory of the judicial function — is well known, but I shall take the liberty of recapitulating it. It runs somewhat as follows. We have a fundamental law in the form of a written Constitution, which overrides legislative enactments that are not in harmony with it. We have a federal system in which powers must be divided between the states and the central government; and a system of separated powers in which the lines must be drawn between the departments of the government, and the encroachments of one on the others avoided. We thus have a system that would result in chaos or tyranny were there no final arbiter. We have, moreover, the danger that men in power will aggrandize their power at the expense of other men, and invade their rights; we have a people safe from such invasion only under the protection of the Constitution. We have, finally, a judicial body, deliberately placed above politics and beyond partisan control, and empowered to assure for us a government of laws and not of men. The fund of knowledge and principles to which this body appeals is to be found in the Anglo-American common law, the precedents of constitutional law, and the "higher law" resident in the "genius of republican institutions."

In its way this official theory is something of a masterpiece, a mosaic pieced together from *The Federalist Papers,* Court decisions and dicta, commentaries by scholars such as James Kent and Charles Cooley, and classic speeches, such as those of Webster. It is a thing of beauty: neat, logical, close fitting, comprehensive — so long as you grant its premises.

Let me set out some of those premises, generally unexpressed. The official theory assumes that a fundamental law must be superior to all legislative enactments, despite the example of the English system, where the line of constitutional growth lies in parliamentary enactment rather than in judicial construction. The official theory assumes that other departments of the government may not be as capable as the judiciary of the task of constitutional construction — assumes, that is, a fund of exclusive and inspired knowledge of the law on the part of the judges. It assumes that the litigant's obligation to accept the Court's construction of a statute extends to Congress as well. It assumes an imperialistic thirst for power and expansion on the part of the executive and the legislature, and despite Justice Stone's agonizing cry of *de profundis* in the *Butler* case ("The only check upon our own exercise of power is our own sense of self-restraint"[6]), despite this cry, the official theory makes no similar assumption about the stake the judges have in their own power. It assumes that all government is dangerous, and thus adopts a negativist attitude toward governmental powers. It assumes that the legal aspects of a governmental problem can be separated and abstracted from its real aspects. It assumes, in short, a closed Constitution in a malignant universe, instead of an open instrument of government in a changing and challenging world.

I have spoken thus far of the formal ideology of judicial power. But an ideology is not merely a series of linked propositions drawn from related premises. Sometimes it draws its greatest strength from allies — in this case, ideas not contained within the official apologia of the Court's power but embedded in the popular imagination. I want to pick four of them for brief discussion: the doctrine of limited governmental powers, the doctrine of the sanctity of property, the doctrine of federalism, and the doctrine of minority rights.

The Constitution was born in a century obsessed with the notion of limited powers, a century overshadowed by Locke and Rousseau. Conservative thought clung to the rights of minorities against the tyranny of the majority, and radical theory, such as that of Jefferson and the great European rationalists, took the form of belief in the perfectibility of man and the malignancy of government. But the pattern of the century contained a curious inner contradiction in its thought. The prevailing economic policy was mercantilistic, with all the close and comprehensive controls that the mercantilist state exercised over economic life, and with all its resulting concentration of authority. The prevailing political thought, however, was atomistic, with its emphasis on individual liberties and governmental dangers. The men who framed the Constitution and ran the government that it created were trapped in this contradiction. Their conservative economic interests dictated a strong, central, mercantilist government; the prevailing ideas of the time, fortifying their fear of democracy, made them place that government of expanded powers within an intellectual framework of limited powers. Hence, to a large extent, the confusion of the constitutional debates. The interesting fact is that judicial ideology still clings to the doctrine of limited powers, even in a world where to act on it would be grotesquely tragic, and where the popular impulse is to abandon it.

When we pass to the doctrine of the sanctity of property, we find that "property" has assumed a variety of forms in our history, but that the protection and support it has accorded to the Supreme Court has been continuous. American life has pushed forward along a variety of trails — farm, frontier, and factory; plantation and city; trade-route, logging-camp, and mining-town; corporation and co-operative. But common to all these has been a persistent and pervasive sense of property. It first took the form of the land mysticism and land hunger of Physiocratic thought, deeply embedded in the whole movement of colonial settlement from which Jefferson eventually drew much of his support; then, the sense of vested rights and the deep sense of contractual obligation to which Marshall gave doctrinal expression in his "contract decisions," and which, using and twisting somewhat Sir Henry Sumner Maine's terminology,[7] provided a new sort of status for an age of capitalism; then, the sense of property individualism, born of the movements for European liberation, blessed with the approval of Protestant capitalism, flourishing in the wilderness of the American frontier, and turned into laissez-faire by the conditions of a reckless and exploitative capitalism; and finally, when individualism could no longer thrive as an idea because it had been extinguished as a fact of economic life, property took the sense of clinging to the profit system and the cash nexus as bulwarks against social anarchy and the destruction of the social fabric. This sense of property, even when its widespread social base has been so largely destroyed in the age of absentee ownership, is still a powerful ally to and of judicial power.

When we turn to the theory of federalism and states' rights, we are dealing with a powerful intellectual and sentimental force that the Supreme Court at times has had to fight but more latterly has been calling to its aid. We are all acquainted with those old arguments that, like ghosts, are continually materializing in the world of ideas even though we are aware that they no longer represent actualities. The idea of free opportunity under capitalism is one, and it lingers on even in a world dominated by monopoly. In the political realm the most potent and assertive American ghost is still federalism. Although most of its former functions have been stripped from it, it haunts a nation in which every force drives toward centralization, both economic and political. I do not mean it is no longer a fact to be reckoned with. The strength of a ghost rests in its capacity to make itself believed; and that, in turn, depends more than anything on our own fears. The fear of overcentralization, of the wiping out of the traditional political and cultural landmarks of the states, is a very real fear, especially in the light of what the fascist dictatorships have done to federalism. It is a fear that the Supreme Court, as witnessed in the AAA case,[8] has not been averse to exploring and exploiting.

About the doctrine of minority rights and individual liberties it might be said that recent events have given them, or seem to have given them, even greater meaning than they once possessed. The tradition of minority rights has always been an important source of strength for judicial supremacy. The doctrine of vested rights, the sanctity of contract and liberty of contract, the doctrine of due process of law — all have drawn upon this tradition. In fact, most of the Court's decisions invalidating legislation hostile to property might be interpreted as proceeding from its zeal for minority rights, rather than from any untoward zeal for business interests. Nevertheless, so long as a strong rationalization for capitalist power existed in economic thought and opinion, the civil liberties and minority-rights argument was secondary. Now, however, two things are happening to push it to the fore. One is the decline of laissez-faire, both in practice and in thought. The second is the spread of fascism in Europe and the fear of it in America. The first has made businessmen and judges turn increasingly to the rhetoric of civil liberties; the second has made the liberals and the middle classes more ready to accept the Court's guardianship of civil liberties, even if it means a measure of judicial control over economic policy.[9]

All four of these ideological allies of judicial power, viewed historically, have their roots in majority movements and have played a great and even revolutionary role in the history of the Western world. And all four have been turned to the uses of minority rule as parts of the constitutional tradition. Take first the idea of a government of limited powers. The notion of a higher law; the idea of natural rights of individuals, who adhere to them independently of government and even in spite of government, and who must be protected against government; the necessity of disobedience of a government that violates these rights: these had once been living parts of revolutionary movements that swept across Western Europe, from the parliamentary champions of the struggle against the Tudors and Stuarts to the philosophes of the French Revolution. They were majority movements, aimed at limiting the powers of the dying upper classes. They were used to rationalize the actual movement toward parliamentarism in England and toward middle-class democracy in France. But in taking them over, judicial review turned them to quite different uses, to defeat parliamentary supremacy and to hem in democracy with severe limitations — in short, to the uses of minority rule. The same may be said of that sense of property that has been part of the American democratic experience, of the democratic localism that underlies federalism and states' rights, and of the democratic movements that generated the doctrines of civil liberties and minority rights. All have been twisted out of their original context and turned to the uses of minority rule.

I want now to examine more closely three concepts I have been using — democracy (or majority will), minority rule, and minority rights. The relation between these three is central to an understanding of the ideology of judicial power.

Scratch a fervent believer in judicial supremacy and like as not you will find someone with a bitterness about democracy. The two are as close as skin and skeleton. When I speak of *democracy* here, I want to distinguish it sharply from *liberalism*. There is no greater confusion in the layman's mind today than the tendency to identify the two with each other. American history has been witness to a protracted struggle between democratic and antidemocratic forces. Antidemocracy began as aristocratic thought, with emphasis on a neo-Greek elite. Alexander Hamilton, heartbroken because the new American state could not be a monarchy with George Washington as king and himself as kingmaker, sublimated his monarchical passion in a dream of America as an aristocracy of property. And a whole school followed him. But it soon became clear that in a country where a revolutionary war had only recently been fought to achieve democracy, an aristocratic body of thought could not form the base of any party successful at the polls. The collapse of the Federalist Party proved it.

A shift was made, therefore, to liberalism; and so powerful an aid did liberalism become to the antidemocratic forces that even conservatism grew shamefaced and, to survive, donned the garments of liberalism. In the South alone, in the period of tension preceding the Civil War, slavery as an economic base allowed aristocratic theory to linger on. The spokesmen for the slavocracy defended it as re-establishing a Greek republic among the roses and cotton bolls below the Mason-Dixon line. But the Civil War proved by blood and iron that aristocratic theory was, like slavery, an unwelcome survivor from archaic times. The northern financial oligarchy that rose to unchallenged political power out of the Civil War spoke thereafter in the name of an orthodox, if slightly cynical, liberalism. And it has continued to do so.

Let us be clear about it: minority-rights liberalism (which becomes in practice minority-rule liberalism) furnishes the only reasoned defense of capitalist power that we have in America. This liberalism has three facets: it defends individual civil liberties against society, it defends minority rights (including both human and property rights) against the possible tyranny of the government, and it contains a belief in rationalism and in the final triumph of the idea. In the course of the liberal revolutions in Europe, democratic forces sought to carry the implications of the libertarian movements to their logical conclusion for both the middle-class and the lower-class population, not only for political but also for economic freedom and equality. They began to loom as the great threat to the privileged position of the middle classes, which fortunately could find in the armory of liberalism the intellectual weapons they needed for fighting the democratic threat. The basis of democracy is majority will; its premise is that the common man can fashion his own political destiny, and that government must consist of representative institutions to carry the majority will into execution. To this, liberalism has countered with the proposition that the freedom and rights of the individual and the minority are more sacred than the will of the majority. Therein lies the essential distinction between liberalism and democracy.

In their fear of majority will, the propertied groups have depicted the democratic mass movements in the darkest colors of extremism. They have called the Jeffersonians "Jacobins," the Jacksonians "Locofocos," the agrarian radicals "Populists," and the trade unionists "Reds" and "Bolsheviks." The democratic forces, in turn, have responded by calling the propertied groups "monarchists," "plutocrats," "economic royalists." The barrage of epithets has enlivened American politics but failed to illuminate it. Behind the battle of the epithets there has been a very real struggle between majority will —

everpresent in a nation whose collective life has been based on democratic premises — and minority rule.

This has been the basic paradox of American life: the necessity of squaring majority will with minority rule — that is, democratic forms with capitalist power. It has made us, in one sense, politically speaking, a nation of hypocrites. But it has also spurred our wits and sharpened the edge of our political inventiveness. Out of it have emerged our peculiar institution of judicial supremacy and the arguments that defend it.

The mistake we are all too ready to make is to see the Constitution and the democratic impulse as antithetical. We have been led into this error partly by the excellent work of Charles Beard and his school in proving that the Constitution represents the property interests of the minority.[10] That is true enough. But we must also remember that the Constitution, without the accretion of judicial review, could (whatever its origins) have become an instrument of the majority will. The whole animus behind it, despite the system of checks and balances, was a flexible one. It was meant to adapt itself to the changes and chances of the national life.[11] It is significant that the majority groups, who were first rather sullen about it, and then accepted it after affixing to it a Bill of Rights guaranteeing individual liberties, finally became enthusiastic about it. Jeffersonians as well as Hamiltonians and Marshallians vied in their praise of the Constitution.[12] What they differed about was judicial power. The real antithesis is between the democratic impulse and the judicial power. With Jefferson and the so-called Revolution of 1800, which saw the triumph of Jeffersonianism, began that series of democratic thrusts, upsurges of the majority will, that have enlivened and vitalized American history. In Jefferson and Jackson, notably in the Bank War and the Dorr Rebellion, in Lincoln, to an extent in Cleveland, in the Populist movement and William Jennings Bryan, in Theodore Roosevelt and Woodrow Wilson, in Eugene Debs, in Franklin Roosevelt and the New Deal, and in John L. Lewis and the Congress of Industrial Organizations, we have had repetitions of that democratic thrust against the seats of minority power. It became the task of the propertied minority to ward off those thrusts, and they have thus far been able to do it through the instrument of judicial supremacy, the ideology that surrounds and defends it, and especially the ideology of liberalism.

Judicial supremacy has smoothed the way for minority rule in two senses. In one specific instance after another, measures of policy that the majority has desired have been invalidated by the Court. If the people of Georgia wanted to undo a corrupt grant of land,[13] or the people of New York wanted an eight-hour working day in bakery shops,[14] or the people of Oklahoma wanted to restrict the number of ice plants,[15] their wishes were so much dry stubble to be trod underfoot by the minority will of the Court.

But there is an even deeper sense in which the Supreme Court has acted as the final barricade against the assaults of democratic majorities. We must remember that the process of the triumph of the democratic majority is a long and tedious process, as majority leaders from Jefferson to Franklin Roosevelt have discovered. It involves displacing the enemy from one position after another. There is the vast inertia of the party system, with an autonomous force of its own even after popular sentiment has changed; there is the political apathy of the masses, the tendency they have of forgetting to remember. There is the pressure of special interests, blocking up committees and arranging filibusters. There is the control that the vested interests exercise over our newspapers and our very patterns of thinking. And there is, finally, the effective weapon the propertied minority has in withdrawing capital from investment and thus paralyzing economic process. And after all these positions have been captured, the anti-democratic forces retreat to their last barricade — judicial review. There, behind the safe earthworks of natural law, due process, minority rights, the judges can in the plenitude of their virtue and sincerity veto and outlaw the basic social program of the majority.

3

During intervals of lucidity, the democratic forces of the country have known what they were up against and what they were fighting. But in addition to all the difficulties of mustering the necessary electoral battalions, they have become increasingly confused recently. And their confusion has arisen from the fact that the rationalizations used to explain and defend the Supreme Court's power flow from the premises of liberalism — that minority rule uses the theory of minority rights, and manages somehow to equate them.

Minority rule has recently had to work very subtly to defeat majority will. In Alexander Hamilton's day, the antidemocratic theorists could say frankly, when confronted with the accusation that they had defeated the people's will: "Your people, Sir, is a great beast."[16] Or they could speak more gravely, as did Fisher Ames, of "a government of the wise, the rich, and the good,"[17] as if all three were coterminous. Later they had to convert the Bill of Rights and the Fourteenth Amendment, the heart of the protection of minority rights, from a charter of liberties into a charter of property protection. The task was a difficult one and involved two major intellectual somersaults: twisting due process of law from a procedural meaning to a substantive meaning, and endowing the corporation with all the attributes of human personality. While the task was well done, it was done with a certain cynicism, as is particularly apparent in the political commentaries between the Civil War and the First World War, as well as in the court decisions of that period. Now, however, in the midst of world tensions, democracy has taken on a new meaning and a new prestige for us, and it needs to be more subtle in defense of minority rule. The new defense is therefore not only a plea of minority rights, powerfully evocative in itself in these days, but a new interpretation of majority will as well.

That interpretation is to be found in its most polished form not in the Supreme Court decisions, when it is always implicit, nor even in scholarly commentary, but in the work of two popular commentators, Mr. Walter Lippmann and Miss Dorothy Thompson. It is significant that Mr. Lippmann embodies it in his book *The Good Society,* which is an attack on economic planning, the most dangerous threat to the economic power of the minority. Even more significantly, Miss Thompson's theory, which is the more sharply delineated, can best be found in a series of three articles that form a critique[18] of Mr. Roosevelt's Roanoke Island speech.

The new theory (I use Miss Thompson's articles as a model) reinterprets the democratic principle so that it becomes something quite different from the naked principle of majority will. First, not only must minorities be protected from majorities, but also majorities must even be protected from themselves. Second, if true democracy does operate in terms of majority will, it is not the will of a numerical majority, but a very different conception. Third, the notion of numerical majorities really smells of fascism. And having arrived at that position, one falls back in fright on minority rights, even if it involves scrapping the Tennessee Valley Authority, the Wagner Act, the Securities and Exchange Commission, and the Labor Relations Board.

When we say that majorities must be protected from themselves, the premise is the antidemocratic one — that the common man may be good material for being ruled but that he has no capacity for governing.[19] When we go on to talk of "true" democracy, as distinguished from majority will, what are we saying? We are saying that democracy is nothing so vulgar and demagogic as a counting of heads, but that there is a "real" national will, as distinguished from the one that expresses itself at the polls. That real national will is somehow a trusteeship of the minority, for the few know what is in the interest of the many better than the many know themselves. This whole concept of the national will as something transcending numbers and having no traffic with the felt desires of the day is essentially mystical.

It has always been a characteristic of reactionary thought to retreat to a mystical conception of the body politic, as witness Burke, de Maistre, Adam Müller, and the French Catholic school. Mystical notions enable one to escape from the fact of the naked majority will. And conservative minority groups have always regarded the majority as unsavory, strident, and as mechanical as the clashing of weapons through which the primitive Germanic tribes indicated their assent by the greatest noise.[20] What is novel is the fact that all this is now said — and believed — in the name of liberalism. And yet it is not so novel if we consider the extent to which the ingredients of liberal thinking — that is, minority-rule thinking — have entered into the traditional defense of the judicial power under the Constitution.

In America, an extrademocratic structure of economic reality has been built that dares not operate through the democratic machinery, for the democratic machinery is too easily turned into an instrument for leveling economic privilege. When this extrademocratic structure (an academic phrase for the structure of corporate power) is challenged, and an attempt to take our democratic theory literally and nakedly is made, how will it respond? To my mind, this is the most important issue facing the Constitution in the calculable future, an issue more dangerous than any it has confronted since the Civil War. Does the economic interest of the corporate groups so far outweigh their sense of commonwealth as to make them ready either to keep their minority rule or to scrap the whole democratic framework? My own conviction is that this is the case, and that they will insist on one or the other of these alternatives. When a corporation cannot win its fight against democracy by economic means, it may resort to military and political means and become (if I may give the term a twist) the corporative state.

If this is so, the new attack on the majority principle represented by Miss Thompson and Mr. Lippmann takes on a disquieting importance. A counterthrust against a successful labor government, for example, will look for a theory to which to anchor itself. Here is a theory ready-made. The naked majority principle, Miss Thompson tells us, is really fascist; it is part of a totalitarian state. I find there is a readiness in surprisingly intelligent quarters to accept this paradox. If that readiness spreads, corporate power will not lack those intellectual garments that it needs to stave off a socialized democracy — intellectual garments that the liberals are now spinning just as assiduously as the Parcae once spun other fateful garments.

1937

5

Keepers of the Covenant in Mythic America

When I wrote the first of these two essays for the original edition of my book America as a Civilization *(1957), I intended it to be the centerpiece of the book's legal and constitutional analysis. The New Deal was over, as were World War II and the postwar tensions. It was the time of Truman and Eisenhower. America was experiencing the only period of relative equilibrium it would have until the first Reagan term, and I seized the chance to take some accounting of it. If readers compare this with my earlier essay, "Constitution and Court as Symbols," they may find I had arrived at a longer perspective and a less combative style.*

I continued, nevertheless, to affirm the thrust of democracy, as I had done in the earlier essay. As for judicial power, after the constitutional impasse of the 1930s had been resolved, I noted that the Roosevelt, Vinson, and early Warren Courts had practiced a mix of Black-Douglas-Warren liberal activism and Holmes-Frankfurter-Jackson centrist restraint.

I was content at the time with the tentative equilibrium between them in the early Warren Court. Only when the later Warren Court broke the equilibrium, especially in cases on criminal procedures and penalties and on hiring quotas, did I feel that the liberal-activist component in the majority decisions had overcome the component of restraint. (For my response to the Warren Court's changes, see the preface to Part III and to the essay, "The Career of the Warren Court.")

The second excerpt here, which is from the 1987 edition of the same book, marks a thirty-year jump into a time frame that included the political-cultural revolutions of the 1960s and 1970s and the information-communication revolutions of the 1980s. The prevailing theme is polarization: in lawlessness countered by the rule of law, in a breakdown in values, in a liberal political-constitutional culture having to operate within a broad resurgence of conservatism.

Amid these polar currents, the continuity of the basic American myths that work for cohesiveness while so much of the civilization moves toward fragmentation has been remarkable. Still to be found at the center of this mythic America, even in a centrifugal time, is the myth of the covenant and its Supreme Court keepers. It has, if anything, gained in urgency since I first presented its perils and promise with some fervor in my 1937 essay.

1

At the apex of the American legal system stands the Supreme Court as interpreter of the Constitution. Walter Bagehot said that every government must contain something of the "dignified" or "majestic" principle, rooted in men's emotions and in what we might today call the irrational mind. Its purpose is to give government a cohesive force that can outlast political change. This element is enshrined in the Constitution, and amid all the turbulences of history, the Constitution as eidolon has remained a fixture in the American mind.

It need no longer be argued vehemently that there is a political cast to many Supreme Court appointments, but the argument is often greatly oversimplified. Certainly the Supreme Court has never been "democratic" in the sense that appointments represent a cross section of the nation. Nor is the Court democratic in the mechanically responsive sense of changing with the shifting waves of popular opinion: one of the reasons for giving the judges life tenure and putting them beyond the reach of political and popular vindictiveness was to fashion a judicial independence without which any effort to interpret the basic frame of constitutional principle as principle would be a sham. There can be too much flexibility in judicial interpretation, as well as too little, especially if the flexibility represents opportunism and a surrender to the passions of the moment.

The great appointments have been those whose judicial statesmanship grew on the bench. Sometimes, as in the appointment of Oliver Wendell Holmes by President Theodore Roosevelt, the choices were made on the mistaken assumption that the judge would go along with the political policy of the president. (After Holmes's dissent in the Northern Securities case, T.R. is reported to have cried, "I could carve out of a banana a justice with more backbone than that.") In other instances the political purpose of the appointment is well known and is carried out, as when Jackson appointed Taney or when Truman appointed Vinson. Sometimes a judge has started his judicial career inauspiciously — as when Hugo Black admitted to membership as a young man in the Ku Klux Klan — and grown to judicial greatness. Sometimes a series of remarkably able appointees have been followed by a series of mediocrities, as with the general level of President Truman's appointments (Burton, Vinson, Clark, and Minton) when compared with the general level of the Roosevelt appointments (Black, Reed, Frankfurter, Murphy, Douglas, Jackson, and Rutledge). Sometimes, as with Stone and Cardozo, the unmistakable sentiment of the whole legal profession has made the choice of a particular man inevitable.

Yet on the whole it has been true of membership on the Supreme Court, as it has of the presidential office, that the garments of office have expanded or shrunk with the dimensions of the wearer. Some of the great judges, like Marshall, Harlan, Stone, Hughes, and Warren, might well have made greater presidents than the presidents who appointed them. No member of the Court has ever been elected to the presidency, although Hughes came close and Taft reversed the process. On the whole, however, it has been a healthy tradition that the Court should not be considered a pathway to presidential office. The very fact that the Court does have decision-making power of vast political consequence makes it even more important for the justices to be invulnerable to the charge of playing for political advantage. It takes great courage to fill the role of final constitutional arbiter with an eye to the enduring lines of national growth and greatness, rather than to any particular group, pressure, or power.

It is not necessary for biographers wholly to unclothe the justices to show the street clothes under their traditional robes. A Supreme Court judge is a human being, which means he is a thinking and valuing animal, with emotions about his fellow human beings and often very decided convictions about the processes of government. Their earlier careers — as corporate and utility lawyers, as governors and senators, as attorneys general or heads of administrative agencies, as law school teachers, as crusading reformers — are usually a pretty good indication of the kind of justice they will make. As an example, I will take an instance almost at random of a mediocre judge who was nevertheless an efficient chief justice: Melville W. Fuller, a northern Democrat who had been a prosperous business lawyer. He had opposed both abolition and secession, had disapproved of the Fourteenth Amendment, and had been a vehement champion of the doctrine of "hard money." It was not too hard to foretell that he would vote to hold the Federal Income Tax Act of 1894 unconstitutional.

Or take a more eminent instance: after the nation's experience with Taft as president, it was not hard to predict that he would make a highly political Supreme Court justice. Taft later boasted that during one term as president he had been lucky enough to make six Supreme Court appointments, while his successor Woodrow Wilson could make only three in two terms. One of those three, McReynolds, who had shown social fervor as attorney general, turned the tables on the guessers and became a conservative (although still unpredictable) justice. But Taft regarded the other two, Brandeis and Clarke, as "of socialist tendency" (the leaders of the legal profession and the holders of economic power agreed with him about Brandeis, as witnessed in the massive effort to kill his nomination, first in the Senate Judiciary Committee and then in the vote on the floor). Taft saw shrewdly that one of the high stakes of the 1920 election was the fact that four of the justices had passed the retiring age and would probably have to be replaced. "There is no greater domestic issue," he said about the 1920 campaign, "than the maintenance of the Supreme Court as the bulwark to enforce the guarantee that no man shall be deprived of his property without due process of law." Harding's election underscored the political realism of Taft's view, for in three years there were four new appointments, including Taft himself, Sutherland, Butler, and Sanford; these four joined three other conservatives to form a bloc of seven who consistently outvoted and isolated Holmes and Brandeis. When Taft met his colleagues as chief justice he told them in conference, "I have been appointed to reverse a few decisions," and (he wrote later), "I looked right at old man Holmes when I said it." Even after Coolidge had appointed Stone, who seemed at first relatively "safe" but developed into a fearlessly independent member of the court, there was still a minority of only three at best on crucial cases. When Hoover appointed Cardozo the potential minority became four, but his appointments of Roberts and Hughes kept the majority safe. This political approach to court appointments evoked the drastic and equally political counterapproach of Franklin Roosevelt's court-packing proposal and, later, his deliberately political appointments of New Dealers to the Court.

I have given some detailed scrutiny here to the appointments in one period of the Court's history, but the same would be true to a much higher degree of the earlier periods. During the whole stretch of Republican presidential power from 1860 to 1912 (except for Cleveland's terms) the proportion of property-minded, business-minded, and corporate-minded judges who reached the Court was, needless to say, very high. The striking fact is that great justices do manage to emerge from this process — Marshall, Taney, Miller, Harlan, Holmes, Hughes, Brandeis, Stone, Cardozo, Black, Frankfurter, Douglas, Warren. (There were also judges like Van Devanter, who was a brilliant craftsman although a reactionary one and unable to write.) It would be hard to find a governing group in any society to match these men in talent, character, vision, and statesmanship. They have proved a fit corollary to the gallery of great presidents.

The task of the chief justice is especially difficult, since he must make the Court as cohesive as possible, iron out differences that need not be aired, avoid too-public splits, assign the writing of the majority opinion (here he can exercise a subtle influence of great importance), and set the whole intellectual tone of the Court. Marshall, Hughes, Stone, perhaps Vinson, and certainly Warren lived up notably to the dimensions of this great office. The case of Harlan Stone is especially interesting. He was appointed attorney general to sweeten the stench left by Harding's Harry Daugherty; he campaigned for Coolidge with speeches that were stilted and stuffed-shirtish; he performed his job as attorney general with distinction, yet when he was appointed to the Court, a few liberal senators, like George Norris, who were distrustful of his having had the Morgan Bank as a client, opposed his confirmation. "I have always been sorry," Stone said later, "that I didn't have the Morgan House for my client more than I did." And Norris, in 1941, voted to confirm him as Chief Justice: Stone had shown the capacity to rise above his earlier conditioning.

One of the problems of the Court has been the overwhelming pressure of judicial business. In 1925 Congress reorganized the Court's work, and later changes were made so that the Court would not have to remedy the wrongs of every litigant on appeal, but could choose the cases involving important principles of constitutional interpretation. The real question has always been what approach the Court would adopt to these principles.

The traditional "great split" between the liberal and conservative views of the Court's function, which Franklin Roosevelt phrased in popular terms as a split between those who cared about property rights and those who cared about human rights, still retains a good deal of its meaning. But in recent years the livelier controversy, which split the liberal camp itself, was the conflict between the school of social "activism" or "dynamism" and that of "judicial self-limitation" or "self-restraint." Both schools went beyond the earlier pretense that there is something fixed and known called "the law," which judges make known to the people. They recognized what Charles E. Hughes meant when he said that "we live under a Constitution, but the Constitution is what the Supreme Court says it is." He gave the simplest possible definition of what has come to be called judicial supremacy. The two schools differed, however, in the method by which they could best live up to their task of interpreting constitutional powers, rights, and immunities.

The self-limitation school, deriving largely from Justice Holmes and notably championed by Justices Frankfurter and Jackson, rested on Holmes's insistence that the justices should minimize their role, stay out of the social struggles as far as possible, accept state and federal legislation unless clearly outside the powers of the legislatures, and decide cases on technical and procedural grounds where possible, to avoid committing the Constitution to principles that may later prove mischievous. The philosophy of the school was well expressed by Justice Stone when he warned his colleagues that "the only restraint we have is our self-restraint." Ultimately it is based on the premise that judicial supremacy can become a form of tyranny, that justices are frail and ought to discipline their sentiments, that all of government and human life is a fragile process, and that the Court acts wisest when it raises as few broad controversial issues of principle as possible.

One difficulty here, of course, is that even the decision to use self-restraint is an exercise of judicial power, and even a judge like Robert H. Jackson, who carried this principle far in most of his opinions, broke it when it came to the case involving the religious liberties of the Jehovah's Witnesses. Another difficulty is that the principle of staying away from principles, and of narrowing every constitutional issue to the minimum one compatible with the immediate facts, can make the judicial process a bleak function. The danger of the doctrine of judicial restraint is that it becomes judicial abdication. Still another danger is that when it is applied to the problems of legislative or administrative interference with civil liberties, it leaves the field of action open to arrogant or frightened and sometimes hysterical legislative majorities, often acting under the pressure of intense minorities in the population.

The activist school, championed by Justices Black and Douglas, was derived largely from Justice Brandeis and held that the Supreme Court had a positive role to play not only in guarding civil liberties but also in setting a legal frame for the quest for a greater measure of economic and social democracy. This approach was strengthened by the philosophy of the New Deal and the appointments that Franklin Roosevelt made to the Court. At base it represents an instrumental approach to the judicial process, and it candidly makes a distinction between the protection of individual freedom and economic and social progress. In the latter case, judicial activism is willing to go along with legislative majorities and administrative action on the theory that these broad issues have been hammered out after long public debate and represent the response to the needs of the time. But in the case of civil liberties, where freedoms of long standing may be threatened by emotional new doctrines expressed through hasty majorities, it holds that the role of the Court is to protect the old freedoms against the new dangers. For example, in the field of administrative law, which has recently grown rapidly, the school of judicial restraint is unlikely to go beyond the findings of fact by administrative agencies and will restrict itself to questions of law; the activist school, on the other hand, will review findings of fact if it suspects that they conceal an instance of arbitrary power by the agency. Just as the weakness of judicial self-restraint is that it may become a form of abdication, so the weakness of judicial activism is that it may become a form of arbitrary intervention by the Court itself into the other areas of government and into state action.

There has been considerable recent debate about whether the Supreme Court is a democratic or an undemocratic instrument of government. The most convincing argument seems to be that it is democratic in its response to the larger fluctuations of public opinion, and in its accessibility to changing presidential regimes. Yet for long stretches, especially from the 1880s to the 1930s, it lagged behind the best legal and judicial opinion. In essence what this means is that the Court is both part of the changes and chances of its time, and also part of the power structure in society as a whole. It was this quality, of being part of the power structure, that made the social activists of the 1930s and 1940s attack it as "undemocratic." On balance one may say that the Court is part of American democracy, but that it has had a tempering influence both on attempts at social and economic change and also on attacks on the freedom of the person.

The ideal justice is the one who maintains the kind of skepticism of ideas that Holmes had and the impulse to restrain his own power that Stone had, but who believes that within this frame of skepticism and restraint the Court has both the duty and the opportunity to make judicial action square with the kind of social humanism Brandeis strove for. This means that there can be no single formula for the judicial process, and that the judge ultimately needs to weigh his intellectual caution and skepticism against his social boldness and his moral faith in human possibility.

The unanimous decision in the school segregation cases, written by Chief Justice Warren, is the best example of that balance. It represented a sharp break from the turn-of-the-century segregation decisions but without any apparatus of protective citation, and without the hypocrisy of trying to "distinguish," so that an actual judicial change would seem to be no change at all. It was a political decision, yet not in the narrow spirit of being a partisan one. North and South, Republicans and Democrats alike, joined in it, because it aimed to sum up the conscience and progress of the nation in the area of civil rights, and because it was the culmination of a long line of decisions. It went outside traditional legal categories by citing studies by psychologists and sociologists that showed that separate and segregated schools could not be "equal," and that their separateness scarred the minds of the schoolchildren, Negro and white alike. It was not a decision reached in haste, but it directed that the states and the local school districts carry it out "with all deliberate speed."

Brown v. Board of Education proves the Court has an important role to play as a national educator — setting standards of social control taken from the best levels of thought and asking the nation as a whole to measure itself by those standards. The Court cannot ever place itself at the vanguard of social thought. Its job is to distill what has been thought and done and to translate that into legal norms. But neither need it wait until the bold has been frustrated or the novel become archaic. The task is creative in that the Court must recognize when majority action is valid and when it is dangerous, and it must seize upon the thinking of the creative minority to hold it up as a standard for the majority to follow. No Court has ever sustained this balance, but it is not an impossible ideal.

1957

2

As a society wedded to law grows more complex, its discontents express themselves increasingly in attacks on the administration of justice. Their bitterest resentment is the rankling sense of injustice. The more reflective Americans understand that the roots of violence lie deep in the psyches of the dispossessed and alienated, and in the absence of limits in an anything-goes morality. They are alarmed by the growth of a drug culture that feeds on the crime culture, in turn is fed by it, and corrupts their children. They are enraged that a loophole-riddled justice system seems more efficient in protecting the procedural rights of the accused than in guarding the victims, and has turned the home into a fortress and the streets into a jungle.

It has become a familiar syndrome. In a liberal democracy, with its stress on civil and human rights, the legal culture takes its cast from the political culture. The "civil religion" remains love of country and God, of freedom, equality, and democracy. But in practice state legislators and local police have felt at a disadvantage because the judges have the final word. The popular perception is that brutal crimes are going unpunished, plea bargaining is flourishing, deterrence has languished, the jails are crowded, and a revolving-door policy puts offenders back on the streets.

The new America, still a government of laws as its founders intended, has suffered dislocating social changes, broken institutional structures, and eroded values. It has not reached a healthy equilibrium between its competing legal patterns.

The central pattern is the rule of law, which is radical in the best sense — that of showing (as in the classic civil rights cases) that the poorest and weakest are not outside the protection of the law, and (as in the case of the Nixon tapes) that even the most powerful are not beyond the reach of the law.

Yet with this comes a corollary pattern — that of procedural due process, even in the face of a local community's rage at a crime. The judicial decisions that threw a blanket of protection around due process were the glory of the Roosevelt Court after 1937 and the Warren Court of the 1950s and 1960s, both known for their activist liberalism. They were taught at the great law schools and have empassioned generations of law students.

Inspiring though they were, they raised a haunting question: could Americans strike a balance between the substantive protections of the Bill of Rights and the perfectionist cult of procedural rigidity? Civilizations have been broken when the government and judiciary have been cut off from their culture, from those with a real sense of injustice. Only a living constitution capable of meeting social changes flexibly but strongly can survive the impact of those changes.

The battle over constitutional interpretation is one of the great continuing doctrinal debates, but it is not a bloodless battle of legal categories. Presidents have come to understand that their judicial appointments endure longer than anything else they do. Every president marches to the drumbeat of federal judges who have outlived a series of presidential terms. John Adams's appointment of "midnight judges" to spite the Jeffersonian Revolution has since become standard practice on every federal judicial level.

What is at stake is not only patronage and power, but also a judicial principle that reaches beyond the political parties and angles of vision. The Earl Warren Court, from Presidents Eisenhower through Lyndon Johnson, embraced a liberal "judicial activism" that forced the Constitution to keep pace with a highly modernized economy and society, and in the process expanded the Supreme Court's powers. But Justices Felix Frankfurter and Robert H. Jackson, working from the Holmesian tradition of "judicial restraint," formed a counterforce. Using this as a springboard, the Warren Burger Court, from Nixon to Reagan, moved to a more conservative version of restraint. The Senate battle over William Rehnquist's confirmation as Chief Justice showed how high the stakes were in the struggle over the composition of the Supreme Court.

Basically it was a battle over the role the federal courts should play in mediating the power of other branches — the executive, Congress, and especially the state legislatures. An activist "broad construction" of the Constitution was translated into greater interventionism, with a concern for the rights of minorities. The "strict construction" of the judicial-restraint school mediated the will of state and local majorities through the prism of legislative intent and long-range constitutional precedent.

In the end what resulted was a polarity, not a duality: they are what make the constitutional struggles of a tangled and complicated democracy so dramatic.

There are no judicial giants left to create new doctrinal positions in the manner of Holmes, Brandeis, Black, Frankfurter, Douglas, and Jackson. Nor could the constitutional crises of the 1980s match those of the years from the New Deal to Watergate. But in an information era and a turbulent world of power, the challenges are bound to come. A new judicial doctrine might well emerge to meet them, bringing activism and restraint into synthesis.

1987

6

Some Perspectives on the Court

This essay is the product of a pinch-hitting assignment. In 1979 the editors of the Journal *at Southwestern University Law School (in Los Angeles) organized a constitutional conference of national scope to which they invited several hundred judges, lawyers, and law professors. Robert M. Hutchins was scheduled to give the keynote address but was stricken with his final illness. The conference organizer, Ronald K. L. Collins, asked if I would take his place. I agreed.*

Interpreting my assignment broadly, I sketched four major ways of looking at the Supreme Court and ventured to add my own as a fifth. I later fleshed out the speech's thin frame into an expanded version for a volume on the conference in the Journal.

The reader will note that I retraced some paths taken in my earlier essays. I have, however, let the overlappings stand, because the venture was basically a fresh one for me. I was not interpreting the Court, its decisions, and its history. Rather, I was dealing with methodologies in constitutional history and law. I was not laying down the "truth" about the Court but was attempting to show the diverse ways of getting at it.

When I added some reflections of my own as a "fifth way" of looking at the Court, I risked some hubris. Yet I had to express my discontentment with schools of thought of which I had to some extent been part. Much had happened in the human sciences — in organizational behavior, developmental psychology, in semiotics and myth studies, in paradigm theory and civilization theory — that was bound to affect constitutional law. I thought it essential to bring the strands together.

In the mid-1920s, when I was a graduate student in Washington, Justice Brandeis would invite several of us to his Sunday afternoons at home. It was not the Brandeis of the "Brandeis briefs" who talked to us, or of the opinions heavily documented with statistics about social actuality. It was the Brandeis who spoke of Pericles and the Greek city-state, of Palestine and the Hebrew prophets, of Jefferson and the early, compassable American Republic, and of the conditions that had created them. I got a hint of the personal and social passion that — if you knew how to recognize it — somehow broke through the screen of detachment and statistics he had built against it.[1]

Adjoining our graduate school was Justice Holmes's house. I used to wait, often toward noon, until he emerged on the arm of his law secretary for his daily "constitutional." Since then both buildings have been torn down, but much in Holmes's thought has endured. We miss a good deal about him by stressing only the antiformalist theme — that "the life of the law is not logic; it is experience." That which made him speak of the "felt needs" of the time, and made him cut the knot of the activist-neutralist problem by saying that it was not unreasonable for a legislator to take account of those needs.[2]

But what counted for Holmes even more was struggle and risk. He saw risk taking in all social experiments, not only in the "insulated chambers of the states" but also in the Constitution itself, which, he said, "is an experiment, as all life is an experiment." He saw law less as contract than as wager, in which a potential infringer bets on what will or won't happen to him — the "hypostasis of a prophecy." It was a mixture of Darwin, William James, his own "can't helps" of belief, and a considerable mystique about what was enduring and prevailing in the Constitution and the nation, as in human life as a whole.

After the arid 1920s, the New Deal period was one of intense constitutional crisis when, as during the Civil War, there was a real question of whether the polity itself could survive. Franklin Roosevelt had great success in carrying the people with him in a crusade against the "economic royalists" and the "money changers in the temple," and hoped to have the same success in a judicial crusade against the "Nine Old Men" who were blocking the constitutional acceptance of necessary social legislation.

But he miscalculated with his "court-packing" plan. What he didn't understand was the difference between his economic reforms and his constitutional proposal. The people saw the first as a necessary change of the machinery. They saw the Constitution and Court not as a mechanism but as a living entity. But there was a saving sense of this inside the Court — at least in the timely "switch" of Justice Owen Roberts — and also inside the legal intellectual community. Thus Roosevelt lost his battle but won his war, and the people could retain their sense of the organism even as it changed.

A series of crises in constitutional history stretches back to *The Federalist Papers* and the decisions of the Marshall Court, through the slavery crisis and the Civil War, through the New Deal and the Roosevelt Court, all the way to the Warren and Burger Courts and to Richard Nixon and Watergate. The pace and frequency of these constitutional crises have quickened, and the interval between them has narrowed. The popular reaction to them has changed even more quickly. There was an élan about the New Deal crisis even at its seamier points that didn't exist in the crisis of the Pentagon Papers and the Nixon Watergate cases. I suggest that a "crisis approach" to studying the Supreme Court is neither complete nor intelligible unless we use it as a way of viewing its organic connections to the society in which it is enmeshed.

Consider this sentence from Oliver Wendell Holmes's brief but elegant 1901 talk commemorating John Marshall: "A great man represents a great ganglion in the nerves of society, or, to vary the figure, a strategic point in the campaign of history, and part of his greatness consists in his being there." What struck me when I first came upon this was the militaristic phrase "campaign of history."[3] What strikes me now is another phrase — "a great ganglion in the nerves of society." Holmes speaks casually of varying the metaphor, but beneath the skin of a metaphor may be a paradigm. A battlefield is a wholly different image than a neural ganglion, and from that difference a number of consequences can flow. As I have just suggested, Roosevelt would have fared better in his efforts to change the Supreme Court had he seen the Court less as a battlefield and more as an organism.

In his presidential address to the American Historical Association, Carl Becker used the phrase "every man his own historian," to describe the historical memory of ordinary people. It emerges from their pride and discontent, their conscience and guilt, their sense of their ideal mission as a people. It conditions how they see the past. History is a living faith.

Better even than the Roosevelt Court, the Warren Court illustrates the truth of Becker's theme. If it operated, as I think it did, on the assumption of the need to bridge the gap between a Court changing too slowly and a rapidly changing society, then it acted as a delayed session of the Roosevelt Court. The fact that its two prime activist justices — Hugo Black and William O. Douglas — were carry-overs from the Roosevelt Court is emblematic of the continuum.

The Warren Court — and indeed the whole decade of the 1960s of which it formed a part — illustrated the need to counter rigidity in a civilization. "When the leaders of a people," said Harold J. Laski, "ask their followers to die for a dream, they have a right to know in whose behalf the dream is being dreamt." Great civilizations have died from a failure of belief among those who wondered whether the dream was being dreamt in their behalf.

In long-range terms, the Warren Court decisions bolstered two themes in America's history: equal access to equal life chances (not equality of result but of opportunity), and equal justice before the law. In fending off some of the rigidifying forces, the Warren Court gave the civilization a base in belief.

Yet some queries remain. The Warren Court moved from a Bill of Rights seen as containing freedoms, to one containing equalities, and finally to one containing entitlements. Daniel Bell's quip about "a revolution of rising entitlements"[4] has a sharpness of edge here. The social-cultural revolutions of the 1960s raised claims and ex-pectations among classes that had in effect become wards of both public employment and public subsidies. By doing away with the Hohfeldian distinction between "rights" and "privileges," the Court turned the privileges into rights and thus brought into being "the new property."[5]

The criminal law decisions of the Warren Court created another area of popular disaffection that cannot simply be brushed aside as a stamping ground for the lunatic fringe, though it did result in the crackpot movement to impeach Earl Warren. The Warren decisions were the expression of one phase of the democratic dilemma — how to protect the procedural rights of every accused person and yet remain rigorous enough to ensure domestic tranquility, to keep the Hobbesian fear from unsettling the social contract, which is as nec-essary in latter-day America as it was in seventeenth-century England.

The Warren Court, no less than the pre-Roosevelt Court, pre-sented the nation with a constitutional crisis. Both crises came out of the excessive activism of the Court. The pre-Roosevelt Court used the activism of the traditionalist Right to strike down needed social legislation, while the Warren Court used the activism of the positivist Left to break established precedents in order to safeguard the procedural rights of the accused. The popular recoil, which has left a residual deposit in the culture, reflected the conflicting messages the Court sent out to the people. The same Court that produced a general feeling of liberation among a large section of the population caused an even larger section to feel it had administered a self-inflicted wound, and in the process injured the social organism.

These two areas involve the Court's role in the acceleration of social change. Elsewhere I have called this the "Tocqueville effect" — during periods of rapid change the passion for change feeds on itself, and legitimizing it by law doesn't moderate the passion but excites it.[6] Alexander Bickel was among the first in America to express a Burkean sense of the fragility of the social organism and the dangers of discontinuities in history and absolutisms in doctrine. His *Supreme Court and the Idea of Progress* is straight out of Carl Becker, and depicts a heavenly city of the Warren Court that goes back to Becker's heavenly city of the eighteenth-century French philosophes whose utopian visions spurred revolutionary fervor. In American intellectual history, too, there is the Calvinistic strain of redemptive history, with its "journey of the elect" to a salvation beyond history, and a "covenant of salvation" that sees the society as redeemable if its people are perfectible.[7]

The most recent of the Court's crisis periods was the crisis of presidential power and authority in the later Nixon years. Here one must grasp the consequences of the power element within the democratic imperium that started with Theodore Roosevelt's sense of America as a world power and Woodrow Wilson's grand domestic reforms and his moralism in war policy. It reached its height in the period after Franklin Roosevelt, when America began operating as an imperium (a power mass) in a world of power and ideological struggle. The term *democratic imperium* comprises several elements: a dominant role in world rivalries, a liberal welfare society, a polity of pressure groups, a frame of national security needs and of intelligence policy within that frame, and a centralized and augmenting presidential power.[8]

Although Nixon brought about the constitutional crisis within the democratic imperium, he didn't create the entity itself. The imperium had grown out of the needs, realities, and imagination of the past half-century and longer. It is not an outgrowth of reactionary trends in the society but of the liberal image of the conditions of the good life for all, and of Jefferson's historic sense of "an empire for liberty." Nixon himself was a conservative, but his five predecessors — starting with FDR and including the liberal Republican Dwight Eisenhower — believed in the liberal tradition and in the liberal intellectual tradition.[9]

Nixon was aware of this and used it to the hilt. In his *apologia pro vita sua*, both in his David Frost interviews on television and in his book, *The Memoirs of Richard Nixon,* he defended his conduct in part by saying that his presidential role made the liberties he took with the Constitution legal, and in part by appealing to the precedent set by Lincoln during the constitutional struggle of the Civil War. In the 1864 presidential campaign, when his enlistment of black soldiers was under attack, Lincoln had written that only by saving the Union first could he save the Constitution.

Even in Lincoln's graceful prose, this was tortured logic. With Nixon, the parallel falls apart. The civilization was not caught in a civil war and fighting for sheer survival. The survival of the nation was not at stake, however much Nixon inflated his sense of the crisis. What was at stake was the survival of his own power. He lost the distinction between political opponents of the regime and enemies of the republic. It was the ultimate corruption of political language.

If I have traced this succession of constitutional crises and of social-cultural climates too rapidly, I trust I have not omitted the crux of it, which is the need for a *contextual* approach to constitutional history. I have also several times referred to the *organismic* character of the polity, society, and culture in which law is imbedded. Man is not a machine but an organism. So are his institutions, his societies, his cosmos. Nowhere is the unsatisfactoriness of the machine model more evident than in judicial decisions and constitutional history.

Yet there is a mechanistic element even in those models that purport to recoil from mechanical jurisprudence. I find this element in an economic determinism that puts both history and society into boxes in which human will and initiative become helpless. I find it among the legal realists who were so bent on unmasking all forms of "myths" within institutions, including capitalism, government, and the law, that they left only "realism" itself unmasked. I find it in the psychoanalytic approaches that strip away everything except repression and the unconscious mechanisms.

The time is ripe for an *organismic model* that sees constitutional law — as it sees human beings, institutions, and societies — as a living matrix of change, growth, illness, homeostasis, decay, and the eternal recurrence of death and rebirth.

If my final model for the Court is contextual and organismic, it is also an *integrative* model. The reality we must all address is actually very complex. The power of the great economic aggregates, the pressures of a pressure-group polity, and the power of the courts themselves all have parts to play. So do the climates of ideas and opinions within which Supreme Court decisions are reached, and the contexts of class, status, ethnicity, and all the other associative clusters that make up a society.

Then there are the basic human drives and propensities, and the subjective ways in which we perceive reality and attach meanings to it, in the values and belief systems we commit ourselves to, in the symbols and myths by which we live. All of these condition our attitudes toward the Constitution, the courts, and the living reality of the law.

We need a multidisciplinary approach from which none of the life sciences or human sciences is excluded. One might call this a *holistic* view, using the term from Jan Smuts that is making as much headway in medical theory and practice as it is in psychology. Or one might call it a *total systems* approach, taking over the model of systems analysis.

Either would be useful, though each must attempt to answer the question of what is the *constitutive* or *integrating* principle in the assemblage of elements. Hence my preference is for an integrative model by which we study the legal case, decision, doctrine, or principle in its context, but with the intent of finding the organismic interrelationships that make it a living entity, not a dead and reductionist abstraction.

If I end with the role of the symbolic and mythic, it is because they are more powerful than anything else in shaping what I have called the constitutive, integrative principle in the approach to law. Almost fifty years ago I wrote a law review article — entitled "Constitution and Court as Symbols" — exploring the hold that both institutions still retain on the popular mind. I believe now more than ever in what I wrote then. All through the Watergate crisis, when presidential authority was eroded and congressional authority impaired, the authority of the Constitution and its interpreters held steady. Despite the fact that four of the members of the Supreme Court, including the chief justice, were Nixon appointees, the Court's response to the challenge far transcended political partisanship, and the people's response to the Court, in turn, was supportive.

In the end this comes down to myth and to the symbols of faith.

We tend to use the Calvinist ethos as a frame for our thinking about the American national character, and this sometimes leads us to explain the symbols' importance in economic terms. But they represent the deepest level of human experience. *Imaginatio facit casum:* the imagination creates the event.

This, then, is my own way of looking at the Court — contextual, organismic, integrative, even mythic. In constitutional concerns, as in much else, the stuff of our imaginings gives meaning to our daily experience. It represents the ultimate reality, because it comes closest to the ways in which we create the meaning of our existence. It is the source of many of our collective fantasies and can therefore be dangerous and destructive, but it is also the source of constitutional strength and viability.

PART II

A GALLERY OF GREATS

PREFACE

THERE ARE TWO FACES TO CONSTITUTIONAL LAW, ONE THAT DEFENDS the existing power structure and another that legitimizes revolutionary change. It can be the shield of the tax evader and the rich wrongdoer, but it can also be the protector of the impoverished and helpless. It can be a sword wielded by the powerful, but it can also (as we learned under Richard Nixon) strike down men in high places.

That is why the young no longer scorn the law and are going to the law schools: to learn how to use it. For its true meaning goes beyond the conservative and the radical, to the core of equal justice without which we are not a society but a jungle of survivors scrambling for power and place.

I got to Yale Law School, myself, but tarried there only briefly — long enough to discover that legal practice and I were not meant for each other. I went off to pursue other dreams. I made my choice in terms of social conscience: economics and politics seemed to offer a faster road to change than legal practice. In my younger days I was a Supreme Court buff of sorts, haunting the Court sessions, reading as many of the reports as I could lay my hands on, and spending many delightful hours trying to gauge the intellectual quality and social outlook of the judges behind the decisions.

American political thinkers have concerned themselves with the quality of presidential greatness, but there has been little in constitutional writings on the nature of judicial greatness. Hence this "gallery of greats."

One reason there is little written about judicial greatness is that the lawyer's eye is on the decision itself and its power as precedent, rather than on the justice who wrote it. Another is that while we all vote for presidential candidates, justices are chosen — and not by the people but by the successful president with the help (or hindrance) of what has become a tortured confirmation process that concerns itself little with greatness.

So we look back at the history of the Court as a fait accompli, and we try to decide who was great or near great, who counted for less — and why. The essays that follow show that it is the *why* that has attracted me. I might add in passing that while I had more than a fleeting acquaintanceship with three of the justices I discuss — Brandeis, Black, and Frankfurter — I have tried to keep it from affecting my judgment unduly.

I start with the fact of the necessary limits of great judicial art.

It is a strange kind of discipline that demands of its greatest practitioners that they work within the severely limited form of textual interpretation and yet leave the imprint of their style and innovativeness. In this sense, constitutional law can be compared to poetry or music. It is exactly because of the strictness of the limits, and the need to apply the same text to changing situations while transcending one's own agenda and values, that the juristic art becomes so demanding. What I saw in all my "greats" was the inspired use of exigent forms to contain personal styles and intellectual visions.

There is no recipe for judicial greatness. Yet if hard pressed, I should settle for someone with a flexible mind, a compassion for the walking wounded, a refusal to be cowed by power, a capacity to live with the contradictions of life and to separate the permanent from the transient.

This is what I should call a passionately judicial temperament, and only a few have had it.

7

John Marshall and the Campaign of History

My essay on John Marshall was written during the four years span-
ning the New Deal's constitutional crisis. When the urgencies of that
crisis were over, I could see Marshall's relation to his time and ours
more clearly, for the resolution of the crisis marked the effective end
of the judicial review controversy. Attention turned to what kind of
judicial review should be undertaken and with what politics and what
judicial doctrine. It turned also to Marshall as the great exponent —
the greatest we have had — of the national constitutional power.

Marshall has had to be rescued from Oliver Wendell Holmes's
too-grudging judgment (in a memorial speech about him) that his
greatness came from the accident of historic placement — that he
came first.

Today more than ever I feel that this was a giant, equipped with
all the necessary wiles and stratagems of the trade, but guided also
with the necessary shaping visions.

He exercised a magnetic force on his Court contemporaries and
on his time. All greatness has a historical referent, a context. The
question is what a man does with it. It is hard to envisage any other
judge doing as much as Marshall did, and with his unmistakable
flourish of grandeur.

*Remembering that you cannot separate a man from
his place, [I] remember also that there fell to Marshall perhaps
the greatest place that ever was filled by a judge.*[1]

THE EDUCATION OF JOHN MARSHALL

John Marshall's first act as chief justice was at once characteristic
and ominous. He changed the established practice, borrowed from
England, by which each justice in turn delivered his opinion on a
case, and he substituted for it "the Court" or "the unanimous Court"
speaking through a single member, usually himself. He wanted to
present to the world the serried ranks of a united Court. And for
thirty-five years he was to cast over his associates on the bench a
spell whose persuasiveness seemed almost diabolical to his contemporaries.[2] The Supreme Court had been in existence for twelve years
before Marshall came on the bench in 1801. Yet when he left it, in
1835, the Supreme Court was no longer a straggling group of lawyers
but rather an institution and a power.

John Marshall did not seem earmarked by fate to play the great
role he did. He was a frontier boy, born in 1755 on a small backwoods
farm in western Virginia, but of good propertied stock.[3] His education
was a frontier education; his economic horizon was bounded by the
self-sufficient backwoods plantation; his moral ideas were those in-
culcated by upright parents, based on self-improvement and steeled
by the rigors of their venture.

Marshall's formal schooling throughout his life amounted to less
than two years, including a year with a family tutor. He imbibed
every homily that an idealistic family environment could impress on
him — of law and order, of moral uprightness, personal loyalty, and
sturdy independence, of respect for authority and the identification
of authority with respectability. Being self-taught, he developed the
resourcefulness and the wide sweep that often characterize self-taught
people, but also their narrow self-confidence and dogmatism. To this
was added an innate sense of purpose and an unruffled consciousness
of stature that were to give him the dominating personality so magnetic to friends and terrifying to opponents.

His reading was family-selected and reinforced the compulsions
of property and authority. By the age of twelve he had copied out

Pope's *An Essay on Man* and knew most of it from memory. At seventeen he read Blackstone's *Commentaries* assiduously with his father, who had subscribed to the volume less on his own account than on that of his son. During the debates on the ratification of the Constitution, he studied carefully *The Federalist Papers,* and we know him to have been greatly influenced by Hamilton's reasoning. While he was practicing law in Richmond he read, as did every fervent Federalist, Burke's *Reflections on the Revolution in France,* and in his *Life of Washington* Marshall reproduces an essentially Burkean view of the impact of Jacobin ideas on the American mind. Marshall was not a man of extensive reading, although Justice Joseph Story assures us in his memoirs that his friend cared a great deal for literature, and we know that later in life he liked Jane Austen's novels.[4] But while his genius was not bookish, the three English writers he read in his formative years left an unmistakable mark on his thinking.

That they did so is of some moment. Alexander Pope's poem has a political content: it "depicts the universe as a species of constitutional monarchy."[5] From it Marshall could get his individualistic psychology, of a world ruled by egoism restrained by reason; his sense of "general laws" as governing human conduct; and an ethical bolstering for his authoritarian conservatism ("whatever is, is right"). Sir William Blackstone held to the tough and crabbed English tradition of a tenacious concern for property. He was the legal theorist of a landed aristocracy that felt its power slipping and sought to retain its hold by entrenching itself behind legal earthworks. As for Edmund Burke, he was a titanic figure whose genius it was to translate a morbid hatred of change into undying political theory, and whose defense of the existing order was more compact of passion than any revolutionary attack on it could be. In these writers — poet, lawyer, political theorist — was stored up the heritage of conservative English thought that was to pass through Marshall's mind into the fabric of American constitutional law.

In such an education the Revolutionary War was a curious interlude, a sort of shadow play in which Marshall went gallantly through all the motions of a minor young hero, experienced Valley Forge, and came home to Virginia. Marshall was young when the war came and scarcely more than a stripling when it ended, but he was quickly responsive to the ebbing of the revolutionary fervor in the leaders whom he followed — men like Washington and Hamilton, who were his archetypal heroes. It was natural in the turbulent years of the Confederation that he should, with them, be dismayed at the agrarian unrest or at the prospect of a military revolution becoming a social revolution.

His political career up to the time he became chief justice was solid and eventful if not distinguished. He settled in Richmond to practice law; became a member of the Virginia legislature; fought valiantly for the Constitution in the Virginia ratifying convention; served a term in Congress; went to France on the unfortunate but eventually highly publicized XYZ mission; was a member of John Adams's ill-starred cabinet, serving in the last years as secretary of state and working heroically to rally the remnants of the badly beaten and demoralized Federalist forces. For a time it looked as if Marshall were only a second-string Federalist politician, caught like the other Federalists in a blind alley of history.

He had much in common with them. His classrooms were theirs, although his disarming democratic ways, casting a spell over his biographers, have tended to obscure that fact. He was outwardly the frontiersman — a charming, gangling Virginian, rustic and unpretentious in his manner, simple in his tastes, careless and even unkempt in his clothes. But in actuality Marshall was a man of substance, with a deep personal and psychological stake in property. He stood heir, by descent, to a long proprietary tradition; he continued this tradition, bought huge landed properties, and was always involved in suits over land titles. By marriage, too, he had become related to landowners, speculators, and financiers. His business and political connections were with the men of funds and funded income, the lawyers and rentiers, the landowners and speculators, the shipbuilders, the merchants and manufacturers. Marshall's habits were molded in the back country of Virginia and among the impoverished farmers who made up Washington's ragged little army at Valley Forge; but his social theory was fashioned among the lawyers in Richmond, and the wealthy planters who traveled there to litigate land titles, and the Brahmins and tiewigs of the New England financial aristocracy with whom Marshall threw in his political fortunes.

In several respects Marshall's career was a good preparation for his work on the Supreme Court. His political experience did him no harm: like Taney after him, he illustrated the general rule that the great justices have also been skillful politicians. He gained a sense of political realities and an adroitness in manipulating them. As the ranking member of the cabinet during the last demoralized years of the Adams administration, he practically ran the government and the campaign of 1800 as well. He grew accustomed to handling large political issues in an audacious way, he mastered the technique of the devious attack and the strategic retreat, he learned the grand manner in politics. His talents were long in maturing. They proved substantial rather than brilliant. He was at his best, as he showed both on the French mission and in the Adams cabinet, in a small group where he could bring to bear the massive influence of his personality.

Much has been made of Marshall's nationalist feeling, especially by his biographer, Senator Albert Beveridge, who uses it to pattern Marshall's entire career. For others as well it seems to be the far-off divine event toward which, as toward a fatality, the whole of Marshall's life moved. Nevertheless, we must not conclude that nationalism was the primum mobile of Marshall's being. It must be remembered that he was to show himself, on the bench, to be the best of the Federalist strategists. And nationalism, however fatefully it may have been rooted in his personality, was above all good strategy. Marshall learned this primarily from his experience on the XYZ mission.

The mission itself was a curious one; the emissaries were sent over in 1797 by the Federalist administration to the French revolutionary government, to protest against French depredations of American commerce and to iron out treaty difficulties. Marshall was a curious choice for such a mission; he thought the French Revolution criminal, French diplomacy diabolical, and Jacobin ideas anarchistic. He went because his land litigation had left him in financial straits, and the 20,000 dollars he got were, in his own phrase, a "Godsend." The mission was doomed to failure. Talleyrand's foxlike tactics met their match in Marshall's stubbornness and conspicuous honesty. The open bid by the French for a bribe proved a boomerang. Marshall came home to find himself a national hero, toasted everywhere.

The French had insulted our national pride, and the insult was skillfully publicized by the Federalists. Marshall learned that the common man, who would not respond to Federalist aristocratic theory, would respond to the same property interests when they were clothed in the rhetoric of the national interest.[6] It was a crucial discovery, and Marshall was to make the most of it on the judicial front, where in the name of nationalism he was to fight the battles of the propertied groups.

Nor must we be confused by Marshall's apparent libertarianism. That too, like his nationalism, was probably sincere enough. Marshall carried over the English constitutional tradition. He thought of himself as a fighter for liberty, and drew his inspiration from the struggle against Tudor and Stuart despotism. There is in every man, even the inveterate Tory, a desire to associate himself with some ringing defiance, to attempt a Promethean struggle against the unjust ruling divinities. Marshall saw himself in combat against the legislative and executive tyranny of Jeffersonian democracy, and he must be accorded his vision of himself. He was full of forebodings about the future; his letters throughout his judicial career breathe a dark pessimism.[7] It was his fate to come to the fore in the councils of the Federalist party in the declining years of the Adams administration. He must be seen symbolically as the dying Federalist who, out of the reckless strength of that dying, made the way safe for the path of American capitalism.

When John Adams in those fateful closing days of his administration looked about at the political terrain, he saw the Federalists, defeated and fleeing everywhere before the new legions of Jeffersonian democracy. Only the judiciary remained. The Federalists "have retired into the judiciary as a stronghold," wrote Jefferson in what has become a famous prediction, "and from that battery all the works of republicanism are to be beaten down."[8] There can be no doubt that Jefferson saw clearly. And there can be little doubt that Marshall was a party to the Federalist councils and plans. When the chief justiceship of the Supreme Court fell vacant, Adams sought one man after another to fill it. Finally he told Marshall that nothing remained but to send his name to the Senate.[9] Marshall, able as he was, never really found himself until he reached the Court. And the Court was where he belonged. The task before him was an unusual one, but he brought an unusual equipment. For his mind was not that of the great lawyers of history, with their heavy erudition, their tortuousness, their narrow legalism, but the mind of a man of action, with its powerful concentration on a single purpose. He had mastered the art of finality. He possessed a large resourcefulness in the service of a singular tenacity of purpose. He was to be a magnificent dictator, dwarfing and uniting his colleagues, polarizing around himself as a dominant personality the forces that were later to be institutionalized in judicial review.

He seems miraculously to have turned up in history just at the point where a rising capitalism most needed him. "A great man," said Justice Holmes of Marshall, "represents . . . a strategic point in the campaign of history, and part of his greatness consists of his being there."[10] Marshall's role was to effect a nexus between the property interests under an expanding industrialism and the judicial power under a federal system of government. He was to be the strategic link between capitalism and constitutionalism. And for occupying that position in the campaign of history, his education and the nature of his mind fitted him superbly. Rarely in American history has the exterior tension of events been matched so completely by an interior tension of preparation and purpose on the part of the exactly right man.

COUNTERREVOLUTION AND JUDICIAL SUPREMACY

There was a grim irony in the fact that Thomas Jefferson, riding the crest of the revolutionary wave of 1800, was sworn into office by John Marshall, his archenemy and the archenemy of his doctrine. That tense moment represented the climax of one struggle — the political-economic struggle between Federalists and Republicans, and the beginning of another — the judicial-economic struggle between the vested interests and the common man.

The owning classes were in a panic. Their defeat at the polls made it imperative for them to draft their best leadership for the crucial judicial battles to come. Marshall had been designated for the most strategic post. In 1798 he had refused to become an associate justice of the Court; in 1801, when the Federalists had been ousted both from the presidency and Congress, he had no choice as a party man but to accept the chief justiceship. The necessity he yielded to was the last-ditch necessity of the Federalist propertied groups. And as soon as he was on the Court he moved swiftly to his purpose. "The Democrats," he wrote to Charles Pinckney on the morning of the inauguration — and the solemnity of the occasion should have made him weigh his words — "The Democrats are divided into speculative theorists and absolute terrorists. With the latter I am disposed to class Mr. Jefferson." This version of Mr. Jefferson seems to have influenced the historians as well, for the early part of Marshall's incumbency is generally characterized as "Jefferson's attack on the judiciary." In reality it may with fully as much justice be called the judiciary's attack on Jefferson. Marshall's appointment was only part, if the most important part, of an extended Federalist plan embracing the passage of the Judiciary Act of 1801, the creation of new judgeships, and the eventual affirmation of the power of judicial review.

Jefferson was no inconsiderable opponent. He had a well-disciplined party machine, he controlled mass opinion, and he was himself a supple and seasoned warrior in this sort of battle. For all his revolutionary talk he was no revolutionist. He had come into office on a popular landslide. The enemy was beaten and demoralized. Yet his inaugural address breathed a honeyed humility. "We are all Federalists," he said, "we are all Republicans." But before he had been half a year in office he had determined to change his tone. Charles Beard found among the Jefferson manuscripts the last draft of his message to Congress in December 1801 before the final revision.[11] It included a statement of the doctrine of the separation of powers in as sharp a form as was to be found in the Kentucky Resolutions, the right of each branch of the government to interpret the Constitution after its best lights, and his intent to declare the sedition laws of the previous administration unconstitutional and void. While admitting that the Supreme Court, as a coordinate branch, could check the power of the other branches of government, the message would nevertheless have denied that the Court had the exclusive right of construing the Constitution.[12] Jefferson had already signed this draft when at the last moment he lost heart, struck out the entire passage, and wrote in the margin for posterity: "This whole passage was omitted as capable of being chicaned, and furnishing something to the opposition to make a handle of." Henry Adams, writing before this draft of the message was known, nevertheless lays the blame for Marshall's victory on Jefferson himself and the fact that he faltered in his determination to crush his most dangerous opponent. He might, writes Adams, have had Congress declare the Alien and Sedition Acts unconstitutional; he might have asked for an annulment of the dangerous Section 25 of the Judiciary Act of 1789. He might even, although it would have been more risky, have had a constitutional amendment passed giving the judges a fixed tenure of years — four or six — renewable by the president and the Senate. In fact, this was the suggestion that Jefferson finally made, desperate and defeated, four years before he died, when he understood more fully the extent of Marshall's victory.

Not daring the larger plan, Jefferson dared the lesser. He moved to have Congress repeal the Judiciary Act of February 13, 1801, which had reorganized the lower federal courts, creating additional circuit judgeships and filling them with staunch Federalists. He could count on a congressional majority. He could count even more on popular opinion, which was already militantly aroused against the highly partisan charges by the judges to juries in cases involving the

Sedition Act. It must be remembered that the excesses of the French Revolution had produced an antiradical scare, and that the Federalists had sought in the Alien and Sedition Acts to use that scare as an instrument against Jeffersonianism. The victory of Jefferson at the polls showed how crude the Federalist tactic had been. The Jeffersonians now moved along two lines to undo the work of the Federalists. They sought the repeal of the Judiciary Act, and they moved for the impeachment of the more blatantly partisan judges. The first line of action reached its climax in the "Great Judiciary Debate" in the Senate, in January 1802; the second, in the impeachment proceedings against Justice Samuel Chase in January and February of 1805. Between these two events came the memorable decision in *Marbury v. Madison* in 1803.

The Great Judiciary Debate of 1802 furnished the stage setting for *Marbury v. Madison*. The problem of judicial review was no new problem when Marshall came on the scene. The Federalists, fearing the majority sentiment, had hitherto not dared to face the issue. Seeing themselves swept out of power, however, by the "revolutionary" wave of 1800, there was nothing for them to do but fall back on their last line of defense. Of Jefferson it may be said that he did not so much fear the judiciary as hate the Federalists. He saw that the Federalists had retreated behind judicial entrenchments, had passed a last-minute act reorganizing the judiciary, had created new circuit judgeships and filled them with the bitterest die-hard Republican-haters they could find in the country. When he saw this, he knew what he wanted. He proceeded to move for the repeal of the act and the offices.

In the debate the Federalists for the first time in our history openly and insistently claimed for the judiciary the final and exclusive power of interpreting the Constitution; some of the Republicans restated the extreme states'-rights doctrine of the Kentucky Resolutions, others steered shy of the discussion. The Federalists did the best talking, but the Republicans had the votes. The act was repealed and the stage was set.

The stage was set, but not even the Federalist claque could have foreseen the brilliance and audacity with which their leading actor would play his part. John Marshall hated Jefferson, but respected Jefferson's strength. Jefferson had talked equivocally in his inaugural address, but he was obviously willing to dislodge the Federalists from the judiciary. Congress had repealed the Federalists' act of reorganization, and had provided that the Supreme Court was not to meet until February of the following year (1803). There was talk of impeaching some of the more extreme Federalist judges. Marshall had to move swiftly and with daring. The *Marbury* case gave him his chance.

The case of poor Marbury (if he was poor Marbury and not a Federalist stooge) was raked by the cross fire of Federalist and Republican *Machtpolitik*.[13] Marshall was faced at once with an opportunity and a dilemma. It was a chance to administer a rebuke to Jefferson, assert officially the judicial power that the Federalists had claimed in the debates, and place the judiciary in a position of control. If Marshall denied Marbury's commission it would be an admission of judicial powerlessness. But if he upheld it, Jefferson (through Madison) would simply refuse to comply. He might say what Jackson is reputed to have said thirty years later, "John Marshall has made his decision, now let him enforce it,"[14] and thus make Marshall and the Court a laughingstock.

Marshall seized his problem with a maneuver in which he managed to administer a public spanking to the administration, assert judicial supremacy, and leave Jefferson helpless to strike back. Marbury's commission, he said, was a valid one; even without the delivery of the document he had a vested right to it, which it was the function of "a government of laws and not of men" to protect; having a right, he had also a remedy, which was mandamus. But the Supreme Court, by its reading of the Constitution, could issue such a writ only where it has appellate and not original jurisdiction. Section 13 of the Judiciary Act of 1789, which sought to confer original jurisdiction on the Court, was therefore unconstitutional.

It mattered little to Marshall that if his conclusion were valid and the Court had no jurisdiction, everything before it would be superfluous — a vast obiter dictum that was sheer political maneuver. It mattered little to him that none of the opposing counsel had argued that the section of the Judiciary Act was unconstitutional, and that to declare it so he had to wrench it beyond all principles of statutory interpretation. He was setting the classic example of what has since come to be called "judicial statesmanship." He had disarmingly picked a portion of a Federalist statute to declare unconstitutional, and he had picked one beyond the reach of the executive — one whose application depended on the judiciary itself. There was, moreover, a movement afoot in the Jeffersonian Congress to capitalize on the popular feeling against the lower federal judges and abolish the lower courts entirely, parceling out their functions among the Supreme Court and the state courts. Marshall sought to quell this movement by asserting the finality of the Supreme Court's decisions on all matters of jurisdiction.

From a legalistic standpoint alone, *Marbury v. Madison* has a nightmarish fascination. If ever the history of the Court is written with the proper cosmic irony, here will be the cream of the jest. Upon this case, as legal precedent, rests the power of judicial review. Yet every part of its reasoning has been repudiated even by conservative commentators and in later Supreme Court decisions, which nonetheless continue to exercise the power it first claimed. "Nothing remains of *Marbury v. Madison*," writes Professor J. A. C. Grant, "except its influence."[15] Everything else has been whittled away. But its influence continues to grin at us from the darkness like the disembodied smile of the Cheshire cat.

It remains to ask how much *Marbury v. Madison*, and through it Marshall, contributed to judicial review. Marshall did not originate judicial review, nor did he single-handedly succeed in establishing it beyond all dislodgment. There are precedents for judicial review, both in colonial and English decisions. As for reasoning, Marshall's argument added nothing substantial to the argument of the Federalists in the Great Debate of 1802. Ultimately, the whole of the theory may be found in number 178 of the *Federalist*, written by Hamilton; in fact, much of Marshall's entire career may be summed up as a process of reading Hamilton's state papers and dissertations. Yet Marshall's decisive achievement is his translation of these ideas into judicial action.

As for the permanence of his work, I find much in Louis B. Boudin's forceful contention that judicial review as we know it is primarily a post–Civil War creation, and that *Marbury v. Madison* decided only the Court's power to determine its own jurisdiction.[16] The permanence of Marshall's work is not to be judged wholly in legalistic terms. The influence of the case went far beyond its strict legal effect. Marshall found judicial review a moot question: he left it an integral part of the constitutional fabric. The Court did not again use judicial review against Congress ("national" judicial review) until the *Dred Scott* case, more than half a century later, because in all economic matters the property interests favored expanding the national power. Where judicial review was used effectively during this period was against state power ("federal" judicial review). In these decisions the reasoning of *Marbury v. Madison* and the increased strength and prestige of the Supreme Court worked powerfully. Marshall's role in this entire process was to give judicial review a foothold, to use it for the immediate interests of the capitalism of his day, to tie it up with the strong appeal of nationalism, and to entrench it where a later stage of capitalism could take it up and carry it further for its own purposes.

Marshall's decision has been described as a revolutionary coup. It was daring and ultimately decisive, but it was not an isolated act. Marshall's decision was the high point of a counterrevolutionary movement that stretched back to the Constitutional Convention. The maneuverings of Federalists and Republicans were not just the attempts of propertied groups and agrarian-labor masses to salvage or hem in the consequences of the revolution: they were part of a worldwide movement of social struggle fought out in France and England as well as in America. For the history of this period can be written adequately only if it is seen as world history.

Marshall and his fellow Federalists (and Marshall was by no means the most extreme) viewed the Republicans as Jacobins, Jefferson as Robespierre, and his letter to Philip Mazzei as the sure mark of the Antichrist.[17] Jefferson, on the other hand, considered the Federalists oligarchs and despots, and he feared Marshall's implacability and cunning. Jefferson was exasperated that his victory at the polls should be frustrated by the judiciary. He never forgot that the Federalist judges had used the bench as a hustings for election speeches.[18] His attempt to impeach these judges failed, but it was as characteristic of the politics of the day as was the united front that the Federalist bench and bar offered — a front so united that the government had difficulty finding counsel to prosecute the impeachments.

The situation was made more grave by the specter of a war with France or England, and by threats of treason. Jefferson meant to avoid war and repeatedly stressed the joys of peace and family life in his public speeches. He rightfully felt that America's borders were endangered by foreign invasion and by internal disaffection. The Burr conspiracy proved how close the danger was, and the Burr trial proved how determined the Federalists were to embarrass the administration. Jefferson's efforts to get a conviction in the Burr trial were met by Marshall's resolutely partisan behavior.

Thus the first six years of Marshall's term — 1801 to 1807 — witnessed the battle of two giants in a setting of world revolution and counterrevolution. The Alien and Sedition Acts, the Judiciary Act, the *Marbury* decision, and the decision in the Burr case were Federalist moves; the victory of 1800, the repeal of the Judiciary Act, the attempt to impeach Chase, and the Burr trial were Jeffersonian moves. Out of the melee there emerged a great and enduring result: the enunciation of the power of judicial review.

LAND CAPITALISM AND MERCHANT CAPITALISM

The great threat to the property interests lay in the action of state legislatures, which since colonial times had been the enemy of the creditor and the moneyed class. The state legislatures had sought to control business and had threatened both the ratification of the Constitution and the dominance of the moneyed groups in the new government. These legislatures had an unseemly habit: they were responsive to the economic plight of the common man. What was needed was a way of using judicial review to keep them in check.

Marshall found the answer in the "obligations of contract" clause in the Constitution.[19] He seized upon it, brought in a "higher law" theory to give a moral afflatus to sanctity of contract, and ended by creating the doctrine of vested rights as an implied limitation on state powers. To do this he had to stretch contract far beyond its contemporary meaning, but he was equal to the task. Sir Henry Maine once said that the progress of society is from status to contract.[20] If that is true, Marshall must rank as one of the great heroes of humanity, for he gave contract a sanctity overriding every consideration of public policy or economic control. Next to judicial review itself this conception of contract — broadened into a doctrine of "vested rights"[21] — is probably the most important invention in the history of the Court. It dominated the constitutional scene up until the Civil War, both in state and federal courts; it served as a model after which later doctrines of implied limitations on state power, such as due process of law and freedom of contract, could be fashioned.

The first of the contract cases[22] to stir attention, *Fletcher v. Peck*, has been described as "a corner-stone of legal structure laid in mud."[23] Behind it lies one of the most malodorous episodes in American history — that of the Yazoo land frauds. The Georgia legislature of 1796, in what Beveridge has described as a "saturnalia of corruption," disposed of a strip of Native American land half the size of New England, comprising most of the present states of Alabama and Mississippi, to a land speculating company for about a cent and a half an acre. Every legislator except one had received a large bribe of land stock, which could be disposed of for cash. The scandal broke;

the people of Georgia, in a fury, wrote a new constitution, elected a new legislature, and rescinded the corrupt act. But meanwhile the speculators had sold their stock to purchasers in New England and the middle states. The latter proceeded to attack the legality of the rescinding act, and made many unsuccessful attempts in Congress to get compensation. Finally, on the basis of an opinion prepared by Alexander Hamilton,[24] they contrived an obviously trumped-up suit and brought it before the Supreme Court. Joseph Story, later to become Marshall's *fidus Achates* on the Court, represented the New England speculators, but it is a safe guess that the opposing attorney did not trouble himself to present too formidable an argument.[25]

Marshall's decision is breathtaking. He ignored the obvious collusion by which the case had been brought before the Court. He held that the Court could not concern itself with the alleged corruption of the Georgia legislature, thereby inaugurating the Supreme Court tradition of maintaining, when convenient, a decent ignorance of events outside the Court. What counted was that the sovereign state of Georgia had, through the original legislative grant, entered into a contract the obligation of which could not be impaired by another act. Against the legislature's power to rescind its own act, Marshall argued that there was a higher moral duty to stand by the sanctity of contract. That moral duty flowed both from the specific sanctity of vested rights under a contract and from more general considerations of "the nature of society and of government," which prescribed limits to the legislative power. Thus a decision that had started by throwing moral considerations out of the window ended by admitting them again through the back door.

It is not difficult to say why the framers of the Constitution inserted the "obligation of contract" clause. They had been distressed by the state legislation repudiating debts and placing moratoria on their payment, by paper-currency legal tender laws, and by installment and commodity payment laws. They had been annoyed even more by "special acts," through which the legislatures had intervened in pending lawsuits and set contracts aside. To meet this problem of moratoria and other debtor relief laws, they counted on a sound and plentiful monetary supply, which would be achieved by giving the federal government a monopoly of coinage. But as if to make doubly sure, they adopted also, at the motion of Rufus King, a clause probably suggested by the contract clause in the recently enacted Ordinance of 1787. The interesting thing is that the contract clause got little enthusiasm in the discussions at the Convention but seems to have been the product mainly of an agreement within the Committee on Style. In the discussions attending ratification there was not much clarity about the meaning of the clause, except for a general agreement that it referred only to private contracts. The prevalent notion of contract at the time was a far narrower one than at present. In fact, contract as a basic concept of law was not developed until the period between the 1830s and 1860s. Little was thought about the contract clause until Alexander Hamilton, retained as counsel by the New England purchasers of the land stock, submitted an opinion in 1796 that for Georgia to rescind its act was a violation of the contract it had, by implication, entered into not to rescind the act.

This was the reasoning Marshall adopted, in a halting and hesitant way. The argument is even more rickety than that in *Marbury v. Madison*. He ignored what was the common understanding that the contract clause applied to private and not public contracts, and that it applied only when an obligation had been undertaken in a contract that the law protected and that had not yet been fulfilled. But having determined to assert his principle, Marshall went the whole way and brought already executed public contracts within the scope of constitutional protection. He ignored also the fact that it was an established principle of the English common law that a legislature could rescind an act when fraud was involved, and the fact that British parliaments had done so repeatedly.

Despite its logical weakness, however, Marshall's decision takes on meaning in the economic context of the day. Gambling in land values represented the principal financial activity in expansionist America at the turn of the nineteenth century, before industrialism came to overshadow everything else. Some of the most prominent men of the day had been involved in the Yazoo land scandal, including James Wilson, an associate justice of the Supreme Court, who was up to the neck in the business: "When the deal was consummated," says Beveridge, "the Justice held shares to the amount of at least three-quarters of a million acres." Nor is this surprising. America was still an agrarian nation at the time, living by the soil and hoping to build its heaven from the soil. For the common people, land meant a livelihood; for the landed squirearchy it meant a social position and a way of life; for a large intermediate group it meant easy profits. "Stock-jobbing" in land was much moralized over and was considered one of the evils of the day, but it was an evil that involved wide circles in its participation. The great families were landowning families, who had obtained their titles in some cases through fraud and in most cases through privilege. But their seigneurial estates could not be run profitably in the North with free labor; so they had turned to land speculation, where their political influence and their social and financial connections would be of account. The "aristocracy of patronage and paper," as John Taylor of North Carolina termed the new banking and financial group, also found in land speculation a source of revenue. The fever spread to workers in the northern cities; in fact, many of the people who had bought the Yazoo stock had invested the savings of a lifetime.

The economic fluctuations up to the Civil War were largely to be the history of land booms and busts, the result of land speculation. The organization of the Yazoo land deal foreshadowed later methods of corporate promoting. The legislature was bought with "gifts" of stock, while promoters granted themselves large blocks of stock for promotion. Northern men were hired as decoys in marketing the stock, and were paid in stock "gifts." This was agrarian capitalism of the sort that spearheaded the emerging industrial capitalism. Marshall's decision was not merely the decision of a man who knew land and loved land — in whose circles of friendship, land speculation was the breath of life. It was also a decision in harmony with the progress of an exploitative merchant capitalism.

It is noteworthy that at the time *Fletcher v. Peck* was being fought out in the courts, Marshall was himself involved in land litigation. Sometime between 1794 and 1800 he had bought from the heirs of Lord Fairfax their claims to two or three million acres of Virginia land between the Rappahannock and the Potomac; these lands had been granted by Charles II in 1673 and had been taken back by Virginia after the Revolution and parceled out to returning soldiers as homesteads. The same had happened to the claims of the Penn heirs in Pennsylvania and the Granville heirs in North Carolina. Marshall, before he became chief justice, acting with his brother and Robert Morris — whom William K. Dodd, the Virginia historian, has called "a shameless speculator of Philadelphia" — bought the Fairfax claims and carried the litigation time and again to the Virginia Supreme Court, which decided unanimously against him. After he became chief justice, the case was carried to the Supreme Court. The issue involved in both cases was the same: the power of a state legislature to revoke a grant made by a previous sovereign body. The principle invoked was the same: sanctity of contract as overriding legislative sovereignty. When Marshall was deciding the case of the Yazoo land frauds, he was in effect setting a precedent for the decision in his own case. When that case came up for decision in 1813, as *Fairfax's Devisee v. Hunter's Lessee*,[26] Marshall quite properly refrained from sitting on it. The opinion of the Court was written by Justice Story, who had been one of the counsel for the land speculators in the reargument of *Fletcher v. Peck*, and it was an opinion upholding the claim of the Marshall brothers on essentially the same grounds as the Yazoo case.[27]

I am not urging a personal interpretation of Marshall's land decisions. Marshall was a man of stubborn integrity. He would undoubtedly have ruled as he did in *Fletcher v. Peck* even if his own land speculations were not concerned. But the fact that even he was involved in such speculations shows how deeply the substance of the issue reached into the economics of the period, how directly it was part of its ethos. And as the frontier of settlement moved further west and south after the Louisiana Purchase, the principle of *Fletcher v. Peck* and *Fairfax's Devisee v. Hunter's Lessee* was extended to the land claims of speculators that were based on flimsy and often corrupt Spanish titles. In *United States v. Arredondo*,[28] *Chouteau v. United States*,[29] and *Soulard v. United States*,[30] an exceedingly liberal interpretation was placed by the court on the power of Spanish officials to grant land deeds, regardless of the written limitations of their authority, and on the validity of the titles based on those deeds. The result was that the bribing of officials and the forging of deeds became a common method of obtaining land titles, and the Supreme Court, in accordance with its principle of not examining the ethics behind a contractual grant of a sovereign, gave those titles authenticity.

Marshall and his Court felt, no doubt, that in thus placing the sanctity of contract above every adventitious consideration of policy or ethics they were encouraging economic stability. Actually they were encouraging the reckless development of American economic resources and the flagrant corruption of state politics that were to characterize the opening of the American continent throughout the nineteenth century.

The *Dartmouth College* decision is one of the most famous that Marshall handed down.[31] The little New Hampshire college, established in 1769 to educate and Christianize the Native Americans, found itself in 1815 without any Native Americans but with a Christian college community split to the center by a cleavage that ranged Congregationalist Federalists against non-Congregationalist Jeffersonians. The issue, as could have happened only in New England, where politics was theology and theology politics, was fought out in a bitter state campaign. The Republicans won both the governorship and the legislature, and they proceeded in 1816 to pass an act amending the college charter, increasing the number of trustees and thus taking control away from the Federalist Old Guard. Jefferson, from his Monticello retreat, applauded: to do otherwise, he wrote, would be to hold "that the earth belongs to the dead and not to the living."[32] The case was fought out before the highest court in New Hampshire, which held the law valid, on the grounds that the college was a public corporation, devoted to public purposes, and that its charter could therefore be amended as public policy shifted. *Fletcher v. Peck*, it was held, did not apply; that related only to legislative grants involving the property rights of individuals, and not to grants of power for public purpose.

The case went to the Supreme Court, where it was argued with eloquence for the college by Daniel Webster, at that time (at thirty-seven) reaching the height of his powers. Every schoolboy knows Webster's reputed eloquent plea ("It is, Sir, as I have said, a small college. Yet there are those who love it.") and how Marshall, whom the Yazoo land scandals had left cold, found his own eyes suffused with tears as Webster, overcome by the emotion of his words, wept.[33] But few schoolboys know that the case had ultimately less to do with colleges than with business corporations; that sanctity of contract was invoked to give corporations immunity against legislative control, and that business enterprise in America has never had more useful mercenaries than the tears Daniel Webster and John Marshall are reputed to have shed so devotedly that March day in Washington in 1818.

After the argument, the judges found they could not agree. The case was continued. Webster, who had ways of knowing, guessed that at least three of the seven judges were safe. Justice Henry Brockholst Livingston was crucial. Since he leaned heavily on the advice of Chancellor Kent of New York, whose learning was as well known and almost as greatly admired as his conservatism, steps were taken to argue Kent out of his view that the New Hampshire court was right in holding that the college was a public corporation. When the Court reconvened the following February, Marshall read the opinion of four justices. The opinion held that the charter was a "private" contract; that the trustees represented the original grantees, whose vested rights to the money and effort they expended required protection; that no one would give money to found a "private eleemosynary institution" such as Dartmouth College unless the charter that was granted would run in perpetuity.[34]

There were holes in the argument, especially where Marshall

agreed that Parliament, which had granted the charter, could legally (not morally) have amended or revoked it, and that as a result of the Revolution the state of New Hampshire was the successor to the sovereignty of Parliament. While Marshall's opinion did not even mention *Fletcher v. Peck* (the concurring opinions of Story and Washington did), that case was assumed. What the *Dartmouth College* decision did was to apply *Fletcher v. Peck* to corporate charters. Once it was clear that a charter was a contract within the meaning of the contract clause, the exemption of public contracts could not have exempted the charters of business corporations from the operation of the rule.[35] What was important was the ruling that a charter of incorporation was a contract. Marshall scarcely discussed this, although it was addressed by Story and Washington. Yet this took the *Dartmouth* decision a step beyond *Fletcher v. Peck,* because it extended the contract clause.

The *Dartmouth* decision was an extension not only in constitutional terms but in economic terms as well. *Fletcher v. Peck* threw the protection of vested rights around the capitalism of land speculation, and allowed it to operate on any terms it chose. The *Dartmouth College* case did the same for corporate business enterprise. I am not speaking in terms of specific intent. The corporation in Marshall's day was not the preferred unit of business enterprise. It was not to become so until after the Civil War. However, it was increasingly important given the grant of charters for turnpikes, canal companies, railroads, bridge construction companies. The *Dartmouth College* decision operated to make an initial grant of power, of tax exemption,[36] and of government lands a permanent one. Later developments, principally Chief Justice Taney's decision in the *Charles River Bridge* case,[37] stripped the decision of some of its starkness. Taney ruled that while charters are contracts, they must be strictly construed in favor of the public interest, and that no power may be exercised that was not expressly granted in them. State legislatures also learned how to insert "reservation clauses" into constitutions and statutes — provisions reserving to themselves the right to "alter, amend, or repeal" the charters they granted. But the inescapable fact is that the *Dartmouth College* case set up an inviolability of corporate charters that has had to be qualified, instead of starting at the opposite pole with a rule of legislative discretion and control. By putting all the burdens on the original wording of the charter, the decision encouraged an interaction between corporate interests and legislative greed that has been one of the peculiar marks of American capitalism.

The contract cases made Marshall the most hated man in the country. State bankruptcy laws, squatter laws, and tax laws fell under the interdict of "vested rights." The decision that aroused the bitterest feeling was *Sturges v. Crowninshield,* ruling that a state bankruptcy act violated the contract clause as it applied to existing ("retrospective") contracts. Marshall's opinion sought to apply this even to contracts made after passage of the act. But this was too much even for Marshall's usually obedient colleagues; in response to a storm of popular protest, they repudiated this obiter dictum eight years later in *Ogden v. Saunders.* Marshall, however, held out to the end and found himself the solitary dissenter. His dissenting opinion in *Ogden v. Saunders* gives the clearest statement of his philosophy of contract as the basis for the doctrine of vested rights. The opinion is steeped in a Rousseauist natural-rights mysticism. It represents the most explicit statement we have of the transcendental sources of the sanctity of contracts, which Marshall finds to be "original and pre-existing principles . . . anterior to, and independent of society." The obligation of contract, he says, is a moral obligation dictated by reason or nature. In short, in the words of a commentator, "It is not the state that gives validity and force to the contract, but, conceivably, a contract which gives validity and force to the state."

Marshall was clearly riding an obsession. His primary drive was to protect private property from governmental encroachment. His struggle against the powers of the state legislatures was an instrument for this purpose. But the pursuit of even a secondary objective over a longer period of time may transform it eventually into an independent objective. States' rights finally became Marshall's bugbear. He came to believe that every concession to the states' regulatory power sapped the Constitution. He had begun his Supreme Court tenure in the shadow of Jacksonian democracy. Increasingly his letters and conversation were filled with dark forebodings about the future.

Yet he had done his work. Vested rights remained an operative doctrine in state judicial review until the Civil War, especially in such industrial states as New York. And after the Civil War the due process clause of the Fourteenth Amendment more than took the place of the contract clause. But the interpretation that the Supreme Court was to place on the due process clause would not have been possible without Marshall's establishment of the power of judicial review, and the calm audacity with which he had transformed the genius of business enterprise into a set of implied limitations on state power.

8

The Great Ganglion
That Was Holmes

"A great man," Oliver Wendell Holmes said of John Marshall, "represents a great ganglion in the nerves of society." I like the metaphor enough to apply it to its own author, who was usually more taken with strategic thinking than organismic.

The reader will readily discover that of all the figures in my gallery, it is Holmes who has had the strongest influence on my own thinking. In part it was his style, literary and personal, in part the larger judicial approach that helped me untangle the issues in decisions other than his own.

I still find his doctrine of judicial restraint (or self-limitation) enormously useful as a guide through the jungle of judicial interpretation. Yet as early as 1936 I came to recognize that judicial restraint could become a form of judicial austerity that ignored the tangled context of many of the "hot" social issues and placed a too unrealistic emphasis on the workings of majoritarianism.

Nor have I been indifferent to the role that a tooth-and-fangs social Darwinism played in the Holmesian universe.

Surrendering his commission after being thrice wounded was the young Holmes's most wrenching Civil War experience. It carried with it an unexpungeable guilt, but also a compensatory glorification of all the martial virtues that became the Holmes mystique, alongside his Hobbesian view that pre–social contract man was the ultimate reality in history.

I am aware of these deep splits in Holmes, and have written about them in the epilogue to this volume. But they come with the

*Holmesian territory, much of which is still terra incognita, open to
further exploration.*

In 1902 Justice Horace Gray retired from the United States Supreme
Court. Since Gray was a Massachusetts man, it was natural for President Theodore Roosevelt to turn to another Massachusetts man to
replace him. Roosevelt at once thought of Oliver Wendell Holmes.
He was attracted by the combination of the scholar with a distinguished military career, and the statesman with a literary and historical bent: after all, he found himself to be the confirmation that
such a blend was a good one. He was attracted also by Holmes's
high reputation for legal ability and learning. And as for the dissents
that Holmes had returned in the labor cases and that had brought
down upon him the contumely of the men of substance, Roosevelt
was not one to balk at that. In fact he probably saw that he could
turn it to advantage. The temper of the country was far more radical
than any of the Republican presidents had been able to understand.
Roosevelt was getting into the swing of his trust-busting phase. He
knew, deeply conservative as he was, that his social order could be
preserved not by turning his back on the storm but by riding and
commanding it.

The hitch lay in one speech that Holmes had made — the one
on John Marshall. It was undoubtedly one of Holmes's great utterances and one of his justest judgments of a man's talent and his place
in history. But to Roosevelt it seemed ominous. Roosevelt liked Marshall's broad interpretation of the national power. He saw him as the
very archetype of the judge, "a constitutional statesman believing in
great party principles, and willing to continue the Constitution so
that the nation can develop on the broadest lines." Roosevelt knew
that Holmes was a nationalist, and had long before written ecstati-
cally to Henry Cabot Lodge about Holmes's fervid 1895 speech
celebrating the martial qualities. But his comments on the Federalist
chief justice bothered Roosevelt. Holmes had preferred to view Marshall not so much as a single hero but rather as "a great ganglion in
the nerves of society, or, to vary the figure, a strategic point in the
campaign of history, and part of his greatness consists in his being
there."

What Roosevelt did not want on the Court, his letter to Lodge
continued, was a Taney who was "a curse to our national life because

he belonged to the wrong party." What he wanted was "a statesman of the national type," "a constructive statesman, constantly keeping in mind . . . his relations with his fellow statesmen who in other branches of the government are striving . . . to advance the ends of government." Roosevelt wanted assurances. "I should like to know that Judge Holmes was in entire sympathy with our views, that is with your views and mine and Judge Gray's, for instance." To select a man "who was not absolutely sane and sound on the great national policies" would be "an irreparable wrong to the nation." Roosevelt instructed Lodge to show his letter to Holmes "if it became necessary." There was no indication that he did: Lodge's answer must have been reassuring enough to assuage Roosevelt's doubts. The President probably made more inquiries during the month that followed Gray's resignation. Finally, having obtained the imprimatur of Senator Hoar of Massachusetts, he announced Holmes's appointment in August 1902. It went to the Senate early in December, the Senate acted on it in very short order, and Holmes became a member of the United States Supreme Court on December 6, 1902.

For a while all was well between the president and his new associate justice. Roosevelt liked to have artistic and literary men around him and made Holmes part of the group of "Roosevelt Familiars," which at one time or another included Lodge, Albert Beveridge, John Hay, Augustus Saint-Gaudens, Owen Wister, and Jules Jusserand, with Lincoln Steffens and Finley Peter Dunne on the margin. He seems to have warmed to Holmes, with his background of Civil War battles, his wit, his epigrams, his talk of books and etchings. The Holmeses, who settled in Washington in 1903 and bought the house on L Street in which they were to live to the end, were often at the White House entertainments. But Holmes made no commitments, whether outer or inner, whether political or intellectual. The honeymoon was doomed to be short-lived, and in a little more than a year it was rudely shattered. What shattered it was Holmes's dissent in Roosevelt's great trust-busting case involving the Northern Securities Company. Despite the hopes Roosevelt had pinned on him, Holmes voted against the government, writing one of the two dissenting opinions in the case. Roosevelt was furious. "I could carve out of a banana," he is reported (apocryphally) to have cried, "a justice with more backbone than that."

He was wrong. Holmes had enough backbone to stand up against the man who had appointed him only a short while before, and who had showered on him the lavishness of his warmth and personality. Roosevelt was so single-minded in his determination to have his way in the *Northern Securities* case that he was obtuse in his judgment of what made Holmes tick.

Nevertheless the whole Roosevelt-Holmes relationship — including the president's letter to Lodge, his doubts, his final decision to appoint Holmes, and his fury at Holmes's dissent — deserves some analysis. It involved questions that cut deep into the nature of the American governmental system and into the personality of both principals in the affair. The commentators have tended to deal too harshly with Roosevelt. The curious thing is that among those most vehement in condemning him have been the liberals. At the same time that they assert that a Peckham or a Sutherland reads his economic view into the Constitution, they condemn Roosevelt for having acted on a similar assumption. It is time that we stripped ourselves of the latent hypocrisy in this. Present-day constitutional writers pretty generally recognize that presidents do tend to appoint justices whose thinking runs along their own grooves, and that justices cannot wholly escape reading their social views into their opinions. If both these propositions are without truth, then a quarter-century of constitutional commentary has been either wasted or misunderstood.

There were, however, extraordinary items in this instance that must qualify the propositions just stated. One was Roosevelt's brashness. He had the temerity to take the assumption on which his predecessors had acted implicitly, at least since John Adams appointed John Marshall to the Court, and to put it quite explicitly in his letter to Lodge. Roosevelt thought of himself as a good deal of an iconoclast. The man who said that he could not show J. P. Morgan or Carnegie or Hill the same regard he had for Peary the explorer, or Bury and Rhodes the historians — the man who brought cowboys and prizefighters and big-game hunters into the White House much as his kinsman-successor brings movie stars — was not a man to balk at putting down on paper the hidden assumptions on which his predecessors had acted. He was writing to Lodge as one man of the world to another. He was at that time in earnest about his antitrust crusade. He knew that there was lined up against him on the Court a minority that might easily be turned into a potential majority, and he was determined that he would not willingly appoint to the Court a judge who might consciously turn the tide against him.[1] As Charles Beard has pointed out, Roosevelt wanted to see the harshness of corporation law tempered by a humanistic jurisprudence. Unless a president believes in government by deadlock, which he is not likely to do, he must appoint to the Court judges who are roughly of his own persuasion — not necessarily from his own political party but within the orbit of his own worldview. Only thus can he keep the various parts of his administration moving together as an administration. In our own time we have had a dramatic illustration of this in the New Deal constitutional crisis and in the Court appointments following it. Franklin D. Roosevelt found out that justices with a worldview reaching back decades before the era of the Depression and the fascist threat were able to burke the whole meaning of his administration.

The second item was that Holmes was not the ordinary judge, any more than Theodore Roosevelt was the ordinary president. Holmes had a judicial method that was developed to a greater degree than any other judge's of that day. He had already shown this quality on the state court, as the president might easily have discovered had he studied his opinions. He had shown an impassioned indifference to the "hydraulic pressures" that converge on "great cases," a meticulous regard for the strict legal profile of a case, an inclination to let the legislature have its way, a sophistication that prevented him from projecting his economic philosophy and calling it the Constitution — and that in an era when it would have been easy enough to identify his views with the welfare of the nation.

But this did not mean that Holmes was of austerity all compact, a god who had pierced beyond the human impulses in him. If Roosevelt had relied on Holmes to give the Sherman Act full sway because he had practiced judicial laissez-faire toward other legislative acts, he failed to reckon with the fact that Holmes was not an Olympian but a philosopher — a wholly different creature. His judicial philosophy of leaving the legislature alone came from a deeper belief in leaving the cosmos alone. And when the strict meaning of restraint of trade in the common law coincided with this philosophy, Holmes was clad in a double armor of conviction. Roosevelt might have anticipated Holmes's *Northern Securities* dissent had he studied Holmes's Massachusetts labor dissent. Taking into account Holmes's Darwinism and his sense of accepting the limits that the universe imposed on him might well have given warning to any president hellbent on antitrust enforcement. Holmes's opinion may reveal a lack of economic realism. But it was natural for Holmes, who approached the case without a feeling for the realities of economic power involved, to accept monopolies as well as trade unions as part of the laws of the organization and the equilibrium of life. Holmes's reasoning from the history of the common-law doctrine of restraint of trade unions was learned and subtle. But the real logic of his *Northern Securities* dissent was poles apart from the logic of the justices who made up the rest of the minority, and from the logic of Roosevelt. The other dissenting justices acted from a vision of an economic universe. Holmes acted from a vision of a philosophic universe. And because he had so firm a nucleus of conviction, he was unperturbed by Roosevelt's concentrated fury.

HIS APPOINTMENT TO THE UNITED STATES SUPREME COURT WAS FOR Holmes the culminating opportunity in a career of thought and effort. Behind him was a long row of cases — thousands of them; before him stretched thousands more. Each case required courage of heart, sharpness of mind, wisdom of judgment, cunning of hand in contriving the right words.

It was because Holmes felt thus that he was troubled by the comments in the press that greeted his appointment. The appointment itself went through the Senate smoothly enough. But when Holmes's name was first announced, he was irritated by the quality of the "stacks of notices." "The immense majority of them," he wrote to Sir Frederick Pollock, "seem devoid of personal discrimination or courage. They are so favorable that they make my nomination a popular success but they have the flabbiness of American ignorance." They generally mentioned Holmes's *Vegelahn* dissent, about which one wrote that its author "has partial views, is brilliant but not very sound." Holmes's response in a letter is a rare instance of a *cri de coeur:* "It makes one sick when he has broken his heart in trying to make every word living and real to see a lot of duffers . . . talking with the sanctity of print in a way that at once discloses to the knowing eye that literally they don't know anything about it." Thus Holmes had his taste of running the gauntlet of lay opinion on a national scale. It was not a severe ordeal as such things go. Chief Justice Taney before him went through a far worse one when his nomination came to the Senate and an outcry arose that he had been Andrew Jackson's "pliant instrument" in the bank controversy. Justice Brandeis was to have an even bitterer cup to drink when the corporate powers and their spokesmen in the Bar Association sought to block his appointment in a protracted Senate fight in 1916. For Holmes's sensitive spirit, either of these major attacks would have been a catastrophe; his own minor one was sufficiently galling.

Holmes was not a young man when he took his place on the Court. He was sixty-one. Two members of the Court, Justices Edward White and Joseph McKenna, were younger than he. Of the rest, there was no one as much as ten years his senior. It was not a brilliant Court nor an enlightened one. The two great justices who had made judicial history in the last decades of the century — Justices Samuel Miller and Stephen Field — were both gone. Those who were left were not even half-gods. Chief Justice Melville Fuller was a nonentity. Of the rest, only Justices John Harlan, Henry Brown, White, and McKenna had more than average ability, and of these only White and Harlan had real stature. All of them, with the exception of Harlan, were deeply conservative, if not reactionary, in their social outlook. The main outlines of judicial strategy had already been laid down — first in the battle over the interpretation of due process between the cohorts led by Field and those led by Miller up until the middle of the 1880s, and then by the sequence of decisions in the 1890s that breathed a bleak laissez-faire philosophy. It was clear that the whole duty of a Supreme Court justice lay in filling in the outlines of these decisions and in using constitutional law as a way of entrenching the system of economic power.

Holmes refused to live up to the rules of a game so conceived. He had no intention of conscripting the legal Constitution as he saw it to the uses of the economic Constitution, any more than he would conscript it to the uses of a political program. If he disappointed President Roosevelt in the *Northern Securities* case, he had many more disappointments in store for those on the other side of the fence. His first opinion in 1903 (in *Otis v. Parker*) showed clearly his intention to give state legislative action a broad margin of tolerance, even if it implied a system of state regulation of economic activity. But it was not until 1905, in the *Lochner* case, that Holmes found his real stride on the Supreme Court.

THERE WERE THREE IMPORTANT TURNING POINTS IN HOLMES'S career on the Supreme Court. One was the *Lochner* dissent in 1905, the second was the coming of Justice Brandeis to the Court in 1916, the third was America's entrance into the war soon after, bringing in its wake a group of civil liberties cases that were to occupy Holmes from 1917 for almost a decade. Each of these is worth more than passing mention.

With the *Lochner* case Holmes really began firing his big judicial guns. Up to that time no really great issue had arisen, although Holmes had given distress to the camp followers of both sides. The *Lochner* dissent marked a turning point. It had every index of having been painfully thought out. It had the clarity of a trumpet call after which there could be no retreat. There have been those who have read Holmes's dissent as mainly an exercise in satire. Charles Beard, for example, speaks of Holmes "allowing his genial wit to melt the frosty verbalism of the law." "Genial" is a curious adjective to apply in this case. Similarly when a few years earlier Thorstein Veblen published his *Theory of the Leisure Class,* the critics had viewed it as an elaborate literary satire. Like Veblen, however, but in his own very different way, Holmes was very much in earnest. He had not entirely forgotten the military strategy of his Civil War experience. He knew that the thrust against the enemy must be sudden and sharp, made with all your might. "When you strike at a king," Emerson had told him long before, "you must kill him." Holmes was striking not only at Justice Peckham's majority opinion in the *Lochner* case but also at the whole dark and intolerant judicial tradition that Peckham was expressing.

While Holmes's motivations were those of a legal craftsman determined not to see his craft distorted, the consequences of his opinions reached to the living standards of the common man and his struggles for dignity. And the *Lochner* dissent did not stand alone. In the quarter-century of judicial labors that remained to him, Holmes fought for the right of the legislature to promote equality of bargaining power for workers, for the right of social experiment, for state and federal social legislation, for the right of the people to develop an effective tax administration, for adequate governmental power in peace and war. He fought with courage and with subtlety. Where by yielding ground slightly he could get the rest of the Court to go along with him, he did so. But where no compromise was possible, he continued to speak out with a magisterial manner and a summary brevity that infuriated his opponents just as much as it delighted his followers.

And followers he did have. For the young lawyers and the students still in the law schools who were looking about for some figure who rose above the deadening plains of legal commercialism and judicial complacency, some veteran who could give them hope that they would not become the mercenaries of a corporate economy, Holmes became a symbol. His opinions were caught up by the law journals, which were just becoming a force. Those who fought to temper the harshness of corporate power and those who, whatever their views, sought in law a vitality that he restored to it, combined in homage to him. They read him avidly, they quoted the Holmesian nuggets they discovered, they wrote about him. Holmes was deeply pleased and yet basically unmoved. His real motivation came from deep within, from his craftsman's conception of judicial power, his philosophy of its place in a limited universe, his unflagging sense of being but part of the long campaign of history.

BUT IT WAS A LONELY FIGHT. FOR A DECADE AND A HALF, ASIDE FROM occasional support from Justice Harlan and later from Charles Evans Hughes, Holmes stood pretty much alone. In 1916, with the appointment of Louis D. Brandeis to the Court, this was changed.

The relationship between Holmes and Brandeis was a complex one. Brandeis brought to the Court a first-rate legal mind, an arduous education in social realities, and a wealth of economic knowledge. He also brought a seriousness of intent and an unwavering will. While there can be no question that Brandeis exercised a substantial influence over Holmes, we must remember that not only the contours of Holmes's mind but also its basic propulsions had already become fixed by the time Brandeis came to the Court. Brandeis's influence was vastly overestimated by men like Chief Justice Taft, who allowed his judgment to be swayed by fear and prejudice. When he wrote in a letter that Holmes enabled Brandeis to cast two votes instead of one, it was a peevish utterance and unjust to both men.

Holmes and Brandeis had known each other in Boston when Brandeis was a young lawyer just out of Harvard and Holmes was a state court judge interested in the affairs of the school and its graduates. After that, except for Brandeis's appearances before the Court in Washington as a counsel, they had little contact until Brandeis became a colleague. There can be no question that Holmes was struck by Brandeis's complete integrity, his vast knowledge, his ethical sense, and by his almost agonizing determination to do the right thing. "There goes a *good* man," he would say to Mrs. Holmes when Brandeis left their home. But the differences between the two were profound.

Brandeis was an economist, Holmes a philosopher. Brandeis was austere where Holmes, except when he was deeply aroused, tended to be whimsical, paradoxical, and gay. Holmes was the author of *The Common Law*, "The Soldier's Faith," and numerous delightful and discursive letters to Sir Frederick Pollock and others. Brandeis was the author of *Other People's Money,* and when he wrote letters they were like communiqués from a battlefield, with the rattle of artillery sounding in their one-two-three memorandum sequence. Holmes thought in terms of an infinite universe of which man was only an infinitesimal part, as were his efforts, including those for social reform. Brandeis saw the threat of a concentrated corporate power within the commonwealth, of a state within a state, and bent every effort toward making real his dream of a Periclean democracy on the American plains. Brandeis was Holmes's conscience, and Holmes still had enough of the Puritan in him to have a slumbering conscience that could be awakened and fortified. But while Brandeis, as a conscience, bolstered Holmes's legal views and strengthened his more liberal impulses, he could not change Holmes in essentials. Despite all his proddings, Holmes could never read any of the economic treatises Brandeis urged on him. They were "improving" — an epithet Holmes applied to anything that disturbed his sense of a human universe.

In a perverse way Holmes prided himself in his ignorance of facts. "I never knew any facts about anything. . . . My intellectual furniture consists of an assortment of general conclusions which grow fewer and more general as I grow older. I always say that the chief end of man is to frame them and that no general conclusion is worth a damn," he wrote to his good friend Pollock:

> Brandeis the other day drove a harpoon into my midriff with reference to my summer occupations. He said you talk about improving your mind, you only exercise it on the subjects with which you are familiar. Why don't you try something new, study some domain of fact. . . . I hate facts. . . . I have little doubt that it would be good for my immortal soul to plunge into them, good also for the performance of my duties, but I shrink from the bore — or rather, I hate to give up the chance to read this and that, that a gentleman should have read before he dies.

The tone of this was partly the result of Holmes's love of paradox. But partly it came from his thirst for the mainstreams of thought and feeling rather than for the tributaries of economics and law. This was so deep in Holmes as to amount to a tropism. And to this tropism one must ascribe the quality of his writing.

"I think it a heartbreaking task," he wrote of the job of composing judicial opinions, "to give an impression of freedom, elegance, and variety." In his letters, as in his opinions, he succeeded. His colleagues on the Court didn't always appreciate the amenities of his style, however. "The boys," Holmes wrote about the other justices, "generally cut one of the genitals out of mine in the form of some expression that they think too free." But Brandeis was not among them. Brandeis he considered one of the "onward and upward" fellows. The tastes of his friend Sir Pollock, although he was not nearly so deep a person as Brandeis, were nearer his own.

Holmes's letters to Pollock reveal the deep and contradictory currents of his thought. An economic conservative, Holmes started a revolution in American judicial thought that was one of the great forces in making possible the present Supreme Court. Nevertheless, the letters show that he undertook it all with the aristocrat's disdain for overearnestness, with no reformer's zeal, and almost as if it were an avocation. He had a pervading sense of human limitation and hated every form of moral imperialism, but along with this there was a magisterial briskness and impatience. There was a note of toughness in his thinking, and he saw through the fluffiness of "transcendental" thought. And yet there remained a persistent strain of idealism. Holmes never seemed to be able to make up his mind as to whether he was a naturalist or an idealist. He spoke at times as if man were no higher than any other living creature, subject to the laws of matter, and at other times as if it were man alone who gave value to the universe. He defined truth variously as "what I can't help believing" and elsewhere as the affirmation of the majority. This faultline in Holmes's thinking does not detract from his greatness. The issue he was unable to resolve is one that still baffles the best minds among us.

WITH THE OUTBREAK OF THE FIRST WORLD WAR, THE COURT WAS confronted with new problems. Holmes had never been an antimilitarist. He had always seen peace as "a little space of calm in the midst of the tempestuous untamed streaming of the world." "High and dangerous action," he had said, "teaches us to believe as right beyond dispute things for which our doubting minds are slow to find words of proof." If Holmes had been less of a philosopher, he would have come close to being something of a firebrand. He had been increasingly troubled by noting among the young secretaries who came to him from the Harvard Law School, part of whose job was to read aloud to him and with whom he discussed life as well as law, an increasing skepticism of patriotic values. He had scant belief in this "experimenting in negations." And yet it was characteristic of him that while with the outbreak of the war he had far fewer words to eat and fewer attitudes to erase than anyone else, he did not go as far as others in uncritical glorifications of the war. This was partly because his whole method was to proceed by continuities rather than by mutations, partly because his critical mind sought always to balance the excesses he saw around him. It was also characteristic of Holmes that one who all his life had had a fighting faith should now be so moderate in trumpeting it and so wary of its abuse.

He had always liked the English without being an Anglophile. In England's moments of greatest danger during the war, Holmes in his letters to Pollock rejoiced with the English victories, expressed concern at the reverses and the bombing raids on London, shared Pollock's impatience with President Wilson's conduct of foreign affairs in the years before America's entrance into the war, and would probably have preferred his former colleague Charles Evans Hughes in the presidency after 1916. He was, to be sure, civilized enough not to let the war wipe out his feeling of esteem for the German legal scholars and historians whom he had known. But when the hour of decision came for America, Holmes had no hesitation. "Between two groups that want to make inconsistent kinds of a world, I see no remedy except force."

Holmes did not idealize the actual experience of war. He had learned what it was like. But he knew long before our own discovery of it the slackness of individual social will out of which the pacifist impulses grow. Philosophically he accepted war as part of his universe. He had, moreover, a belief in the toughening effect of warlike sports and pursuits ("a price well paid for the breeding of a race fit for leadership and command"). To most of us today such words will seem dangerously close to imperialism. But Holmes was more concerned with national cohesion than with conquest. He thought that the war experience gave the individual once more a sense of being part of "an unimaginable whole." These quotations have been from the Holmes of the 1890s. But as late as 1913, in his speech, "Law and the Court," he expressed an "old man's apprehension": that "competition from new races will cut deeper than working men's disputes and will test whether we can hang together or can fight."

Because of these convictions, the war, when it came to the Supreme Court, did not catch Holmes intellectually unprepared. As a judge there were two principal problems he would have to face. The first was the question of the positive powers of a wartime democracy. For all his relativism, Holmes saw the war as a struggle for our conception of civilized values. He could not see, therefore, how the network of government regulation of industry and the daily lives of people fell outside the Constitution or was a prohibitive price to pay for the survival of these values. The opinion that best expresses this belief is found in *Missouri v. Holland,* the migratory bird treaty case, and in *Block v. Hirsh,* the leading Emergency Rent Law case. That Holmes would have extended the same logic from the congressional power to the presidential war power follows from the analogy of his reasoning about the governor's power in *Moyer v. Peabody.*

A more difficult problem that came before Holmes and the Court was that of civil liberties in wartime. As a Massachusetts judge, Holmes had dealt with the regular run of civil liberties cases, and in one, *Commonwealth v. Davis,* he had written a legal opinion that was much cited later by those wishing to restrict by municipal ordinance the right to use public property as a forum for discussion. It was by no means a foregone conclusion, therefore, that Holmes would, with the war cases, become a champion of civil liberties.

That he did may be traced to several strands of influence. One was Holmes's sense of critical balance and his dislike for the excesses committed by wartime patrioteers. A second was his admiration for the civil liberties of the English tradition, and for the temperate manner in which they handled problems of intellectual freedom. A third was the influence of Brandeis, who brought to the Court a fierce determination that nothing should destroy the right of criticism on which democratic change depends. One may guess that in this association Brandeis helped enrich Holmes's grasp of the social values of the problem, and Holmes's contribution was to give the conception legal contours and his unique gift of form. And finally there was Holmes's growing sense that men could do little by repression to divert the movement of events. This comes out most sharply in the closing paragraph of his 1925 dissent in *Gitlow v. New York:* "If in the long run the beliefs expressed in proletarian dictatorship are destined to be accepted by the dominant forces of the community, the only meaning of free speech is that they should be given their chance and have their way." Here he sees free speech as the core of the succession of political power in a democracy, and the larger function of government as being to give expression to the struggle of life.

To these factors must be added Holmes's sense of legal crafts-manship and his devotion to legal values. That this was a real devotion is clear not only from the great personal reluctance he felt about his opinion in the *Debs* case, but even more from his brief memorandum on refusing a stay of execution for Sacco and Vanzetti in 1927. There is very little that Holmes added to the philosophical conception of intellectual freedom in a democracy, although he gave it a literary sharpness. His creative work lay in reducing the nebulousness of philosophical concepts to usable legal standards. In the *Schenck* case, and after that in the *Abrams* and *Gitlow* dissents, Holmes worked out the tests of clear and present danger and of actual intent that may serve as a point of departure for Supreme Court action in this area. It is a tribute to the mark that Holmes has left on us that in much of the current controversy over free speech in wartime the fires of doctrine should rage over how Holmes would have interpreted the problem and what he would say if he were alive today.

As he grew older, Holmes liked to joke about being an old man. His letters to John C. H. Wu are especially revealing. They are the letters of an old New England aristocrat, laden with years and honors, to a young Chinese student of law and philosophy. We see an old man, concerned about his age, expecting to die any year, but gallant, generous, graceful — taking the time to dip into his rich experience and nourish an eager and hungry youth; we see a general in the campaign of life painstakingly teaching a new recruit the rules of warfare; we see a man who has found success and a deep core of peace within himself gently nurturing the troubled spirit of a young man just starting out; we see a teacher writing to a student with infinite frankness and infinite tact.

He writes of law as "a statement of the circumstances in which the public force will be brought to bear upon men through the courts." Of justice: "I hate justice, which means that I know if a man begins to talk about that, for one reason or another he is shirking talking in legal terms." The tough-minded note is sounded especially when he is talking of political realities. He has scant respect for talk about equality. "I hardly think of man as so sacred an object as Laski seems to think him. I believe that Malthus was right in his funda-mental notion . . . every society is founded on the death of men. In one way or another some are always and inevitably pushed down the dead line." He hated also talk of neighborly love, and wrote it down as humbug. He had "an imaginary society of jobbists, who were free to be egotists or altruists on the usual Saturday half-holiday provided they were neither while on their job."

Nor did he think much of "the human ultimate that man is always an end in himself":

> . . . We march up a conscript with bayonets behind to die for a cause he doesn't believe in. And I feel no scruples about it. Our morality seems to me only a check on the ultimate domination of force, just as our politeness is a check on the impulse of every pig to put his feet in the trough. . . . When it comes to the development of a *corpus juris* the ultimate question is what do the dominant forces of the community want and do they want it hard enough to disregard whatever inhibitions may stand in the way.

This was the ripe fruit of an idea he had planted more than fifty years before, in 1873, in his comment on the gas stokers' strike.

> This [Herbert Spencer's] tacit assumption of the solidarity of the interests of society is very common, but seems to us false. . . . In the last resort a man rightly prefers his own interest to that of his neighbor. . . . All that can be expected from modern improvements is that legislation should easily and quickly, yet not too quickly, modify itself in accordance with the will of the *de facto* supreme power in the community, and that the spread of an educated sympathy should reduce the sacrifice of minorities to a minimum. . . . The more powerful interests must be more or less reflected in legislation, which, like every other device of man or beast, must tend in the long run to aid the survival of the fittest. . . . It is no sufficient condemnation of legislation that it favors one class at the expense of another, for much or all legislation does that.

Thus his view of politics and law is seen as a curious compound of social Darwinism, the Marxian class concept, and a pragmatic semi-Austinian recognition of the realities of a social system, all tempered by a tolerance of other people's views and a humorous unwillingness to erect his own notions into absolutes.

But Holmes never tired of saying that he saw law and politics as only parts of the cosmos. It is with the cosmos that his letters are most concerned. His attitude toward it was always that of a gallant humility, and a shrug of the shoulder that did not preclude the most arduous effort. "A man must accept limits," he writes. And again: "We begin with an act of faith, with deciding that we are not God, for if we were dreaming the universe we should be God so far as we knew." But within these limits that the cosmos imposes, he believed in human heroism. "If . . . you bear the fire in your belly, it will survive and transfigure the hard facts."

The hard fact of age concerned him. Holmes feared outstaying his competence on the Court, as others before him had done. Increasingly, of course, he had to conserve his strength, particularly after a major operation he had to undergo in 1922. In 1929 his wife died. Life was drawing to a close for him. In 1931, on the occasion of his ninetieth birthday, honors and tributes were heaped upon him from all sides. On January 12, 1932, he retired from the Court. He said he felt like a schoolboy released from his duties. He could no longer write letters by his own hand, but he continued with the aid of his secretary to read and to keep in touch with the new figures on the intellectual horizon. With his zest for life scarcely diminished, he waited serenely for death. It came on March 6, 1935. Two days later he would have been ninety-four.

Is the influence Holmes left transitory? And are we in danger of accepting him too uncritically? We have had warnings lately about the development of a Holmes cult. And yet, if the materials for a cult are there, the warnings will do little good. Despite the strictures on Holmes and the skepticism about him from skeptical minds, there will be in every generation young men to read Holmes's words who will not read the words of warning about him. And their minds will be captured not by the words alone but by the personal image of Holmes that emerges from them. What is this image? Borrowing the notion of a guardian angel, one might say that Holmes, with his Apollonian serenity and his irrepressible high spirits, was watched over by one of those grave-gay deities of the Greeks. What disappoints many about Holmes is the absence of passion and of a feeling of dedication, the lack of the pattern of torture and complexity such as the generations following Dostoyevski and Nietzsche have come to expect of the modern hero. To use Nietzsche's dualism, there was very much of the Apollonian in Holmes and very little of the darker urges of the Dionysian.

He had a serenity even in his moments of anger or near despair, an assurance even in the midst of skepticism. It is a chastening thing to read his writings over the span of his life — to see how slow has been the movement toward a workable democracy, how many obstructions have been placed in its path, how unmalleable have been the interpretations placed on the fundamental laws by the dominant judicial caste, how spirit breaking the efforts to fight against complacency and blindness. But if it is chastening, it is also heartening, particularly today when the young need to be heartened about the future of a militant democracy: heartening to see how at the high tide of capitalist materialism there were still those who stood by their faith in social reason and in the competition of ideas, their belief in the steady, if slow, march of social progress. Holmes was one of these. He was at once buoyant and unfooled. The most striking thing about him was that he refused to live in a private universe. He was a great spokesman for our constitutional tradition because he was a great enough conservative to enlarge the framework of the past to accommodate at least some of the needs of the present. He saw himself as part of the army of historic movement, whose "black spearheads" he saw "stretching away against the unattainable sky."

That is different, however, from saying that he was a warrior in the armies of social change. To lay violent siege to history was as little in his temperament as to shake his fist at the cosmos. He accepted the limits both of history and of nature, and within those limits he found his freedom in a free world. He was part of no movement. What he said and his writings did not grow out of the current social experience of the emerging cultural forces. They were, rather, the reaping of past experience and the extraction of its full implications by a man who was content enough with life, but who did not feel himself to be god enough to hem in those whose passion for changes was greater than his.

At the core of every culture's existence is a poetic attitude toward the world. This attitude has often been better expressed by literature and art than by the urgencies of political or economic doctrine. The poet can often distill into his symbols even the experiences of which he has not been a direct part, particularly if he has in him a sense of the past and a sensitivity to the mood around him. Many have wondered how an aristocrat like Holmes, who would have nothing to do with the mechanical gadgets of American life, who refused to read the newspapers and identified himself with none of the political or economic movements of his time, was nevertheless able to distill into his writings the sense of American libertarian democracy. I venture the belief that the son of Dr. Holmes turned out to be more of a poet than his father, if by poet we mean someone who pierces the appearances of life and expresses his vision in living language. And if this sheds some light on Holmes, it should be not without meaning for his age that one of its poets should work in the intractable material of legal rhetoric.

Despite this — better, because of this — Holmes has had a great impact on our constitutional development and history. For a time it seemed that his work, however gallant, would prove futile. The Supreme Court majority continued to show glacial hostility to his basic constitutional attitudes, and the country as a whole, indifference to his fighting faith. But the constitutional crisis of the New Deal and the struggle over the Court reorganization plan of another Roosevelt have cleared the way for the complete adoption of Holmes's views on constitutional law.

Holmes created the means for his vindication. Yet his vindication, in turn, will tend to reduce that sense of wonder on which a man's éclat in history depends. Holmes wrote in his essay on Montesquieu that "because his book was a work of science and epoch-making, it is as dead as the classics." Similarly, in some of his letters to Pollock on the difficulty today of reading the classics, he pointed out that what has been borrowed from them and built into the structure of our own thought strips them of the sense of newness and surprise. That may well happen to Holmes himself in the next few generations. And yet despite what familiarity may do to his thought, there is beyond the thought the imprint of a unique personality and of a poetic image.

There are those who compare Holmes with John Marshall. The comparison is unjust to both men. Unlike Marshall, Holmes was a great man regardless of whether he was a great justice. He will probably leave a greater effect on English style and on what the young men dream and want than on American constitutional law. Marshall's reputation stands or falls with the vested interests he defended and with the viability of the system of economic relations that leans heavily on his constitutional interpretations. The greatness of Holmes will survive the vested interests and their constitutional bolstering. It will stand up so long as the English language stands, so long as people find life complex and exciting, and law a part of life, and the sharp blade of thought powerful enough to cleave both.

1943

9

Frankfurter on Holmes
and the Austerity Theory

NO BOOK THIS YEAR (1938) WILL BE READ BETWEEN THE LINES MORE intensively than Professor Frankfurter's. In fact many people are likely to probe the interstices who have no mind for the lines themselves. We owe this fact to the accident (or is it an accident?) that the foremost scholar on recent Supreme Court history is also the most assiduously discussed prospect for filling the current Supreme Court vacancy.[1] We owe it also to the paradox that one of the most controversial figures in American life has always, despite the persuasive stream of his private conversation, been reticent about the public expression of his views. This man, whose mind has touched and influenced so many others in law, government, business, and education, has a way of making every word count. The more the magazines and news-papers write about him, the less he seems to write for them, by a sort of Gresham's law that dictates that bad writing drives out good.

Those who come to the book for the light that it sheds on Felix Frankfurter as well as on Oliver Wendell Holmes will not be dis-appointed. For no one can write about another without writing at the same time about himself, and everyone who has written about Holmes has managed to write something of himself into Holmes. But Mr. Frankfurter has done more. He has written a good deal of himself into his discussion of the Supreme Court and the judicial process, and he has done it courageously. Never in our history has anyone so prominently mentioned for appointment to the Court writ-ten in so critical a tone of its conservative tendencies.

There is no indictment, no finger pointing. Mr. Frankfurter's method is one of deadly objectivity. In each of his three lectures he considers a phase of Holmes's work on the Supreme Court — his views on property and society, on civil liberties and the individual, and on federalism. He begins each lecture with a brief introduction providing a factual social setting for the Court's work in each field, and then proceeds to Holmes's views. The effect is to show that one can be human and reasonable, although a Supreme Court judge, and to reveal the chasm that separated Holmes and some of his liberal colleagues from the Court majority during his years of tenure. It is as if there were, in the sense in which Disraeli spoke of the "two nations" in England, two Supreme Courts instead of one. Without this factual context, Holmes's opinions are great utterance; with it they take on, in addition, the accents of inevitable statesmanship.

Mr. Frankfurter's eye is always on Holmes and his opinions. Yet the book is also a study of the judicial process, in the sense in which a book on Keats would have to contain at the same time some theory on the creative process in poetry. Mr. Frankfurter loves the judicial process, whatever he may think of some of its practitioners. And he is plainspoken about its frustrations, since he believes so deeply in its possibilities. It is partly because of this *odi et amo* at the base of Mr. Frankfurter's attitude toward the Supreme Court and partly because the book is about Holmes that it contains his best writing thus far. The sentences crackle and glow, the argument moves swiftly, and there is a sustained brilliance of phrase that gives an edge even to his poised and balanced judgments.

There can be no quarrel with the estimate of the greatness of Holmes's opinions. But since the book is also an inquiry into the nature of the judicial process, I am inclined to linger over his analysis of how Holmes arrived at his judgments. Mr. Frankfurter underscores Holmes's capacity to "transcend personal predilections and private notions of social policy" — what I call the "austerity theory" of the judicial process. But if Holmes was so completely above the battle, it would seem harder to apply Mr. Frankfurter's social-context method of approach to him than to any judge in the Court's history. It fits the early Brandeis or the present Black; one can even use it for the inverted sociology of Justices Field or Sutherland. But it is surely one of the prime paradoxes about Holmes that one who averted his eyes from social needs should have written opinions that coincided with those of Judge Brandeis.

There are several hypotheses for this. One is that Holmes was a socially neutral Olympian whose credo about the Court's power happened, by the merest accident, to jibe with our deepest social needs. I say "by the merest accident," for if Holmes were a completely disinterested mind who always gave the legislatures carte blanche, there could be no strictly logical relation between his decisions and the needs of America; for all we know, the legislators might have wholly misgauged the social needs, and judicial tolerance would have been no blessing.

Mr. Frankfurter seems inclined to a second and more forceful view of the austerity theory. He points out that Holmes's tenure on the Court coincided with an upsurge of regulatory legislation in the interest of "bringing to the masses economic freedom commensurate with their political freedom." Thus Holmes's policy of taking a laissez-faire attitude toward the legislature would be likely to have the same social consequences as a more affirmative method of deciding cases in terms of their social context. Holmes's opinions took on, as it were, the color of the legislature's sense of social need. Such sociology is still strongly tinged with the accidental, but it is accident geared to historical trend.

My own leaning would be away from either of these explanations and toward a third. It may be true, as Mr. Frankfurter observes of Holmes, that "he had an artist's craving for perfection and sought it through an austere observance of the demands of judicial self-limitation." However, I am less impressed with Justice Holmes's austerity than with his shrewd Yankee sense of strategy. Holmes had a genius for economy of effort. He knew the extent to which a judge's constitutional doctrines were shaped by his social views, and his social views by his training and his sense of economic interest. He knew his brethren on the bench, and how their narrow lawyers' intelligences could play havoc with the broad demands of social growth. He knew how hard it was to hope for anything from a head-on encounter with them over social policy. And he must have known that, given the power of judicial review, the best way to keep them from meddling overmuch with the processes of social adjustment was to limit their activity as censors. Thus Holmes became the father of judicial self-limitation.

I am the more inclined to this view by several other considerations. One concerns the difficulty we have always had, on the premise of Holmes's uncompromisingly judicial austerity, of explaining the fault line between his property decisions and his civil liberty decisions. The problem is this: how to reconcile Holmes's toleration of legislative restrictions on property with his refusal to tolerate legislative restrictions on civil liberties? Mr. Frankfurter's resolution of this paradox is brilliant, but it stays within the limits of the austerity hypothesis. "Just as he would allow experiments in economics which he himself viewed with doubt and distrust," he says of Holmes, "so he would protect speech that offended his taste and wisdom." But surely that is either stretching austerity too far and making self-denial almost an end in and of itself, or shifting the ground from the principle of judicial self-limitation to the actual social values to be preserved, whether of economic experiment or intellectual experiment. I incline to the latter view as the more adequate, and I wish that Mr. Frankfurter were more consistent in holding to it. Holmes had a way of keeping his eye steadily on the object. He did not make a fetish of the policy of judicial tolerance because, in cases of legislative infringement of civil liberties, he found his colleagues all too willing to pursue such a policy. What was good strategy in regard to the economic restrictions, because it led to good social consequences, became bad strategy in the civil-liberty restrictions, because it led to bad social consequences.

Moreover, there were even cases in the economic arena where Holmes dropped his protective mask of judicial tolerance and acted clearly in accord with his views of economic theory. These were, to be sure, cases where the question was of interpreting rather than invalidating legislation; yet we all know that the Court has shown its power as much in its interpretation of statutes as in its veto of them. One instance was Holmes's opinion in the *Northern Securities* case, which did so much to whittle down the effectiveness of the Sherman Antitrust Act. It is interesting also to read Holmes's opinion in the *Dr. Miles Medical Company* case, and to see the similarity between his views and those that undermined the effectiveness of the Federal Trade Commission. Mr. Frankfurter himself mentions some further instances of Holmes's archaic views of economic theory. Taken together, these cases remain marginal and do not reflect on Holmes's greatness. Yet they do indicate that Holmes was not wholly austere in his approach to legislation, that he had economic notions and applied them directly in his opinions. Most often, however, he found it better strategy to let the legislature have its way, so long as it was safe to do so.

I do not want to press too hard this view of Holmes as a strategist. He was neither schemer nor dreamer. He was an aristocrat caught in a dilemma. As an aristocrat, he would not go out of his way to concern himself with mass welfare; however, neither would he let the *novi homines* of capitalism have things to themselves. The best gesture was at once generous and Olympian — to let the legislature lead. He saw the uses to which he could put the philosophically aristocratic doctrine of judicial laissez-faire, and to give it substance he added to it the philosophically aristocratic concept of the reasonable man, borrowed from the common law of torts, changing it into the concept of the not-unreasonable legislator.

He was not the greatest judge we have had on the Supreme Court. Marshall was more formative. He had too much skepticism, too little fighting faith, and too little part in the emerging forces of our economic life to be able to shape those forces with an unquenchable will. But he was probably the greatest mind and the most complete and human personality we have had on the Court.

If I have a quarrel with Mr. Frankfurter's masterly study, it is for the tendency I have pointed out to take Holmes's rhetoric of austerity at face value, and the tendency to deify him. I think I understand what lies behind this tendency. There is Mr. Frankfurter's own knowledge of the man, and his love for him. There is the fact that the Holmes method of judicial self-limitation, so long neglected by the Court majority, has come into the ascendancy in the present Court, and Holmes may be viewed somewhat as the judicial prophet now vindicated. Finally — for no work today can help being an *oeuvre de circonstance* — there is the author's desire to hold Holmes up as a model of tolerance and social rationality in an irrational and sadistic world.

One may agree with all this and yet ask whether it is not time to bring Holmes down to earth. There he belongs and there, I think, he would prefer to be.

1938

10

Justice Louis D. Brandeis and Judicial Activism

I first came to know Justice Louis D. Brandeis during the years 1925 to 1927, when I was a graduate student at the Brookings School. He invited me to his Saturday "at homes," and I always sat, slightly dazed, as he talked of his favorite (nonjudicial) themes.

The essence was the "curse of bigness" and the creativeness of the compassable community. His first instance was Periclean democracy, his second the America of the founders, his third the Israeli settlements that were developing their own life forms. I saw — and was drawn to — the patriarch and prophet in Brandeis. In the graduate classroom his opinions, particularly his civil liberties dissents, along with those of Holmes, became our sacred writings.

Although we still think of Holmes and Brandeis as allies, Brandeis has had a more lasting influence. Holmes left principles. Brandeis's contribution was a workaday method — the emphasis on the social context of the case; the effort to grasp the urgencies, injustices, and dislocations that it involved; the scanning of possible responses; the use of judicial decision when necessary to resolve it. I add the paradox that, for later generations, the workaday method assumed the proportions of a lofty philosophy, and Brandeis now looms for many as a visionary.

Since Brandeis was, among other things, the originator of the "Brandeis brief" and the contextual decision, he may well be regarded as the authentic father of liberal judicial activism. This should be qualified. Brandeis shaped much of the conservative judicial activism that overturned the majoritarian statutes. But later liberal activists hailed him as their leader, and the historical fact is that he fathered their basic approach.

On First Amendment freedoms Holmes and Brandeis came largely to stand together, both in dissenting minorities and in the majority. But they reached the same result by different paths, with Brandeis always broadening the base of his libertarianism. Of the two roads, it is Brandeis's that has proved the one "more traveled by."

Since the First World War the American legal world has had three outstanding names: Holmes, Brandeis, and Cardozo. Of the three, Brandeis is the last to lay down his shield. The other two had more in common with each other than either of them had with Brandeis. Literary flair, philosophic sweep, elegant simplicity, the flashing phrase — these are not notable in Brandeis. His opinions are not examples of great writing. His philosophy is generally implicit.

Justice Brandeis has specialized in advocacy and judicial decision, not philosophizing. In fact he is one of the most aphilosophical of jurists — a thinker whose thought is always directed to eventual action, a judge in the great tradition of Anglo-American case law who proceeds from the facts of the concrete case to a particular decision. He has said of his own mental processes that only after he has found himself confronted with a specific set of facts and has thought his way through them has he found his conclusion to coincide with some well-recognized philosophical "principle."

When he theorizes about democracy and the individual, and when he calls for new ethical codes in business, his exhortations and theories sound like others we have read. His writings lack that personal imprint of greatness that stamps his conversation. But this should not blind us to Brandeis's real greatness. He has brought economic emphasis into legal thought, and in the process has evolved a usable philosophy and a technique transmissible to future generations of judges and lawyers. The philosophy is that individual rights and group claims are neither absolute nor unchanging and must be weighed in terms of the need for checking and democratizing our corporate capitalism. The technique is to interpret the constitutional phrase and the legal doctrine within the context of legislative history and economic facts from which laws emerge. The philosophy has basic links to the tradition of American democracy since Jefferson. The technique is deeply rooted in our pragmatism and our hard-headed statistical bent. Together they have reinvigorated American law. Holmes and Cardozo will be read and quoted by eager students for generations, but their discipleship will be limited to those with rare gifts of sensitiveness, imagination, and literary talent. Brandeis, on the other hand, will live on by becoming part of the institutional fabric.

Brandeis's record has written itself into the history of the American progressive mind. The earliest influence in fashioning the mind of Justice Brandeis — and perhaps therefore the deepest and least eradicable — was a strain of romantic liberalism whose essence was a gallant and optimistic struggle for certain supposedly basic human rights.[1] It was a liberalism compelling enough to lead his parents to emigrate to America from Bohemia after the unsuccessful revolutions of 1848. Those revolutions, aptly characterized by George Trevelyan as "the turning point at which modern history failed to turn," were in spirit constitutional, humanitarian, idealistic. They presented a renewal on Continental soil of the egalitarian ideals of the American and French revolutions. Carried back to the United States by the emigrant groups of the midcentury, they imparted freshness and vigor to the American tradition of civil and political liberties. Freedom and justice and democracy as homegrown varieties had wilted a bit in the hot climate of American experience; but when similar doctrines were transplanted from Europe they took on new growth. They were terms that retained a genuine and simple content for those naive newcomers. Justice Brandeis grew up thus in an atmosphere of what might be called primitive Americanism.

This Americanism took the characteristic form, in the semi-frontier Kentucky society in which the Brandeises lived, of a deeply felt individualism, an individualism as varied as the liberating sources from which it sprang. To be allowed finally to do what one had always dreamed of doing — to talk or criticize or worship as one pleased, to see an immediacy of relation between economic effort and economic reward — reinforced one's sense of the dignity and sovereign importance of the individual. Slaves provided living symbols for border-state abolitionist groups, of what it meant to lack liberty. And Justice Brandeis recalls how violent his reaction was when, during a brief sojourn in Germany as a young man, he was reprimanded by the authorities for whistling at night. The reprimand was more than a personal reproof; it was an insult to a complete and cherished way of life.

One does not easily become disengaged from a way of life so deeply learned. The whole early career of Justice Brandeis, with its emphasis on hard work and study and success, runs in the best tradition of American individualism. In fact, all the events of his first forty years conspired to make him an idealistic yet successful liberal and civic leader, whose conspicuous ability justified his excess of zeal, and whose mastery of the hard facts of business leavened his somewhat tiresome sermonizing. It is true he showed at times a disquieting curiosity about matters into which a Boston gentleman rarely pried — as when in the 1880s he began to talk with labor leaders, and to regard the labor struggle from the worker's point of view. And he showed also a somewhat unusual tendency to interpret the lawyer's function as more than mere advocacy, and to set himself up now as judge and now as arbitrator. But all his offenses stayed within the limits of tolerance.

The genuinely formative years of Justice Brandeis fell in the "social justice" period of American history, in the latter part of the 1890s and the first decade of the twentieth century. They were years that witnessed both the rise of powerful vested interests and the expropriation of American resources by capital acting under a laissez-faire philosophy of government, and such movements as populism, muckraking, trust-busting, and the "new freedom." To minds educated in the dialectic of liberalism, it seemed obvious that the situation could be best explained in terms of a conflicting duality: the captains of industry and the masters of capital, and the landmarks on the terrain of American liberty that in the exultation of success, they wanted to sweep away. And it seemed clear also that the only recourse for liberals lay in an attack on all fronts — an attack on bankers, on corporations, and on politicians corruptly allied with them, a pitiless campaign of investigation and publicity.

It was amid this turmoil that Brandeis's worldview took shape. After the critical struggle to establish a legal practice was won, his mind, whose Hebraic sense of righteousness had been reinforced by his background of Continental liberalism, turned more and more to issues of social justice. He would never take on a case without turning it about in every direction, seeking to understand it. Similarly, he could not live and work in a society without seeking to uncover its foundations. And the deeper he dug, the deeper became his conviction that it was the concentration of economic power that was responsible for the social blockage. It stood, a menacing giant, in the path of democratic action; it snuffed out the hopes for a decent individual life.

He set himself, David-like, to fight this giant. The only weapon he had was his mind — concrete in a legal brief, swift and sure before a judge or an investigating commission, merciless with a witness — an architectural mind that laid brick on brick until the argument became a structure that could not be torn down. In Louis D. Brandeis, the able Boston lawyer, the forces of liberalism gained no mean ally. I say ally, because a simple, unquestioning soldier he could never be; a stern individualist who cared more about the integrity of his personality than about anything else, he had to fight in his own fashion.

He mastered the intricacies of corporation finance, because he saw that it was a key to the economic and therefore the social structure. Equipped with all the information one had reckoned was one's own, he was a terrifying opponent to encounter. From a few published figures and with weeks of work, he reconstructed the accounting system of the New Haven Railroad with such deadly accuracy that the opposing attorneys thought he must have had access to the books. For twenty years, from 1896 to 1916, he fought the trolley car companies, the public utilities, the railroads, the life insurance companies, the Money Trust. It was never a vindictive fight and never an aimless one. He had what Graham Wallas called "social inventiveness," and was always ready with a plan by which the railroads could be operated more efficiently or life insurance could be furnished to workers more cheaply. He took on the causes that did not pay, and became the "people's attorney." At sixty he was a public figure without having held public office — living proof of how great a man can become if he loves justice and masters arithmetic.

He was effective. Of that there can be no doubt. The minutes of legislative hearings and investigations, the records of lawsuits in which groups of citizens, organized as a "league" of some sort or other, applied for court action against an encroaching corporation, the newspapers that reported his speeches and activities, and the journalists who commented on them all attest to his effectiveness. There was room in that struggle for every sort of talent — for a Bryan, a La Follette, a Roosevelt, a Steffens, a Hapgood, a Wilson. But when most of the brilliant legal minds of the country were being enrolled in the service of the corporations, the talents of a first-rate legal and statistical mind were worth more than the talents of all the politicians and journalists. Brandeis was comfortable with the sort of problems that had to be mastered. His career, weaving together one set of financial and political intricacies with another, took on something of the fiber of the period.

If Brandeis stands out as a unique and heroic figure in the populist thought of the period, it is not for the raking fire of his cross-examinations, or for the brave assurance of his analysis of the "money trust";[2] not even for that stubborn command of facts and figures that made men call him the mathematician of the movement.[3] It is rather because of the stress we find him laying, even in those early days, on the necessity for the continuous application of social intelligence to social problems, and on the inadequacy of any solution that did not have behind it the creative will of the people.

But it was Brandeis's misfortune to try to fashion a social philosophy in the midst of a crusade. The banners wavered for a moment, fluttered anxiously, but were immediately carried forward. He was himself caught up in the contagion, and might have remained merely one of the adherents of a "fighting faith" that had had its day and given way to another. But the fervor of the crusade had reached to the White House, and when, on the death of Mr. Justice Lamar in 1916, President Wilson looked about for a successor, his choice fell on the Boston lawyer who had displayed such ability and courage and who, without holding public office, had already led a crowded public life.

The appointment changes our whole perspective on Brandeis's work. It transformed him from a free lance into one of the ruling powers. It gave direction to his energies and meaning to the wide scattering of activities that had constituted his career.

From one point of view, Brandeis's contacts with labor unions, corporations, and bankers, with the toiling workers and the vested interests, constituted an exploration of modern industrial society unique in the education of justices of the Supreme Court. He gained an understanding of the gap that lay between the haves and the have-nots, and some notions about its implications.[4] He had a realistic grasp of the meager life-style of the vast armies of labor. And he saw the dangers posed by the growing institutionalization of life as it was embodied in the corporation, the trade union, and the centralization of government. His education taught him also that there was invested in the American economic system more hard work and experience than any novel scheme of control could command, and that it was dangerous to drive beyond the bounds within which initiative and skill could be continuously exerted.

There was much that Justice Brandeis did not learn during those years of his crowded career. But considering the blind chance that fits or misfits our haphazard educations to the crucial tasks that somehow fall to us, the education of Justice Brandeis appears amazingly apposite. The social context within which his thinking would have an effect was more complex than that in which either the Constitution or the body of judicial precedent had been formed. A system of industrial organization, so much more developed than that of the nineteenth century as to take on the aspects of a second industrial revolution, had also created a "great society" that was unique in its problems and temper. Here was a man who was uniquely qualified to understand the processes of change and the instruments of control.

Enough opposition was raised to Brandeis's appointment to make it something of a cause célèbre. There was much more in the struggle over the appointment than a conflict of personalities. There was a historical rationale behind the protests of the seven ex-presidents of the American Bar Association, the petition of the Boston men of affairs, and the editorials in the financial papers. They argued that his candidacy was unsuitable because of infringements of legal ethics, unjudicial temperament, and even chicanery and dishonesty. There was an investigation undertaken by the Senate Judiciary Committee, in which some fifteen hundred pages of testimony were taken.

The protest against the appointment of Brandeis was a crucial recognition by the old order that the new order was arriving. For half a century, the propertied class in America had known the conditions under which they could operate and expand. The rules of the game, however advantageous they may have been, had been fixed. Surely they could not now be revoked. A man who had formed and expressed opinions on most of the great issues of national policy that were likely to come before the Court was dangerous, especially when those opinions were original, unconventional, and held with moral fervor.

The appointment was thus more than the filling of a vacancy. It represented a turning point in the American judicial process. For whatever Justice Brandeis might or might not do, he could not be expected to cleave to the tradition that a Supreme Court justice should maintain a decent innocence of the world outside the Court. Despite the protests, Brandeis's only sin was that he had beaten the corporation lawyers at their own game of amassing a fortune in legal practice. Yet he had done this while increasing the time he devoted to the service of the common people in fighting the giants of monopoly.

So great has his work been as a justice that we forget how great was his work as a lawyer. He transformed constitutional pleading through the "Brandeis brief."[5] But he also transformed legal practice by becoming a successful lawyer who did not have to lay his personal idealism and his practical social sense on the shelf while out making money. What Holmes was exhorting youngsters to do, in winged rhetoric at law banquets, Brandeis went ahead and did. His 1913 testimony before the Pujo Committee and his book *Other People's Money* (1914) together form two of the classic analyses of American finance capitalism. They gave content to Woodrow Wilson's phrases about "the new freedom" — hence the historical justice in Wilson's appointment of Brandeis. On the Supreme Court, Justice Brandeis similarly geared his analysis to economic change and his directives to social action.

It is in doing this that Justice Brandeis has made the sharpest break with the classical tradition of the Court. Whether interpreted by a tory or a liberal mind, the classical tradition was concerned with the interpretation of the Constitution as an instrument of government. In the hands of Marshall and Story, Taney and Field, it produced widely variant results, but it seems fair to say that their differences stemmed from differences in political theory — the "narrow" or the "strict" construction of the Constitution, centralization or states' rights, the clash of sections. Fortifying each of these positions were, to be sure, a social philosophy and an understanding of economic circumstances. But these remained in the background. On the fighting line were the competing political and constitutional theories. It is Justice Brandeis's achievement to have appreciably altered the basis and the terms of the conflict. He has been the first to face squarely and consistently the problem of the relation between social change and judicial action.

He is thus preeminently the jurist of a transitional society, in which change is the dominant, the obtrusive fact. His thought is geared to social change. Not that Marshall and Taney lived in a static world. But the realities they and their colleagues wrestled with were the realities of constructing, consolidating, and reconstructing the foundations of the American polity. The principles of constitutional interpretation had themselves to be outlined, and they occupied the foreground, despite the social changes that accompanied the beginnings of industrialism in America. The maturity of industrialism brought an unparalleled pace of change, and as the task of adjusting legal thought and institutions to economic development grew more difficult, it grew also more imperative.

To adjust the body of legal rules to a world of bewildering change requires, to begin with, the fixed sense of social value and social need that accompanies a strongly functionalist way of thinking. Institutions often develop their own principle of growth, not necessarily related to the need that brought them into existence, and the original need has commonly to be rediscovered and redefined. Justice Brandeis is peculiarly qualified for such a task. For example, in *United Railways and Electric Co. v. West* (1930), amid the variety of conflicting practices regarding depreciation, he sought the underlying function that a depreciation account serves.[6] In a case involving the abolition of private employment agencies, *Adams v. Tanner* (1916), he sought to get at the functional purpose of all labor exchanges: "The problem which confronted the people of Washington was far more comprehensive and fundamental than that of protecting workers applying to the private agencies. It was the chronic problem of unemployment — perhaps the gravest and most difficult problem of modern industry. . . ."

But a jurisprudence built around social change requires, even more, an intimate and realistic knowledge of economic organization. Without subscribing to the economic interpretation of that social process, Justice Brandeis believes that the forces that create new tasks for law are mainly economic. Chief Justice Marshall had a strong realistic sense of American political problems and processes; and Justice Holmes, with his mordant insight into human motives, is a consummate psychological realist. Justice Brandeis's realism is chiefly economic.

His realism is concerned with effecting a rapprochement between law and the institutional life to which it is directed. Viewed typically and schematically, Justice Brandeis's thinking sees the process of public law as an interplay of relationships among three entities: society, out of which disputes and problems arise; legislative bodies, acting alone or through administrative commissions they create, which purport to crystallize social experience in their enactments; and the courts, which interpret the application of constitutional and common law principles to the specific case. He always goes beyond the superficial facts of the case in the matrix of need, maladjustment, or agitation, from the object itself to the social landscape that gives it perspective. Such a method has a tendency to reorient the preoccupation of the Court. Anxiety about freedom of contract gives way to an analysis of wages and the conditions of labor, due process to waste and scientific management, discussion of principle to recital of fact.

This shift of emphasis was marked dramatically by the Brandeis brief in *Muller v. Oregon* (1908),[7] but it runs through the body of Mr. Justice Brandeis's decisions as well as his advocacy. The *Muller* case involved an Oregon statute limiting the working day for women to ten hours. It is interesting to note that the mass of material that the brief presented as "the world's experience upon which the legislation limiting the hours of labor for women is based" was offered to the Court as "facts of common knowledge of which the Court may take judicial notice." Justice David Brewer, for the Court, wrote: "We take judicial cognizance of all matters of general knowledge." The "economic briefs" were thus admitted into the mansions of the law through a side entrance.

One of the consequences of such a conception of judicial interpretation is the allowance of greater latitude for the enactments of state legislatures and the rulings of administrative commissions than Justice Brandeis's thinking would have seemed to require. If anything, his experience with state legislatures during the years he was fighting insurance companies, railroad companies, and trusts must have cast some doubt on the disinterestedness of the ordinary legislator and on the extent to which he represented the wishes of the "people." Nor does this broad tolerance — not unmixed with respect for the sovereignty of a morally self-sufficient group, with which Justice Holmes regards state legislative acts — occupy a central place in Justice Brandeis's thought. He is not a states' rights advocate, nor, with his distinctly humanitarian and reformist trend, does he have that skepticism about the superiority of one form of social action over another that might dictate a laissez-faire attitude toward legislatures. His tendency to relax the rigor of the constitutional limitations on state legislative action as hitherto interpreted proceeds from another source. The recent trend of legislative action, especially in the western states affected by the populist movements, has responded to the pressure of social change much more adequately than have the legal concepts handed down in the common law. Forced to choose between the two, Mr. Justice Brandeis could have no hesitation. In the test of reasonableness, as applied to state legislation, he has found an effective instrument ready at hand to bring about some approximation of realistic jurisprudence.

The emphasis on context is so constant an item in Justice Brandeis's method that "institutionalism" or "contextualism" might serve as readily as "realism" to describe the method. The context of a "felt necessity" for the particular legislative enactment is represented in a large number of his opinions — for example, the felt necessity of suppressing private employment agencies (*Adams v. Tanner* [1916]),[8] or of regulating unscrupulous steamship-ticket agents (*Di Santo v. Pennsylvania* [1926]),[9] or of discouraging corporate business organizations by levying a state tax on corporations (*Quaker City Cab Co. v. Pennsylvania* [1928]).[10] In the *Quaker City* case, he said:

> There are still intelligent, informed, just-minded and civilized persons who believe that the rapidly growing aggregation of capital through corporations constitutes an insidious menace to the liberty of the citizen; that it tends to increase the subjection of labor to capital; that, because of the guidance and control necessarily exercised by great corporations upon those engaged in business, individual initiative is being impaired and creative power will be lessened; that the absorption of capital by corporations, and their perpetual life, may bring evils similar to those which attended mortmain.

Context may even involve the prolonged agitation by interested groups to secure the enactment of the law, as in the account Justice Brandeis gives in *Duplex Printing Press Co. v. Deering* (1920);[11] the state's experience in the administration of its weights and measures (*Jay Burns Baking Co. v. Bryan* [1923]);[12] the excesses of competition and the disorder such competition produces (*American Column and Lumber Co. v. United States* [1921]);[13] the state's wish to protect its workers and its limit on the use of the injunction in labor cases (*Truax v. Corrigan* [1921]);[14] the state's wish to protect its cotton growers from exploitation by private gin owners grants (*Frost v. Corporation Commission* [1928]).[15] The context of the case most seriously attracts Justice Brandeis's attention. He presents it with sympathy and with an engaging persuasiveness.

Invariably, the significant elements in the social setting of a case are what Justice Brandeis probes to determine whether the legislation in question had reasonably weighed conflicting social values. His questions revolve around the goals of a particular piece of legislation, the need for it, the character and extent of the public opinion behind it, the psychological milieu in which it was passed, its possible consequences. "Nearly all legislation," he writes, "involves a weighing of public needs as against private desires. . . . What at any particular time is the paramount public need, is necessarily largely a matter of judgment."[16] Where the judgment is not demonstrably clear, he appeals to the experience of other states or countries, to the consensus of practice within relevant groups, or to the consensus of enlightened opinion.

The study of the context and the appeal to consensus are intellectual techniques holding out such great possibilities for the judicial process that it is important to note their ultimate subservience to the social philosophy of the judge. They aid him in arriving at an opinion, but they are also almost inevitably themselves preconditioned. To the detached political psychologist there is little difference between the pressures to obtain privileged legislation exerted by an agricultural community in a time of low profits, and the hysterias that in time of war result in criminal syndicalist legislation or the suppression of radical agitation. Various individuals will sympathize with one type of legislation or the other, depending on their intellectual temper; a respectable array of social experience and a consensus of judgment could with discretion be marshaled for both. Yet Justice Brandeis has consistently upheld the reasonableness of legislation in the former type of case and consistently rejected it in the latter.[17] He finds it difficult to reconcile an encroachment on fundamental civil liberties with any possible reasonableness in the legislation.

A significant social philosophy today must do more than bridge the gap between institutional change and legal development. That is, to be sure, of inestimable importance, especially in cases involving submerged groups, such as labor, whose interests have not been incorporated in the fashioning of legal rules. But it does not offer a technique for dealing with the problems emerging from the active development of business enterprise. The world that the Court operates in is a world of accomplished fact, with which one must come to the best terms possible. But it is also a world continually in the making. To direct the flux of economic life and to turn it into socially accredited channels becomes the task of the modern state and, under our constitutional system, preeminently the task of the Supreme Court.

In this sphere Justice Brandeis is easily our outstanding figure.

He has stood firmly for holding business enterprise rigorously to its social responsibilities. He has remained sensitive to trends in economic organization and exercised the imagination of genuine statesmanship in envisaging their meaning for the future. He has applied on the judicial front the ideas developed in economic thought and built up a technique of control that has appreciably added to the resources of our administrative law.

There would seem at first sight to be a contradiction between such an instrumental conception of legal function and Justice Brandeis's well-known and fervent individualism. But the contradiction is resolved when it is recalled how far his individualism is from the quietistic attitude of laissez-faire economics. While he still borrows heavily from classical economic thought, he has discarded completely the Ricardian faith in the unassisted working of the economic order. He believes competition is good for the competitors, good for the consumer, and good for the industrial process. But he does not fall into the nineteenth-century error of believing that the economic mechanism can be left to itself. He believes instead that only through the judicious intervention of the state under the proper circumstances can it function smoothly.

Justice Brandeis's philosophy of control looks to no comprehensive and continuous organization of economic life in terms of state power, no system of either planning or paternalism. He is entirely in accord with what he conceives to be the normal functioning of the present economic setup; his animus is directed only against its pathology. The huge and unwieldy corporation, the industrial monopoly, the unfair competitor, the overcapitalized public-utility company, the pyramided money trust — these are diseases requiring cures. They represent unbridled economic aggrandizement and antisocial economic power. To Justice Brandeis they are not what they are to critics of capitalism — natural growths from capitalistic organization, and its characteristic products. They are rather excrescences — tumors in a world where no formula and no system can ensure perfect health.

Justice Brandeis has had to work out his theory and technique of control in the course of interpreting the application of constitutional principles to the operations under the Sherman Act and the rulings of the federal and state administrative commissions. He has had to determine what the scope and the powers of the commissions are under the laws creating them, and in passing upon the validity of their rulings, he has had to crystallize in his thinking the principles to be applied in the regulation of business.

At the base of Justice Brandeis's attitude toward the problem of regulation is his conviction that no rights are absolute. This conviction was expressed in his opinion in *International News Service v. Associated Press* (1918), which involved the copying of Associated Press bulletins by the International News Service. Because the Associated Press had unusual and even exclusive advantages in the gathering of foreign news, Justice Brandeis felt that, in the absence of legislative regulation, no new property rights should be vested in news. In the pitting of public welfare against property rights, he insists that there is no absolute right to make profits. The state grants qualified rights in certain property, in return for which the corporation assumes corresponding obligations of charging fair prices, engaging in no discriminations or unfair practices, and allowing a field open to all competitors. The resulting system is one of individualism, in the sense that it premises a regime of profits, competition, and private enterprise. But it is also one of an ethical individualism — emphasizing responsibilities and duties. When the conditions for vesting property rights are unsatisfactory, the courts must await legislative action by which a system of regulation can be imposed.

Justice Brandeis's attitude toward control stems from his adherence to the idea of competition. Wherever monopoly has taken hold, he wishes to restore and maintain competition; where unfair practices threaten the competitive equilibrium, he wishes to curb them and so maintain the plane of competition; where competition is impossible or undesirable, he wishes to pattern the system of control as closely as possible on the model of a putative competition. The first of these three spheres of action for government control roughly parallels the operation of the Sherman Act, the second the Federal Trade Commission, and the last the Interstate Commerce Commission and the various state public-service commissions.[18] In all of them he projects the competitive ideal into situations where it functions with difficulty, even to the extent of introducing competition as a fiction — very much as the social contract was a fiction — to rationalize regulatory practices in the field of public utilities, where, in most cases, it would be drastic or impossible to maintain competition.

Justice Brandeis's conception of his task has as much to do with economic statesmanship as with judicial interpretation. Stare decisis has played a less important part than the decisions on industrial development and business initiative; far from hesitating to read his notions of public policy into the Constitution, he has deemed it his first duty to formulate a just and statesmanlike policy. There is an admixture of economic romanticism in his gallant wrestling with "these great issues of government." A less vigorous mind might have flinched from them and taken refuge in a safe judicial "objectivity." A more sardonic mind might have concluded that, amid an economic welter such as ours, government can at best seem to bring some semblance of order to what are really the workings of chance and chaos. But Justice Brandeis, knowing man must master economic circumstance, is involved in the gigantic struggle we are waging here to subjugate every natural and human resource to the uses of the nation.

His principal concern has been with the creation of sound conditions for the maintenance of a healthy system of business enterprise — composed of small, independent, individual units that will achieve continuous advance in the industrial and management arts through the incentive of profits and the mechanics of competition. To this end he has favored the introduction of every device that makes for efficiency, the dissemination of trade and market information, and the toleration of price maintenance. Just as he has seen in Big Business a dangerous and irresponsible force, he has looked to a business kept at its legitimate functions and proportions to take on the attitudes and the ethics of a profession.

All his efforts have been directed thus to the creation of a socialized, regulated welfare capitalism. One may discern that to achieve this ideal he has thrown his energies in two directions: he has sought to socialize and ethicize business, and he has sought to gain for labor an equality of position at a bargaining level. To do this he has had to work in two camps at once. To confront the philosophy of the entrepreneur and the stockholder, a new philosophy representing the aspirations and outlook of labor crept into the body of judicial decision. But alongside this is a vision of the economic system, not as a militant and dominant labor group but as a self-reliant body of independent businessmen.

That these two streams of thought meet and flow strongly together in Justice Brandeis's own thinking is indisputable. What is disputable is whether an economic philosophy that involves the balancing and synthesizing of such diverse tendencies will have any evocative power in a world that must take sides or grow apathetic.

Above partisanship himself, Justice Brandeis runs the risk of appearing partisan to both extremes. He is little short of an antichrist to the big corporations. And to many in radical circles, his refusal, on ethical grounds, to intervene in the Sacco-Vanzetti case seemed equivocal.

Such contemporary opinion may be of small importance to a long-run appraisal of the validity of Justice Brandeis's economic philosophy. And any point of view that has been forged by a lifetime of active thought and is the product of mature experience must seem equivocal when viewed from the anxious passions at both the left and the right. But there is a significance in such criticism, because the object of it, in pursuing the integrity of his own thinking, may have lost touch with the emotional trends of his time; and the emotional trends of a period often come close to being a reflection of its deeper institutional trends.

A very large body of American liberal opinion has made an idol of Justice Brandeis and acknowledges the leadership of his thought. But there are evidences that widening gaps in American life may ultimately leave this body of opinion isolated and powerless. The crucial premise in Justice Brandeis's economic thought — that the things he is fighting are excrescences to be lopped off, pathological diversions of energy to be brought back to their normal channels — finds less and less confirmation in the *Spätkapitalismus* stage of American economic organization. Agglomerations of capital grow more monstrous, mergers have become the order of the day, the pyramiding of economic power goes on, the individual finds himself increasingly shut out. In the face of such tendencies, Justice Brandeis's attempt to hold a scrupulous balance between what is legitimate in business enterprise and what is an encroachment on the liberties of the individual seems somewhat indecisive, and his denial to capitalists of further increments of that power of which, as an interpreter of the Constitution, he could not divest them seems a gallant but hopeless attempt to bridge two worlds.

In the face of a task of such proportions, Justice Brandeis has been remarkably successful. He has not altogether kept the Supreme Court from appearing to liberal opinion as something of a Heartbreak House. But he has drawn the issues clearly, taken a positive and constructive stand, and polarized every liberal tendency in the Court. A more radical philosophy, a less statesmanlike attitude than his might have failed utterly. Justice Brandeis's intellectual creed, although always clear-cut and decisive, contains that admirable balancing of tradition and innovation that represents the greatest assurance of eventual success. There has been no intent in it to break with the essential Supreme Court traditions. Justice Brandeis's doctrine of stare decisis is mature as well as flexible. He has adhered to the American tradition of individualism, redefining it to suit the realities of the age. In his emphasis on democracy and freedom, he has insisted that as a nation we bid fair to alienate ourselves from the psychological drives that have conditioned our history. The pragmatic cast of his thought and its ethical strain have set up responses in the American mind. His method — factual, experimental, inductive — strives only to assimilate law into those other procedures that already have those characteristics. He has advocated not the creation of new institutions but a procedure that will use law to bring out the best in existing institutions.

It would be strange indeed if twentieth-century America, which has in almost every field of thought and art produced its characteristic expression, should fail to do so in jurisprudence. Justice Brandeis has admirably evoked and summed up contemporary tendencies in legal thought. It seems likely that the future of judicial decision lies with these tendencies rather than with those that have opposed them. But if that should prove true, will Justice Brandeis's work, in the phrase James Fitzjames Stephen used of Bentham, "be buried in the ruins it has made"? To the extent that his thought merely merges with contemporary trends, that is likely. But there is permanence and distinctiveness in Justice Brandeis's conception of "living law." His realistic method of shifting the battle from the barren ground of precedent and logic to the higher ground of social function and social situation must prove an enduring contribution to the process of constitutional interpretation. Even the epigones when they come will find it a technique that they can use.

1939

11

The Education of Hugo Black

Hugo Black's was one of the most independent and daring minds the Court has seen. An implacable reader of history, philosophy, and political theory, he was determined to use his learning to bolster the views he brought with him. He cared about history and "original intent" when it supported the "incorporation" of the Fourteenth Amendment — and expanded its prohibitions on the federal government. He also cared passionately about the strict meaning of the language of the Constitution, yielding to no qualification of absolutism to the rights in the Bill of Rights.

Legal scholarship has suggested that his reading of history was sometimes wrong. And when he felt impelled (in his later years) to add qualifications to the freedom of assembly and establishment of religion clauses, he did so in as magisterial a way as when he had denied them.

Expansiveness was his saving capacity and kept him from rigidity. More than any other justice, Black managed to combine a tough-mindedness about history and language with a belief in judicial activism, and he carried it off with a Whitmanesque disdain for contradiction.

I add a personal note. Some articles I wrote played a small role in his defense during the crisis over his Klan membership. But my assessment of his judicial potential and achievement stood on its own. I would have preferred him to be less of an activist, but over the years I accepted him for what he was — and still do.

It was in mid-September 1937 that President Roosevelt, in his second term, decided to change the direction and complexion of the Supreme Court. To fill a welcome vacancy, he made the unlikely choice of Hugo Lafayette Black, senator from the redneck Alabama hill country and radical New Dealer. Black was more distinguished for his political militancy than for his judicial temperament and experience.

Roosevelt didn't mind riling the opposition. He was deep in a battle to permanently change the voting patterns of the Court. He enjoyed frustrating his enemies by making them seat on the Court the eighth child of a Confederate dirt farmer — a nominee as radical as Louis D. Brandeis, around whose confirmation a storm had swirled in 1916. FDR knew that a Democratic Senate couldn't turn down a southerner and one of their own.

I was political editor of the *Nation*, too young for mellowness, delighting in battle as a New Dealer and championing Black's positions in his Senate brawls. Naturally, I hailed the appointment.

Then the cyclone hit. A journalist named Sprigle, acting on a good tip, did a beautiful job of digging up the fact that this fervent New Deal senator, now a month-old associate justice, had been a Klansman, having joined the hooded ones in Birmingham in 1923. My fellow editors on the *Nation* were ready to throw Hugo to the wolves. I counseled cool. I learned that Black, on a London vacation, was visiting my friend Harold Laski. I wrote Laski about how the cyclone had hit New York and offered to fly to London. Laski cabled me to sit tight and meet Black's boat at Newport News.

A couple hundred other press and radio reporters were there too, all in quest of a mass interview with Hugo. I felt lost and surrounded. Black sent out word that there would be no interview. I bribed a steward to get a note into the stateroom, and back came word on how to make a getaway. The tide of media humanity swirled about him but we extricated ourselves, and I walked down the gangplank with Hugo and Josephine Black, and off we went to Alexandria.

He talked. Why had he refused the press conference? Because he had learned in politics never to meet an attack on the enemy's ground. He would go on the air and answer in his own way, on his own terms. It was a sound democratic instinct. And because he followed this instinct, he turned what might have been a figurative lynching into something like a triumphal homecoming.

I shall not easily forget an extended conversation with Black on the evening following his arrival. Journalists learn to be skeptical of the drama of events, and yet there are moments when men and occasion combine to leave an ineradicable mark. This was one. Justice Black's biography, as I have pieced it together from this and other sources, is one of the most moving and contradictory records in our history. Since the sources were sympathetic, the record I am setting down may contain a degree of bias or rationalization. I offer it not as a final critical account but as a personal history, in which I have sought to view the action as the actor might have viewed it.

Hugo Black was born in 1886 on a farm in Clay County, Alabama, the youngest of the large family of a desolately poor farmer. He was of Scotch-Irish and English descent, and his Irish ancestors had been driven out of their country for their religious beliefs. When Hugo was five, his father moved to the county seat at Ashland, bought a small store, and became a tolerably successful merchant. The county was poor; it had neither bank nor hospital, but it did boast a primitive sort of academy called Ashland College, which provided the boy's schooling from six to sixteen. He studied medicine for a year but had always preferred law, and so he left medicine to complete a two-year law course at the University of Alabama. In 1907, at the age of twenty-one, he settled down to a career as a Birmingham lawyer.

There followed intense work at law, reading crowded into the night hours, rapid political success. Birmingham was the school that taught him. He made close connections with the trade unions: in 1909 he represented the miners' union in its first Alabama strike; later he was attorney for the carpenters' union in another important suit. He loved the techniques of the law, mastered its procedure, began to build statewide fame. This led naturally to politics, and Black was elected police judge in 1910, at age twenty-four, and prosecuting attorney in 1914. He had been absorbed with politics ever since he could remember; he recalls staying up all night as a boy of ten to listen to the election returns for probate judge. He was a hard and tireless campaigner. In the 1926 election he campaigned for thirteen months, dropping all his work, covering every county in the state, some of them twenty times. His opponents learned to fear him, because his appeal was that of someone who knew his audiences and loved to match wits with them. In fact, as I talked with him I had a notion that when he came to make his radio statement he would feel isolated before the microphones. He would, I think, have preferred to carry his answer to actual audiences all over the country, face to face with the people to whom he responded and who responded to him.

That a man like Black should have come to join the Klan is one of those facts monstrously hard to grasp until you approach it not as a moral problem but simply as a piece of political behavior. Black's career was that of a progressive in politics, and in the South in the decade after the First World War such a career inevitably crossed that of the Klan. For the Klan had not inconsiderable roots, although twisted ones, in the popular mind. Its superpatriotism fitted the anti-radical mood after the war; its law-enforcement plank was strong in the period of Prohibition racketeering; in regions of economic distress, its nativism seemed an insurance against the competition of immigrant labor; amid the decay of religious faith, its mystical spirituality had an appeal; its attitude toward the Negroes was integral to the southern psychosis of "white supremacy." In such a soil, the Klan grew with an intoxicating speed that seemed its own sanction. Many of the younger southern leaders felt helpless before it. They had to either ride the whirlwind of the Klan or surrender, and they had no thought of surrendering.

It is easy to call their acquiescence contemptible. It was a tragic mistake, and it is clear that Justice Black thinks so now. But it is easy to be wise after the fact. In Alabama at that time not only the farmer and merchant were Klansmen; 90 percent of organized labor in Birmingham was enrolled. The common people had been captured by the Klan, for it buttressed them against problems they could not understand, with principles that seemed eternal. The Klan assumed, moreover, a radical attitude on many specific issues that appealed to the progressives. Like the fascist movement in Germany, it combined a spurious radicalism with terrorism. Those who leaned toward the first were often able to shut their eyes to the second. But as the Klan madness took its swift and terrible course, and as it became the prey of racketeers and hoodlums, its fascist character grew ever clearer. Before that process had gone far, Hugo Black had left the Klan, but he could not escape the shadow of it.

He was from the very beginning a "joiner." Even before he was of age, he had put in his applications for the Knights of Pythias and the Masons. He had a youthful fervor for those secret societies. Somewhere around 1920 he was approached to join the Klan. He pleaded lack of time; he was then Grand Chancellor of the Knights of Pythias and an officer of his Masonic lodge. He was skeptical of the Klan's exclusion of Jews (the Masons admitted them), eager to know the character of its members, suspicious that they might take the law into their own hands. The matter was dropped, but soon a close friend approached Black again, and this time overcame his objections. But it was not until two years later that Black actually attended a meeting and paid dues. He went to very few meetings, and when he spoke it was to warn against lawlessness and religious intolerance. Finally, on the eve of the Senate race, he resigned altogether.

He resigned, but he did not openly repudiate the Klan. To have done so would have taken greater political hardiness than Black possessed. And he accepted in his election the support of the Klan people, because he needed the votes of the workers and farmers who made up its members. In 1926, after the election, he was invited by the head of the state lodge to address a meeting in Birmingham at which Governor-elect Bibb Graves was also to speak. He went to it, as he went to similar meetings of other societies. He was in a jubilant mood after his victory, and he thanked the audience for its support as he had thanked many other audiences. His speech, if the Sprigle version of it is correct, pulsed with a vague spirituality and an over-accented brotherly love, but little more. After that, he never attended another Klan meeting, and his relations with the Klan grew steadily worse. In 1928 his support of Al Smith went directly counter to the Klan's policy. In 1930, when James Heflin ran for the Senate, Black stumped the state against him, further embittering the Klan, which was openly backing Heflin. Black's opposition defeated Heflin, as Heflin has himself admitted, and elected Senator William Bankhead.

Hugo Black is no Klansman. Everything that he has stood for in his eleven years in the Senate runs counter to what the Klan has stood for. The Klan hates him bitterly now, as the Alabama employers hate him, and it has evidently lent its records with great willingness to the "investigators." Black has supported human rights in their crucial aspect in the America of today — the right to have a job, get decent wages, and not work excessive hours. He has fought for adequate relief for the unemployed from the ravages of the Depression. He has fought to give Negroes in the South the same economic status as whites, and to save them from discrimination in the provisions of the wage-hour bill. He has fought for the consumer of public-utility services. He has fought for the liberation of the common man from the oppressive weight of the giant corporation lobbies. Throughout his career in the Senate, Black has been more than a politico who pays lip service to the tenets of liberalism. He has been a passionately sincere humanist, guided throughout by his understanding of the fundamental truth of the new militant liberalism — that the basic approach to human rights lies in securing for the individual that economic freedom on which alone the dignity of the individual can be based.

Hugo Black was not born to this knowledge. He was no New England Brahmin, no western populist, no New York intellectual. He did not have in his blood and at his command the traditions of intellectual enlightenment that Justice Holmes, Senator La Follette, Justice Cardozo inherited. For what he is, he has had to sweat and fight. He has come up from the ignorance and bigotry of the southern masses. He has fought his way from a rudimentary schooling and a small-town law practice into national prominence. He has had no one like Emerson near him to discuss Plato with, as Holmes did, no Harvard training as Brandeis did. He has had to grope his way unaided through books, see through their platitudes, get at their truths. On his visit to London, the man he sought out was Harold Laski, the place he sought out was Toynbee Hall, the books he looked for in the bookstalls were a volume of Grote's *Aristotle,* which was missing from his collection, and Thucydides' *History of the Peloponnesian War.* Between the philosophical radical of today and Black's origins in the little town of Ashland, Alabama, stretches an enormous span. The story of how that span was built is the story of the education of Hugo Black. And in that education the Klan incident was an episode, blunderingly entered upon and now bitterly paid for. But the results of that education hearten us with a renewed belief in the possibilities of American life.

Black's Senate record was such as to wipe out, in his own mind as in the minds of those who valued his liberalism and humanity, all concern with, if not all memory of, the brief Klan years. When the nomination to the Supreme Court came to him, he accepted it as a recognition of his work as senator. If he did not mention to the president his former Klan membership, it was because by the side of his Senate career it seemed irrelevant. We may regard such a judgment as an error, but it was understandable.

There are some who feel more strongly about his failure to tell the Senate about the Klan connection when the issue was raised. But the same sense of relative unimportance would have operated in Black's mind with respect to the Senate. There would be, in addition, his unwillingness to involve the administration in a row over an episode that seemed to have lost all meaning, and a feeling of pride that the least his own colleagues in the Senate could do would be to judge him on the basis of their associations with him.

When the Sprigle series broke, as I have said, Black was in

London. He knew that groups similar to those behind these articles had, in both of his senatorial campaigns, sent investigators to Alabama to scour the state for something they could use against him. In fact the Sprigle material itself was not new. Most of it had been made public in Alabama during the last Senate fight. Knowing this, Justice Black was inclined to give the American people more credit for keeping their heads than we turned out to deserve. When he found that the articles were raising a storm, he had to face a bitter choice between making a statement and remaining quiet. But it is clear that to put the charges in their true perspective would have been impossible from across the ocean; the only item that would have survived transatlantic passage and the mercies of the newspaper moguls would have been the admission that he was once a member of the Klan. And Hugo Black has had as good a training in political tactics as the next man. He knows that when you are unscrupulously attacked, instead of answering at a disadvantage, it is better to wait until it is your show and then strike dramatically and hard. Hence the wait and the eventual radio speech.

There are several ironies about the whole episode. The obvious one is that so militant a New Dealer should be accused of being a reactionary. Another is that this man, charged with hostility to Negroes, would have faced defeat in another senatorial contest because he had fought too strenuously for raising the wages of Negro mill hands and lumber workers. But the greatest irony is that the most fervent Senate admirer of John Stuart Mill and the liberal tradition should be charged with being a bigot and an enemy of civil liberties. Mill's *Autobiography* and his essay *On Liberty*, Plato's *Dialogues*, and Grote's *Plato* — these are the books on which his mind dwells. But there are two authors whom he has read even more assiduously: Jefferson, whose set of writings in his library is completely marked up; and John W. Draper, whose highly libertarian *History of the Intellectual Development of Europe* he has read four or five times. The curious may even now turn to the *Congressional Record* for 1929 and read Black's fervid speech against the Treasury bill for censoring books from abroad, in which he quoted Draper's account of the burning of the Alexandria library, and then compare it with Heflin's speech on the subject.

I do not mean to say that Justice Black is all of one texture. In fact, the remarkable thing about him is that he is so full of contradictions. He is not a simple man to understand. His critics have called him slippery, but I found a man who is confident of his strength. I found a quick and elusive intelligence that defied whatever rules I had built up for categorizing people.

Such a man could do much to vitalize the Court and to broaden himself further in the process. He is on the Court now, and he means to stay. He knows that he belongs there, and he feels that the majority of the people want him there. The impression has been built up that he is not of high legal caliber, and that his talents are only those of the police judge and the prosecutor. That is not true. He never had a Harvard Law School training and never was an operative in a New York law factory, but he has come up against the smart lawyers and the corporation lawyers, both in his practice and in the Senate; and the encounters have not left him with a feeling of inferiority. Justice Black is no backwoods lawyer.

There were many among Justice Black's friends who wanted him to go slow when he came to the Court, wanted him to establish his position before he began applying his drastic progressivism to the judicial process. This applies to several of Black's friends on the Court itself, and who received him with a mixture of welcome and trepidation. They regarded him much as a Social Register-ite might regard a relative fresh from the sticks, arrived for a protracted visit — talented and high-spirited, but uncouth, unpredictable, and a questionable addition to formal parties. They wished he would give himself a chance to mellow. Several are reported to have said that, given five or ten years in which to master the lure of the Court and steep himself in its traditions and spirit, Black would make a great justice.

Black didn't intend to wait that long. Outwardly he has proved malleable enough. His relations with his colleagues have been personally cordial. The chief justice went out of his way to be friendly. Only Justice McReynolds is still hostile. He regards Black as a renegade southerner. And well he may, for their two social philosophies are as widely removed as the antipodes. Responding to the friendliness of the other justices, Black has been almost hypersensitive to the Court tradition about personal discreetness. He surrounds even his casual contacts with elaborate safeguards. He is still suffering from the trauma of having people forever on his trail during the agonizing weeks of his cause célèbre.

But while eager to play the game in all personal matters, Justice Black has challenged the rules of the game so far as constitutional law is concerned.

Of the twenty opinions in which Justice Black's name has thus far appeared, six have been dissents and six have been concurring opinions in which he disagreed with the Court's reasoning but agreed with the conclusion. In eight, he wrote the Court opinion. This is a high ratio of divergence, especially for a new justice. I shall pass over the cases in which Black has written the Court's majority or unanimous decision, because the cases assigned to him have been relatively unimportant. It is as a dissenter that he has most sharply broken the Court's patterns of thought and most distressed even his liberal colleagues.

The case involving the "obligations of contracts" clause (*Indiana ex rel. Anderson v. Brand*) does not at first sight reveal the importance that it possesses. In 1927 the Indiana legislature passed an act establishing a certain tenure for teachers, and then, in 1933, it passed another act excluding township schools from the tenure provisions. A teacher in a township school who had lost her job sued on the ground that the 1927 act established a contract whereby she could not be discharged except under certain conditions, and that the 1933 act had impaired the obligation of the contract and was invalid. The Supreme Court, reversing the state court, held with her, but Black dissented. A comparison of his opinion with the majority opinion written by Justice Roberts shows disagreements as to the construction of both the state legislation and the Indiana precedents. But basically the disagreement was over the extent of state sovereignty as against the overriding sanctity of contracts. And there, for Black, is the nub of the matter. He believes in legislative supremacy, state or federal, as against judicial supremacy and the rigid hold of contract doctrine. Intellectually he knows where he stands in the struggle, begun in America more than a century ago with *Fletcher v. Peck* and the Dartmouth College case, between those who would freeze our order through property institutions and those who would keep it fluid through legislative change.

But the struggle over the contract clause is more an echo of past battles than an expression of present conflicts. More central in Black's judicial career are his opinions in the utility cases. Two of them stand out — a dissent in *McCart v. Indianapolis Water Company* and a concurring opinion in *United Gas Public Service Company v. Texas*. The *Indianapolis Water* dissent created a flurry in legal circles on procedural grounds, for Black did the unprecedented thing of dissenting from a per curiam decision, in which the Court speaks as a whole rather than through any particular justice. With a sharp, clipped severity the Supreme Court held that the lower court, in upholding the state commission's schedule of water rates, had erred in not allowing for an upward trend of prices between 1933 and

1935. The rates had been held not confiscatory in 1933; but — the per curiam opinion argued — they might have become confiscatory by the time the 1935 decision was handed down. Black's answer to this decision forms the best opinion he has thus far written. Full, detailed, statistical in the best Brandeis manner, it cuts through the overgrowths of legal jargon that screen the fact that ultimately the consumer pays for the impotence of the regulatory system. It had taken six years for the commission's order to reach the Court; now it was being remanded. At that rate, it would be back in the Court again in 1943. But Black preferred to settle things then and there — and he did so on the basis of the prudent-investment principle that Justice Brandeis has developed in his classic dissents. In the process he wrote a severe condemnation of the Court's whole practice, since 1890, of invalidating state regulation of utility rates.

The Texas gas case was the second round of the utility fight between Black and the Court. In a separate concurring opinion, he pointed out that the company is an affiliate of the Electric Bond and Share, that the salaries paid to the holding-company officials are set down in operating expenses for the subsidiary and are paid by the consumer in the form of inflated rates. This opinion is notable also for its defense of the jury trial as a method of fixing the validity of commission rate-setting (Justice McReynolds, in one of his *ex tempore* speeches from the bench, called it "little more than a farce").

But the dissent that has proved most impressive is that in *Connecticut General Life Insurance Company v. Johnson*. The California legislature laid a tax on reinsurance premiums that was aimed at corporations from other states. The Court overruled it as violative of the Fourteenth Amendment, which provides that "no state shall . . . deprive any person of life, liberty, or property without due process of law, nor deny to any person . . . the equal protection of the laws." Black states quite simply: "I do not believe that the word 'person' in the Fourteenth Amendment includes corporations." And thus he sweeps away fifty years of Supreme Court history and strikes at one of the props of corporate power.

But he does so only after an interesting survey of the legislative and judicial history of the amendment. I believe he is on solid ground so far as history is concerned. For some time there has been a controversy among American historians as to whether those who framed the amendment intended it as a protection of corporate property rights. That such was their intent was the argument of Roscoe Conkling, one of the members of the congressional committee that drafted the amendment in 1866, when he appeared before the Court in the *San Mateo* case in 1882. This would imply something of a conspiracy on the part of the committee, for the purpose of the amendment was clearly the protection of the newly granted rights of Negroes against hostile state legislatures. Conkling's thesis was accepted as Court doctrine in 1886 in the *Santa Clara* case. Black challenges it as irrelevant. Whatever individual members of the committee may have thought or intended, he points to the indisputable fact that the Congress that passed the amendment, the states that ratified it, and the people in whom the amending power rests were told that it was to protect Negroes and not to remove corporations from the regulation of state governments.

Black's argument is good. There are, however, three things that trouble me about it. One is that, in the face of fifty years of Court history, it is likely never to be more than a courageous gesture. This is not merely because of the time that has elapsed; it is due to the fact that the personality of the corporation has become an integral part of our constitutional law — right or wrong. The second thing is that his opinion would have been more complete had he taken account of the fact that where "person" has been used previously in the language of the law and of lawyers, it has also been construed to include the corporation. The third is that the more strategic line of attack on the abuse of power by the courts would have been to insist that "due process" should be interpreted only to mean procedural safeguards and not substantive determinations of social policy. That was the direction of the Holmes approach, and an economic realist such as Black could carry it out even more completely.

There remains the question of Black's impact on the future. He is not the sort of person who, like Holmes or Brandeis, can build a liberal minority around himself. His liberal colleagues are not ready to go with him; he is too acid, too impetuous. He ruffles judicial sensibilities. Like the child in the story, he cries out that the king is, after all, naked, and it has been the whole function of constitutional law to weave imaginary garments for the nakedness of corporate power. Added to that, there is the fact that while his decisions are clear and well written, they do not have the brilliance of phrase and the sure legal touch that Holmes's had, or the scrupulous solidity and genius for procedure that Brandeis's have.

All of which means that Black has become a judicial crusader before he has come to maturity as a judge. His strength lies in the areas in which he was strong as senator — his feel for economic realities and his intrepid belief in popular democratic government as against any sort of oligarchy. He seems to belong in the Jacksonian period of the Court, when the democratic upsurge brought to the bench tribunes of the people, who had fought for them in the legislatures. Black has proved himself, in the deepest sense, a tribune of the people — ever watchful over their interests, zealous in protecting legislative power, reducing utility cases to the final problem of the interests of the consumer, zealous for government regulatory power over corporations.

There is a new doctrinal struggle going on within the Court's own ranks. A "new left" has emerged in the decisions of Justice Black, reaching even further in its implications than the "new left" of Justice Brandeis in 1916. Justices Brandeis, Stone, Cardozo, and Reed represent a social liberalism sharply defined against the reactionary background of the Court's tradition or the grudging "liberalism" of Justices Hughes and Roberts, but primarily they have aimed at a decent amount of judicial restraint and self-limitation. This is an excellent principle when contrasted with the history of the Court's previous thirst for power. So, also, is the present majority's courage in overruling past decisions, which was revealed most dramatically in *Erie Railroad Company v. Tompkins* (304 U.S. 64 [1938]), where the court declared it had been wrong for nearly a century on the question of recognizing the construction of common law by state courts.

The weakness of this attitude is that it is negative and belated. It lacks the clear-cut and affirmative outlines of a fighting faith that can keep pace with changes in governmental power. Such a faith has emerged in Justice Black's opinions. The real doctrinal struggle within the Court is no longer between a "broad" and a "strict" construction of federal power. The Supreme Court revolution has, at least for the present, decided that struggle in favor of the broad construction. What we have now is a struggle between a negative and an affirmative attitude toward the process of governmental activity, between two views as to the pace of social change. It is here that the real meaning of Justice Black's much-discussed dissent lies. Leafing through the Court records for the term, one is impressed by the courage, integrity, and consistency of his position, which, in terms of constitutional doctrine, signals the emergence of a militant left-wing democratic and labor movement and its bid for continued national power.

1938

12

Felix Frankfurter and the
Essential Tension

Of all the justices I have dealt with, Felix Frankfurter tried hardest
to maintain what Thomas Kuhn calls "the essential tension"[1] between
polar pulls, an effort that reaches deep into the arts of inquiry and
interpretation. Frankfurter's method often gave the impression of
being an agonized inner struggle to achieve a balance between the
conflicting judicial schools. He didn't wholly succeed, perhaps because his inner intensities constantly strained him beyond his ability
to play such a role.

Yet it would be hard to name another justice who could rival
his ability to scrutinize tradition and change.

He was the only justice whose heart was equally divided between
taking a judicial position and a role as adviser to Franklin Roosevelt.
He carried over into politics the respect for tradition that he had as
law teacher and judge. He also carried over into law the obsession
with strategy that he shared with his presidential hero.

I first met Frankfurter when I taught briefly at Harvard College
in 1935 and 1936. We maintained a mostly epistolary friendship for
many years. He sent me his opinions and would return my letters
with comments scribbled across them. Despite my differences with
him in my reviews and columns, he never gave me up as a lost cause.
I shall always remember him as a dancing bundle of conflicting energies — and that was his Court role as well. In both he was memorable.

Some time ago there was a serious theft from the Library of Congress, of papers and diaries of the late Supreme Court Justice Felix Frankfurter. Whatever their money value, they were of great historical importance. The shrewdness with which the choice was made of the stuff to be stolen, leaving the rest, showed it was a scholarly larceny. Jack Anderson wrote of the theft in his column, and in response to his appeal, someone — presumably the scholarly felon — has now sent him copies of the stolen letters, but not the precious diaries.

The legacy of Felix Frankfurter can be found not only in the letters and diaries but also in his books, his court opinions, his basic approach to law and society, and — most of all — in his personality: highly charged, vivid, irrepressible, playing a behind-the-scenes role in most political dramas over a span of a half-century. He had a flair for friendship, a capacity to spot the flowering talents of young men and to direct them into public service, and a genius for using legal skills (his own and those of others) at the exactly right points in the governmental process.

Coming to America from Vienna at age thirteen, just before the turn of the century, Felix Frankfurter crowded his high school, college, and law school into a few meteoric years, worked under Henry Stimson, served in Washington under Woodrow Wilson in World War I as a troubleshooter in labor relations, and found his exactly right niche at the Harvard Law School, teaching labor and administrative law. But his energy, interests, and friendships burst the bounds of law itself. He was, directly or indirectly, an adviser to presidents from Taft to Kennedy. He was on terms of intimate friendship with creative men in the law firms, the academies, the government, including Holmes and Brandeis, Laski, Learned and Augustus Hand, Henry Stimson, Dean Acheson, Archibald MacLeish, and dozens of others. He maintained a constant stream of correspondence with hundreds of prominent figures from England to Israel to India. There was scarcely a legal or political sparrow that fell anywhere in the world without his noting it and trying to do something about it.

He was an activist if there ever was one — but he drew the line at the judicial process, which he regarded as having its own inviolate tradition of personal restraint. He learned from Brandeis the belief that the process of history can be moved and changed by the actions and convictions of a few men, provided they are the right men, with the right skills and understandings, at the right spots. He had a passion for the concrete detail as against the vast abstraction.

Curiously, he first became known to the larger American public as a kind of radical, through his writings on the Sacco and Vanzetti case in the 1920s. For him the fact that the men were anarchists was of no moment, one way or another. What counted was the due process of law, for them or anyone else, especially in the postwar period of antiradical hysteria. But the radical tag clung to him.

During the early New Deal days he became almost a one-man recruiting service for the great talent elite — the first since Wilson's — that drafted and administered the necessary New Deal legislation. His young men — dubbed the "Hot Dogs" — were close to every phase of the Roosevelt program. He himself remained in Cambridge for the first five years, the only quiet spot in the whole tornado. It was there I first came to know him. He tried to set me right on a number of topics on which I persisted perversely in being wrong. This continued for many years.

It took an act of courage for Roosevelt to appoint him to the Supreme Court, because of his associations with Sacco and Vanzetti, Laski and the Boston police strike, the Hot Dogs. As in the case of Wilson's appointment of Brandeis, there was a flurry of opposition in the Senate committee, but there was no real struggle against confirmation as there had been with Brandeis. By every suffrage of lawyers and judges, however much they might disagree with his views and career, Frankfurter's scholarship and legal brilliance belonged on the Court.

It is sad that he could not have kept going on the Court another decade or more, into his nineties, as did his mentor and model, Justice Holmes. His judicial temperament — and he showed again and again that he had it — lay in his heroic effort to achieve a kind of judicial austerity, to which his own political and social preferences were subordinated for the sake of orderly change in the law. It did not lie in any shrinking from controversy. His was a salty personality, whose favorite conversational divide was that of genial insult and assault. He loved a fight, and liked to recall the words of Civil War veteran Justice Holmes: "The final test . . . is battle in some form. . . . It is one thing to utter a happy phrase from a protected cloister; another to think under fire — to think for action upon which great interests depend."

The enemies he fought hardest were cant, stuffiness, "paralyzing abstraction," dogma, and category thinking. On the question of his "liberalism" or "conservatism," one may see him best as an administrative and economic liberal (witness his influence on the ideas and personnel of the New Deal) but a judicial conservative. This is all the more interesting because his hero, Justice Holmes, was exactly the reverse: an economic conservative and (in his day) a Bill of Rights liberal.

Yet in the long view of Court history, his place will be with Holmes rather than with Brandeis, who influenced him greatly on administrative and social issues.

The great difference between Felix Frankfurter and the groups around Justice Black and Chief Justice Warren is not a difference in their visions of the good society or the good life. It is that while the Black group primarily responds to present urgencies and willingly takes big judicial risks in meeting them, Frankfurter responded to his picture of the long-range future and felt that the protection of the human spirit is best served by refusing to break the all-too-fragile judicial safeguards that have taken centuries to shape.

As it happens, my own sympathies on many matters are with the Black-Warren view. But I deeply respect Justice Frankfurter's concern with the legal fabric, and I have only scorn for those who, in their quick and shallow intolerance, attacked him as some kind of antediluvian stick-in-the-mud. Only ignorance of the law and of Frankfurter's whole intellectual stance could justify the way in which some of his critics have tried to dismiss him.

A Felix Frankfurter saga is in the making, and the newest chapter in it concerns the most important judicial decision of the century — *Brown v. Board of Education*. Every great decision carries a story inside it. We knew that there was turmoil among the judges on the eve of the case, making it unlikely that a majority could be found to attack and overrun the *Plessy v. Ferguson* fortress of "separate but equal" schools. We knew also that Chief Justice Fred Vinson had been hostile to any new doctrine on school equality, and that his death and replacement by Earl Warren had opened the possibility of getting the needed majority.

Now comes a *Harvard Law Review* piece about Philip Elman, a Justice Department official who was a former law clerk to and close friend of Justice Frankfurter. The gist of the article is that Frankfurter and Elman worked together to contrive a strategy that would make the *Brown* case a turning point in the history of access to education for all children.

The challenge was to avoid a divided Court and a decision that would split the nation. Frankfurter told Elman that Justice Hugo Black, Alabama liberal that he was, wanted a new doctrine but had warned his fellow justices that if the Court overruled *Plessy* and also mandated the integration of the nation's schools, it would mean open rebellion in the South. The Klan would ride again.

Frankfurter was enough of a realist to take Black seriously. He also knew that only a unanimous decision could summon the moral authority to rally the nation and cushion the shock.

Ever the law professor, Frankfurter found an eager listener in the new chief justice, Earl Warren, as he portrayed for him the chance that the case offered the court for an act of statesmanship. The Court ordered the school cases reargued and asked the Justice Department to submit a brief — which Elman wrote.

Its crucial proposal was for the Court to put a legal end to segregated schools — but not mandate their immediate integration. Instead, the Warren opinion for a unanimous court in 1954 ordered integration "with all deliberate speed" — an ambiguous phrase Frankfurter suggested and that has become famous for the way it provided the nation with breathing space and face saving.

It took several decades — the resistance fought a series of rearguard actions — but the federal district judges proved strong and held to their purpose.

It was a watershed decision. America became the first multiracial nation to resolve its major racial inequality by constitutional means.

Did Frankfurter overstep the bounds of judicial propriety in his talks with his former law clerk? Clearly he did. But Elman's answer rings true: "Without that little impropriety you would not have had this enormous contribution to American constitutional life of the 20th Century."

In his book *The Brandeis/Frankfurter Connection*, Bruce Allen Murphy chronicled an earlier impropriety by both men in a long private partnership to effect social change together. Murphy quotes a 1943 Frankfurter diary entry in which he notes that a justice is like a monk who "leaves all sorts of worldly desires behind him," and that "this court has no excuse for being unless it's a monastery."

Does the Elman account turn Frankfurter into a hypocrite? Perhaps. But I see the diary entry as a cry from the warring heart against a fate that made him work always in the shadows.

Frankfurter was at bottom a political activist and strategist, whether as law professor, collaborator with Brandeis, adviser to Roosevelt, or Supreme Court justice.

Proprieties are not trivial. In government they are necessary as norms. But it would be a foolish nation that makes its rules of propriety so rigid as to exclude propriety-breakers like Brandeis, Roosevelt, and Frankfurter.

1965, 1986

13

The Mind and Style
of Robert H. Jackson

*Justice Robert H. Jackson's flaws, both as political warrior and ju-
dicial statesman, were not those of mind but of personality and
judgment. Unlike Holmes's classic verdict on FDR ("first-rate temperament, second-rate mind") Jackson had a first-rate mind and a
second-rate temperament. His abilities carried him far — to the attorney generalship and to the Supreme Court. His ambitions aimed
higher, first to the presidency, then the chief justiceship. The fact that
he failed to become either left a deep scar on him.*

*A man in a high judicial post is supposed to be personally ju-
dicious. Jackson wasn't. He was combative, much like Black. But
Black was a seasoned veteran of political infighting, while Jackson
became a victim of his temperament. As a constitutional thinker
Jackson ranks not far below Frankfurter and Black, and his prose
style has more bite than either of theirs.*

*Jackson's constitutional journey took him from playing an active
part in Roosevelt's court-packing scheme to holding a relatively isolated position on the Warren Court. The result of this journey is
evident in his heart-searching inner debate over* Brown v. Board of
Education. *Initially he felt that the Court opinion emerging from*
Brown *was a "political" one, and was scornful of adding to judicial
supremacy by playing politics. But it was testimony to his more
mature judgment and strength that he rose from his hospital bed to
be there in person when the Court handed down its unanimous* Brown
decision.

Robert H. Jackson served the New Deal brilliantly and militantly in a succession of tax and antitrust administrative posts. He drafted much of the Roosevelt legislation and served formidably as U.S. solicitor general (a post in which he won a legendary number of cases) and then as attorney general. He testified in favor of Roosevelt's court-packing plan and wrote a book highly critical of the expanding judicial power.[1]

The echoes of the Court fight during those years seem muted now. But those who followed the constitutional wars know that they were not bloodless battles of categories. They were struggles for power and struggles over order. Mr. Justice Jackson saw this clearly. That was why he chose to write not of judicial review but of judicial supremacy. He was willing to accept the former as part of a working scheme of government, but not the latter.

Where does the distinction lie? Perhaps no sharp distinction can be drawn. Judicial review means the power of the courts to review acts of the other branches of the government. Judicial supremacy is the position of overlordship that results from that power. The power of judicial review is nothing if not supreme. But therein lay Jackson's dilemma. Judicial review may, if kept within bounds, be a perfectly good instrument of government. He was sure this was so in the protection of civil liberties and in keeping the states from acts of petty economic tyranny and anarchy that would pulverize the federal structure. What, then, remains? According to Jackson, the courts must be kept from judicial supremacy, that is, from "unwarranted interference in the economic affairs of the country."

"As the decisions now stand," Justice Holmes once admonished his colleagues, "I see hardly any limits but the sky." And Justice Stone put the same thought in different words when he said that while the executive and legislative branches were checked by the judiciary, "The only check upon our own exercise of power is our own sense of self-restraint." Jackson ultimately falls back on the Holmes-Brandeis-Stone-Frankfurter doctrine of self-restraint to draw a line of distinction between judicial review and judicial supremacy.

Perhaps it is as good a formulation as you can get — and the rest has to be spelled out not in doctrinal terms but in the history of the Court in action. In his book, Jackson divides the New Deal judicial war into four phases. The first was the period of uncertainty, in which the Court hesitated between two worlds, with four justices definitely living in the old, three in the new, and Mr. Chief Justice Hughes and Mr. Justice Roberts commuting back and forth. That was in 1933 and 1934, when reform legislation was being upheld by the Court by a five-to-four vote and everyone was on tenterhooks. The second phase was in 1935 and 1936, when the commuters decided to settle down and the Court, in Jackson's words, "nullified the New Deal." The succession of blows the Court inflicted on the majority will — the "storm signals" in the hot-oil and railroad retirement-pension cases; then "Black Monday," May 27, 1935, when the Court handed down in a single day adverse opinions on farm debtors' relief (*Louisville Bank v. Radford*),[2] the President's power to remove appointees (*Humphrey's Executor v. U.S.*),[3] and the National Relief Agency (NRA). The locust swarm was set loose. In the lower federal courts, a single judge might sabotage the results of a national effort. In succession followed the Agricultural Adjustment Administration (AAA) decision, the Jones stock-fraud decision that almost turned over the Securities and Exchange Commission applecart (*Jones v. SEC*),[4] the *Carter Coal* decision (*Carter v. Carter Coal Co.*),[5] the municipal bankruptcy decision, and, as a climax, *Morehead v. Tipaldo*,[6] outlawing the New York minimum-wage law. In the *Morehead* case, the Court was saying, in effect, that neither the national government nor the state governments had the authority to deal with sweatshop wages.

The third phase of crisis was what Mr. Jackson calls "the challenge" of the president to judicial supremacy — the reorganization plan. Clearly it was a counterattack against the justices. Jackson had defended the plan before the Senate Judiciary Committee, but he was chary of any real argument except one: that there was plenty of provocation for it. The alternative to the plan, once it became the center of a battle, was not some other sort of Court reform but none at all. For the rest, he deemphasized the plan itself, contenting himself with the fact that the president ultimately won the war.

This victory marked the fourth phase of the crisis — the retreat of the Court into judicial review. In 1937, in another long and dramatic line of cases, the Court sought to undo all the damage it had done in 1935 and 1936. Justice Roberts switched back again, and the minimum-wage law of the state of Washington was ruled constitutional in *West Coast Hotel Co. v. Parrish*,[7] whereas exactly the same law in New York had formerly been unconstitutional. The same temper was shown in the Labor Board cases: *NLRB v. Jones and Laughlin*,[8] *NLRB v. Fruehauf Trailer Co.*,[9] *NLRB v. Friedman-Harry Marks Clothing Co.*,[10] and *Associated Press v. NLRB*.[11] Moreover, the change from supremacy to review was accomplished without a single new appointment by the president. The old Court had reformed itself. With that reform, the New Deal constitutional crisis was at an end.

Jackson's book gives us a history of a particular constitutional crisis, but there were others — in Jefferson's time, in Taney's, during the Civil War, at the time of the income-tax decisions. What do they have in common? The answer lies in whatever it is that makes our system of constitutional interpretation too rigid for the imperatives of social change.

Mr. Justice Jackson saw all the implications of the New Deal crisis. He saw that litigation had become an organic part of our political system, a way of shaping social policy, and he did not like it. His solution was that we deny judicial review to the lower federal courts, that we restrict it to a single court and provide some means for a prompt settlement of the constitutionality of social policy, so that there would be no doubt and no long delays. His remedies rely mainly on restraint. In this, he shares the same position as other spokesmen of liberal judicial thought. My feeling is that we shall still have to tackle the power of judicial supremacy in a constitutional crisis that may crop up once more in our generation. Jackson must have thought so too. His book discusses how the arrogance of Justice Taney in rendering the *Dred Scott* decision prepared the way for the Civil War and therefore for the humiliation of Taney in the *Merryman* case.

Jackson was appointed to the U.S. Supreme Court in 1941. Until his appointment, he seemed a model of a Roosevelt Court justice. He was populist, antimonopoly, and anti–holding company. He had risen with meteoric brilliance through a number of major New Deal posts. He was a superb legislative draftsman. He was canny about all the dodges of interpretation that judges used to clothe the interests of the dominant economic class in judicial sanction. Yet he surprised everyone by turning out to be a very different kind of judge. At heart, he was a maverick who refused to do the expected. He broke away from Black and Douglas, mocking their efforts to rewrite past precedents in the language of liberal philosophy. He became an opponent of the judicial activism of his colleagues, whether in the area of property rights or personal freedoms. His philosophy of judicial restraint was closer to Justice Frankfurter's, and together they fought a continuing feud with Black and Douglas. Yet he could also mock Frankfurter's sometimes long-winded attitudinizing. As an individualist, he was first among his peers on the Court. He was the best stylist. The ironic smile that seemed settled on his lips translated into dissenting and concurring opinions that were contemptuous of the rhetoric of judicial self-righteousness. His constitutional views cannot be categorized as either liberal or conservative, since he felt that both labels had lost much of their meaning. He could take strong positions against the anti-Communist oath in the Taft-Hartley Act, in support of the "right of irreligion" as well as of religion, and in support of rape defendants who had been "convicted" by press headlines. He spoke out with a canny realism against illegal searches and police lawlessness. But in the Rosenberg espionage case and in the Smith Act convictions of top Communist leaders, he took the hard-nosed view that the Constitution was not intended as a suicide pact.

More than anything, he was moved by a passionate commitment to the role of law as setting limits — around swollen economic power, swollen governmental and even judicial power, swollen, dehumanized nationalism. It was the last of these that led him to fly to Nuremberg in 1945 and establish the framework for the prosecution of Nazi war leaders, thereby bringing closer the idea of a world law representing the conscience of humankind. At least in part, he was moved by a feeling of restlessness on the Court. He saw himself as an icon-smasher, and his political hero was another Jackson — Andrew — who had brought a frontier vigor into the White House. In 1937 there had been a boomlet of support for him to be governor of New York, but nothing came of it. He was generally recognized as Roosevelt's own choice to succeed him in the presidency, but when Roosevelt moved to a third term nothing came of that either. Jackson later felt that Hugo Black had stopped a movement to appoint him chief justice. Out of this sense of frustration came his ill-conceived cable from Nuremberg with its bitter blast at Black, whom he accused of organizing a cabal against him.

He returned to the Court to serve under Chief Justice Vinson and later under Warren. His last two years were hindered by illness, but while he had doubts about judicial lawmaking, he insisted on sitting with his colleagues to dramatize the Court's unanimity in the *Brown* desegregation decision in May 1954, several months before his death.

1941, 1974

14

William O. Douglas:
True Militant

William O. Douglas saw himself as the true Court militant activist, often working closely with Hugo Black but very much a man on his own. I met and interviewed him early, when the Yale Law School professor was chosen to head the Securities and Exchange Commission. The result was a magazine piece I called "Diogenes on Wall Street."[1] *When Justice Brandeis decided to retire, he singled out Douglas as his successor. The young Douglas (only forty) still seemed to focus his intensity on the strategies and evasions of corporate finance and law.*

Yet with all his talents, and they were many, Douglas's problem was one of diffusing them too broadly. He seemed determined not to allow his Court post to interfere with his real ambition — to be a Renaissance man, a free-floating, many-splendored cluster of talents seeking to affect everything in American life.

To his followers he remained a brilliant and provocative path-breaker throughout. Yet he lacked the quality of gravitas, the weightiness of judgment and action in a sustained involvement with the grand themes of the law.

In his basic method, Douglas followed the Brandeis path of contextual activism. His strength lay in his capacity to explore the areas of individual and cultural protections that could be turned into constitutional rights. Thus his most signal contribution came in Griswold v. Connecticut *(1965),*[2] *in which he managed to transform the freedom in the use of contraceptives into something larger — a "mystical right." He borrowed this wizardry — and the phrase itself — from the classic early article on the "right of privacy" by Louis D. Brandeis and Charles Warren. But out of it Douglas shaped policy, law, and history.*

William O. Douglas has been one of the most liberal and militant justices of the Supreme Court, early in his career a reforming administrator of the laws governing securities, and throughout a vigorous, controversial writer. His life had the makings of an American success story: the fatherless child, overcoming an early bout with polio, supporting his widowed mother, working his way through high school and college, riding a freight car across the continent to attend Columbia Law School, graduating into a prestigious New York law firm, sweeping away all before him as he reached the successive rungs of the ladder — law school professor, SEC commissioner, Supreme Court justice — in the eyes of many, clearly bent for the presidency.

Yet the real meaning of Douglas's life lay in the opposite direction, not in conventional, single-minded success but in unconventional many-faceted fulfillment, always challenging whatever establishments he encountered.

As an economic reformer he linked the populist tradition of the Northwest with the Brandeisian tradition of curbing those financial interests whose power was swollen by the use of "other people's money." He linked that in turn with the economic philosophy of FDR's New Deal, which he himself did so much to formulate. His memorandum on corporate reorganization, submitted in the early days of the Securities and Exchange Commission, was an eight-volume document detailing the ways in which investment bankers involved in reorganizations secured both profits and power from the companies. In his brief tenure as SEC chairman he had a chance to translate his corporate knowledge into regulatory rules. As a Supreme Court justice (appropriately, he succeeded to Brandeis's seat) he unswervingly led the struggle to control corporate power when it threatened the worker, the consumer, or the small businessman. He did so, moreover, as an insider who knew all the dodges and strategies.

As a judge, Douglas's strength lay in a forthright liberalism that rarely left any question as to where he would stand, especially on cases involving the Bill of Rights. His judicial career had contained four phases: he was an active leader in the Roosevelt Court, both in dissent and in majority; he was a dissenter on the Vinson Court, especially in the cold war cases; he was a militant member of the majority on the Warren Court; and he was the leader of the liberal minority on the Burger Court.

The proposed impeachment of Justice Douglas bruited by Representative Gerald Ford — and more than hinted at by Vice President Spiro Agnew — raised questions about the intent of the Nixon administration. How far did it dare go in politicizing the Supreme Court? The Court was caught in a web of political maneuvers more involving than any in the previous thirty or thirty-five years.

Douglas's reading of the First Amendment was, like Hugo Black's, an absolutist libertarian one. On freedom of religion, on the rights of accused persons, on the one-man-one-vote cases, on the right of access to contraceptive information, on obscenity cases, on school desegregation and other civil rights issues, Douglas sought to protect rights of dissent, privacy, equal access, and freedom of political action, even in cases that seemed extreme to his fellow liberals. He did it partly as a judicial activist who believed that the Court must be a sword as well as a shield, and partly because he was a rebel, and this gave him a strong empathy for other rebels.

His liberalism had a more sustained militancy than that of the other Roosevelt appointees to the Court — Black, Frankfurter, Jackson — but it had a one-dimensional quality, less brilliantly resourceful in constitutional stratagems than Black's, less learned and tortured than Frankfurter's, with less statesmanlike depth than Jackson's. His judicial style is muscular and combative, very much as his writing style in his many books. But it is not memorable.

The judicial career of Douglas represents only one phase of an almost Jeffersonian many-sidedness that encompassed teacher, naturalist, traveler, explorer, mountain climber, writer, lecturer, political man. He was Faustian in his appetite for life. Both by precept and by example he scorned the traditional view that a judge should lead a gray and neutral life lest he be accused of being a partisan. Douglas gloried in his partisanship, as he gloried in a flamboyant life that included four marriages and three divorces. Inevitably this aroused conservative hostility. Several times enemies sought his impeachment, but after some flutterings and flickerings the attempts died out.

The war against Douglas was a dangerous game, bound to cost the nation heavily. Douglas made mistakes. It was a serious mistake to become and remain a director of a foundation whose funds had a shady source, even though it spent them for high-minded purposes. But if Ford, Agnew, and others thirsted for his blood, they should have moved right after the Abe Fortas case and had the whole issue out when it might have seemed a moral one. Instead they waited — after the rejection of Clement Haynsworth and Harold Carswell. Maybe the attackers had higher purposes, but it was hard to avoid the conclusion that they were out for political blood.

They had an added issue against Douglas — the intemperate

closing pages of his last book — *Points of Revolution.* I didn't take these pages seriously. It was foolish of Douglas to reopen the war against George III, to equate the revolutionary anarchists of today with Tom Paine 200 years ago and to give them any moral support at all.

But Douglas has been on this line for some years, and no one has impeached him. Maybe he was disappointed at never having reached the presidency, as he might have through Truman and the vice presidential path. Maybe he was captivated by the worldview of young rebels, as seen through his youthful wife. Whatever the motive, it enriches the Court to have one member who bridges the world of the young and the old, the radical and the traditional.

I caught a glimpse of Justice William O. Douglas on TV the other day, in his wheelchair, on his way to his Supreme Court duties. He seemed very frail, but gallant in his courage, as he told the old story about Holmes and Brandeis on a street corner in Washington. The wind had whipped a pretty girl's skirt around her knees and while Brandeis went on in earnest conversation, the ninety-year-old Holmes had sighed and said, "Oh, to be seventy again." It was Douglas's way of pointing to the "Yankee from Olympus," who had stayed on the Court until a later age than his own.

I write this in Douglas country, in the shadow of Douglas's youth. A half-hour drive from here is Yakima, Washington, where this extraordinary man grew up and had his early life struggles, before he heeded the call to "Go East" and invaded Columbia and Yale law schools. The tenacity with which he holds on to his Court post in the face of his partial paralysis and the ups and downs of improvement and relapse is one of the dramatic stories of Court history.

Clearly Douglas wants his tenure on the Supreme Court to outlast Gerald Ford's in the White House. President Ford is damned in his eyes for a double reason: he inherited the presidency from Nixon, and when he was in Congress he led the Nixon administration's effort to impeach Douglas. These would seem reason enough for Douglas's enmity. But in addition he seems convinced that the judge Gerald Ford would pick to succeed him would be one more vote added to Nixon's four court appointees, and would provide a five-judge majority for conservative decisions.

This isn't the first time a judge has reasoned politically when he had to decide about retiring. Politics is never very far from the Supreme Court, from the time a president starts to pick a new judge right up to the time that judge gives way to another. In the case of

Justice Douglas, his refusal to retire just happens to be more nakedly political than usual.

But it is also something more. Douglas doesn't want to give up his self-image. He is frail. He needs physical therapy. He sits silently through the sessions when once he asked barbed questions from the bench. Despite all this, he still sees himself as he once was — the daring young man defying the Establishment.

He has done everything, been everywhere. He has broken whole clusters of rules — in his marriages, his activism, his flirtations with presidential politics, his walking tours, his travels, his mountain climbing, his lecturing, his writing myriad books.

There is an often-told story about Justice Stephen J. Field, a West Coaster like Douglas, but unlike him one of the Court's most committed conservatives. Justice Robert Grier was not only getting old, he was also a man of confused mind, who showed some of his confusion in the historic legal tender cases. Field headed a committee of his brethren formed to persuade Grier to retire. Years later, when Field was old and sick and his fellow judges reminded him of his role in the Grier retirement, Field shot back, "Yes, and a dirtier day's work I never did in my life."

None of Douglas's colleagues will do a Field on him, not his liberal friends who treasure him, not the Burger group, which feels it's best not to intervene. Douglas must himself decide the point at which his tenacity will no longer be a symbol of courage and will begin to hurt the Court's image as well as its work.

He has had a longer service on the Court than any judge in its history. He knows that until a newly elected president is inaugurated there will be a period during which those who do not agree with him could decide who will take his seat. He feels that to yield power now to the wrong person would defeat the purpose of his whole judicial life.

So he hangs on in anguish and the nation waits, watching his lonely debate.

1975

PART III

THE INTERACTION OF COURTS AND CULTURES

PREFACE

WHERE THE FOCUS IN THE FIRST CLUSTER OF ESSAYS WAS DOCTRINAL (the search for the foundations of constitutional thinking) and the second was personal (an assessment of the stature of some of the judicial "greats"), the focus here is on the interaction between justices and their doctrines, and on the gritty stuff of social context. One way to organize this approach is by "Courts," using whoever is chief justice as symbol and embodiment. I paid some attention in the earlier essays to the Courts headed by Chief Justices Charles E. Hughes and Harlan F. Stone. I turn now to their four successor Courts — those of Fred Vinson, Earl Warren, Warren Burger, and William Rehnquist.

For each Court one can trace a "career" — the trajectory of a shifting community of judges as they ponder the cases, maneuver for position, and choose between alternative ways of interpreting the Constitution. The tenure of a chief justice may be an artificial way of demarking this process, especially when that justice isn't the dominant figure of the Court. Yet each Court takes on a character of its own as its members compete to leave their imprint on constitutional history.

In this cluster of essays I am chiefly concerned with the cases that affect the direction of constitutional law, the justices who write the decisions and quarrel over them, the justices the presidents pick to assure their own place in history, the tangled politics of the Senate confirmation process, and the history of the issues and pressure groups that orbit around the "great cases." In the end, I am concerned also with the crises that test the resilience of the constitutional system and society.

I use the term *culture* here to describe how a community grows around a unifying principle, how members of a culture perceive themselves, and how they seek to cultivate and protect their shared interests. I am of course most concerned with the legal and constitutional cultures, subsets of the larger intellectual culture that intersects the political and media cultures. All of these cultures are encompassed by the "knowledge" class (sometimes called the "new class"). I used to feel that the most important distinction lay between the constitutional culture and the dominant business-corporate class. I am now more inclined to locate the critical distinction between the constitutional culture and that larger segment of society that deals with ideas, symbols, and power. Intersecting both are ethnic, religious, and economic interest groups, which stand in relation to the Court as both clients and masters. These interest groups exert pressures on the nominees, members, and decisions of the Court. This complex array of interacting entities forms the context in which all federal courts operate.

As much as possible, I have favored the narrative sequence, moving from the trial and execution of Julius and Ethel Rosenberg at the start of the 1950s to the storm over President Reagan's attempts in 1987 to fill the seat vacated by Justice Lewis Powell. Most of the writings that follow first appeared as newspaper columns. Often I wrote from texts of the decisions supplied by my friends on the Court, who were writing them. Not infrequently they told me when they felt I had misstated their positions or guessed wrongly about their reasoning and motivations.

While I could have provided a neater, more continuous, more "detached" account, such an account would miss the immediacy that came from writing about the Courts, justices, and cases at the point when they made their entrance into constitutional history, *currente calamo,* in the thick of the swirling currents of life.

15

The Vinson Regime, Caught in Midpassage

The following piece, "The Tragedy of the Rosenbergs," narrates a moving personal experience that raised some questions about the impact of the American justice system on the cold war and the claims the two world powers and their systems made upon the commitment of the young.

The pieces on federal school aid and religious freedom may be read as background for the continuing struggle over the "double wall of separation" between church and state that rages still, even in an era of a strong return to the sacral in the American belief system.

THE TRAGEDY OF THE ROSENBERGS

Ford Madox Ford began *The Good Soldier* with "This is the saddest story I have ever known." I thought I had known many sad stories, but there are few sadder than that of the Rosenbergs, who were sentenced to death last week for espionage.

I have spent the weekend reading a startling book that includes this story. It is factual, 222 pages long, made up mostly of courtroom and official testimony. It is called *Soviet Atomic Espionage* (published by the U.S. Government Printing Office), and it is a report prepared by the staff of the Joint Congressional Committee on Atomic Energy, released today. It is an even more important document than the report on the Canadian atomic spies.

The theme of this book is the tragedy of treason. The report notes with pride that there have been no known breaches of American espionage security since mid-1946, when the law creating the Joint Committee and the Atomic Energy Commission was enacted. But before that there were a number of cases, including the famous ones involving Klaus Fuchs and Allan Nunn May. On the British side there is also an account of the recent flight of Dr. Bruno Pontecorvo, the Italian-born British scientist, to the Iron Curtain countries.

The case that is foremost in our minds now is that of David Greenglass and the Rosenbergs. The testimony in it takes up almost half of the report, pages 50 to 162. The question is: Why did they do it? And, having done it, why have they persisted to the end in denying it?

One possible explanation is the poverty and the slum areas of East Side life in New York. I don't think this is an adequate one, however. For every East Sider who is involved here, there are hundreds of thousands who never transformed the bitterness of poverty and deprivation into treason. You have to invoke something more decisive than the neighborhood environment.

The answer, if I may suggest it, lies in a seemingly crazy paradox. There are some who become spies for money, or out of vanity, megalomania, ambition, or a desire for thrills. But one malady of our time is that there are those who become spies out of idealism.

That, so far as we can judge, was the case with Julius Rosenberg. He came out of the East Side and fought his way through college. His father was religious and patriotic, but the son's rebellion was against the father as well as against society. He was bright and he was tough-willed, and at some point he came to identify his life's meaning with the cause of world communism. In Ethel, he married a girl who, as her mother put it, had "always fought hard for everything." Together they were Communists, and together they spied, and were caught, and now together they face death in another six weeks, evidently with no trace of remorse.

The case of David Greenglass and his wife, Ruth, is different. David is Ethel's young brother, the archetypal Kid Brother who liked to putter with chemistry and was never much of a thinker but who looked up to his sister and worshiped Julius as a hero. Julius used the Kid Brother ruthlessly. He was usable, he was pliable, and, as luck would have it, he was in the army working as a machinist at Los Alamos. What he gave the Russians, especially the drawings and descriptions of a lens mold for the atom bomb, was second in value only to what they got from Klaus Fuchs.

Who can doubt that in the end he did what he had to do? Yet I shouldn't like to be in the shoes of a man who, in trying to make some amends for his treason against his country, has had to send his sister to her death.

Judge Kaufman, too, did what he had to do. The sentence is drastic, yet it is scarcely possible to challenge its justice, especially after reading the detailed testimony in the Atomic Committee document. My real dissent from Judge Kaufman's speech to the accused has to do with his evident belief that the death penalty will deter others like the Rosenbergs from committing similar treason. This is to skim the surface of their action and ignore its deeper sources.

APRIL 9, 1954

I witnessed something on Tuesday night that stirred me both to anger and to compassion. I went to Flatbush, to the meeting held by the so-called Committee to Secure Justice in the Rosenberg case. The meeting was run and dominated by the Communists, and my anger was at the cynicism with which they exploited the emotions of good people for an evil cause. My compassion was for the people who came to the meeting, almost all of them Jewish residents of Brooklyn, not knowing that the Communist clique who ran the meeting cared no more for the Rosenbergs than they had once cared for the Alters and Ehrlichs who had been murdered by the Russian commissars.

The case of the atom spies Julius and Ethel Rosenberg is one of almost unrelieved ugliness and degradation; during the whole Flatbush meeting one listened in vain for a single hard fact that would cast a serious doubt on their guilt. The speakers stressed that those on whose testimony the Rosenbergs were convicted had betrayed the close ties of blood. It is a true fact, and a shattering one. Yet it is a sword that cuts both ways. David Greenglass could not have sent his sister to her doom unless she had involved him in a real conspiracy to steal atomic secrets for the Russians.

Albert Kahn made the collection speech. He read a message from the Rosenbergs, and when he got to the payoff sentences his eyes filled with tears and his words stuck in his throat. A heap of five- and ten-dollar bills, and hundreds of dollar bills, came to the platform, $3,500 worth.

Yet I do not think the primary purpose of the meeting was to milk these people of their greenbacks. The main purpose was to spread the Communist legend that the American government is anti-Semitic.

I am fed up with that legend, and with the efforts of the Communist clique to exploit the fears and sensitivities of American Jews. The note was struck in Rosenberg's letter from prison. "We are as innocent of espionage and treason," he wrote, "as were our six million brothers and sisters who were put to death in the gas chambers of Europe." The same note was repeated in almost every speech. It is time that someone denounced the lie that it is. What has happened to the Rosenbergs had nothing to do with their being Jewish.

The climax of the evening was a speech by a little orthodox rabbi, Meyer Sharff, of Williamsburg. He wore a skullcap and a long black coat with prayer shawl under it and a magnificent growth of beard. He was the prize catch of the cynical men who ran the meeting. He spoke in English with long Hebrew quotations from the holy books. No one could accuse him, he said, of being a Communist — and the crowd laughed. The reason, he explained, was that the Communists in Russia had killed his sixteen-year-old son for being bourgeois — and no one laughed a bit. What seemed to weigh in his mind was that Judge Kaufman, who passed the death sentence on the Rosenbergs, was himself a Jew and inclined to lean backward. I agree that the death penalty was unprecedented and harsh. But I wondered how loudly the Communists would complain even if the judge happened not to be Jewish.

I looked around the room, and what I saw were vultures and victims. The vultures were the half-pint commissars, exploiting the emotions of unsuspecting Jews. The victims were the lower-middle-class men and women, huddled together in anxiety. I keep thinking of the little orthodox rabbi. He seemed to me to be a genuine person, with a religious passion and a sense of kinship with his people. He knew that the Communists hated and destroyed Jewish communities everywhere behind the Iron Curtain. Why did he let himself be used by them?

I think it was because he had dwelt so long on the memory of the centuries of abuse his people had suffered. Even in a free America, it is a hard thing to erase their memory. That is why it is so unforgivable for the Communists to keep spreading the lie about the Rosenberg case. It is an insult to the overwhelming number of American Jews who hate every form of totalitarianism, and it is a mockery of the millions of Jewish martyrs in Europe.

JUNE 19, 1952

The last-minute appeals of the Rosenbergs to the courts have been dramatic, but there is every sign that they will be futile. The same goes for the clemency appeal to President Eisenhower. There will be no more doors for the Rosenbergs to knock at. This looks more and more like the last mile for them.

I expect to be at Ossining Thursday night, reporting on the execution. I can think of very few tasks I like less. Meanwhile I want to set down here, as honestly as I know how, some thoughts on the eve of the execution.

I don't see how anyone can have strong doubts about the essential guilt of the convicted pair. Communists in every country have spread the story that there was no evidence against them. That is not true. There was strong evidence of their recruiting David Greenglass for spying, evidence of the recognition signal for the meeting with Harry Gold, evidence of the plan for flight.

The argument that Greenglass lied to save his skin seems weak. He could save his skin better by telling the truth. Moreover, the truth could never backfire on him, while the lies might.

The most powerful criticism of the government's case is that of the atomic scientist Harold Urey. He says that Greenglass could not have known enough to submit the plans for the atom bomb to his fellow spies. He had neither the education nor the training for it, nor was he in a position to gather together the many complicated pieces that formed a picture of the bomb.

This does not mean that Greenglass and the Rosenbergs were not spies. It means that the crime of the Rosenbergs is not as stupendous in its consequences as Judge Kaufman thought, and does not merit the death sentence. In fact, it undercuts the whole basis on which Judge Kaufman meted out a death penalty.

As I see it, this is not anything that the Supreme Court can do much about. It would be hard to argue that the Rosenbergs have been denied due process of law, or that our judicial system failed to function. There were mistakes in judgment and policy. The greatest mistake in judgment was, I think, Judge Kaufman's. I say this with humility, and with respect for Kaufman's integrity, but the penalty could as easily have been thirty years as death. Given such a penalty, the worldwide Communist campaign to blacken America's image would have been futile. This mistake of judgment was compounded by President Eisenhower's rejection of the first clemency plea. But it is not too late for him to reconsider it. The president seems to feel that the execution will deter other spies. He has only to study Julius and Ethel Rosenberg, read their letters, watch their behavior, to understand that they are Communist fanatics who would never have been deterred from serving their false cause.

I have been reading the *Death House Letters,* which the Rosenberg Committee has published. They have a pathos especially apparent when the father and mother visit their two boys. But they are stilted, mechanical letters that read like *Daily Worker* editorials. And the effort to exploit the boys themselves is yet more evidence that communism dehumanizes its soldiers.

I need scarcely repeat here what I have so often written — that only the Soviet cause will benefit from the execution of the Rosenbergs. They are worth far more to the Russians dead than alive. One of the clergymen who visited President Eisenhower put it well when he said that the case has by now become symbolic, and the symbolism of the execution would be the worst kind. Let us not needlessly risk the good image that world opinion has of us.

I shall go to Sing Sing Thursday night believing that the Rosenbergs are guilty of espionage, despising their behavior as Communist marionettes, yet firmly convinced that they should not be put to death, because the penalty in this case is both unwarranted and stupid. And whatever they did, I shall go with compassion.

JUNE 17, 1953

Julius and Ethel Rosenberg died in the electric chair in Sing Sing Prison just before sundown on Friday evening.

Julius went first. The first jolt of the current was given him at 8:04 P.M., and he was pronounced dead at 8:06:45. Ethel followed him, taking a good deal longer to die, from 8:11:30 to 8:16.

Since sundown was officially at 8:31, the government had beaten the falling of the Jewish Sabbath by fifteen minutes. Few noted the irony that two people who in their life had turned their back on religious faith should have had their death hour shifted because of it. Both died with the same lack of emotion with which they had spent more than two years on death row. Neither of them made any statement before death. Neither one knew which was dying first. There was only one break in their impassivity. It came when Ethel Rosenberg shook hands with her prison matron, Mrs. Helen Evans, then suddenly pulled Mrs. Evans closer and kissed her. Otherwise she endured her ordeal with composure, and with a faint smile on her thin, tight lips.

Both husband and wife died without any departure from their persistent refusal to make any confession. If the death sentence had been imposed in the hope that the Rosenbergs might shrink from leaving their two little sons orphaned, and might break the story of the atomic espionage ring, that hope was cheated.

Death, as Justice Douglas has put it, is irrevocable. We shall now probably never know the whole story of the spy conspiracy, and there are men in the Kremlin who must be breathing more freely today because Julius and Ethel Rosenberg are now forever silent.

I was one of the several dozen newspapermen permitted to enter the administration building to be briefed on the actual execution by the three wire service reporters who witnessed it. I think the briefing was worse than watching the deaths would have been. What we got in the briefing were words, carefully chosen by skilled reporters to evoke images, but the reality of death that might have given dignity to the words was not there. Some of the questions the reporters asked, in their passion for precise detail, only helped to make the whole experience more sickening. I remember especially the reporter who wanted to know the color of the smoke that rose from Ethel Rosenberg's head after the first of the five electric charges it took to kill her. Ethel died very hard — much harder than her husband. Perhaps, despite the stiff, pedantic preachings of his death house letters and his show of toughness, his wife had a greater will to live than he.

I don't think I shall ever forget the half-mile walk from the prison back to town when the long day ended. The people along the road were out on their porches or on the sidewalk, clustered around their cars, listening to the radio, talking and laughing. I heard one child tell another she wished she could have thrown the switch. There were geraniums in the window boxes, trellises of roses, hedges adorned with the paper cups discarded by the press. A pair of lovers walked down the road, laughing and holding hands.

All over the world, millions of people were waiting for the word that some dreaded, others welcomed. Most of them will attack America, forgetting or ignoring the fact that there have been nineteen reviews and appeals in the Rosenberg case, including two clemency appeals to President Eisenhower.

There is no question that there has been due process of law in this case. Nor can there be any question that the Rosenbergs were involved in atomic espionage. The real question is whether the death sentence was either necessary or wise. President Eisenhower, who does care about psychological warfare, ignored in this case the terrible defeat America has suffered in its psychological warfare with the Kremlin. The Rosenbergs are dead, but the propaganda that exploits their death will go on.

JUNE 21, 1953

IS FREEDOM A LUXURY?

The best way to tackle the majority opinions in the case of the eleven Communist leaders (*Dennis v. U.S.*[1]) is to read them while standing on your head. I must report that only the two dissents (Black and Douglas) make sense to me; that the majority opinion (Vinson) is one of the dreariest examples of confusion of thought and betrayal of values in the history of the Court; and that the two concurring justices (Frankfurter and Jackson) come out at the wrong end of the tortuous tunnel into which they have burrowed.

If Chief Justice Vinson had been candid, he would have said quite simply that we're at war, that the Communists are getting what they've got coming to them, and that all the talk of freedom is fiddle-faddle. But Vinson has chosen to use the famous "clear and present danger" doctrine of Justices Holmes and Brandeis to confound the purposes and values for which they stood.[2] He explains the doctrine with so much subtlety that he refines it out of existence. Vinson tells us that Holmes meant "clear and present danger" not as a test for the protection of a real individual and social value, but only as a way of interpreting evidence. Thus he makes the great discovery that Holmes and Brandeis never really meant what we had always thought they did, and what they themselves said they did. The Vinson contribution to the theory of free speech is a distinction between "discussion" and "advocacy." Meaning that if you wear a cap and gown and turn around on a swivel chair, you can discuss Marx and Lenin. However, if you get serious and go out into the marketplace to hawk your ideas, you break the law.

Vinson knows, of course, that the Communist movement in America is pitifully weak, that its bankruptcy has been shown up, that it is ingloriously on the run. It borders on the ridiculous to argue that Communist teaching may lead to an "attempt" at overthrowing the government. Worse, it subverts our concern for freedom to suppress speech now because someday the conditions of danger may exist. As for the argument that the Communist movement includes spies and saboteurs, the answer is that the real spies are rarely card-carrying Communists, and that laws exist to deal adequately with overt acts of espionage and sedition.

The Court's majority seems to be saying that freedom is a luxury we cannot afford in these serious times. But to treat freedom as a luxury is to miss the meaning of the democratic experience. Throwing freedom overboard when the going gets a bit rough is like throwing love and loyalty overboard when a marriage is put to real tests.

Justice Frankfurter, in his concurring opinion, sees this clearly, and he shows how the hunt for dangerous thoughts is bound to destroy the inner meaning of democracy. The trouble with the Frankfurter essay is that after giving all the reasons that the Vinson reasoning is basically wrong, Frankfurter ends by voting with it. Ditto for Justice Jackson.

Behind both these well-intentioned opinions is the premise that Congress may be wrong, but it has the power to punish any speech that it regards as dangerous. But this surrenders to Congress a duty reserved for the courts. If the courts are indeed the guardians of freedom of speech, they cannot plead that Congress's invasion of that freedom is not unconstitutional. If the courts will not protect our civil liberties, who will?

Because Justices Black and Douglas understand this, their opinions cut through the fog of half-truths and doubts in which the other opinions are enveloped. Obviously, meeting the Communist propaganda attack means balancing social values. If you don't believe that freedom is a crucial value, especially in a crisis, you are sunk before you start. Black and Douglas know this, just as they know that the obvious ruthlessness and baseness of Communist propaganda can shake that belief in freedom. Even amid the urgencies of 1951, the values that have stood the Republic in good stead since its beginning do not date. The distinction between speech and an overt act is still the crucial distinction.

It is a sad reflection that this monstrous backward step in the history of American free speech has been taken by a Supreme Court majority largely appointed by a Fair Deal president. Harry Truman assures his visitors these days that he is passionately concerned about the witch-hunt for dangerous thoughts. Yet the four justices he has himself appointed — Vinson, Burton, Minton, and Clark — need conscript only Justice Reed from the Roosevelt Court to form an unfailing majority against freedom. It is a Truman majority.

The wildest irony is that in the context of the struggle with world communism, this is exactly the kind of decision that will undermine our fighting strength. One need only think of how news of the decision will be greeted in Paris, London, Brussels, Oslo, Rome, and New Delhi. The most powerful weapon we have in the competition with the wretched faith of the Communists is the image of a free society. If people of the free world conclude that we are selling our tradition of freedom cheap, at cut-rate prices, because of some fancied sense of security, they will conclude that what you sell cheap you value cheap. And that will be worth more to the Kremlin than the miserable little group of men who are now being sent to prison.

JUNE 6, 1951

I want to turn now to a second and related argument. There are many who feel that a liberal policy on free speech may have made sense in the days of Holmes and Brandeis, during the generation of World War I, but that we are now on the brink of World War III and times have changed. Has the world changed so radically that the old guarantees of freedom have become outdated?

There seems to be a growing, somewhat fashionable view that it is very unchic and unsophisticated to keep your old convictions about freedom. Obviously the generation of 1950 lives in a world that would seem strange to the generation of 1920. Communism is no longer the flaming ideal it was to many then. It has become a cynical organization of power, propaganda, and conspiracy, centered in the Kremlin.

But the dangers of the Bolshevik Revolution were just as vividly felt in the years after 1917 as the dangers of the Kremlin are felt now. In fact, when the Communist idea still seemed the symbol of a dawning new world that would sweep away the ancient injustices, it had a stronger appeal to our young people than it has in these days of cynical ruthlessness. The intervening period has stripped many of the masks and illusions from Communism. And it has shown what can be done in our own country — through an expanding economy and a New Deal — to reaffirm faith in democracy. That is why Communism has met with so stony a response from Americans.

When talking of the difference between the world of 1920 and that of 1950, many Americans are off on the wrong track. They think the important change is the shift in the Communist technique, from exhortation to internal subversion. But no one except Senator McCarthy takes seriously the prospect of Washington falling into Communist hands in our lifetime. That is why the whole discussion of the "clear and present danger" doctrine had such an unreal ring in the *Dennis* case.

There have been two important changes in world communism since 1920: first, the growth in the Kremlin's power and the hardening of the police state under Russian communism; second, and more important, the shift of Russian hopes from internal subversion in highly industrialized countries like America and England to colonial revolution in undeveloped areas.

If I am right about this, the Supreme Court's opinions were arguments in darkness. The way out is not in the piddling negativism of sending a dozen ineffectual and deluded men to jail, but in taking the ideological offensive all over the world against the police-state bleakness of communism. Had the Supreme Court decision reaffirmed our belief in the freedom of advocacy of pernicious ideas, it would have strengthened our hand against communism exactly in those areas where it most needs strengthening. The new conditions of our generation require not a bedraggled retreat from the open society and the open mind but a more militant assertion of their value.

JUNE 7, 1951

FEDERAL AID AND RELIGIOUS FREEDOM

Amid the turmoil of other matters, Americans have made the mistake of almost ignoring a recent Supreme Court decision that deals with issues central to our freedom. It is the case of *Everson v. Board of Education*.[3] By a five-to-four vote, the Court upheld a New Jersey state law (and also similar laws in New York, Massachusetts, Louisiana, Michigan, Indiana, and Illinois) according to which public tax funds can be used to pay for school buses serving parochial schools as well as public schools.

There is no more essential doctrine in the American tradition than the separation of church and state. We have always recognized that this has a double meaning: the state must leave the churches free, but the churches must also be kept from meddling with the state, and especially from using state funds. That doctrine has now been broken, under sufferance from a bare majority of our nation's highest court.

In fairness to Justice Black's majority decision, the doctrine of the separation of state and church is reasserted several times in the strongest terms. But in its reasoning and its conclusion, the decision legalizes an act whose essence is to give church education the support of the state. As Justice Jackson in his dissent wryly comments: "The undertones of the opinion . . . seem utterly discordant with its conclusion. The case which irresistibly comes to mind as the most fitting precedent is that of Julia, who, according to Byron whispered ' "I will ne'er consent" — and consented.' "

At once the deepest and most brilliant treatment of the whole issue is in Justice Rutledge's thirty-five-page dissenting opinion. In the decade since Justice Brandeis's resignation from the Court, I do not recall an opinion that more satisfyingly combined historical thoroughness, legal acumen, logic, and moral passion. "This is not," writes Justice Rutledge, "just a little case over bus fares." I agree.

Americans suffer from too easily forgetting how strenuous and costly was the early struggle to lash down the principle of the separation of church and state. The same year that saw the Declaration of Independence — 1776 — also saw the great Virginia Declaration of Rights, in which James Madison and George Mason joined to assert that religious freedom is not merely to be *tolerated,* but is an *inherent right* of the person. Ten years later, in 1786, Madison led a fight in the Virginia assembly against a bill to tax Virginians for the support of religious education. In his campaign against the bill, he wrote his famous *Remonstrance.* The bill was defeated. Madison then succeeded in getting the assembly to adopt Jefferson's measure banning state support of any church. In 1789, Madison led the fight to add a Bill of Rights to the new United States Constitution. The result is the very first amendment in the present Bill of Rights: "Congress shall make no law respecting an establishment of religion, or prohibiting the free exercise thereof."

Where does "the little case over bus fares" fit into this framework?

There is a new tide rising in American thought that ignores the tradition of Madison and Jefferson, and that is ready to surrender to an uncritical and mystical demand to bring the state back into religion and bring the church back into public education. That movement has two facets. First, it is demanding the introduction of religious teaching in the public schools, under the "released time" program. Second, it is searching around for state subsidies for church schools.

Back in 1925 the epochal Supreme Court decision *Pierce v. Society of Sisters*[4] established the right of the Catholics and other religious sects to maintain their own schools (if they so wish and at their own expense) outside the public school system. That was a weighty decision to make in a democracy founded on the community's stake in public education for all, but it was all to the good in the interests of religious freedom. The question now is whether freedom to run sectarian schools also includes the right to use general tax funds for that purpose.

Does the school bus issue involve the First Amendment, forbidding any "law respecting the establishment of a religion"? I think it does, and this is also strongly the view of the dissenting opinion in the *Everson* case. The purpose of all sectarian education, Justice Rutledge points out, is the propagation of a certain brand of religious belief. The means used are not only teachers, books, classrooms, and school equipment, but also transportation. The transportation is, at least in the rural areas, as essential as the teaching. For the public to pay transportation costs out of taxes is as much a support of sectarian education as it would be for the public to pay the teachers.

Justice Black, however, argues that the support of school business by the township or state is just another public safety issue or welfare measure and that the state must be neutral in applying such measures to children. This is the heart of the majority decision. Justice Rutledge leaves it a shambles. He points out that the purpose of the First Amendment is to *exclude* religion and religious education from the public functions supported by the state. If it is a "public function" to provide religious schools with bus transport, then why not also (he argues) provide them with school lunches, payment for teachers, and everything else? (There is little comfort in Justice Black's assurance that he does not mean to go any further than bus transport, and that this "approaches the verge of the state's power."[5])

It will be a disaster if America yields any further to the drive for state support of religious establishments. As Madison pointed out long ago in his *Remonstrance,* the whole point of separating church and state is to take the question of religious education out of politics. Once it is admitted, sects will compete for state funds, state support, and, eventually, for state power. Religious controversies are fatal to democracy. The only way to avoid them is to maintain a rigid separation of church and state, and especially of church schools and state funds.

There is a double price, as Justice Rutledge points out, that we must pay for religious liberty. One is the immense effort to keep the state from interfering in the way people worship their God. The other is the equally immense effort to keep the churches from using state strength to propagate one particular version of religious truth. Let us not forget that to assure religious freedom in the first sense, we must assure it in the second also. That the road away from one also leads away from the other has been amply shown, not only by the religious despotisms in the Europe of Jefferson's day, but also by the even more terrible despotisms Europe has seen in the twentieth century.

FEBRUARY 20, 1947

The bills now before Congress providing for federal aid for education bring up one of the great questions of our time. It is this: When you give federal subsidies to parochial schools, are you shattering the wall separating church and state in America?

It is too late to argue about the general merits of federal aid for education. The nation has been roused to its importance for at least a decade. But for a decade, federal-aid bills have been drawn up, sent to committee, discussed at hearings — and allowed to die without (except in one year) ever reaching floor debate. Why? Partly because of the "states' rights" cry, and the fear of state and local administrators that a federal bureaucracy would supplant them. Partly because there has never been enough urgency behind an aid-to-public-schools bill to get it over the hurdle of the opposition from the parochial schools. If ever that urgency was felt, it is now. For now, as never before, Americans have come to understand some facts about their school system.

They have come to understand that teachers need higher salaries and schools need better equipment; that the American teacher who makes a decent living will soon be as rare as the bison; that our teaching standards are too low; that a child who grows into an ignorant and intolerant adult is as much a menace to his community as an unquarantined case of smallpox; that federal aid means help and not control, and would not take education away from the localities, any more than the GI Bill has taken education away from the colleges. The big question is no longer, Shall we have federal aid? It has become, What kind of federal aid?

There is a spate of federal-aid bills before both houses. The big differences between these bills may be reduced to three: whether they try to *equalize* the educational differentials between states; how much of a federal program they take on; and finally, what they do about parochial schools.

It is true that dangerous inroads have already been made on the principle of the separation of church and state. The first step was taken when the Supreme Court decided that a religious group could not be compelled to send its children to the public schools, and that it could run its own schools at its own expense. Two values conflicted here: the nation's stake in having a common democratic education for all its children, and the principle of freedom of conscience in education. The latter won.

This should have meant the end, but the inroads have gone further. Every state except one has now allotted "released time" for religious education at public expense.[6] School-lunch subsidies are given to both parochial and public schools. School bus transportation is being provided for out of both state and local tax funds, and in the fateful *Everson* case, the Supreme Court decided this was a constitutionally permissible state action.

For each of these encroachments, a specific reason was somehow found for getting around the general principle. But now the issue goes to the root of the principle, for what the parochial schools (mainly Catholic, but to some extent Protestant) are demanding is that while they keep their schools wholly to themselves, running them so as to indoctrinate their children with a particular religious and political creed, they be allowed to do so at federal expense. They want to share in all the federal aid benefits given to schools run by the whole community.

This demand is breathtaking. For years the strategy has been to whittle away at the principle of separation of church and state. Now with the defenders lulled and confused, the assault is directly on the citadel. Once that is taken, the rest of the city — the city of man, of secular democratic education — will not easily be defended.

What are the arguments used? They all follow the same pattern: the parochial schools are not asking for subsidies as schools, but are asking only that there be no discrimination against Catholic children in the use of public funds. This is an appealing argument, and one hard to resist. I detest anti-Catholicism as I detest anti-Semitism or racism. There is no room in a democracy for discrimination on the basis of religion or color. All must be treated equally.

Yet the argument is none the less fallacious. No one is proposing that Catholic children in the public schools be treated differently from others. That would be monstrous. The real point is that the parochial schools *are not part of the public school system* in a democracy. *They are part of a religious establishment.* To deny public subsidies to church schools is not to deny equality but to insist that the granting of a special privilege should not carry in its wake the commitment to subsidize that privilege.

In a democracy, schools develop civic ideals, transmit cultural heritage, mingle youngsters of every race and religion so that they can learn to live together. When public funds are used, they are used for these purposes. Any religious group that wants to secede from the public school system can do so — at its own expense. It can, if it wishes, transmit not the whole Western cultural heritage, but only that small section of it devoted to certain "absolute truths." It can refuse to expose its children to the community's ideas. But if a church makes this choice, it must stand by it and not expect that the community will both allow the secession to take place, and underwrite it with public money. That is not a demand for equality but a request that the community commit suicide.

Can we in all honesty take any other position? Catholic clerics accuse the Protestant leaders who oppose federal subsidies for parochial schools of being "divisive." That is a curious argument from a group insisting on its right to split off from the general school system, and at the same time keeping up a continuous attack on the "irreligion" and "moral emptiness" of that school system. They point out also that they spend many millions for education, thus decreasing the community's school expenses. True: but they spend those millions on their own decisions, for their own church and educational purposes, not for those of the community.

I sympathize with the plight of the parochial schools. They need more money, just as every school does. With rising costs, they find it hard to compete with the publicly supported nonsectarian schools. They would like to shift part of the burden of cost to the community as a whole.

But that will mean all of us are supporting the schools of a particular religious group. The framers of the Constitution knew that once the government begins to tax people to support a church and its special ideas of sin and salvation and truth, it opens the door for unending religious strife; democratic harmony becomes impossible. The encroachments on that principle have already proven its truth. To demonstrate it further would invite disaster for the religious freedom of all of us — Protestant, Catholic, Jewish, agnostic.

American students, teachers, and schools need help badly. If the parochial schools cannot maintain their present burden, their children are always welcome in the public school system. It would be tragic if the insistence of one church group, however powerful politically, were to prevent a federal-aid bill from being passed.

MAY 10, 1947

THE STEEL SEIZURE CASE: PREDICTING A DECISION

All hunger for theater, and when old John W. Davis gets up in a crowded Supreme Court this afternoon to argue the steel company's case against the presidential seizure, it will be great and historic theater. It is almost like the old days of the New Deal cases, when almost any day the nine judges of the court would be listening to fervent invocations of Magna Charta and King Charles I, and when every expensive lawyer preparing for a big corporation would end his plea in a dark prediction of certain doom for the republic under the presidential dictatorship.

I notice that all are pinning their hopes or fears on the Court's decision: those who expect it to save the republic from Hitlerism or Stalinism, those who expect it to solve all strike threats in crucial industries, those who expect it to bring certainty and order to a troubled world. Even the more intelligent commentators are saying, in effect, "Now we will know just how much power the president has or doesn't have."

Would that it were that easy, but alas, it isn't. Presidential power is a shifting thing. It isn't marked out beyond peradventure, like the path of the constellation. The reason is that American government is not parliamentary government but presidential government. The main axis of power lies with the presidency, which more and more has had to give direction to what might otherwise become chaos or deadlock. That is the effective criticism of Judge Pine's ruling against the government in the steel case: you cannot really talk of limited presidential power in a government in which the crucial leadership has to come from the White House. The presidency is more than an enumeration of powers. It is a set of functions. The real question about a particular presidential act in any crisis is whether the president could have performed his function in that crisis without it.

Every president has had different notions about the extent of his powers. The "strong" presidents, like Jackson and Lincoln, Teddy Roosevelt, Wilson, and FDR, have stretched them as far as they could. The "weak" presidents have preferred to let Congress give direction to the government. Yet even a president like Jefferson, who believed, in principle, that Congress should overshadow the executive, has extended the president's powers — as witness the Barbary War and the Louisiana Purchase. In the case of Lincoln, who was not a dictator at heart, presidential powers went very far in meeting the war emergency. In his treatment of the war governors, in raising a federal army, in the habeas corpus cases, in the Emancipation Proclamation, Lincoln knew that his true judge was to be history.

This will be new ground that the Supreme Court will be exploring. You can't decide what power the president has in the steel crisis by quoting Andrew Johnson or Theodore Roosevelt. Neither can you decide it by talking of the tyranny of the Stuart kings.

I don't envy the justices their job. The president has one of the hardest jobs in the world. But the nine who sit on the Supreme Court have a hard job too: they must find the arguments to back up how they believe a democracy ought to operate. Just as each president has exercised his powers differently, so each justice brings to the case his whole life experience — and then looks around for precedents.

One fact is clear: it is the Court that will decide, and the president who will listen, because (as Harry Truman has said) he is a constitutional president. This running of the gauntlet of judicial review has not always proven a happy experience in our history. But in the present phase of the world, it is a triumph to know that the president's powers — however great — are subject to the law of the land.

MAY 12, 1952

You can never figure how the Supreme Court will vote on a case by studying the questions the justices throw at the lawyers, but at least they provide a clue. Sometimes the justices indulge in a bit of intellectual fun at the expense of the poor, sweating counsel (like Solicitor General Perlman yesterday), and sometimes at the expense of each other. Sometimes, no matter how clever you think your guesses about them are, they cross you up on decision day.

If the Court decides the constitutional issue of the president's right to seize an industry like the steel industry, it looks now as if the decision will turn on the answers to three questions. First, what test is there to show it is an emergency? Second, has the president exhausted other methods? Third, what is there to determine where the president will stop? These were questions thrown at the solicitor general yesterday.

The most pointed questions seem to come from the liberals, including four of the five Roosevelt appointees — Justices Black, Douglas, Frankfurter, and Jackson.

Black, who belongs to the populist tradition of the South, has been a consistent liberal on both economic and civil liberties issues. If he thought the emergency were real, he would not hesitate to uphold a broad conception of executive power. But he is skeptical of the president, and, given his brilliant experience as Senator, Black's first impulse is to see most issues involving the separation of powers with the eyes of a legislator.

Douglas, too, is suspicious of the president and the group around him. He has spoken out against the fears behind what has been called a national emergency, endangering civil liberties. He is likely to keep asking, as he did yesterday, where the limits to the president's power are.

Justice Frankfurter used to teach law at Harvard, and he still likes to act the professor in the courtroom, peppering the attorneys with a steady stream of caustic, witty, and sometimes involved questions. He gave the solicitor general a bad time yesterday. An expert on procedural matters, Frankfurter likes to avoid deciding broad constitutional issues, holding that the nation is better served if the justices refrain from too many sweeping decisions.

As for Justice Jackson, he is the Bad Boy of the Court and seems to relish the role, taunting his colleagues and pointing out that their opinions make them sound like dolts, nincompoops, and worse. Of the Douglas opinion in the released-time case, he remarked, for example, that it would be more useful to future students of psychiatry than to those of constitutional law. He is a stylist with gaiety and abandon, but he can also be bitter. I think he will cast an acid anti-Truman vote.

Justice Burton can be counted on for the fifth, making a majority. A gentle, inconspicuous Republican, he kept hammering yesterday at the president's failure to use the Taft-Hartley law. As for Justice Reed, who is pedantic and unimaginative, the absence of a clear statute on which to base seizure will probably sway this "swing judge" in the same direction.

Which leaves three judges for the minority — the last three Truman appointees. The leader of the trio, Chief Justice Vinson, is good-natured and politically shrewd, and may yet figure out a strategic way of saving the president from a bad drubbing. The other two, whose opinions have been utterly without distinction, will probably go with Vinson.

MAY 13, 1952

Six of the nine judges of the Supreme Court have written separate opinions justifying slapping down President Truman's steel seizure. I assume that this is not just because of the feverish literary impulse of the prolific brethren, but because of their recognition of the decision's historic importance. They used different routes to arrive at the common view that Harry Truman has blunderingly (though innocently) tried to take hold of a dangerous extension of presidential power.

The anti-Truman and pro–steel company press would do well not to celebrate too hastily. The majority has not denied that the government has the right to seize an industry, or even that the president might do so when Congress has failed to provide for other action. But where Congress has spoken, the Court tells us, even the commander-in-chief has no power except as directed by Congress. The Court has thus grappled directly with the massive issue of the division of constitutional powers in a state of crisis. Here was no occasion for legal coyness, but for a frontal attack. Future presidents will not be grateful to Harry Truman for having raised the issue of the scope of presidential power through a case riddled by irrelevant matters and resting on so shaky a foundation.

The legislative emphasis of Justices Black and Burton found expression in their opinions. So too did Justice Douglas's fear that the power used today against the corporations might be used tomorrow against the unions. Justice Frankfurter, always aware of how complex the task of government is, was swayed by the evidence that Congress had consciously withheld the power of seizure. Justice Jackson went for the jugular when he showed what it could mean if the president had the same power in domestic affairs he already has over foreign policy.

Where I went sadly wrong was on Justice Clark. I thought that he, and not (as it turned out) Justice Reed, would be the third dissenter, along with Justices Vinson and Minton.

Chief Justice Vinson's dissent, upholding the president, was neither fainthearted nor apologetic. It dealt its blows lustily at his colleagues. They had behind them the Jeffersonian fear of swollen executive power. The chief justice, in turn, had behind him the tradition of effective executive action in a crisis, reaching back to the great authors of *The Federalist Papers*. By painting the president as only a temporary trustee of the power of Congress, to keep its legislative intent from being destroyed, Vinson showed strategic skill. But where he was most effective was in his contemptuous rejection of the "messenger-boy concept of the presidency," which sees the president as running to Congress with a message whenever decisive action is needed.

Charles Curtis once called the Supreme Court justices "lions before the throne." The lions have roared, defending the throne of liberty. They have put a bad crimp into the expansion of presidential power, which has been going on since Lincoln. They have elevated Congress to a position of supremacy in the scheme of government that it has not had for a long time. Congress is the new and glittering Golden Boy, for whom the whole creation moves.

JUNE 3, 1952

POLITICIAN IN A ROBE

In Europe they have a word for it, *Grenzemensch,* or "border man" — someone who feels at home in a number of languages, cultures, customs. Chief Justice Fred M. Vinson had a kind of borderman skill and mentality. Coming from Kentucky, he carried with him the authentic flavor of the southern border state. He established a reputation for being middle-of-the-road about everything. This was not out of detachment, but out of canniness. Vinson was less a judge than a first-rate politician.

I say this without wishing to be ungenerous about a deceased public figure. But the fact should be set down that Vinson was neither a great jurist nor a good chief justice. What can be said about him as a judge is that he was the best of the Truman appointees — the fabulous quartet of Vinson, Burton, Minton, and Clark. Truman had many merits, but picking Supreme Court judges was not one of them.

Vinson got the job of chief justice because of the famous feud between Justices Robert Jackson and Hugo Black, which resulted in the incredible Jackson cable from Nuremberg. The man who had been Chief Stabilizer and coordinator of production during the difficult war years was called in to ride herd on the unruly jurists. He tried very hard to get his associates to stop writing so many dissenting and concurring opinions. Further, he tried to cut through judicial wrangles by using his influence to reject many of the cases on which the Court should have heard argument. The result was a greater massacre of the writs of certiorari (requests for hearings) than ever in the Court's history.

But it was no use. The Court may have written fewer opinions, but they were just as scrappily contested among the judges. I never could quite grasp just why Vinson wanted to cut down on judicial opinions, as if you could treat a Supreme Court case as a public relations affair.

To have done his job as chief justice with distinction, Vinson would have needed something of the legal and personal skills Charles Evans Hughes possessed. He didn't have them. The Roosevelt appointees on the Court — Black, Frankfurter, Douglas, Jackson, and Reed — could not be kept in check by a politician, however skillful, who was not also a master legal technician. I once interviewed every member of the Vinson court, and I came away with the conviction that at least five of them knew more law than the chief did.

The story of his rise was just as characteristically American, and as incredible, as those of his friends Truman and Eisenhower. His father was a small-town jailer, and he told me how he grew up in the atmosphere of Kentucky-courthouse politics. He learned to be soft-spoken, and to tell the stories that later used to keep his cronies amused when they were playing cards or talking policy on the presidential yacht. He was a minor-league baseball player before he ran for political office. His passions remained the "three B's" — baseball, bourbon, and bridge.

But it was the war that catapulted him to a succession of high positions. He had the skill for them — until the last one. He had great weight in conference. John Maynard Keynes told me just before his death that in discussions over a British loan, he had found Vinson one of the toughest negotiators with whom he had ever dealt. The British papers even hinted that Vinson's toughness had hastened Keynes's death.

I hope I have not left the impression that he was a small man. He had stature, but it was political, not judicial. His decision in the United Mine Workers case was atrocious law, a political stick with which to beat John L. Lewis. His handling of the Rosenberg case was mainly intended to end, not resolve, that crisis. In the current cases involving Jim Crow schools for Negroes, his objective was to avoid a head-on encounter with the South.

Governor Earl Warren, if he succeeds to the job, will also be a political leader. I wish him well, but I have my fingers crossed about a politician in robes.

SEPTEMBER 9, 1953

16

The Career of the Warren Court

In constitutional scholarship, a court-watcher's assessment of the Warren Court has become the test of where he stands and why. My own view evolved in part because I was writing a syndicated commentary, which meant that my view of the Court was frequently exposed to public view. The essay in this section on Warren's appointment is dated September 30, 1953; my essay on the occasion of Warren's death is dated July 12, 1974. It was a crowded and turbulent stretch in the history of both the Court and the larger culture.

The critical fact is that during its early phase — roughly its first half — the Warren Court was, in personnel and doctrine, an extension of the Roosevelt Court. Its four "stars" were Hugo Black, Felix Frankfurter, William Douglas, and Robert Jackson, all New Deal "liberals," though two of them (Frankfurter and Jackson) were traditionally more centrist than liberal. Three others were Eisenhower appointees — Earl Warren himself, William Brennan, and John Harlan — two of them liberals, Harlan a centrist. President Kennedy's two appointees — Arthur Goldberg and Byron White — completed the Court as it functioned before Kennedy's death.

In my writings on the Warren Court's beginnings, on the Brown *school desegregation case, on the Little Rock episode and southern resistance to it, and on the reapportionment cases (the essay, "One Man, One Vote"), I identified strongly with the Court's majority. I now sense that, doctrinally, I was feeling uneasy about the new philosophy emerging with the reapportionment decisions — about what*

I described with the subtitle, "The Court as Spur, Not Rein." I embraced it in those decisions, as in the school decision, because in the failure of both the states and Congress to act, there was a vacuum that could have caused serious social divisiveness.

But as the Warren Court moved on, in the latter half of its course, after Kennedy's death and with the accession of Lyndon Johnson and his Great Society, I felt increasingly that the "spur" was often constitutionally unjustified. Instead of preventing social divisiveness, it was accelerating it. Hence my assessments of the Court changed. My disagreements were mostly in the areas of affirmative-action quotas and criminal procedures and sanctions.

Whatever my differences with those later decisions, the Warren Court had stature. On the constitutional culture and the popular mind, it left an even sharper image than the Roosevelt Court. The image was politicized to an extent that had not been true since Roosevelt's court-packing plan. I have included some of my pieces here — on Justices Marshall, Goldberg, Fortas, and Douglas, as well as on Warren himself — that deal with the politicizing dimension and set it in perspective.

The later Warren justices made the Court an instrument for dealing with change by judicial policy-making, and thus for shaping the Constitution with no articulated principle of limits. Writing in 1970, at the end of the Warren Court's career, Alexander Bickel was somewhat harsh on its efforts to invent the future for America. "In dealing with problems of great magnitude and pervasive ramifications," he wrote, ". . . judicial supremacy . . . is not possible. . . . It is, in a vast, complex, changeable society, a most unsuitable instrument for the formation of policy." Instead of inventing the future, he suggests, we can "remember the future" by using the full complement of what the American political tradition places at our disposal, rather than the social vision of the Court alone.

Despite Bickel and other critics, and despite the Burger and Rehnquist Courts that followed it, the Warren Court remained the judicial canon during the 1970s and 1980s and still functions as such today. It has retained its glory, and perhaps also its dangers to the organic development of American society.

ENTER, THE WARREN COURT

Earl Warren's appointment as chief justice of the United States is surely one of the most important that President Eisenhower will have made. Here is a man upon whom will descend the mantle of Marshall, Taney, Chase, and Hughes. Is he big enough to wear it well?

My answer is yes. I will not say of Warren what Cardozo said so confidently when the appointment of Charles Evans Hughes was announced in 1930, that it is "a great choice of a great man for a great office." Warren's stature, despite his long years in public office, has never fully been measured. But his record as governor suggests that he will not close his mind to the demands of the great office.

Some will lament the fact that Warren is a political rather than a judicial figure. As I pointed out after Vinson's death, politicians in judicial robes are not the medicine the doctor ordered. Yet this is not a decisive reason to be against Warren. One need not lament the appointment of a strong and able political figure, even to the Supreme Court, but rather the choice of a weak party hack, such as Clark or Minton. Only one of the three great chief justices we have had — Hughes — was primarily a jurist. The other two — Marshall and Taney — were picked because of their political views.

Along with many others, I should have liked to see Associate Justice Robert H. Jackson raised to the chief justiceship, but his chance for the top job was thrown away in his dramatic attack on Justice Black. Were there another federal judge somewhere like Learned Hand — whom both Roosevelt and Truman foolishly passed over — he would have been the inevitable choice. Thus, failing and forsaking all others, the Warren appointment is a logical one.

Warren's abilities for the post are considerable. A chief justice must be a good administrator, and he has shown himself to be one. He must have the capacity to make people work together, especially since four of the seven Democrats left on the court — Black, Frankfurter, Douglas, and Jackson — are men of tough and independent mind. Taft once wrote that the job of a Chief Justice was that of "massing the court," by which he meant holding it in line with some degree of agreement. No one could do it with this Court, but Warren's skill in winning in both party primaries in California shows that he should be able at least to tangle with them.

But all this does not reach to the heart of the matter. The real point is that the Supreme Court, in the coming years, will be tested mainly in the area of civil liberties, which requires a generous spirit and a devotion to the principles of the open society.

Warren has shown his liberalism as a Republican. But, more important, the valiant stand he made in the University of California oath case, where he fought both William Randolph Hearst's regent, Marshall Neylan, and his own reactionary lieutenant governor Knight, showed his belief in civil liberties. If he can maintain this doughtiness, he will rank with the great.

SEPTEMBER 30, 1953

THE CONSTITUTION IS COLOR-BLIND

"An age of storm and tragedy," Winston Churchill called our present era in his Nobel Prize acceptance speech. He was talking of atomic weapons, but "storm and tragedy" were also present in the Supreme Court reargument last week on the school segregation cases. John W. Davis, speaking for the die-hard South Carolina position, ended with an emotional plea for states' rights that made his voice falter and choke; Thurgood Marshall, speaking for the NAACP, told movingly what it meant to be a Negro growing up under segregation.

American race relations have been going through a social revolution without violence. For more than half a century the Negro, who by constitutional amendment had been made a free man and a legal equal to the white man, has had the gates leading to equal opportunity padlocked against him. Now the gates are being broken open. In housing covenants, university education, train service, restaurant facilities, admission to movie houses, access to jobs and public office, equality in the armed services, our generation has witnessed a historic series of legal, political, and social victories, which have been won with relatively little violence. The desegregation of the public schools is the toughest of the battles thus far, but it is also likely to prove the most important one. If this rampart of the caste system is breached, the rest will follow.

I cannot believe that the perplexities of the justices primarily involve the technicalities of constitutional law. The giveaway came when several of the counsel for the southern states asked the Court, should it decide to outlaw Jim Crow in the schools, to allow for a slow transition by leaving it to the local courts to determine the pace. In other words, Jim Crow is in his last agony, but he is trying to win time. And the Supreme Court justices are searching their consciences to decide whether they will kill him "forthwith" or do it by a "gradual adjustment" — that is, by letting him take an unconscionably long time to die.

I don't mean to brush aside the technical legal arguments wholly, especially since I have had occasion in the past to study the art of quoting from dead law cases to shape the future or to prevent it. John W. Davis, who has put his great ability in the service of an unworthy cause, made a strong legal case for "separate but equal" Negro schools as fulfilling the meaning of the "equal protection of the laws" guaranteed to white and black alike by the Fourteenth Amendment. He points out with some force that it is hard to know what was the exact "intent" of the congressional framers of the Fourteenth Amendment on the question of Negro children in public schools. His strongest argument is that if you look not at what Congress intended, but at what it did, you will find that it went on to establish segregated schools in the District of Columbia as late as the 1880s.

But the broad intent of the amendment was to give Negroes the same first-class citizenship that whites have, with the same legal protection and the same standing before the law. The Supreme Court has itself recognized this in a series of cases in the last decade. As Thurgood Marshall put it, the issue is whether the southern states and the school districts shall be allowed to substitute their own mores for the rights that the Negroes have under the Constitution.

The justices know that the mixing of white and Negro children seems to many southerners a defilement of the "purity" of the white children. They also know that the Court has the legal power to put an end to segregation in the schools. But they have a right to ask why Congress has not itself acted to carry through the revolution that has been in process, and why the burden must rest on the nine men who are not even elected.

The answer is that neither the Democrats nor the Republicans — both of whom are wooing the southern tories — have shown the political courage to push a bill through Congress that would express how the overwhelming majority of Americans feel about equality for Negroes. The answer is also that, throughout the whole silent revolution, the courts have had to lead the way, and even southern public opinion has followed. The highest judges of the land will be unable to face their own conscience if they falter now at the last and crucial step.

Justice Jackson fears this will mean a "generation of litigation." Even if this proves true, it would be preferable to another generation of injustice — of scars on the hearts of the Negroes and on the conscience of the whites. Southern governors speak of evading the Constitution by making the public schools "private," but the courts would rule this unconstitutional. The real question is whether the South will accept the future with grace.

DECEMBER 13, 1953

The rebel southerners, making a last-ditch stand against racial equality in education, are calling the Supreme Court school decision in *Brown v. Board of Education* a "political" decision because it overrules the precedents.[1] It is true that the Court has now explicitly wiped out the "separate but equal" doctrine of *Plessy v. Ferguson*. But that doctrine was never a constitutional principle. Anyone who has studied its history knows that it was one of those dodges and devices a democracy often uses to tide itself over in a time of troubles.

By the time of the *Plessy* case, in 1896, the South had passed through thirty years of bitterness over its defeat in the Civil War. On the one hand, there was the Fourteenth Amendment, with its guarantee to the Negroes of "equal protection of the laws." On the other hand, there were state segregation laws and the whole institution of "white supremacy," based on the memory of those thirty years. And so the Court evolved the "doctrine" of "separate but equal" facilities for both races. In practice they were separate and unequal. The doctrine was intended as a mask to hide the ugliness of inequality.

This tricky political stratagem — always opportunist, never honest — has long outlived any decent usefulness. In a world of hydrogen energy, in a military setup where black and white alike share in a democracy of death, in a culture where access to schooling has become the portal to a full life, the *Plessy* doctrine had become a shabby hypocrisy. It was time the Supreme Court swept it away.

The real constitutional principle at stake has always been the "equal protection of the laws." That is why *Brown v. Board of Education* is a historic decision. It was read by Chief Justice Warren for a unanimous court. It is brief, almost stark in its simplicity, with scarcely a memorable or flashing phrase, as if the Court recognized that this moment of sober justice was no occasion for verbal adornments.

For some years the Court has been stalking the doctrine of "separate but equal" facilities. Now it has finally destroyed it, vindicating the great dissent of Justice Harlan in the *Plessy* case, when he wrote that "our Constitution is color-blind, and neither knows nor tolerates classes among citizens." Lincoln once said that "nothing is ever settled until it is settled right." The Court has now settled the issue right.

I want to note how great an influence the social-science studies in our universities had on the final decision. The work of many students of American civilization helped shape currents of opinion that scarcely existed a generation ago. Very much as Justice Louis D. Brandeis used to lean heavily on economics research and labor statistics, so the judges here have used studies by psychologists and psychiatrists showing that segregation has taken a heavy psychic toll from the Negro children.

The mark it has left on the children is the mark of the outsider. Children need to feel that they are wanted and accepted. They like to wear the badges of belonging. They have been made to feel unwanted, unequal, and unused. Feeling inferior and unworthy, they have turned often in frustration against whites and in self-hatred against themselves. By denying them equal schooling, we have denied them the life chances that ought to be open to all. By putting on them the mark of Cain's victim we have committed the ultimate crime in any democracy, which is the crime against children.

That is why I cannot take too seriously the Wailing Wall at which the southern racists are now uttering lamentations and shouting threats. There will be a difficult period of changeover for the schools, but a decade from now it will read like ancient history. Using the triple weapons of law, economics, and conscience, Negro and white leaders together are moving toward inevitable victory. A wind is rising and the waters flow, and as they flow they erase the old landmarks of oppression for the Negro and shame for the white.

MAY 19, 1954

SCARS ARE FOR THE YOUNG:
LITTLE ROCK AND THE SILENT SOUTH

What haunts me about the integration riots in the southern schools is what must be going on in the minds of the children themselves —

the Negro children in the schools of Tennessee, Texas, and the other states, around whom the tides of the race battle are surging. Have you seen their faces in those pictures the papers have been running? There is the one showing a little group of Negro boys about to enter the high school at Clinton, passing a line of jeering white boys. And there is the one of a Negro girl in the classroom, with empty seats around her, a desolate child, target of a battle not of her making.

Writing in *Ebony* about what he would do were he an American Negro, William Faulkner said he would join his fellow Negroes in picking a child — neatly dressed, well behaved — and have him present himself each day at a "white" school. Well, twelve Negro children presented themselves on the first day of school at the Clinton High School — and an avalanche of terror broke loose. Faulkner was counseling persistence, and he was right. But it takes a lot of stamina for the children who have to carry the ball. You can teach children something about the meaning of what they are going to do, but martyrdom has to be made of older and tougher fabric.

What makes it all the more deadly is that, despite the final outcome, what happens inside the minds of these children can never be erased. Nor, for that matter, can it be erased for the white teenagers either, except that the scar in their minds is caused by hating, not by being hated.

What can we say about the riots, except that they are what happens when a match is touched to inflammable material. The match is not, as many southerners seem to think, the Supreme Court decision. That is the conclusion that the segregationists want the nation to draw, but it is not the true one. The actual match is lit by an aspiring young Goebbels from New Jersey, by the head of the Alabama White Citizens Councils, by whoever may be looking for a thrill or a following. To be sure, there was inflammable material in the small towns of Tennessee and Texas, and the Supreme Court decision made it more so. But there is inflammable material in every culture, and in every human heart — if you know how to light it. These particular mobs had hate stored up in them, ready to explode. The troublemakers knew the right catchwords to set off the explosion.

The thing to remember is that neither they nor the rioters can claim to speak for the South. The sheriff of Clinton, the mayor, the volunteers who organized themselves into a protective wall until the state forces could arrive, the judge who issued the integration order, the governor who sent the National Guard, the senators who backed up the move, the U.S. Supreme Court justice from Alabama who denied a plea to set the integration order aside — these too are south-erners, and we in the North should not forget it when we are tempted to despair of social peace and human decency ever coming to the South.

I should have added, as another southerner, the Reverend D. W. Clark, the young Episcopalian minister who had the courage to cry shame at the crowd in Mansfield, Texas. When he spoke of loving thy neighbor, someone shouted, "This ain't a love-thy-neighbor crowd." The voice was right: the principle that has taken over these little towns is the hate-thy-neighbor principle. When the minister spoke of the effigy of a Negro hanging from the school flagpole, and reminded the rioters that man was created in the image of God, he was mocked.

What the young clergyman said remains true. The segregationists have set themselves against the very God these little communities pretend to worship. There need be no bloodshed, provided two things happen. One is we keep the moral issue clear. The second is our leaders exert the force of leadership. Where there is no leadership on an issue as morally clear as this one, the heart of a child perishes.

SEPTEMBER 5, 1956

Every nation has its deep, corrosive issue. For France today it is Algeria; for Italy it is the cancerous poverty and backwardness of the whole southern region; for Spain it is the closed society and the fear of challenging a dictator; for Russia it is the dark night of tyranny over the Hungarian people; for America it is the effort of some southerners to block the growth of the Negro child. It is a futile, doomed effort.

The Little Rock story shows what a fearful human cost this effort involves. When some hate-drunk Alabama Klansmen pick a Negro at random on a Birmingham street, and use a razor blade unspeakably to emasculate him, they are the bestial survivors of a dying old method in racial hatred — that of physical violence. But when an Arkansas governor, who is too educated to use a razor on a man, calls out troops to surround a Negro child, he is as surely doing violence to life.

Governor Orval Faubus has learned somewhere to turn words upside down, to make them mean the opposite of what they normally mean. He speaks of guarding Little Rock from "violence," when no violence existed until his act of calling out the troops set the stage for it. He applies the term "force" to the painfully slow operation of the law in carrying out the Supreme Court decision in the school case. He accuses the federal courts of lawlessness and plants a martyr's crown on his own head.

His whole course has been a mixture of craft and stupidity — craft in seizing for a brief moment the role of leader of an embattled southern resistance movement, stupidity because in the end he can't win. The final word will be said by the same federal-court system that he has tried to turn into an enemy symbol. He is, moreover, tangling with the presidential office as well as with the courts. He ought to know that if it comes to a showdown, any president who failed to back up the courts with his executive power would as surely be a laughingstock as any court system that backed away from applying the law of a nation.

No one denies that states retain rights under federalism, nor that state governors have powers. But there are sharp limits to both the rights and the powers. The grand constitutional principle is that on economic and administrative matters the states have a "police power" to act for the health, safety, and welfare of their people; but on questions that touch the freedom of the people and their equal rights with others, a state governor cannot behave like a princeling.

Unfortunately President Eisenhower was slow and clumsy in his first response to Faubus's gesture of defiance. It seems incredible that he should have chosen just such a moment to point out that the southerners fear the "mongrelization" of their stock, and that you can't legislate a change of heart. Two days later he swung into a clearer and stronger groove, but Faubus had already entrenched himself by then. This was a time when the nation would have benefited from an Andrew Jackson, who knew how to confront a nullification attempt by a state, or from a Harry Truman, who would have used the right salty, crisp, and decisive language.

In this matter of equal schooling opportunities, the function of the local authorities — primarily the school boards — is to apply the Court formula of "all deliberate speed" to their local situation.[2] It is not to countermand the Court orders or nullify the Court's decision. The function of the federal courts and the president, on the other hand, is to express the policy and the conscience of the people on a matter that concerns the whole nation, not just a state or even a region.

How many Negro children will be admitted each year to the school system, and how quickly the changeover will take place, are matters that can be argued locally. But whether a Negro child shall be isolated from the fullness of intellectual and cultural experience that should be available to every American child — that is now beyond argument. It has been settled, and it cannot be unsettled by Faubus or anyone else. Governor Faubus may think that he can stop the court of history, but will find it a bigger job than he — or any other man — can swing.

VENICE, SEPTEMBER 12, 1957

I have been reading the debates about the power of a governor in the face of the federal power — about how to interpret what Justice Holmes once said in the case of *Moyer v. Peabody*[3] as against what Justice Hughes said later in the case of *Sterling v. Constantin*.[4] But constitutional law is also what takes place in the mind of a youngster growing up in America. The true test of our governments, state and federal, is what their acts do to our young people, white and black alike.

How absurd the nullifiers really are is best shown when you look at the picture — reprinted in every European newspaper and weekly — of Dorothy Counts walking down a Charlotte street with a little rabble of jeering, screaming, and spitting children around her. The apparatus of government, civil and military alike, is reduced to a monstrous evil when it permits anyone to strike terror into Dorothy Counts's heart and leave a scar. Government exists, as society exists, to protect children, not to wound them.

I hope we won't pass judgment too easily on Dorothy Counts's parents for giving up the fight and pulling her out of school. She walked straight in that picture, and her pride seemed to sit on her firmly poised head with a quiet grace. But what the picture didn't show was what was happening within.

It takes a great deal of courage, for parents and child alike, to be in the front ranks of the struggle for equal rights in southern schools. There are white children to throw sticks at you, to spit at you, to chant insults. There are adults from the White Citizens Councils to spur on the tormenters. There is cruelty, of course, in every school. The thoughts of youth are not always tender thoughts, nor are its songs always the songs of innocence. But try to imagine what it would be like to send your child off every morning to be battered by the waves of organized hatred.

We sometimes make a mistake in thinking that conflict is wholly destructive. It isn't. For those it doesn't destroy, it can be a creative experience. The night before Elizabeth Eckford went to school, in Little Rock, she read the lines in the Psalms, "The Lord is my light and my salvation; whom shall I fear? The Lord is the strength of my life; of whom shall I be afraid?" Despite her lonely long walk back from the line of the Faubus militia who kept her out of the "white" school, Elizabeth says quietly that she is not going back to the Jim Crow school. She plans to study law. Another of the Little Rock girls will be a schoolteacher, still another a social worker.

Something does come out of this struggle then, as something has always come out of every struggle for freedom. And this is an education in itself, perhaps a better education than the schoolbooks will ever be able to give. The turning point in growing up is when you discover the core of strength within you that survives all hurt. Am I wrong in thinking that a whole young generation of American Negroes is being hardened in this baptism of fire, and will furnish a new and great leadership in the days ahead?

They might perhaps, at another time, have grown up to be just mediocre people. But history has placed them *there*, at a place and time that will give their lives a meaning beyond anything they might otherwise have had. Even a Faubus has his uses.

I do not mean to pass over the young white children in the South. They too pay a high price for the struggle — the price of hate. But there are a few who sit down by the young Negro newcomers in the classroom, and eat with them in the lunchroom, and walk home with them. It takes courage for them, but it is a courage that redeems.

VENICE, SEPTEMBER 23, 1957

ONE MAN, ONE VOTE:
THE COURT AS SPUR, NOT REIN (1962–1964)

I rejoice whenever the dead hand of the past is withdrawn from the throats of the living. In this case the dead hand was the capacity of state legislatures to freeze permanently into place their old scheme of apportionment, which kept the rural districts in control of the state even after the people had moved out of them into the cities and the suburbs.

Tocqueville noted in the 1830s how restless Americans were,

and they have continued to be a people in motion. Yet the ghost towns and spectral villages from which they have moved, numbering their population only in the hundreds or a few thousand, have kept a power greater than the cities and suburbs with their hundreds of thousands and millions.

The rural majorities in the legislatures have held on to their power over the generations partly by ingenious legal-political fictions, such as giving deserted and populous counties the same unit vote, but mainly by the simple fact of sitting where they are and not budging. They are like the tribal chiefs in some West African areas, who pass on their power through "stool families" and a "stool line."

There has been no reapportionment in Tennessee for more than sixty years. The legislative stool kings have sat with their backs turned toward the future. Now the Supreme Court, which for years had feared getting into the picture because of the doctrine of not passing on "political questions," has got up enough nerve to decide that the matter is within its jurisdiction. Why in the name of common sense, legal rights, and elementary political justice should it not be?

If a modern state is to survive, it must have a modern economy — this is usually recognized. But if a modern economy is to survive, it must have a modern political system that gives its citizens equal representation as well as equal rights and opporunities. Twice in our generation the Warren Court has struck a great blow for equality. The first was in the school desegregation case, eight years ago.

The four militant liberals on the Court — Justices Warren, Black, Douglas, and Brennan — managed to bring over Justices Thomas Clark and Potter Stewart to form a majority of six in the apportionment decision. They overruled the long-standing *Colgrove* decision written by Justice Frankfurter.[5] Not surprisingly, Frankfurter is now the dissenter, and Justice Harlan with him.

I respect Justice Frankfurter's learning and the legal passion that flows from his characteristic vision. His feeling is that majorities come and go, but the Supreme Court must continue to guard the people's liberties. This role, he fears, will be impaired if the Court gets mixed up in "their political thicket" of apportionment. For it now has power other than the "sustained public confidence in its moral sanctions."

This view cannot be brushed away. There is always danger that the Supreme Court's prestige will be diminished in the minds of the people. The question is, from what source will the greater danger spring? From action or inaction?

If the Supreme Court had not finally acted in the economic wasteland and legal no-man's-land of the Depression years to sanction the New Deal legislative program, there would have been no Congress, no executive, no judiciary left, and no governmental powers to divide between them. The American political system was in danger of being paralyzed; the dead hand of the past lay upon it, in the form of the Court's refusal to concede that the economic welfare of the nation might be its judicial concern.

The national crisis may not be so tangible today, but it is real enough. The white light of world attention bears down on the American political process: Will it work in a time of challenge from world communism, not only in arms but in welfare — or won't it? The rurally controlled legislatures neglect and ignore all the great problems of city and suburban life, including housing, transport, education. They lie like a massive glacial weight on the lives and hearts of the people, frustrating their hopes.

Justice Frankfurter argues that "there is no judicial remedy for every political mischief," and that only "an aroused, popular conscience that sears the conscience of the people's representatives" can meet it. We must reply by asking how there would have been any chance of arousing that popular conscience except by removing the dead hand of the past. The Court has now done it, and hope is alive.

MARCH 27, 1962

They will be arguing about *Wesberry v. Sanders* in the law schools for a long time. The subdued but nonetheless urgent passion of Justice Hugo Black is evident in every section of his majority opinion in the historic decision, which will in time compel all the states to get a rough numerical equality between their congressional districts. And the bitter eloquence of Justice John Harlan's dissenting opinion is like a cry of despair from the depths of the Supreme Court minority — an agonized cry, because Harlan feels the Court majority is heady with success and doesn't intend to stop.

It would be satisfying if you could call this a duel between the liberals and the reactionaries, but you can't. It is a struggle between two historic types of judicial liberalism.

This decision again seeks out social injustices and inequalities and tries to set them right, over the Holmes-Frankfurter tradition of judicial self-restraint. The latter tradition tries to limit the Court's reforming powers. It says to the activist group, "Tread softly. Don't try to take over the job of the states or of Congress, even if they are doing it badly: it's their problem and the people's, not the Court's."

Although I have mixed feelings about the law and the logic of the decision, I end (as I did in the case of *Baker v. Carr*) on the side of the Black group.

It isn't open-and-shut. Harlan has written a powerful dissent, and its tight reasoning undercuts Black's essay on the historical intent of the founding fathers. Harlan rightly says that you can argue either side of the case from the historical citations, but the Constitution itself (despite Harlan) is also indecisive. The founders hated the English "rotten boroughs" but made no explicit provision for preventing them in America; Congress has certainly — by its actions and inactions — left the relative numerical size of the districts to each state, but the states have failed to act. In this vacuum the Supreme Court now has the right to act.

Harlan is excessive in his assertion that the whole of Congress has now been declared unconstitutional: the reply is that, as each federal suit is brought, the Court will bring each state into line with its present concept of constitutionality.

Where Harlan's argument falls short is in saying that Supreme Court action to correct a fault that Congress has failed to correct "saps the political process." If both the states and Congress fail to protect a man's right to have his vote count equally with others, their failure should not be rewarded by Court inaction as well. Any other view would perpetuate the power of the men who sit in the seats of obstruction.

The question of whether the Republicans or the Democrats will benefit most by the decision is interesting but not important, although my guess is that the more liberal wings of each party (city and suburban) will benefit, as against the more conservative (small-town and rural). The real question is whether the nation as a whole is willing to see democracy paralyzed by the inaction of every branch, which results in perpetrating a system of plural and fractional voting power. Justice Black has a right to quote *The Federalist Papers*, because he is acting in their spirit: if a democracy is to survive, its government must be effective in meeting the great crises. By removing a major roadblock in the way of equal rights, the Court majority is acting to energize American democracy.

FEBRUARY 19, 1964

"Kill all the lawyers," Jack Cade said centuries ago in England. "Impeach the judges" is the cry today of the radical right, especially after the two drastic Supreme Court decisions on the apportionment of state legislatures. Chief Justice Warren, who has been the target of hostility ever since his opinion for a unanimous court in the school desegregation case ten years ago, has shown unremitting courage in writing the majority opinions in the current Alabama and New York cases.

Warren is not a complex man, just as he is not a timid one. When he is convinced of the justice of a case, he goes for it with all the subtlety of a locomotive steaming down a single track toward its terminal point. He has taken the one-man, one-vote principle that the Court used for congressional apportionment in the *Vandiver* case last February and applied it to the state legislatures — not just to one house but to both.

The decision has stunned legal and political circles in Washington, not because it was wrong (everyone agrees that something had to be done about the shocking imbalance in the weight of rural and urban districts in most states) but because it was uncompromising. But to a lover of paradox, there is surely something delightful in the thought that it took a former Republican governor of California, appointed by a Republican president, to head the most revolutionary Supreme Court in American history. It is also a delicious paradox that all the breaking and making of precedents has been an adventure in radical democracy, carried through by a Supreme Court that is itself nondemocratic, subject neither to electoral choice nor electoral defeat.

Is all this, then, as the Court's accusers contend, a case of usurpation of power by the Supreme Court? Only the fanatics will see it thus. The Warren Court has magnificently vindicated the effective functioning of the curious mixture of elements that we call American democracy.

Not being subject to the whims and passions of the people, the federal courts have always been regarded as a brake on those passions. It was always the conservatives who hailed the Supreme Court in this role. And the life tenure of the judges, making them independent of politics, was what made it possible.

This independence still operates to firm up the courage of the judges. What was not expected was that it might make of the Court not a rein but a spur to democracy. Already in the cloture vote on civil rights, Congress has shown a will to follow up on what the

Court began in the school decision. The executive too, in Washington and in every state capital, is bound to be energized by having a more representative legislature to work with.

Can it be, despite all our croakings about the decay of democracy, that we live in a springtime when all three branches of the government will blossom?

JUNE 17, 1964

EPITAPH FOR EARL WARREN AND HIS COURT

I have put this in the form of a catechism to get away from the smog of cant and distortion that surrounds the Supreme Court and its recent changes.

The "new birth of freedom" that Lincoln saw in a vision at Gettysburg was not rhetoric but a political and social imperative. Equality and freedom have had to be renewed in every generation. It happened in the Jeffersonian revolution and again with the Populists, whose revolt bore its fruit under the first Roosevelt and with Wilson, and again with the second Roosevelt.

In our own time this new birth of freedom has been brought about as much by the judiciary as by the chief executives. If I had to fix on one name since Roosevelt to serve as its symbol, I should say Warren.

Barry Goldwater warned President Eisenhower against appointing as chief justice a man who "hadn't practiced law in twenty-five years, had never been a judge, and was a Socialist." But Eisenhower, who wanted to quiet the Supreme Court upheaval already in process, did pick him. Historians may come to regard it as the most important act of his administration. Eisenhower came to regret it. Robert H. Donovan, who wrote from knowledge, said that Eisenhower was furious with himself for ever having allowed Warren anywhere near the Court.

Ike must have thought ruefully of Harry Truman's remark, "Packing the Supreme Court can't be done, because I've tried and it won't work. . . . Whenever you put a man on the Supreme Court he ceases to be your friend." But for Warren it was not a question of friendship or gratitude, but of fulfilling his self-image.

He was neither an innovator nor a judicial scholar. In his first few terms of Court, there was a struggle between Black and Frankfurter to influence him. It was Black who won, and whose judicial activism gave intellectual form to Warren's leadership. But it was Warren himself who, with his genial good nature, wisdom, boldness, integrity, and moral authority, fleshed out that leadership. If Eisenhower had nominated either John Foster Dulles or Tom Dewey (both had first claim on the chief justiceship but refused it), what a difference it would have made in the history of our time.

For a quarter-century, the Court has been engaged in a struggle between the philosophies of "judicial self-restraint" and "judicial activism." The first was the Holmes-Frankfurter tradition, best expressed in Holmes's own salty words to a younger colleague: "About seventy-five years ago I learned that I was not God. And so when the people (through legislation) want to do something I can't find anything in the Constitution forbidding them to do, I say, whether I like it or not, 'Godammit, let 'em do it.' "

The Warren Court has gone beyond this, to an activist philosophy. When something needs doing badly (desegregating schools, protecting the rights of the accused, reapportioning voting districts, guaranteeing freedom of expression, keeping church and state separated) and unconstitutional obstructions stand in the way, the Court must actively remove the obstructions. The Court majority has known this would provoke pain and rage, but it has stood its ground. Warren departs knowing that the Court of the next decade will not undo the work that his Court, for good or ill, has done.

There is in fact only one issue that will decide Earl Warren's place in history — the question of what the Warren Court did for social progress and to the judicial tradition. My own reply is that the social results justified the wrenching of the tradition.

Warren died at a favoring moment. The people who once wished him dead — or at least impeached — are today caught up in another cause, on the other side of a different impeachment drive. There are more who admired him, who mourn him deeply, and who feel that if his high integrity had prevailed in Washington, there would have been no Watergate and no Nixon impeachment drive today.

I talked with him a few times — at the 1948 Republican convention, in the early 1960s at Brandeis University when he dedicated a statue to Justice Brandeis, and several times after Supreme Court hearings. He always struck me as an American primitive. I mean this in the best sense, in that he went back to the roots of the national identity. In the modern American Babylon, he was a prophet of the "civil religion," which Cushing Strout has located at the point where liberty, law, religion, and morality converge.

His story was a sheer triumph of character over the doubts and divisions of American life. To get the nomination for governor of California from both political parties took some doing. To be appointed chief justice by a conservative moderate like President Eisenhower, and then to turn the Supreme Court into a raging engine for social change, also took some doing.

Ike felt, ruefully, that there had been an element of false pretense and betrayal in it, but he was wrong. It was a case not of betrayal but of growth. Judicial independence enabled Warren to spread his wings. As a politician he had waited a lifetime for the chance, on a national level, to turn progress into law. That is what he did as chief justice. He hadn't changed, his medium had, and it gave him his chance to transcend himself.

Certainly he was one of the great chief justices — on a level with Marshall and Hughes in his command of his colleagues' respect and his capacity to give the Court direction. He didn't pretend to be as learned as Frankfurter, nor to have the historical sense of Harlan, nor the legal acumen of his friends Douglas and Brennan, nor the sheer judicial genius of Black. He was not a lawyer's lawyer nor a judge's judge. But he knew where he wanted the Court to go — and he got it there.

Look in the history books for what the Warren Court accomplished in the sixteen years of his leadership — in civil rights, the rights of accused, reapportionment, voting rights, education. There are a number of constitutional lawyers — among them Alexander Bickel, Herbert Wechsler, Phillip Kurland — who felt that the social gains were real and overdue, but that the judicial cost was too high.

Courts always move, though more slowly, with the changes in the social climate. The Warren Court moved ahead on its own, setting an example for the rest of the society.

After Warren's resignation, President Nixon politicized the court even more subjectively and nakedly with his appointments, but in a different way and direction. Thus there have been two departures from judicial neutrality — Warren's and Nixon's. Despite them, or perhaps because they counterbalanced each other, the striking fact is that the authority of the Court has never been so great during this century.

That may prove Warren's most effective answer to his critics, and his best epitaph.

JULY 12, 1974

17

Watergate as Constitutional Crisis

Of all the major events in my experience, Watergate was the one that combined political and constitutional dimensions in the most intricate fashion. The only other one that came close was the New Deal. Thus, some forty years after the New Deal crisis, my thinking focused again on the fateful interaction of the federal courts with the polity and the culture.

Watergate was tragic for the nation. But as it did for many others, it engaged my constitutional thinking to the fullest. My articles followed the unfolding story for fifteen months (April 1973 through July 1974), and I have chosen here a handful that outline the structure of the crisis. I don't exclude the moments of high theater, like the Saturday Night of the Long Knives. But while the clash of constitutional positions allows little scope for embellishment, polemic, or a show of erudition, it is what counts most for me.

The protagonist, Richard Nixon, appears in each scene, sitting characteristically "in the center of the web," trying to "look as if he can . . . distance himself from the storm raging around him." Yet for me the true center of the drama is not Nixon but the judicial process.

The reader will notice, in comparing this commentary with the sustained essays in Part I, that a marked shift has occurred. The legal issues here are rather narrowly focused on presidential power and its limits. Capitalism and judicial supremacy are no longer central strands of analysis. The activist-restraint polarity of earlier constitutional crises seems almost irrelevant.

I locate the crux instead at the point where law touches national self-perception. Finding a way out of the constitutional maze —

224 /

Ariadne's thread — requires all the resources of logic and critical analysis.

Along with the differences between my old and new approaches, I also see the continuities. The nation could not have resolved the Watergate crisis — nor could I have written these essays — without having witnessed and studied earlier crises. The opinion that Warren Burger read for a unanimous Court was as magisterial and (although it still surprised most of us) as inevitable as the Earl Warren opinion in the Brown *school desegregation case. Like its predecessor, it was an act of judicial statesmanship. Unlike its predecessor, it did not have to overrule a line of precedents. In that sense both judicial activism and judicial restraint were joined in a remarkable fusion.*

Resolutions of conflict are ephemeral. It didn't take long for the new procedures brought about by the Watergate conflict to start unraveling. The Ethics in Government Act, passed in the wake of Watergate to make special prosecutors independent of the executive, instead made them dependent on the judiciary, which would also have to pass on their actions, thus running afoul of the clear intent of the Constitution and the "such inferior officers" clause. This has plagued the Rehnquist Court. It may continue to do so. The radical rule of law is a guideline for judging only when Congress and the president have already agreed on a philosophy for governing.

IMMUNITY FROM WHAT?

The thread of Watergate unravels back to the beginnings of the government. In the historic case of *Marbury v. Madison,* in 1803, when a cabinet officer refused to answer questions put to him about that case, the Court's basic position was that he was bound to answer anything about his "ministerial" function, but not about his "confidential" one. This still makes sense, and it applies both to congressional and judicial inquiries.

President Andrew Jackson bridled when the Senate merely passed a resolution of censure against him, and said it was "an imputation on my private as well as my public character." In 1860, when a House committee tried to investigate possible corruption in the executive branch, President Buchanan said he was as independent of Congress as it was of him. In response, Senator John Sherman said he was a Charles I mouthing that "the King can do no wrong."

Is it true that the Constitution does give "this terrible, secret, inquisitorial power," as Buchanan put it, to Congress? Yes, it is. The power of Congress to investigate almost anything has been upheld, but it must do so decently, fairly, without hounding government officials for their views or politics, and without hurting innocent people by trying their case in the press — as happened with the leaks from the Ervin Committee.

What about the confidential relation between the president and his staff? When the questions do in fact involve it, they need not be answered, but those about other matters must be. Otherwise there would be no limits to staff activities under the guise of presidential secrecy.

When President Nixon claims "executive privilege" (it would be better to call it "executive immunity"), he is saying that, unlike other officials, he and his immediate staff are not required to testify before Congress or the courts. Were they required to, his people would not advise him with utter candor.

There is a good deal to this. An American president has more things to do than any official in the world. Increasingly, he has to rely on his staff. Cabinet officers have constituencies and political ambitions of their own, and career civil servants have to survive from president to president.

It was FDR who first discovered the need for a number of direct assistants with no constituency, no political ambitions, and "a passion for anonymity." Nixon has carried much further what FDR had begun.

But if the staff members are accountable only to him, what happens to their accountability to the people as a whole? Their immunity from the ordinary kind of questioning has become part of the unwritten Constitution. Remember that much of our Constitution is unwritten, and all of it must be respected.

But when there is a mystery that needs solving, like Watergate, and some senators and a lone judge are the only ones doing it, then the president can't hide himself or his staff behind immunity. The presidency itself will cease to be credible.

Consider two possibilities. If the questions have to do with Watergate but not the president, the witness can answer with clear conscience and no breach of trust or loyalty. If the questions have to do with Watergate *and* the president, and the witness refuses to answer, we shall have to conclude that the resident is asking for immunity for his own possible complicity.

APRIL 6, 1973

ON IMPEACHING A PRESIDENT

Try this list of names. William Blount, John Pickering, Samuel Chase, James H. Peck, West H. Humphreys, Andrew Johnson, William W. Belknap, Charles Swayne, Robert W. Archbald, George W. English, Harold Louderback, Halsted L. Ritter. Do you recognize them? Andrew Johnson is the giveaway because of the noise his impeachment has made in the American history books. Otherwise they remain in their merited obscurity. They are the twelve men who, from 1797 to 1936, have been impeached by the House and tried by the Senate.

Irving Brant wrote a learned brief on the constitutional history of the twelve cases, mostly to head off the move for impeaching Justice William O. Douglas. It was published last year — *Impeachment: Trials and Errors* (Knopf) — and it should be read in this Watergate year.

People are starting to talk, gingerly, about a Nixon impeachment. Judging from some recent conversations around the country, I find that while most people skirt it still, it hangs in the air, and you feel its brooding presence when they talk about the agony of Watergate.

By the Constitution (Articles I and II) and by later usage, impeachment applies to the president, vice president, federal judges, and other "civil officers of the United States," but excludes senators and representatives. It is meant for "treason, bribery or other high crimes and misdemeanors." Impeachment itself is a kind of indictment passed down by the House of Representatives. At the Senate trial, it requires two-thirds of the Senators present to convict. The penalty is removal from office and disqualification from holding any other federal office. The president can't intervene, since his appointees are the ones who are being tried.

This may sound simple and clear-cut, but few sections of the Constitution have turned out to be as vexing, tangled, and generally unsatisfactory in their application. In most of the twelve historical cases, the partisan spirit of both houses has had a field day.

"The history of impeachment in the United States," Brant writes, "shows all too plainly that the House and Senate, if restrained only by their own sense of self-restraint, can twist 'high crimes and misdemeanors' into an unrestricted power to impeach for any cause."

This doesn't overstate the case. Not that the men the House picked to bring before the Senate had been angelic. Blount was a senator who got messed up with a filibustering expedition; Pickering, a drunken federal judge who swore lustily from the bench; Chase, no drunk but a politically intemperate judge; Peck, another judge who didn't have much judgment; Humphreys, a judge who joined the Confederacy. Belknap was a secretary of war under Ulysses S. Grant who was not averse to making some money out of his appointments. Swayne, Archbald, and English were all judges and all accused of profiting from their jobs. Louderback was accused of letting incompetent receivers collect high fees, and Ritter got caught up in a net of charges about legal fees while on the bench.

Several from among the twelve were removed from office; the rest got off in the tangle of party politics and constitutional confusion. The worst case of all was that of President Andrew Johnson, who became the target of a vendetta by a cabal of senators who hated him for his reconstruction policies and for refusing to go along with theirs. It had nothing to do with any violation of his oath or with high crimes or misdemeanors. He escaped conviction by a single vote.

It is well worth dwelling on this shabby record before we get ourselves into the bramble bush again. It may turn out that President Nixon can be connected, directly and unmistakably, with actual crimes in the Watergate affair. That would put him in a different category from Johnson. It would not be simply a case of congressional disagreement with his policies.

Even then, an impeachment trial before the Senate would rip the nation apart, as the Johnson trial did, if it came to that. My hunch is that Mr. Nixon would be more likely to resign than to go through a Senate trial.

MAY 14, 1973

For a perilous moment President Nixon seemed to teeter on the edge of bypassing the appeals process and simply refusing to comply with U.S. District Judge Sirica's decision on the tapes. He had one precedent for it in White House history — that of Andrew Jackson, who had disliked one of Chief Justice Marshall's decisions that required executive enforcement, and who had said tauntingly, "John Marshall has made his decision: now let him enforce it."

But whoever may have counseled this in the president's legal entourage, Nixon wisely didn't follow it up. It would have meant an even sharper constitutional crisis than exists now, and could have spelled grief for him. He is caught in a constitutional bind. He insists on the one hand (as Jefferson used to) that the courts are coequal with the presidency, which is not subordinate to them. Yet he has also argued that the Ervin Committee inquiry has violated the due-process rights of the people it has damned by introducing hearsay outside the law courts, and that the Senate committee should give way to the legal process.

Nixon cannot have it both ways. If the executive is coequal with the courts, then the Senate is too, and therefore Ervin doesn't have to move to the back of the stage while the courts move to the center of it. But if the Senate has to defer to the judicial process, the executive also has to. That is the president's bind.

Logically he could have chosen the "coequal branches" road, and defied Judge Sirica and the courts to do their worst. But he would have lost whatever standing he has built with public opinion since his press conference. If there is sympathy for Nixon as the victim of the bad old Senator Ervin, that sympathy would melt away if the bad old Nixon told the courts to go to hell.

Whoever else is winning or losing, the courts are coming out of this mess pretty well. There is a basic radicalism to the idea of law in a functioning democracy — radical in the sense that every man must take his chance with the law, that it must treat every man equally, and that no man can be above or beyond it. This is more deeply imbedded in the American mind than any other single political idea. Nixon is wise not to go against it. He, too, must take his chances with the law. He takes his chances, of course, as president, not as you or I. As president he cannot be tried for a crime or misdemeanor unless he has first been impeached. As president, also, even before any impeaching process, he has the right to argue his "coequal" constitutional position. He is doing exactly that when he argues that Judge Sirica's court had no jurisdiction over the Archibald Cox subpoena for the tapes, because the president's powers — by Nixon's definition — include the right to decide on the confidentiality of his own papers, and their relation to national security.

Without giving up this argument, President Nixon has rightly decided to appeal to the next higher court after Sirica's, and doubtless either Nixon or Cox will be making another appeal — to the Supreme Court. By making the appeal, he submits himself, for the purpose of the appeal, to the very jurisdiction he will keep challenging to the end. The Court will have to make the ruling, both about jurisdiction and about the great constitutional issue of how confidential a president's papers are, and to what degree and in what way the confidentiality can be breached by being made subject to the legal process.

Nixon has an able constitutional lawyer in Professor Charles

Wright of the University of Texas, who is planning and arguing his constitutional strategy. He has an able opponent, also, in prosecutor Archibald Cox. Both men are conscious of their historic roles — as is Nixon himself — and of the high issues that the Supreme Court will be deciding.

Every court, as well as every jury, operates in whatever political and intellectual climate happens to prevail at the time. This will be true of the Supreme Court, as well. Judge Sirica was very aware of that, and it may have shaped what he called his "middle way" approach, with an eye to influencing the higher court. Senator Ervin and the members of his committee would do well to be equally aware of the current climate, if what they want is a favorable Supreme Court decision on the tapes.

SEPTEMBER 4, 1973

THE "SATURDAY NIGHT MASSACRE" AND THE HEART OF THE ISSUE

The stormiest president in American history has precipitated the stormiest constitutional crisis by two acts. By firing prosecutor Archibald Cox, Nixon has placed himself in contempt of Congress, scarcely an impeachable offense. But by refusing to either obey or appeal the court order requiring him to surrender his tapes, he has placed himself in contempt of the federal courts — which may well be an impeachable offense.

In moral terms, Nixon broke his pledge, made via Attorney General Elliot Richardson, of complete independence for Cox. Faced with a "compromise plan" for the tapes that undercut his independence, Cox had no moral recourse other than to defy Nixon and be fired. Faced by Cox's cleaving to principle, Richardson had no honorable choice except to resign.

Nixon used both men, then discarded them when they were no longer needed. Morally it was a shabby business, and if there could be impeachment for a president's moral overreaching, Nixon would be a prime target. But that isn't what impeachment is about.

Nor is it about whom you would like to see in the presidency. There are people so fed up with Nixon that they would ride him out of Washington on a rail, and others who believe him more sinned against than sinning. Still others think he is all deviousness and corner-cutting but a strong president, especially in foreign policy.

None of these go to the heart of impeachment. My guess is that Nixon's recent day of brooding at Camp David went beyond his choice of Gerald Ford as vice president. Was he working out his larger game plan? Had he started with the removal of Agnew, and did he then plan the choice of Ford in his place? And then — in the midst of the euphoria over Ford and the anxiety over the Middle East — did he schedule the maneuver of the Stennis compromise that led to ridding himself of the incubus of Cox?

It can't be proved, but anyone who thinks all this beyond Nixon's capacity for planning and maneuvering does scant justice to the web-like mind of a complex president.

Nixon has contrived a double line of political earthworks against impeachment. The Democrats have to ask themselves whether they will give Ford three years to run the country and entrench himself for 1976. If Ford is rejected, the Republicans have to ask themselves if they want Speaker Carl Albert, a Democrat, to succeed as president. It doesn't demean either man to say that their best friends and greatest admirers have not regarded them as being of presidential stature.

Beyond the moral and political realms there is the constitutional one. Congress had better study well the history of impeachment. Professor Alexander Bickel of Yale — an anti-Nixon liberal who argued the Pentagon Papers case for the *New York Times* — warns that an impeachment based on the firing of Cox will be too much like the hapless Andrew Johnson scenario. In the teeth of a special act of Congress, Johnson fired his war secretary.

I don't agree with Bickel, however, when he says there are no constitutional grounds for impeaching Nixon now. There are more grounds for it than there were for the firing of Cox: Nixon's defiance of the court of appeals' ruling on his tapes.

A president has the right to fire one of his officials, even when he is at sword's point with Congress over that official's acting as a witness. Andrew Jackson fired two secretaries of the treasury until he got a third to do his bidding. But when he is himself suspected of criminal complicity and under a court order to surrender important evidence, then he cannot thumb his nose at the court.

The president's reply has two aspects. One is his often-stated position on the confidentiality of presidential papers. The second is his offer, with the consent of Senators Sam Ervin and Howard Baker, to let Senator John Stennis weed out the confidential matters from Watergate matters, and hand over the latter.

The court of appeals had first urged an out-of-court meeting of minds between Cox and Nixon's lawyers. It remains to be seen whether the substitution of Ervin and Baker for Cox, and of Stennis for Judge Sirica, will satisfy either the court of appeals or Sirica. If it doesn't, and if Nixon is still adamant, then Congress will have a good case for exploring an impeachment.

OCTOBER 22, 1973

THE ESSENCE IS THE JUDICIAL PROCESS

The constitutional crisis of the president and presidency has claimed as its victims not only the palace guard in the White House, three attorneys general (one way or another) and a special prosecutor, and the Senate Investigating Committee, but now also the House Judiciary Committee, which declares itself impotent to prepare impeachment proceedings unless it can get the new special prosecutor, Leon Jaworski, to join with it.

Nixon is not averse to using his allies — Senator W. Kerr Scott (R-Pa.) and Vice President Ford — to hint that he could clear himself if he chose. But instead of choosing to calm the tempest, he has chosen to defy it. Nor has Congress, after its holiday, achieved any further clarity of purpose. Largely this is because the people themselves have not. In three states I have visited — Florida, California, and Ohio — I find people are caught between feeling that the president has probably committed impeachable offenses and being hesitant to push him out, because they don't know what would follow. That, too, is a crucial part of the crisis.

There is only one precedent, more than a century old, and everything has changed since then. There is a dangerous energy crisis, a diplomatic crisis, a strong chance of a worldwide depression. There is an untried vice president in the wings, who seems to suggest that the last thing in the world he wants is to have the presidency thrust on him.

The question of timing is fascinating. Up to now it was President Nixon's opponents who counseled full speed ahead. Now they are unsure. If they wait, the anger and outrage may subside. If they move ahead with impeachment — assuming they can — they run the risk of not being able to drum up the votes in Congress they will need. And in the meantime, what happens to the business of government?

The time element is not the essential element on the question of impeaching or not impeaching. It would be another matter if the president should choose on his own to resign. This would clear the air immeasurably. But his party leaders have not stumbled over themselves to pressure him to resign. Nor is he about to satisfy his opponents by handing them the resignation they hunger for.

If time is not of the essence, what is? My answer is as it has been for some months — the judicial process. The House Judiciary Committee is only now emerging from a slumberous state. It admits that the key to impeachment will be not the committee's files, which hardly exist, but those of Special Prosecutor Jaworski, who seems to know his business.

Jaworski cares about due process. He doesn't refuse the committee the files it wants on the president. However, he also says — and Elliot Richardson backs him up — that this is a grand jury province and that he will only give them up if U.S. District Judge Sirica empowers him to. The next move is Judge Sirica's, as it should be.

I have read some commentators who say that the national interest should override such considerations of judicial due process. Should it? I had thought that the idea of an overriding national interest — under the name of "national security" — was what caused the Watergate mess to start with.

No, let us keep to due process of law, even if it takes us longer to resolve the crisis. It makes a sovereign medicine.

JANUARY 25, 1974

ARGUING AND DECIDING *U.S. V. NIXON*

Hundreds of people lining up overnight to get into the Supreme Court, as if they were a crush of young rock fans: not bad for the stuffy old girl, is it?

They endured the ordeal of waiting, I think, for two reasons. They sense the Court's role as the repository of authority at a time when so many other institutions have lost authority. They also sense that we are in the sharpest constitutional crisis in American history since the Civil War, and that the question of the tapes lies at the heart of the crisis.

Special Prosecutor Jaworski had a hard time with questions from the bench, but he had the better case to present. The president's counsel, James St. Clair, did less floundering, but his case was the less tenable one.

I don't go as far as Raoul Berger in denying that executive privilege ever existed or that it can ever be accorded the presidency, even though it is not mentioned in the Constitution. In the nature of presidential functioning there has to be a measure of secrecy reserved for delicate discussions. But it becomes an absurdity to say that the president alone can decide which conversations or documents he will release, especially when the Watergate matters involve the possible impeachable and criminal guilt of the president himself.

Anything else would be to renounce the accountability of the president, or — what amounts to the same thing — to say that the president must be the judge of his own accountability to the law.

Mr. St. Clair argued that impeachment belongs to Congress, that the Court cannot become involved with it, that any tapes delivered to Prosecutor Jaworski are bound to wind up with the House Judiciary Committee, and that therefore the surrender of the tapes would mean involving the judiciary in the impeachment process. The final judge, he says, of whether the president has made the right decision in withholding the tapes must be not the courts but the people.

He did it well, but it is tortured reasoning. The impeachment power of Congress won't operate effectively unless evidence up to now hidden within the presumably privileged sanctuary of presidential immunity is somehow made available. As for the people, how can they pass judgment on the president's decisions about the tapes unless there is some way that someone other than the president — the prosecutor, the Congress, or a judge — can find out what is on the tapes?

There is a danger that prosecutors and congressional committees might go berserk in their demands for tapes — "insatiable" is St. Clair's term. This has been called the "slippery slope," on which a reasonable release might grow into an uncontrollable one. But it can be avoided by having the tapes or documents handed to the judge — perhaps even to a revolving panel of retired judges — to decide what is relevant.

Some of the Supreme Court justices may well feel that this case is pushing them into playing a political role, by making them settle political questions they have no right to settle. But the time is long past when the Supreme Court should be terrified by political considerations. However political it may be, this one is deeply a constitutional question, and it needs deciding. More is involved than Richard Nixon and his political fate. The nature of constitutional government, the distribution of powers, the accountability of the highest official of the government — all of these are also involved.

St. Clair's argument in his brief — that there is a "special nature" to the presidency — may prove his most important and most vulnerable contention. The positions taken by Nixon's various counsel have all stressed a strict rather than a broad reading of the Constitution. All except this one. St. Clair argues for the broadest possible interpretation of presidential power as being beyond the reach of judicial accountability, because the presidency is the executive branch and therefore has a special nature.

It is a dangerous mystique to invoke and too late in the history of the Constitution, and the presidency, to develop it.

JULY 10, 1974

The Supreme Court has ruled, with commanding authority, that President Nixon will have to obey the law on the tapes — or else. What could be more "definitive" (to use Nixon's own term) than a unanimous court, speaking through its chief justice? The fact that there were no dissenting or even separate concurring opinions, only a single opinion for the whole Court, proves that the judges meant their decision to carry the fullest possible weight.

If Nixon chose not to obey the command of the Court, he would surely and swiftly be impeached and convicted. To prevent this, he could resign. This was the triangle of his options: to obey, to be impeached, to resign.

Nixon wisely chose to obey. What impact the new batch of tapes will have on the House and Senate decisions remains to be seen. Some impact, one must assume. Nixon would scarcely have held out so long on selfless constitutional grounds alone. There must also have been self-interest grounds, because of their content.

The heart of the historic opinion lies in its humbling of the presidency and its assertion of a judicial veto power over the claim of executive privilege. Chief Justice Burger couched his opinion throughout in terms of the demands of "criminal justice."

This was an understandable emphasis, given Burger's known preoccupation with the administrative reform of criminal justice. But beyond this emphasis there was the even more critical act of striking down the claim by a president to an absolute and unlimited control of his papers, tapes, and memoranda.

Wisely or not, the president's counsel, James St. Clair, had put the claim in absolute terms in his argument before the Supreme Court. He drew the line starkly, with no concessions, and he got his answer sharply. He might have fared better had he left some room for compromise and pleaded that the president would hold out only on the marginal and doubtful tapes, and would entrust them to the detached judgment of a judicial panel.

As it worked out, his uncompromising stance seemed an unbending challenge to the judicial supremacy on all questions of law, and the doctrine of executive privilege has come out more badly bruised than might otherwise have been the case.

Whatever their differences, the members of any Supreme Court — and it applies to the Burger Court as well — are likely to sink them when their judicial power is called in question. Hence Burger's repeated reference to *Marbury v. Madison,* in which Chief Justice John Marshall had shrewdly used an unlikely occasion to assert the Court's power of judicial review. *U.S. v. Nixon* rounds out, historically, the process begun by *Marbury v. Madison.*

Thus we have new and creative constitutional law being shaped in the midst of today's great constitutional crisis. The doctrine of the confidentiality of presidential papers and tapes is clearer now than it was: they have no absolute confidentiality, although their secrecy must be preserved when high military and national security grounds can be established. The grounds on which the claim had been made — that without absolute confidentiality no one would advise the president with complete candor — were dismissed as overstated.

As for the separation of powers doctrine, Chief Justice Burger turns it to the Court's advantage by pointing out that the president has the power of vetoing and Congress the power of overriding his veto, but that the courts are entrusted with the supremacy of criminal justice, and neither of the other branches can trench on it.

Chief Justice Warren Burger was wise to recognize the needs of the presidential office, as witness the strict and explicit conditions he laid down to Judge Sirica in regard to sifting the tapes. But to the Nixon–St. Clair argument that the president can be controlled only through impeachment, a political game to be played out between the president and Congress, the Supreme Court's retort is brusque: if the tapes are needed for the process of criminal justice, that is the overriding consideration, game or no game.

Only at a time when the people are so conscious of the swollen powers of the presidency could the Court have taken so unanimous a stand. Whatever its weaknesses, the Supreme Court does respond to the movement of opinion. By doing so it retains its authority.

JULY 26, 1974

THE JUDICIARY COMMITTEE DEBATE: THE NATION, YES

Only a biblical affirmation could express the wave of near euphoria that swept over many Americans as they watched the deliberations, debates, and decisions of the House Judiciary Committee on the impeachment of President Nixon. There was of course a mood of depression and defeat among a minority of watchers. But it didn't dent the prevailing feeling that all was well with Congress, as all was well with the Supreme Court, and that the American constitutional system was working.

The paradox is that the American people were never as sure of the strength of their government as they are today, in the midst of an impeachment process.

It took a major constitutional crisis to make Americans strip themselves of nonessentials, like party, creed, sectionalism, and ethnicity, and get to the core of belief in America's capacity to redress its ills through a deliberate constitutional process. It wasn't easy, for Americans' first reaction to their dawning sense of the full truth of the encroachments on power was a sense of confusion and a loss of confidence.

For many years, from Wilson and Roosevelt through Kennedy, they were taught to believe that the true dangers to their freedom came from the industrial magnates or some military cabal. This was true even under Eisenhower, as witness his warning that the function of the presidency was to protect citizens from the "military-industrial complex." Then suddenly they discovered a danger to freedom in the very citadel of the presidency itself. It shattered their confidence and threatened the authority of Congress and the courts as well as the presidency.

But the courts came through well, their actions rounded out by the impressive, unanimous decision of the Supreme Court on the presidential tapes. Now the TV spectacular of the Judiciary Committee has strengthened the authority of Congress as well. Viewers who had always scorned Congress watched, listened, and were conquered by the obvious preparation of the committee members, the quality of the debate, and the sight of Republicans and southern Democrats crossing party and sectional lines, either because of conscience or because they bowed to the will of the people in their districts.

This was clearly the most important vote that any of the committee members had ever cast, and they rose to the occasion. It made that occasion more than a media event, and promises well for the further use of TV in the rest of the impeachment.

Chairman Peter Rodino, who had come under attack for his presumed loss of detachment, handled himself maturely. Even more impressive was the care that went into the articles of impeachment that were adopted — though some scholars feel that the first article should have been phrased to charge that the president himself authorized and took part in the obstruction of justice.

How can one account for the total performance of the committee? The clearest answer is that the belief in constitutionalism — the respect for the supremacy of the law — is much stronger and more widespread than we had expected. It cuts across all differences. Both conservatives and liberals feel a special relationship to it.

The conservatives fear a power thrust from the revolutionary Left, the liberals from the reactionary Right. But both camps join in feeling that the swollen power of a future presidency may carry such a threat, and that only a scrupulous and forceful constitutionalism can prevent it.

Thus it was a vote that went beyond partisanship. It was the nation — which watched and was watched in the debate — that came through.

JULY 31, 1974

A PRESIDENT'S RIGHT TO HIS PAPERS: A POSTSCRIPT

The Supreme Court decision denying Nixon absolute control over his presidential papers and tapes is the start of a series of adverse court rulings. I can't remember a president who has been, constitutionally, so totally a disgrace.

Three of the decisions will be studied in the law schools for decades — the one on the Pentagon Papers and the doctrine of prior restraint; the 1974 decision ordering Nixon to surrender the tapes subpoenaed by the special prosecutor, which led him to resign; and the current one.

The Supreme Court that is called the Nixon Court, ironically enough, because he appointed four of its nine members, has been a consuming fire, laying waste every plea Nixon has made.

This time, two of Nixon's appointees — Chief Justice Warren Burger and Justice William Rehnquist — made a strong dissenting case against the constitutionality of singling out one president to punish him for his transgressions. This (they said) violated the doctrine that a president is "coequal" with Congress, and could threaten future presidents in their efforts to get candid policy discussion and advice.

But Burger and Rehnquist couldn't find any more takers for this view, not even the other two Nixon appointees, Justices Harry Blackmun and Lewis Powell, who wrote separate opinions but voted with the majority on the central issue.

It was one of those cases that drives constitutional lawyers crazy, where there are almost as many written opinions (six in this case) as there are justices. The major antagonists were Justice William Brennan and Chief Justice Burger, who are at opposite poles on most cases that try a judge's soul.

In this case, Brennan not only brought his usual liberal partner along (Justice Thurgood Marshall) but also the three moderate "swing judges" (Justices Byron White, Potter Stewart, and John Paul Stevens). He had a majority of five right there, and wrote his opinion narrowly enough to keep the moderates with him. That Brennan also netted two of the usual Burger cluster of four judges must have been galling to the chief justice.

Had Brennan tried to argue that there is an overriding public interest in presidential papers, he would have lost his majority. President after president has carted his papers off, housed them in his home state, and decided what would be viewed by whom and how soon. It feeds his ego, perpetuates his memory, gives him a scholarly claque, and pleases the home folk.

Instead, Brennan and the majority held that Congress had the right to pass an act taking control of Nixon's papers and tapes. Nixon had made an agreement with the General Accounting Office, which gave him the right to destroy some of them at some future time. This justified constitutionally the quick response by Congress to head Nixon off. It made him a "legitimate class of one" — a valid special case.

Without at least one of the three judges who wrote concurring opinions, there would have been no majority in the case. All three — Stevens, Blackmun, Powell — argued strongly that the decision must not serve as a precedent for future Congresses with a vendetta against a president. The Stevens opinion is especially important, since he argued that Nixon's resignation and pardon made him a very special "class of one."

Were I on the Court, I would have voted and reasoned as Stevens did, with his warnings about the future. And I would have welcomed Burger's even stronger warning, even while voting on the other side. The chief justice is not primarily a Nixon judge — he is a presidency judge. He doesn't want the power of presidents to be eroded. He overstates his fears, and the Stevens-Blackmun-Powell trio did better on the same point, but there is substance to Burger's view.

You don't have to like what a president does to recognize his constitutional power to do it. Future Congresses and Courts should note this well. Nor do Courts — as Brennan points out — have to like or dislike what a Congress does to recognize its power to do it. This division between personal efforts and constitutional health is the beginning of wisdom in such matters.

Even Justice Brennan would agree that climates count strongly in the deliberations of Courts as well as of presidents and Congresses. Nixon and Congress did what they did in a climate of opinion.

The present Court sits in a different climate and is more conservative on several scores than was the Warren Court. But on issues affecting Nixon, the climate hasn't changed much since 1974, and the seven justices in the majority respond to it.

JULY 1, 1977

18

The Balancing Act of
the Burger Court

The Warren Court was a hard act to follow. The Burger Court couldn't master the interpretive and stylistic talent of its predecessor. Nor did its chief justice have the clear majority that would have enabled him to erase the Warren landmarks by overruling them.

The best Warren Burger could hope for was to arrest the momentum of the Warren Court's activism, and to offer a balancing, countervailing force against it. This he did by raiding the group of "swing justices," which gave him majorities in selected areas such as school busing, criminal procedures, the death penalty, and pornography, when he could count on a surge of anger in the larger culture.

Because the liberal-oriented constitutional culture was hostile to him, Burger never got a fair assessment from it. As Nixon's appointee to fill Earl Warren's seat, he had constantly to prove that he was no right-wing troglodyte. He stood up tolerably in the harsh light focused on him.

In Minnesota, before his Court career, Warren Burger had been a politician, as Earl Warren had been in California. Carrying out a carefully contrived strategy, he distanced himself from some of Justice William Rehnquist's positions on the Right, and showed true independence from Nixon in the Pentagon Papers case and (clinchingly) in the Watergate crisis. He carved out the niche of authority over his brethren that every chief justice must at some point carve. He cut the necessary deals and carried off the necessary maneuvers to exert his influence over who would write the majority decisions — and sometimes the key dissents. With tactical shifts of position, he inched his way closer to the doctrinal center than anyone (including myself) had predicted at the start. He lasted through the Nixon and Carter years and well into Reagan's, and when he resigned to head up the Bicentennial Commission he was no longer the Big Bad Wolf but had almost become a good gray judge.

When Burger became chief justice at the Court, I initially described it with the phrase "Nixon Court" but quickly changed it to "Burger Court." This was a sign that the chief justice had taken command. After the Hughes Court, one spoke of the Roosevelt Court, not the Stone Court, because FDR was so clearly the commanding figure, not only in appointing its justices but also in giving it ideological direction. That was not true in the cases of President Truman, whose chief justice was Fred Vinson, and President Eisenhower, who appointed Earl Warren. Once Warren took his seat, there was never any question whose Court it was. Like FDR, Richard Nixon had strong ideas about his judiciary. Given his number of appointees and the stir made over them, one thought of the Court as his Court. But Burger made it again the chief justice's Court.

The reader may note some shifts in my own assessment of the Court's positioning in the doctrinal spectrum. They were written between June 1972 and August 1974, relatively early in the Burger Court's journey, and they bear witness to the principle of growth in a Court that never became static. As late as 1978, after the Bakke *decision, I still saw it as a "capturable" court.*

I had underestimated the growth and independence of both Justice Blackmun and Justice Powell, who added strength to the "swing" group between the doctrinal camps. But I had no qualms about correcting my estimates after later decisions.

What I missed most in Burger, as I did in Warren, was the play of ideas and the flash of style. As Nixon's prime appointee, the carrier of his ideological heritage, Burger was in a difficult role. His strength was tactical, not doctrinal. He was best at following the barometer of shifting public attitudes, and at using it to strengthen his basic position. That position was primarily one of Frankfurter-Jackson judicial restraint, to which he adhered throughout his tenure as chief justice.

THE NEW COURT

My own reading of the new Burger Court is that it falls into three voting groups. One is the hard-core remnant of the Warren Court, composed of Douglas (an FDR appointee) and Brennan (Eisenhower), with Thurgood Marshall (LBJ) joining them on civil rights and freedoms. The second consists of the two Nixon appointees — Burger and Blackmun — who stick together and are bound to prove a historic tandem, along with Stewart (Eisenhower), who frequently joins them but is capable of surprises.

This leaves a third very loose trio — Black (FDR), Harlan (Eisenhower), and Byron White (JFK). They don't vote as a block: Black is a southern radical on free speech issues; Harlan a Republican liberal whose dominant passion is to protect the sovereignty of the states and their courts; White, a former football star (hence his nickname, "Whizzer"), has little ideology in him. One could call them a swing trio only in the sense that whichever way two of them swing will provide a majority of five — and recently at least two have swung more often than not in the Burger-Blackmun direction.

Burger has been a natural at dismantling what was vulnerable in the Warren Court and consolidating the rest. But as the appointee of a president who was pledged to reverse the Warren decisions — especially in criminal constitutional cases — he has promises to keep, if not literally then symbolically. This keeps him from being quite the kind of unifying chief justice that Hughes and Warren were.

The Warren Court lasted for a generation, 1953 to 1969, extending through the Eisenhower, Kennedy, and Johnson terms. The Warren Court has commanded in three cases: *Brown v. Board of Education* (school desegregation); *Baker v. Carr* (one-man, one-vote apportionment); and *Gideon* (the absolute right to counsel). To *Gideon* we must add *Miranda,* on confessions given without the police first reading a suspect's rights.

Of these three areas, victory has been won beyond redress in the apportionment area. Over desegregation there will still be battles ahead, not only because of a clash of ideologies on the Court but also because leaders outside the Court don't know where they want to go or why. On the rights of the accused, the recent *Harris* decision cut back on *Miranda,* although I can't match Brennan's intensity about the seriousness of the cutback.

Burger would not have been able to get his majorities together — in the *Harris* case, the *James* case on welfare visits, or in the recent conscientious objector case — had the climate of opinion outside the court not changed. The coming decision on women's rights and capital punishment will be largely governed by this climate.

MARCH 29, 1971

THE PENTAGON PAPERS: PRIOR RESTRAINT, EXECUTIVE SECRECY, AND FOREIGN POLICY

By ruling against prior restraint of the publication of the secret Pentagon Papers, the Supreme Court — in an extraordinary set of opinions — reaffirmed a declaration of press independence. Chief Justice Burger felt that the Court had been "almost irresponsibly feverish" about the press cases. My own feeling is that he was wrong. This is one of those "great cases" that made good law, not bad.

In the current climate of widespread disillusionment with both the government and the press, the nation needed some kind of guideline that would delimit the powers of each and restore faith in both. The court weighed two prime national objectives against each other: the right of the people to know and the right of policymakers to keep sensitive matters secret. Six judges decided that prior restraint — blanking the story before publication — is unconstitutional unless the government can make a persuasive case for it on national security grounds. It couldn't.

Thus the First Amendment is given priority in future clashes, and the government is placed on notice that it must carry a heavy burden of factual proof about actual dangers to make prior restraint stick.

The first effect of the ruling will be a flooding of the press with chapters of the Pentagon Papers, on which the *New York Times* no longer has a beat. The second will be a revamping of the overclassified system of classifying confidential government documents.

The best plan still seems to me to be the idea of a cutoff point after three to five years, with a review board of disinterested people — other than the classifiers — ruling on the exceptions. Thus one could make certain that a "top secret" designation doesn't become a self-protective dodge to keep blunders or shenanigans hidden.

Beyond that, the effect will probably be to tighten security inside future administrations, lest similar leaks occur at the hands of disillusioned insiders. The best way to handle that is not by censorship of the press but by picking staffers carefully, and maintaining their morale and their trust. This in turn can be achieved only with greater prudence and greater candor.

An administration that loses credibility with the people will lose credibility with its own staff. Tougher policies won't solve it, because once the cement of trust crumbles, the "leaks" are bound to multiply.

The Nixon-Mitchell decision to ask for a restraining order must look in retrospect — even to the administration officials — like an unwise one. They must have done it as a containment measure, to keep the lid on disclosures beyond this particular set of papers.

The move to indict Daniel Ellsberg was also probably part of the containment strategy. It would have been wiser all around, even politically, for Nixon to say that history is history, that the war decisions were not of his making, that the people deserve to know what happened, and that he would focus on disengaging. But that would have meant a daring and imaginative leap beyond Nixon's habits and personality. Nixon and Mitchell took the more conventional path of bureaucrats, and stumbled.

As for the Supreme Court, it has reestablished its central place. In their questioning of counsel during the arguing of the case, and in their opinions, the judges showed that each is very much an individual. But they are also part of a larger operation, in which they, too — like the press and the administration — must remain credible, if constitutional government is to work.

Presidents make mistakes. Even Jefferson blundered for a while in trying to suppress newspapers for their "torrent of slander." But he regained his balance, and his deepest thinking lay in his querying "whether freedom of discussion, unaided by power, is not sufficient . . . whether a government, conducting itself with zeal and purity, and doing no act which it would be unwilling the whole world would witness, can be written down by falsehood and defamation."

For some years successive presidents have been unwilling for the world to witness the context of the decisions made on the Vietnam War. But the process of resolving the clash between necessary freedom and necessary security has been enabled, with the whole world as witness.

The Pentagon Papers decisions illustrate that the Burger Court is neither radical nor reactionary, but is a centrist court. Its nine members are so intensely individualistic that the prior restraint cases produced nine individual opinions, although six of them added up to a majority court holding.

These opinions should make us discard once and for all the idea that we are in the midst of a Great Repression that is peeling our liberties like a skin off the body politic and leaving it vulnerable to every tyranny. Burke Marshall put it memorably when he said that while there was considerable evidence of "efforts of repression," his feeling was "that the country right now is not repressible, that the repression — to have an effect — requires a mood or an atmosphere or a sort of receptivity toward repression, which doesn't exist in the U.S. today."

To talk of a Mitchell Palmer period of repression in America today misses the crucial fact that in Palmer's day — fifty years ago — the executive, the legislatures, the courts, and most of the public all presented a united repressive front — which simply isn't true today.

The nine judicial opinions, for all their diversity (each judge wanted to have his own opinion inscribed for eternity), fall into three groups. There are those who took an absolute view of the First Amendment — that no security threat, however dangerous, can interfere with press freedom (Black, Douglas, Marshall); those who held that the danger to security would have to be "direct, immediate, irreparable" (Brennan, Stewart, White); and three dissenters (Harlan, Burger, Blackmun) who wanted the cases sent back to the lower federal courts to give them more time to take account of what the executive officers — especially the secretary of state — said might cause death or national harm.

My own feeling is that on most cases, over the long run, the court's groupings are even more complex than this. Whatever group or bloc he falls into, every justice operates in a climate of opinion. At present the wind blows strongly toward freedom of the individual editor's conscience on every matter of national policy and security. The newspapers have said to the president and his staff, "We are as competent as you to decide what is in the national security interest," and while no clear court majority has upheld them (only three judges have; three others have said "watch out for the irreparable harm"), the country's mood seems to run that way.

This individualist mood may fragment society, or it may prove healthy — if in the long run the press takes on the burden of responsibility, and if that forces future administrations to be more candid with the people.

JUNE 23, 1972

BAKKE: QUOTAS AND DIVERSITY IN HIGHER EDUCATION

On October twelfth the Supreme Court judges will have a hot potato on their hands. It is the case of Allan Bakke, who failed to gain admission to the University of California Medical School at Davis, although his scholastic record was stronger than a number of black students who were admitted.

The medical school has a "special admissions" system, which every year allots 16 of its 100 places to minorities. Bakke sued for his constitutional right to equal treatment, and he won his case in the California Supreme Court. Now the nine judges in Washington must finally settle it.

I have just taken part in a conference on constitutional law. Easily the most dramatic discussion centered around the issue of "reverse discrimination." A number of the nation's leading white and black lawyers, constitutional scholars, and high court judges were among the participants, including the deeply respected black federal court judge Constance Baker Motley.

Speaking on the possible effect of the decision on law schools, Terrance Sandelow of the University of Michigan Law School predicted that if the quota system is overturned, the number of black law students in the nation, today at a high of 1,700, would fall to 250. This would be 1 percent of the total enrollment, which was the percentage before the Civil Rights Act in 1964. With a high black crime rate and few black lawyers, it would mean an all-white justice system.

This didn't deter University of Texas professor Lino Graglia's attack on the current system of "racial preference." He stressed that nonwhites graduating from professional schools today have "at least as good a chance" as whites to get placed in the professions, and that lowering the educational standards will help no one.

As for the argument that minority students deserve compensatory treatment because of past racial discrimination, Graglia answered that the burden of this injustice should not be placed on white students by reverse discrimination. The best policy is for schools and governments to be racially neutral.

Dean Louis Pollack of Penn responded to Graglia by raising the question of a time frame for resolving discrimination. He held out hope for a "progressive elimination of caste" only if we continue the affirmative action program. Referring to Justice John M. Harlan's historic comment, that "the Constitution is color-blind," Pollack pleaded that "our society cannot be completely color-blind in the short term if we are to have a color-blind society in the long term."

But how long is the "short term" likely to be? Some have said ten years or possibly a generation. My own guess is that it more likely will require a quarter- or half-century before black students, no longer handicapped by their past, will be able to compete on equal terms with others in professional schools.

Quotas are not a healthy thing in any society. However worthy their purpose, they are socially costly. They carry heavy overtones for the various ethnic and religious groups that experienced them under European tyrannies.

Sandelow and Pollack both argued persuasively that the belief of young blacks in the American system would be undermined by a return to earlier enrollment levels in medical and law schools. But from my conversations, I can testify that among white students the belief in the fairness of the system is now being undercut.

Either way, there will be damage done. As in many constitutional cases, the challenge for the Supreme Court is how to choose the lesser damage and come closest to the central beliefs of the society.

SEPTEMBER 21, 1977

When is a quota not a quota? That was the question thrashed out between the Supreme Court and Archibald Cox, counsel for the University of California in the *Allan Bakke* "reverse discrimination" case. Cox's answer, in effect: a quota is not a quota when it is not a stigma.

The *Bakke* case took two hours to argue before the Supreme Court. Whichever way it is decided, it may take two decades to overcome its divisive consequences. This is one of the "no win" cases in which, whatever side wins, society has to pay a heavy price.

It is the way of a democracy to hang its laundry out to dry in public view, exposed to the angry winds of social passion. To have the Supreme Court make the final policy ruling sometimes cools the emotions, but not always.

The anti-Bakke side was lucky in having Cox there to make his elegant, sophisticated argument in a chamber he knew well. Few constitutional lawyers could have spoken with more authority, though Cox duly made the expected arguments — that blacks need preferred treatment in graduate school admission to compensate for past discrimination, and that their enrollment will be reduced to a "trickle" if the program ends.

But he also gave a new twist to the argument. First, he tried to mute the question of comparative student records by insisting that all the "minority" students admitted were "qualified." What does qualified mean? Simply that they were admitted to fill the sixteen special places reserved for them? That would be begging the question. On the facts of the case, judged by grades and school records, Bakke was better qualified than some who were admitted according to a race-conscious standard.

Cox argued another point subtly. This was no quota system, he said, becauses it didn't "stigmatize" the students as being in some way inferior, as the Jewish quotas had done. It was a quota meant to admit as many of the minority as possible, rather than to keep them out. But Justice John Paul Stevens was quick to point out that the real quota was not the sixteen but the other eighty-four. No stigma attaches to the whites as such, but the practical consequences are the same as if it did.

Cox floundered on the question of numbers in the quotas. If sixteen places out of a hundred are now reserved for nonwhites, how far can this go? Can it go as far as fifty places, or seven more, and still not be "invidious," still not destroy the social purpose it is meant to serve? In the end, Cox had to say yes, it could go as far as fifty. He was caught in his own logic.

Bakke's attorney, Reynold Colvin, arguing his first case before the Court, was not as familiar with the code words that pass for constitutional concepts. When Justice Byron White asked him whether race as a classification is unconstitutional "even if there are compelling interests," he swallowed the trap of "compelling interests" and said yes. Thus he conceded more than he had to, yet remained adamant on the race issue.

Both lawyers were trapped by their own logic, but of the two, Cox's was the more complex. He agreed that there was the danger that the quotas could someday lead to legal "entitlement," assigning a permanent admissions quota to a race in proportion to its population ratio. This would be a body blow to hard work, merit, individual striving.

Possibly the justices will send the case back to the California Supreme Court for more facts, or decide it on narrow grounds, which will offer a face-saving compromise to both sides. If this doesn't happen, and the justices face the issue squarely, my guess is that there will be a blurring of the lines that normally divide the Court into three camps.

The central issue is whether higher education will be organized around individual merit or around categories such as race. Category thinking led America to antiblack racism in the first place.

No one will benefit. Quotas mean rigidifying America at the critical nerve ends of educational growth. When a society grows rigid, it starts to die.

OCTOBER 17, 1977

Landmark Supreme Court decisions sometimes create more problems than they solve. This may possibly prove true of the confusion of separate opinions in the *Bakke* "reverse discrimination" case.

But the prevailing opinion, written by Justice Lewis Powell, is so carefully and ably reasoned that four other judges joined with its central thrust to make it the majority decision.

I can best trace some of its consequences in a series of propositions:

In the case of state programs created by the Equal Protection clause of the Fourteenth Amendment, the burden is on the government to show that a classification based on race is "both constitutionally permissible and substantial, and that its use of the classification is necessary to the accomplishment of its purpose" and that it is "precisely tailored to serve a compelling governmental interest."

In effect the Court ruled against outright admissions quotas in state-supported higher education. All opinions were restricted to education. But the Powell language on numerical quotas was strong enough to make this a case that will influence areas beyond education.

At the same time, there is no outlawing of other kinds of "affirmative action" programs, both in education and elsewhere. Presumably there can be "benign" discrimination as opposed to the kind that leaves a "stigma."

The actual boundaries will be traced out by future Supreme Court decisions. But the millions of people for whom affirmative action has become an important ingredient of their jobs and income need not fear that all is lost. The Supreme Court has ruled against only the excesses of the doctrine that take the form of naked quotas, at least in higher education supported by the state.

The question of a person's ethnic identification — or "race" — can still be counted as part of the equation in admissions. From the standpoint of black leaders, this is a brand saved from the burning. But note how it enters into the total picture — by becoming part of the desirable "diversity" in any total student population.

In the case of medical school admissions, Powell reasons, there are few ways of telling which students would become doctors who would treat minorities. He therefore preferred to base the inclusion of the ethnic factor on the concept of diversity (as in the Harvard College plan) rather than on the delivery of health services.

The Court rejects the familiar argument that reverse discrimination is allowable to redress the past and compensate for historical discriminations.

Finally, Powell rejects the whole concept of ethnic majorities and minorities in American society. The so-called white "majority" is actually composed of many minorities, each of which has had some experience of injustice and discrimination. As for the original WASPs, they are now themselves a minority. It is good to see this rickety construct pushed aside, I hope for good.

An added word about how the Court members voted. There was no clear ideological split. The four Nixon appointees didn't vote as a group. Two of them — Chief Justice Burger and Justice Rehnquist — were part of a group of four that joined in a concurring opinion by Justice Stevens. But both Stevens and Justice Stewart have usually voted as centrists leaning toward liberalism, while the other two have been conservatives.

Note also that of the four dissenting opinions on the liberal side, two were by the hard-core liberals, Justices Brennan and Marshall. But Justice White is a centrist conservative and Justice Blackmun usually votes with Burger.

MAY 10, 1978

EROS DENIED: PORNOGRAPHY AND THE EROTIC

As I read the Supreme Court opinions in the three recent obscenity cases, the majority are decisions permitting the stream of erotic literature to keep flowing, so long as it has any literary pretension and does not wholly lack social value. But they also make an effort to tone down the blatancy with which the stuff is being pushed. By joining the permissive *Fanny Hill* decision with the restrictive *Ralph Ginzburg* decision, Justice Brennan has tried to create a sort of judicial-doctrine double harness: both horses are needed to pull the weight of the new majority holding, and neither can get anywhere without the other.

As it happens, I like the *Fanny Hill* decision and don't like the *Ginzburg* one, but in fairness to Brennan I must add that he has tried to find a way out of the jungle of problems created by pornography and the First Amendment. It probably raises more issues than it settles, and it won't work, but the debate it has started will prove helpful.

Five justices formed the majority in the *Ginzburg* case: Brennan, Warren, Clark, White, and Fortas. Clark came across as a fuddy-duddy in his *Fanny Hill* dissent, and White has been a moderate on most issues, but the other three have fought hard to defend individual freedom in civil liberties cases. It is unfair to accuse them of Grundy-ism or Comstockism. I do charge them with a willingness to make Ginzburg expendable in their effort to distinguish between a marginal publication in a relatively quiet context and one in a shrill, commercial context.

You can see why they tried. In the case of books for relatively serious readers, from *Ulysses* through *Tropic of Cancer* to *The Soft Machine*, there is no longer any way of keeping a book from being published or distributed because of four-letter words and highly erotic scenes. If it has a measure of literary merit, social content, or news value, almost anything can be printed and sold in book form now.

True, there is still not the same freedom in magazines, even in *Playboy*, nor on television, as witness the hullabaloo when Kenneth Tynan used the short, sharp word that fell like a lightning bolt on BBC. Leave it to the studios to protect themselves by running a tape first, from which they can snip off the offending utterance. Nor can you say in a family newspaper what you can say in a book.

Aside from these residual reticences, the dike has broken. In the case of the dirt that gets packaged in the "bondage stuff" and the sadistic and masochistic quickies that infest the racks in drugstores, cigar stores, and liquor stores, the Supreme Court has again cracked down on them in the *Mishkin* case. It is enough to say that they have no literary merit, news value, or social usefulness. But how can you hold back the torrent of marginal books?

Justice Brennan and his colleagues have tried to salvage what is salvageable by scaring off shrill and leering promotion of the bor-derline books. It won't do, because it opens up too many quarrels about what is and is not provocative advertising or cover copy, and it is bound to keep the booksellers in a turmoil of uncertainty. It also won't work because it is simpler and clearer to apply the tests of the *Roth* case and its successors to the book itself as literature. As soon as you probe the motives of the publisher using his method of publicity, you are on shaky ground.

Erotic literature must be allowed, because in life eroticism cannot be cut away from what we think and do, dream and imagine. The only distinction must be between the genuinely erotic and the shabbily pornographic. If Eros is denied in literature, it will be gagged in life, with results far more harmful than some tasteless promotion copy.

MARCH 23, 1964

The liberals have reacted to the Supreme Court smut decisions with almost catatonic shock, the local prosecutors with delight, and most people with a wait-and-see acceptance. For myself, on purely (or impurely) literary grounds I draw a line between the erotic and the pornographic. I want to save the most creative in writing, theater, filmmaking, but I am indifferent to the dreary pornography. If we can't distinguish between them, we ought to throw in the towel as critics.

There are commentators who say they are sickened by smut, but who also attack the Supreme Court for trying to distinguish between the tolerable and the intolerable.

If I thought that the *Miller* and *Paris Theater* decisions left the final definition of pornography to local prosecutors and juries, I should be shocked too. But that is not how I read the decisions. They are loosely phrased and can be interpreted in several ways. Far from closing the door against a rational and workable plan, Chief Justice Burger is seeking one, and has stuck his neck out to do so.

The Burger opinions break new ground on two counts. They move away from the 1966 *Memoirs v. Massachusetts* decision, which held (by a three-judge plurality, not a majority) that an offensive work must be "utterly" without redeeming social value to be pornographic. The new and more sensible test is that it should have "no serious value."

Second, the new decisions allow each state to frame its own statute, following the new guidelines. The sexual conduct proscribed by such a statute must be "specifically defined" and be depicted or described in a "patently offensive way." For all of us who mistrust local censorship, the shocker is that the "trier of fact" (the man the jury has in mind) should be "the average person, applying contemporary community standards."

Clearly the "average person" in some communities will find

books, plays, and films "of prurient interest" and "patently offensive" that others won't. To that extent, smut becomes a kind of local option, much like the local option on the sale of alcohol in some states. But in addition to the "prurient" and "offensive" categories there is a third guideline — that the work has some "serious value," whether literary, scientific, or social.

Here is the rub, and this is where the misreadings and confusions have come in. The "average person's" view of the prurient and offensive is set in the context of his community and will vary with the state and locality. But whether a work has some serious literary or scientific value doesn't vary with states and localities, perhaps not even with nations. The "triers of fact" — that is, the jury — should not have the last word here. The last critical and evaluative word belongs with the critics and scientists. The last judicial word belongs with the Supreme Court.

I fault Chief Justice Burger for not having made this distinction between the first two guidelines and the third clear enough. He does warn of "the ultimate power of appellate courts to conduct an independent review of constitutional claims when necessary." He is saying that if state and lower federal courts get the guidelines wrong, the appeals courts can overrule them.

This is the heart of the protection he offers against whimsical and arbitrary application of the guidelines, but he should have made it clearer that local prosecutors and juries cannot substitute their own esthetic judgment for that of the critics. The critics, and they alone, should be the arbiters of the third guideline, and the courts must try to use those judgments and enforce them.

Justice Burger could have been content with correcting the silly earlier emphasis — and shifted from "utterly" to "serious" — and let it go at that. He would have escaped most of the rotten eggs and tomatoes now being thrown at him. He chose to include the local-option judgment, probably because he felt that hard-core smut couldn't be gotten out of the "adult bookshops" and the "adult theaters" without considerable harassment by local prosecutors.

They are going to have a field day. Some will use it politically to show their antismut muscle; some will go berserk and crack down on works beyond their comprehension — works that will live long after their own wretched sensibilities.

It remains to be seen whether the frenzy of harassment becomes too high a price to pay for Burger's new guidelines. When the dust has settled, we shall still be reading D. H. Lawrence, Henry Miller,

Philip Roth, Norman Mailer, James Baldwin. *Playboy,* too, since its "serious value" has long been established.

Deep Throat will probably become an underground item, and so will most of what its success has spawned. But no one will dare to ban *Last Tango.* The critical audience won't let them, and it is what counts.

JULY 6, 1973

The most treacherous tyranny in any open society may be the tyranny of undefined but powerful words. I say this because, for my sins, I have had to read the 200-page report of the Attorney General's Commission on Pornography — the "Meese Commission," for short.

If I were Edwin Meese III, I would hang my head at a majority report that attaches its folly, rightly or wrongly, to my name.

The commission was misbegotten at its inception, wretchedly chosen and staffed, misplanned, misguided, and basically unresearched. Its public hearings across the nation were less hearings than forums for self-appointed guardians of private morality to get public attention for their repressive sexual and social philosophies.

In its mad rush to judgment, the commission was used as a guided missile by two career antipornography prosecutors — its chairman, Henry H. Hudson, and its staff director, Allen Sears — to recommend a series of wildly punitive law enforcement measures that few true professionals in the field are likely to approve.

One of the more ominous episodes in the commission's short and unhappy history was a threatening letter sent, over the signature of its staff director, to a number of store owners selling *Playboy* and *Penthouse,* citing them as implicated in the sale and distribution of pornography, and in effect daring them to continue. This was an obvious threat of blacklisting, and it led to the craven cancellation of sales, notably by the 7-Eleven convenience stores.

It has also led to several lawsuits against Meese and the commission, including one by *Playboy,* in which the American Booksellers Association and others have joined. If these cases reach the Supreme Court, our right of access to our personal choices in reading materials will be examined more judiciously than the Elmer Gantrys of the Meese Commission and its fanatic witnesses have done.

I hope that congressmen and media commentators who care about this area will read the striking twenty-page minority report by Dr. Judith Becker, a Columbia University psychologist, and Ellen

Levine, editor-in-chief of *Woman's Day*. It is a cool, dispassionate, but devastating document.

It points out that the commission never agreed on defining the key concepts on which its mandate was based. What does "pornography" mean, as distinguished from "obscenity," which the Supreme Court has defined, or from "erotica," which has produced a considerable body of creative literature? What does "degrading" or "exploitative" material mean when applied to sexually explicit drawings or photos of women? What effects, if any, do nonviolent portrayals of sexuality have on deviant or violent behavior among sexual offenders?

Consider two of many choice quotes from the minority report: "The preponderance of existing data indicates that non-violent and non-degrading sexually explicit material does not have a negative effect on adults." And again: "To say that exposure to pornography will cause an individual to commit a sexual crime is simplistic, not supported by the social science data."

This confirms my conviction that the majority pursued their task not only without precise definition but also without adequate research. The crime against the social sciences may have been just as outrageous as the crime against constitutional freedoms. The great waves of change in sexual behavior and relationships roll on, and they create problems. It would be unfortunate if the republic had to rely on the Meese Commission for their solution and its own protection.

JUNE 1, 1986

THANATOS EMBRACED: THE DEATH DECISIONS UNDER WARREN AND BURGER

The revolution in American constitutional law, which the Warren Court has been responsible for, has a deeply humanist philosophy: better that ninety-nine guilty men go free than that one innocent man end up imprisoned or dead. Certainly this is the traditional ethos of the English legal experience from which Americans derived their first principles. Yet my hunch is that the stream of recent court decisions on the death penalty wells up not from abstract legal principle but from a deep identification with the social underdog — so deep, in fact, that it bears some marks of guilt and masochism.

If you look hard at America and England — the two societies that have shown the greatest concern for the accused — you will find they share two traits. One is their tradition of Puritanism; the other is their sense of living in a secure society, where the fabric of law is strong enough to give people the luxury of a protection that leans backward to be fair. Puritanism has left a residue of social guilt that works to the advantage of the accused: without it we would not have had the *Gideon* or *Escobedo* decisions. The sense of security has given us a margin for taking risks with letting some guilty men get away, in order to protect the last innocent man. Hence the Warren Court majority on all these cases.

The trouble is that a countermood is beginning to build up in America — a mood of not-so-quiet desperation about the violence with which people feel themselves surrounded, and the lack of concern the law shows for the victims of that violence.

There is a classic passage by the English criminal theorist, James Fitzjames Stephen, who, as champion of punishment as a form of retributive justice, wrote almost a century ago: "The feeling of hatred and the desire of vengeance are important elements in human nature which ought . . . to be satisfied in a regular public and legal manner." Modern criminologists, of course, reject this as far too bloodthirsty. Yet we had better recognize that a mood of near panic about the treatment of offenders has set in.

This is one reason I hope that the American press will not be too badly hobbled by the new rules governing the discussion of murder cases, even before they go to trial. I am not speaking here of the musty abstraction of "freedom of press," but of the very real and concrete malaise moving across the nation.

Tocqueville, in discussing the American jury system in his *Democracy in America,* felt that for many Americans the jury experience was an experience in weighing and judging human motive, and that it carried over into their public lives, giving them weight and balance as citizens. For most Americans today this weighing of motives comes in newspaper reading. It would be unhealthy to cut that source off too severely.

NOVEMBER 18, 1966

The moral question about capital punishment will not go away. There are about 500 convicted murderers awaiting execution, 70 of them in California alone. No one has been put to death for the past two years, and only three were in the two years preceding. Governors and judges who have to decide on stays of execution are waiting for the Supreme Court to guide them.

There are two constitutional issues before the Court. One is whether a jury system that excludes opponents of capital punishment doesn't result in a built-in bias against the defendant. On the other hand, a policy of admitting them would mean a built-in escape from death, since one holdout juror could always prevent a unanimous first-degree verdict. The other issue is whether the Bill of Rights clause prohibiting "cruel and unusual punishments" doesn't rule out the death sentence. Clearly it was not meant to. Has the intellectual and moral climate changed sufficiently to justify a new interpretation?

Most opponents of the death penalty argue it has no deterrent effect on future murders. I am not moved that way. Deterrence is too difficult to prove either way. In an age of widespread murderousness it is too risky to assume that the death penalty is no deterrent.

More solid ground for abolishing capital punishment is what it does to society's sensibilities when society kills in cold blood. I don't agree with those who say that society must never doom a human life. If you feel that way, how can you morally doom those who may kill more readily because they know they will escape the extreme penalty? No, I see no moral absolutes here. But I do agree that executions have a barbarizing effect on the society as a whole.

On balance I feel we should not rule out the death penalty, but should use it charily, and use clemency and stays of execution generously whenever there are real doubts — as there were, for example, in the Sacco-Vanzetti case. Sirhan Sirhan's defense lawyers labored mightily in his behalf, but I find it hard to share Grant Cooper's near tears about the death verdict. The tears might better have been shed for Robert Kennedy and his family, and for the nation that lost a potentially great leader.

APRIL 28, 1969

Tony Amsterdam became legendary for his crusade to abolish capital punishment. He had a strong hand in winning the decision in *Furman v. Georgia* (408 U.S. 238 [1972]), which toppled the death penalty — at least for a time. The Court's majority reasoning was that death penalties were administered loosely and arbitrarily and thus fell afoul of the Constitution's mandate against "cruel and unusual punishment."

The decision rested at best on shaky grounds, which in the intervening years have become shakier. Chief Justice Burger, dissenting in *Furman,* nailed down the true meaning of the majority (five-to-four) view. If the death penalty is not itself cruel and unusual, but becomes so only because unequally and arbitrarily administered, then the remedy is clear: let the states pass new statutes leaving less up to prosecutor, judge, and jury.

Some have done exactly that. Five cases from southern states — Texas, North Carolina, Georgia, Louisiana, and Florida — have just been argued before the Supreme Court.

Moreover, the climate today is different from what it was several years ago, and in close Supreme Court cases, the social climate counts. A wave of anger over the climbing murder rate, which has risen faster since the *Furman* decision, has been sweeping the nation. It now looms over state legislatures and the Supreme Court itself.

The anti–death penalty cohorts will have a harder time of it now. Justice Douglas is gone. Only Justices Brennan and Marshall remain as the anti–death penalty hard core. Justices Burger, Blackmun, Powell, and Rehnquist are even more strongly entrenched in their propenalty stance. They will need only one vote from among Justices Stewart, White, and Stevens, and they are likely to get it and perhaps even more.

As it happens, I took part in a TV debate on the subject with the Florida attorney general, just before he appeared before the Court to argue for the new Florida law. I knew I was fighting against the national tide. Perhaps that was why I took that side — because it is a faltering but gallant and humane cause, rather than because of any 100 percent conviction on the facts.

I used four major arguments against restoring the death penalty: that we've had it for centuries and it hasn't really deterred murderers; that it is uneven and discriminatory in its operation, especially against blacks and the poor; that it brutalizes the society that applies it; and — most of all — that it is so final.

The weak point of this array of argument is, of course, deterrence. Pro-abolition liberals often make the mistake of ignoring the evidence that now suggests that death as a penalty does, to a substantial degree, deter others from killing. A strong argument for the deterrence view is found in Ernest van dan Haag's powerful and sharply argued book, *Punishing Criminals.*

During the Court argument, Justice Stewart pointed out to Tony Amsterdam that judges have an area of discretion in all penalties, of whatever severity, a discretion that is built into the system. Does that make all sentences "cruel and unusual punishment"? he asked. Wasn't Amsterdam trying to prove too much? No, Amsterdam flung back, "death is different. If it isn't," he added, "we lose the case."

That is, of course, the last battleground — that death is different, because it traumatizes the society that assumes its own right to kill, and because it is so final, so irrevocable.

But here, too, the other side has an answer. Exactly because it is irrevocable, a death sentence deters others while even a life sentence may not, becauses it still leaves a shred of hope.

FOUR YEARS AGO, BY A SHAKY FIVE- TO-FOUR VOTE, THE JUSTICES HELD the death penalty to be unconstitutional because it was "wantonly and freakishly imposed," which made it a "cruel and unusual punishment." But ruling on three redrawn statutes in *Gregg v. Georgia,* it has found the death penalty in itself not inherently unconstitutional and that, where the statutes are well drawn, the penalty is valid.

The condemned men in three states — Georgia, Florida, and Texas — asked for a rehearing to decide whether the particular statutes did in fact meet the Court's criteria. This is what the Court has just turned down.

There may be some rejoicing among a number of state law enforcement officials, but it makes little sense to rejoice about something as grim as death, whether in private or public killings. The hundreds waiting on death row must feel that their fate has been sealed by forces outside their present conduct. Many more people feel that the death penalty differs from others, both in its impact on society and in its sheer finality. They won't rejoice either.

Yet we can't leave it at that. The Court didn't act whimsically. Writing after the 1972 decision against the death penalty, I noted that while Chief Justice Warren Burger was in the minority, he had written the crucial opinion. He pointed out that the majority decision didn't hold the death penalty to be inherently unconstitutional, but only so because it was carried out waywardly. The message he sent to the state legislatures couldn't have been clearer: to revise their statutes and procedure and try the courts again. This they did.

Almost exactly four years later, the Court spoke again. This time it said yes to the death penalty, by a wider margin (seven to two) than its earlier no. This time, even the two "swing" judges who had controlled the earlier majority decision — Justices Stewart and

White — didn't find the new state laws to be either wanton or freakish.

Chief Justice Burger, assigning the writing of the majority opinion to Justice Powell, was in control. He has remained there. Make no mistake about it: this is a Burger Court.

I suggest that we have viewed the death penalty decisions too narrowly, from a legal and constitutional viewpoint. The fact is that each side in the controversy is moved both by a revulsion against one facet of death and a denial of another. The "liberal," antipenalty camp recoils from the brutalizing effect of the penalty, but finds it can live with the brutality of the crimes. The "hard" or propenalty camp recoils from the enormity of the crimes, but finds it can live with the finality of the penalty.

I feel that we need to face both realities and both brutalities — of the crime and of the punishment — and acknowledge the heavy price we pay for what we want. The crucial shift in popular opinion reflects a new belief in the deterrent quality of death as a penalty. It comes from the life experience of ordinary people, but also from recent research studies. The Supreme Court justices, I suspect, are themselves influenced by this shift.

In the long historic debate on the death penalty, the great liberal voices have spoken out against the penalty. The weight of the intellectual community today is also against it, including the law faculties, judges, and most psychologists, psychiatrists, and penologists. My own searing experience was the long, tense wait at the Ossining Prison, along with a group of other reporters, for word that Julius and Ethel Rosenberg had died in the chair.

The abolitionists base their opposition to the death penalty on the argument that human life is sacred, including even that of the most vicious murderer; that there is a finality about death that leaves no room for correcting errors or rehabilitating the criminals; and that an execution degrades society.

It is a strong position, strongly felt. Walter Berns has tried to answer it in a new book called *For Capital Punishment: Crime and the Morality of the Death Penalty.* Berns feels that the life of the victim is just as sacred as that of the murderer. He has little faith in the rehabilitation of most murderers, less in the prison system, and no tolerance for the view that the murderer is a patient and society the criminal. He presents a strong case for death as deterrence against other murders, basing it on the statistical work of Isaac Ehrlich.

But his argument rests mostly on the rock-solid morality of law, holding that the best deterrence is built into the hearts of people by the awesomeness of both the crime of murder and the penalty of death.

It is a powerful argument, put with learning and elegance, not to be easily dismissed as conservative or heartless. Berns is a humanist who believes that the morality distilled in Shakespeare's view of the enormity of Macbeth's crime is better than the one found in Albert Camus's novel, *The Stranger,* about the absurdity of a death penalty in a universe "benignly indifferent" to anything human.

There is irony in the fact that Berns, a deeply religious man, takes his most effective quote from Nietzsche's *Beyond Good and Evil:* "There is a point in the history of society when it becomes so pathologically soft and tender that it sides even with those who harm it, criminals, and does this quite seriously and honestly."

MAY 30, 1979

THE BURGER BRETHREN . . . ALL TOO HUMAN

There are two types of "inside" information in the Bob Woodward–Scott Armstrong book, *The Brethren.* One is how the judges feel about each other, and who does and says what about whom. It doesn't interest me terribly to be told that Justice Brennan regards Chief Justice Burger as a "dummy," and once made an obscene gesture with his finger to describe him, nor that Justice Douglas had a low opinion of Justice Rehnquist, nor that most of his brethren were embarrassed by Douglas's pathetic efforts to hold on to his job after his stroke. These people have lived for years in an unholy group wedlock with each other, and their inevitable irritations are not terribly important.

The other kind of information is more important. I mean the stuff about what happened behind the scenes in the discussions of the capital punishment cases, or those on abortion or busing or pornography, or whatever the gut issues are that divide and plague these human, fallible men.

Sometimes friendships and enmities cross ideological lines, as in the close relationship (in an earlier Court) between Hugo Black and John Harlan, who didn't usually vote on the same side. But the classic occasions of enmity — like the long feud between Black and Robert

Jackson — were as much due to doctrinal as to personal intolerance of each other.

Despite the petty stories the authors tell, no enmities on the Burger court — not even the Brennan-Burger feud — approach the grandeur of the Black-Jackson verbal shoot-out. Brennan probably couldn't be a great chief justice, any more than Burger is. The only member who might have been able to handle it is Justice Lewis Powell, who has the respect of all three groups on the court — Left, Right, and Center.

Clearly Woodward and Armstrong, and the law clerks, stacked the cards against Burger and his conservative colleagues, whom they try to terminate with extreme prejudice. Further, the failure to cite sources as evidence goes against the journalistic as well as the scholarly and legal tradition.

Despite this, the book doesn't detract from the respect one must have for the basic process of judicial review. In fact, the spectacle of the judges — maneuvering, conspiring, bargaining, trading, conniving, forming blocs and alliances, canvasing strategies, weighing legal and social consequences — is a good picture, not a bad one. It shows that the Court is representative of a democracy that is pluralist and tangled in its composition.

The infighting shows that vanities abound. But here are also men who fight hard because they care about the stakes and results. The book rips away the altar vestments and reveals not gods but humans, striving, struggling, caring. Since I didn't expect to find the gods, I am not disillusioned about finding the humans to be all too human.

1974

19

The Rehnquist Court
Enters History

The Rehnquist Court began as a real entity only in 1986, when sitting justice William H. Rehnquist was confirmed as Ronald Reagan's choice for chief justice. President Reagan's first Court appointment five years earlier, Sandra Day O'Connor, had been uneventful: Judge O'Connor was a conservative moderate, and the historic event of her being the first woman named to the Court made her less vulnerable as a choice.

Rehnquist, an outright conservative with a stormy constitutional journey behind him, was hard-pressed at his confirmation hearings on the "character" and "fitness" issues. The political nature of the questioning was scarcely concealed: the confirmation offensive of the mid-1980s had begun. What saved Rehnquist was the fact that Republicans still controlled the Judiciary Committee.

It also saved Antonin Scalia, nominated for Associate Justice, who was just as deeply committed to conservative restraint as Rehnquist. Had either nominee been held over until after the November 1986 elections, the stories of both might have been different, as Robert Bork's was when his turn came.

In its doctrinal groupings, the Rehnquist Court began to take a shape strikingly similar to that of the Burger Court. If anything, Justice Scalia is more uncompromisingly a believer in judicial restraint than even Warren Burger was. While Justice William Brennan was still on the Court he showed an uncanny skill of maneuvering in his ability to reach beyond his natural alliance with Justices Thurgood Marshall and (very often) Harry Blackmun to recruit two or even three of the capturable middle group (John Paul Stevens, Byron White, even O'Connor at times).

In fact, in one of my last brace of essays I raised the question of whether the control of the Court had stayed with Rehnquist or shifted to Justice Brennan. The appointments of Scalia and Anthony Kennedy strengthened Rehnquist's position by bringing two able new justices to the Court. The addition of Justices David Souter and Clarence Thomas strengthened it further. But Thomas's alliance with Justice Scalia on the far libertarian Right of the Court, with its strong base in natural rights and the historical readings of a case, offer the prospect of a challenge to Rehnquist from the doctrinal Right.

In one area, Rehnquist is bound to move in the same direction as Burger — in fighting off the encroachments of the congressional and judicial branches on the executive. This applies especially to the conduct of foreign policy, to the "war powers" issue, and to the "faithful execution of the laws." It goes beyond the "special prosecutor" issue to the broader question of how to give the tormented office of the presidency some maneuvering room in a rapidly changing world.

WHO AUTHORED THE REHNQUIST MEMO? A POSTSCRIPT TO A MYSTERY

During the Senate hearings on Justice William Rehnquist's nomination, there was a to-do over a 1952 memo on the school desegregation cases, initialed by him when he was law clerk to Justice Robert H. Jackson. There was a minor tempest over it, since it argued for reaffirming the separate-but-equal doctrine of *Plessy v. Ferguson*.

Rehnquist's letter to Senator Eastland explained that it was a kind of aide-mémoire for Justice Jackson, summing up Jackson's own views after a discussion with Rehnquist, to use at a conference with his colleagues. P.S.: Rehnquist was confirmed.

All this is ancient history. But working recently on an interpretive article about Jackson, and rereading the memo, I add a footnote to that ancient history.

The memo, as Justice Rehnquist notes in his letter, is not a law clerk's painstaking tracking down of cases and precedents. It is, rather, a quick, glancing statement — less than a thousand words — of a way to interpret the great historic cases on judicial review.

While none of it is new or world-shaking, it does have a caustic irreverence about it, and a sharp cutting edge. As such, it could have been the product of a seasoned ironic mind, like Jackson's, or of a bright young iconoclastic law graduate's, like Rehnquist's — or both.

The memo notes that the post–Civil War decisions of the Supreme Court were efforts to protect business interests against state legislatures, as if — in Justice Holmes's phrase — the Fourteenth Amendment had enacted Herbert Spencer's *Social Statics*. This had rightly come to an end, it says, because the judges were reading their own conservative economic views into the Constitution. In the school desegregation cases the same thing was happening, with a new twist — the judges were reading their liberal sociological views into the Constitution. It notes that this would make the current Court differ from the old McReynolds Court "only in the kinds of litigants it favors" — that is, blacks instead of corporations.

It goes on to argue that you can't create a special situation for minorities and stick to it unless the majority chooses to stick; that 150 years of Court efforts to protect minority rights, "whether those of business, slaveholders, or Jehovah's Witnesses," have always ended the same way; that "one by one the cases . . . have been sloughed off, and crept silently to rest."

Then comes the crashing conclusion — that at the risk of being "excoriated by 'liberal' colleagues . . . I think *Plessy v. Ferguson* was right and should be reaffirmed. If the Fourteenth Amendment did not enact Spencer's *Social Statics,* it just as surely did not enact Myrdal's *American Dilemma.*"

End of memo, and almost end of Rehnquist. That is, if he hadn't added that salvaging letter to Senator Eastland that gave his supporters a chance to save their face and his judicial hopes. Not only was the memo not his own view, he insisted, but he fully supports "the legal reasoning and the rightness of the *Brown* decision."

Senator Birch Bayh unsurprisingly felt that Rehnquist's "candor and veracity" were in question, noting that Jackson was dead and couldn't challenge his former clerk. There is no documentary evidence either way.

My own reconstruction of what probably happened is as follows: the ailing old warrior and his bright young conservative law clerk had a long conversation. Jackson found it fun to talk with him because they could both gibe at Justices Black and Douglas. They had a rollicking time of it, each egging on the other to wickedly pungent epigrams.

Neither may have gone all the way with the argument they concocted together, but each was half persuaded and half fascinated by it. Jackson then asked his clerk to put it down, thinking to bait some of his colleagues with it in their discussions and exchanges.

In the end, as we know, Jackson voted with them. Frail and ailing, he came to the Court on the *Brown* decision day, on that fateful May day in 1954, to dramatize the Court's unanimity.

I don't know Rehnquist. I did know Jackson, and talked with him several times in chambers. If this were his own memo, he wouldn't have turned a somersault on it, as he did. It must have been a joint product. Alexander Bickel noted shrewdly that Jackson's questions, put to the appeals counsel (which included Thurgood Marshall) during the arguments of the case, showed he had doubts whether the Court could do what the legislature had failed to do.

Evidently Jackson resolved his doubts. Evidently Rehnquist did also. Each had the right to. But over the course of the years, and under the spur of the hearings, Rehnquist may have magnified Jackson's role in the memo and more than slightly sloughed off his own.

FEBRUARY 9, 1973

REAGAN'S FIRST APPOINTMENT

It was an irony that it should have been left to Ronald Reagan to appoint the first woman to the Supreme Court. Reagan had made a passing promise during the campaign, but most expected him to delay fulfilling it. By choosing Judge Sandra D. O'Connor he has again shown his capacity to catch both his opponents and supporters off guard.

The New Right stalwarts, like Richard Viguerie and the Reverend Jerry Falwell, feel betrayed by the appointment. When Judge O'Connor was Republican majority leader of the Arizona Senate, she showed signs of backing the Equal Rights Amendment and was less than adamant in her opposition to abortion. But that surely did credit to her legislative realism, and it offers the margin of independence that will make her more credible as a member of the Court. If the New Right leaders had any real sense, of either history or politics, they would understand this. But what makes them what they are is that they don't.

When President Woodrow Wilson appointed a liberal Jewish lawyer, Louis D. Brandeis, to the Supreme Court, there was a far greater uproar. Past and present presidents of all the bar associations signed a tirade against Brandeis, on the grounds of his being "irresponsible." Yet the decisive count against him was doubtless that he was a liberal and a Jew. I would guess that the fact of Judge O'Connor's being a woman is as rankling to the New Right as the bitter tea of her betrayal of simon-pure conservative principles.

Yet her being a woman is also, symbolically and historically, more important than her degree of conservatism. For more than a quarter-century — in law school, legal practice, politics, the legislature, the state courts — she has been the living embodiment of her determined will to function beyond a "woman's place" in society.

Her appointment brings to the Court the experience of all women as women, just as Thurgood Marshall's appointment by Lyndon Johnson brought to the Court the experience of all blacks as blacks.

JULY 10, 1981

THE TWO AYATOLLAHS IN COMBAT: MEESE VS. BRENNAN

Long after many of Ronald Reagan's gambits and decisions and summit conferences are forgotten, his influence on federal judges and their interpretation of the Constitution still will be with us.

Already Reagan has appointed roughly a third of the total number of federal judges. Before 1989, he may have appointed half. This is one reason that Justice William Brennan — the Ayatollah of judicial liberalism — decided to break the tradition of Supreme Court privacy and go public in a speech that was as much political as constitutional. It was an answer to a July speech by Edwin Meese — the conservative Ayatollah of the Justice Department — that attacked some "bizarre" liberal opinions of the present Supreme Court.

During the New Deal constitutional crisis, I broke several lances jousting against the conservative court majority, which was using the doctrines of "higher law," "due process," and "freedom of contract" to protect corporate interests. Franklin Roosevelt, with his four election victories, appointed enough liberals to the Supreme Court to create a Roosevelt Court. Dwight Eisenhower added, along with Justice John Harlan, Justices Earl Warren and William Brennan — an act that had historical consequences he had not intended. John Kennedy and Lyndon Johnson added other liberals, and the result was the liberal Warren Court, whose influence still lingers in the largely Nixon-appointed Burger Court, which tilts toward conservatism but has no clear majority either way.

In their judicial fusillades, Justices Brennan and William Rehnquist — the heavies of the strongly liberal and conservative loyalist blocs — get media notice by slinging rhetorical insults at each other. But behind the rhetoric there is a skillful tactical maneuvering to win votes from the "swing judges" — Byron White, Lewis Powell, and John Paul Stevens.

With one new Reagan appointee, the conservative bloc may be able to overturn *Roe v. Wade,* the Blackmun abortion decision. With a second, they may overturn the school "moment of silence" decision and revise some of the "technical" court safeguards for defendants, safeguards that drive law enforcement officials up the wall.

That's what the shooting is all about between the Brennan and Meese cohorts.

Meese is gung ho to call the Brennan bloc "activist" and to establish a "judicial restraint" doctrine for the federal and Supreme Court judges still to be appointed. Brennan is equally gung ho to attach the stigma of "arrogance" to Meese's doctrine of reading the Constitution's provisions in the light of the "original intent" of the framers.

By conscripting the imperative of change and of "twentieth-century Americanism," Brennan wants to protect the social-legislative and welfare state. Meese wants to replace it with looser regulations, tighter law enforcement, tougher traditional values.

There is a kernel of truth in what both Brennan and Meese hold to and what they throw away. The Constitution must be both flexible enough and principled enough to enable a democracy to survive and flourish.

OCTOBER 26, 1985

THE YOUNG STALWART BECOMES CHIEF JUSTICE

In deciding to leave the Supreme Court at this moment in history, Chief Justice Warren Burger probably made his most vulnerable decision. He gave a Republican president the chance to name both a chief justice and a new associate justice. He also gave a Republican-led Senate a chance to affirm them with little media tumult.

Had he waited until the November elections and a possible Democratic-led Senate, it could have forced the two Reagan appointees to run a harsh gauntlet. Had he waited until mid-1988, the Senate might have done to lame-duck Ronald Reagan what it did in 1968 to lame-duck Lyndon Johnson — refused to accept his choices and waited for the next president to make them.

The nominee for chief justice whom the Senate rejected then was Abe Fortas. The chief justice it had to accept when Richard Nixon became president in 1969 was Warren Burger. That was how the Warren Court ended and the Burger Court was born. And that is why the Burger Court ends now and goes quietly into history, as the Rehnquist Court enters history.

The obits on the Burger Court have it that it began with a bang and had a chance to establish its own identity, but failed to do it. Clearly Burger, who managed to keep the Court from fratricide for seventeen years, lacked the commanding qualities of the great chief justices — Marshall, Hughes, Stone, and Warren. The result has been a standoff between the cluster around Justice Rehnquist and the rear-guard action that Justice Brennan and his forces have mustered.

Seen in the perspective of history, President Reagan has been prudent in picking Chief Justice Rehnquist and Justice Antonin Scalia, as he was earlier with Justice Sandra O'Connor. He has not chosen cronies nor hacks but a trio of patently intelligent professionals, whose political and judicial conservatism becomes secondary. When added to the attested ability of Justices Brennan and Powell, this forms a group of five, which may spell the difference between a mediocre Court and a distinguished one — whatever the politics of the resulting decisions.

Most of the recent commentary has run in terms of that politics, because there a struggle for judicial power is being waged. Beneath that is an ideological struggle between two sets of what Justice Rehnquist has called the "tacit postulates" — the competing clusters of principles and assumptions within which judges frame their decisions. This goes beyond the stereotyped question of "original intent" or the talk of a "changing court." The struggle is between the "judicial activists" of the Brandeis and Douglas brand, now best personified by Brennan, and the "judicial restraint" school that runs from Holmes through Frankfurter and Harlan and Jackson, now best expressed by Rehnquist, who was Jackson's law clerk.

It is a war of legal philosophies, and its victors will claim the suffrage of generations of law students who are the judges to come.

THE HIGH STAKES IN THE SENATE'S CONFIRMATION HEARINGS FOR Justice William Rehnquist as chief justice have been clear from the start.

Here is the star conservative justice of the past fifteen years, and here is a popular president, who has picked him as his legacy for the Court's future. How can the Democratic Left use the hearings to put a crimp in Reagan and his cause? Obviously by rejecting the portrait of Rehnquist as the "Right Stuff" and portraying him instead as an unacceptable and extremist "Man of the Right."

It was an unenviable task but not one that Senators Edward Kennedy and Howard Metzenbaum could refuse. Their strategy was to attack Rehnquist as an extremist in his political philosophy, the inference being that anyone so political cannot be judicial.

It doesn't follow. There have been strong liberals politically as well as strong conservatives on the Court, and it hasn't kept them from being good judges — sometimes even great ones. Rehnquist, politically conservative, has been a brilliant judge for fifteen years. His becoming chief justice won't shift the political balance of the Court.

Yet it will, of course, give him additional leverage in assigning majority opinions, building a consensus, administering the Court system, acting as a symbol. Will that be bad for the Court and the nation?

We need to distinguish between Rehnquist's political philosophy and his judicial philosophy. Politically he has been, in his career, a Goldwater-Nixon-Reagan conservative. But what is significant is his philosophy of judicial restraint in judging cases and shaping the judicial tradition.

His mentor was Justice Robert H. Jackson, a New Deal Democrat close to FDR. A judge doesn't have to be a political conservative to believe in the legal doctrine of judicial restraint, as witness Justice Felix Frankfurter, another New Dealer.

The issue of character has been raised by Senators Metzenbaum and Kennedy, who have dwelt on his role as a Republican-election lawyer in Arizona a quarter-century ago. A cloudy issue at best; the real target is not character but political philosophy.

No one denies the power of the Senate to grill a nominee, especially for a crucial lifetime post that will affect the lives of millions. But neither Senate nor party prestige is enhanced when the motives are partisan and the spirit niggardly.

Rehnquist has a measure of the necessary qualities that have served important chief justices in the past — the ability to form a working majority when possible, to make the law intelligible on issues of great concern, to pull the Court together, and to dispel some of the clouds of ambiguity around it. He will remain a militant on judicial philosophy, competing for the Court's soul, but he will do it without fuzziness and hypocrisy.

JUNE 4, 1986

THE FATE OF *ROE V. WADE:* WHY AGING JUDGES HOLD ON

Justice Harry Blackmun, of *Roe v. Wade* fame, had to undergo another wrenching ordeal when he took on the challenge of the Pennsylvania antiabortion statute in *Thornburgh v. American College of Obstetricians and Gynecologists* and rejected it in a five-to-four majority opinion. This Nixon appointee is a monument to the proposition that lifetime tenure often turns conservative judges into creeping liberals, just as it may turn liberals into creeping conservatives.

Reaffirming the landmark *Roe v. Wade* of 1973, which affirmed a woman's constitutional right to an abortion, the decision was a dubious victory for the pro-choice forces. It moved Chief Justice Warren Burger dangerously into the minority, in a dissent in which he warned that next time he might vote explicitly to overrule *Roe v. Wade.*

Will there be such a "next time" when Nemesis, now breathing hard on the necks of the pro-choice majority, will overtake it? If there is, the Reagan forces will be able to carry through a judicial turnaround not only on the abortion issue but also on church-state questions, and on state legislation in the murky area of freedom of access to sexually explicit material.

These all turn on the "social agenda" of the evangelical Right. The Reagan administration's ties to it represent the darker side of the Reagan moon.

In an age of information revolution, the striking fact about the opinions in the Pennsylvania case was that they all turned on the amount of information that could constitutionally be made available by a doctor to a woman making an abortion decision.

Justice Blackmun interpreted the information mandated by the Pennsylvania statute as meant to "intimidate" the woman. All four minority judges, speaking through three dissenting opinions, saw the same information as expressing valid health, family, and public interests. Chief Justice Burger fears that the majority's trend since 1973 has been toward "abortion on demand," and Justice Blackmun fears that the efforts to intimidate freedom of choice will keep mounting.

It is a dangerous polarization. It is also an avoidable one. We need a social strategy that protects the right of choice but doesn't fend off all other information from the woman as if the right were an absolute.

JUNE 19, 1986

WILL THE CHIEF JUSTICE TAKE TRUE COMMAND?

Again the empire has struck back. I am talking of the Santa Clara, California, gender-discrimination decision. I see in it the resurgence of the empire of the liberal judicial culture, which pretty much has held power since FDR appointed Justice Hugo Black.

The hold of the liberal judicial empire was strongest in the 1960s, with the Earl Warren majority, and was weakened by the Warren Burger Court in the 1970s. When Burger was replaced by William Rehnquist there was widespread fear that a Rehnquist Court would inaugurate a new Dark Age.

Now, only a year later, it isn't at all clear whether a Rehnquist Court exists. A string of recent decisions, culminating in the *Santa Clara* affirmative action case, offers evidence that the Court is more truly a Brennan than a Rehnquist court.

What makes this remarkable is that, except for Justice Byron White (a Kennedy appointee) and Justice Thurgood Marshall (a Johnson appointee), all of the justices have been chosen by Republican presidents. It is a tribute to the strength of the judicial empire that the thrust of its liberal culture has undercut the vaunted power of "political" choice and the dogma that "the Supreme Court follows the election returns."

What happened, then, to the Rehnquist Court? Partly, it was undercut by the clumsiness of Attorney General Edwin Meese's shotgun attacks on the Supreme Court liberals, and his blundering sorties into the jungle of constitutional doctrine. In the judicial culture, it is marginality that counts. It is the marginal third of the Supreme Court — comprising Justices Powell, White, and Stevens — that must be won over by either the Rehnquist or Brennan ideological camp. Meese scared the marginal justices he should have wooed.

Nor did Rehnquist help. He has an able constitutional mind, but was a poor witness for himself in the drawn-out Senate confirmation hearings. It is now clear that he is anything but a tactician, unskilled in wooing the borderline judge the way Burger could. Wooing involves casting your vote to make a winning majority, and using well your power to choose who will write the decision — thus bending it in your direction. Rehnquist seems too rigidly involved in his own doctrine to do it.

As for the *Santa Clara* case itself, the Court may now have passed the critical point in affirmative action decisions, abrogating its earlier moderate guidelines. Justice Antonin Scalia's scathingly brilliant dissent points out the irony of leaving male white workers unprotected — "the predominantly unknown, unaffluent, unorganized."

Thus, some sort of constitutional crisis is sure to arise in the next few years. The pity of it is that the 1964 Civil Rights Act and its "affirmative action" could have served as a bridge from an unequal discriminatory society to a meritocracy balanced by a deep concern for equal access. It is again a case of high intentions leading to unintended and scarring consequences. Eventually, the Court is bound to change direction.

APRIL 1, 1987

We've just had a brace of Supreme Court decisions worth studying, a unanimous one on the Falwell-Flynt First Amendment case and a six-to-two decision on the *San Jose* rent-control case. Remarkably, in both the signature of Chief Justice William H. Rehnquist led all the rest.

Court watchers are asking themselves what has happened to the hitherto unshakable leader of the Court's conservative bloc. Since President Nixon appointed him, Rehnquist has seen his job to be reversing the liberal-activist tilt of the Warren Court heritage. He has written strong majority or concurring opinions and scathing dissents, all of them contained within a coherent judicial philosophy.

Are we to read the new message from him as signaling that he is creeping — (or slouching) toward the Bethlehem of judicial activism?

It is an accepted generalization that once a justice gets his life tenure, the course he will follow is unpredictable, whatever his president may have hoped of him. Few students of the Court, however, have felt this about Justice Rehnquist, who withstood the waves of hostility from his critics. Is this a man who will now reverse his image?

What Justice Rehnquist is doing, I suspect, cuts deeper than the hypothesis that he is a defector from the conservative camp. If he were simply following the unpredictability model, he would have started his tilt long before this. I prefer another view, which turns on the question of what it means to become a chief justice.

As associate justice, Rehnquist served under Chief Justice Warren Burger, who in turn modeled himself on the great chiefs of the century — William H. Taft, Charles E. Hughes, Harlan F. Stone, Earl Warren. They understood that a chief justice has to corral the votes of his fellow members and tame some of their wildness, and that he can do it only by controlling his own doctrinal impulses.

Using his power to assign opinions when he is in the majority, a chief justice has to be a wily strategist, striving whenever possible to speak for the Court, building coalitions with the "swing" judges, and keeping the important opinions from embodying the reasoning of his major adversaries.

Something else, however, must be added. Rehnquist's mentor, Justice Robert H. Jackson, wrote a book about "judicial supremacy" over the other two branches. He and his close friend, Justice Felix Frankfurter, fought the philosophy of court activism, whether its political source was liberal or conservative, and whether it overrode executive or legislative action. In the *San Jose* case, where rent control came as a local legislative act, Justice Rehnquist could salve his conscience by feeling that Jackson would have approved.

As for the Falwell-Flynt case, one must note the references to Justice Holmes's great *Abrams* dissent, and his concept of "free trade in ideas." The chief justice now accepts the basic distinction between libel in the province of fact, where truth and falsity are evidentiary, and freedom in the province of opinion and ideas, where they are not. It is an important step for him.

A step toward what? Chief Justice Rehnquist has, I think, come to recognize the power of the political culture, which has made the protection of opinion a near absolute. One must recall that Justice Frankfurter, and, in the end, Justice Jackson, came to recognize that power in the *Brown* school desegregation decision thirty-four years ago.

There are faits accomplis in the larger culture that a realistic justice, especially when he is chief, must come to terms with as an act of judicial statesmanship. This is especially true now, when the conservatives have thus far failed to fashion a political counterculture to challenge the dominant liberal culture effectively.

MARCH 2, 1988

20

The Bork Wars
as Confirmation Crisis

The nomination of Robert Bork to the Supreme Court by Ronald Reagan precipitated a brief but intense crisis, spanning two failed nominations and a finally successful one. I didn't know Bork, nor did I identify with the positions he took in his writings in the late 1960s and the 1970s. I felt closer to those of Alexander Bickel, at once his antagonist and mentor, with whom he had crossed swords at Yale Law School. But I did agree strongly with both in their basic philosophy of judicial restraint. And I liked the risk taking that characterized their constitutional journeys.

They were not academics who had played it safe, running with the dominant gang in the liberal-activist law school culture. They had independent minds, worked at constitutional law, lived it, explored how far they could push it and still hold their intellectual universe together.

Bork had made his blunders, had paid for them and learned from them. So I broke a lance for him, as I had done for Hugo Black in the extremity of his Klansman crisis. My liberal friends in 1938 hadn't liked my Black position any better than my liberal friends in 1987 liked my Bork position. My sense of continuity with my own past was, in the fine Holmes phrase, not a duty; it was only a necessity.

The nature of the opposition to Bork confirmed for me that something of more than the moment was at stake. As it intensified, so did my own conviction that it was an unhealthy opposition, based on the principle of confirming or rejecting Court appointees by interest group pressures, and that in the end it was a sort of plebiscite.

I felt it could imperil the independence of judges, conservative and liberal alike, and politicize them.

My conviction grew as the whole grotesque scenario unfolded, from the Bork hearings — so skillfully tilted against him — and his rejection by the Judiciary Committee and Senate, through the ill-fated Douglas Ginsburg nomination that collapsed from a whiff of marijuana, to the confirmation of Anthony Kennedy. By that time the activists had won their war and were willing to cede a nominal battle. Besides, all passion was spent in both camps.

This crisis has to do with the present structure of political consciousness, which makes something like what happened in the Bork hearings possible: that near-hysteria, fired and fed by the leadership of pressure groups, could destroy a nominee of distinction whose record as a judge was ignored, and whose present constitutional outlook was distorted because of passionate resentment of his past positions and actions.

We can't know yet whether this plebiscitary trend in judicial confirmation will get beyond control. I know I shall be part of the effort to check it during what remains of my constitutional journey. I am beyond caring about what party and power stakes are involved with a particular nominee. What I care about is the freshness of the energies a candidate has put into the constitutional process, and the stature of the justice and the Court that are formed by them.

ROBERT BORK'S INTELLECTUAL JOURNEY

I don't recall this much commotion over a Supreme Court justice since the battle over Hugo Black's Ku Klux Klan membership. Robert Bork has no personal shadow to dog him, as Black did, and their political philosophies are far apart, but their legal acumen and constitutional grasp put them in the same class, as strongly innovative thinkers.

We have had fewer psychological profiles of judges than we have of presidents. But for those whose lives have been most closely studied, the best lead can be found in the ideas they pursued early. With Bork, there was a mixture of earnestness and awkward ambition as he struggled to understand the relation of law to society and power. His vision was primarily an economic one, derived from an encounter with the free-market thinking of a University of Chicago teacher, Aaron Director.

Politically Bork became a conservative, and philosophically a libertarian. Yet like his economics, these were segmented, prismatic colors in a complex and questing mind. Intellectual excitement eluded him in his lucrative corporate legal practice in Chicago, and he left to teach antitrust law at Yale. There he worked out a treatise on the economic efficiencies of combines that was meant to topple much of the passionate liberal antimonopoly tradition. Looking for a second course to teach, he chose constitutional law.

A joint seminar taught with Alexander Bickel proved critical in shaping his thinking and his career. Bickel's own intellectual journey was very different. A refugee from Hitler, he had served as clerk to Justice Felix Frankfurter and had been at the heart of the tumultuous Warren Court, which he later dissected with icy elegance.

Bickel became Bork's seminar antagonist and in time his closest confidant and mentor. Students crowded in to watch the rapier duels between them. Bickel displayed his clinical skills in the diagnostic fine-tuning of the key decisions. (Bork described him as "a mixture of Edmund Burke and Fiddler on the Roof.") Bork stuck to his libertarianism and his free-market philosophy, attempting, impossibly, to fuse them into a framework for the unruly flux of constitutional decisions. In time Bickel wrestled Bork to the ground, leaving him to work out a philosophy much closer to Bickel's.

When Bickel died of cancer, he left behind a cluster of books on the Warren Court, whose liberal activism was the prime target of both thinkers. Bork carried on his legacy, but in his own characteristic way — more political and career conscious, more hungry for recognition, more restless and tortured.

Bork's encounter, as solicitor general, with Richard Nixon and the "Saturday Night Massacre" probably taught him more than he wanted to know about politics played to the hilt. He somehow salvaged both his conscience and reputation and returned to Yale. The hostility of the law school establishment and the liberal judicial culture of the mid-1970s further embittered him.

For anyone who has staked his philosophical claims in the law reviews, the final test is judicial battle. The chance came when Ronald Reagan gave him a coveted seat on the Washington, D.C., appeals court. Bork must have viewed it as the perch before the final flight. But just as Gerald Ford had passed him over in filling William O.

Douglas's seat, so Reagan passed him over for his first two Supreme Court vacancies. Everyone knew Bork was better equipped than most others, but he carried confirmation peril with him. With the third vacancy, the nomination finally came to the scarred veteran who, at sixty, had almost given up hope.

"Wreak yourself upon life," Frankfurter had told Bickel, and he had passed it on to Bork, whom it fitted better. It should be read as an injunction from an older to a younger man to think boldly and assertively and to leave an impression on the world. Bork has done it and drawn the lightning that comes with it. One of the bolts has come from Ronald Dworkin (in the *New York Review of Books*), who calls him a "radical" bent on breaking and overruling the continuity of the liberal legal tradition in the service of a reactionary far Right. This is the kind of Chicken Little polemics that will doubtless saturate the hearings. The fact is that there is now an "activist" judicial culture that is mostly liberal and a "judicial restraint" culture that is mostly conservative. Bork, at least in rhetoric, champions a restraint philosophy that will be politically "neutral."

We need to tread lightly here. The results of social upheaval are often tricky and always hard won, but once in place, they are not easily dislodged. In any case, since the New Deal, and especially since the 1960s, America has suffered not from sclerosis but from an accelerating change that has strained its cohesion.

This has led the liberal activists to say that the Court must "adapt" the constitutional text to a "changing social reality." Anyone who doesn't "adapt" to change, in this litany, becomes "reactionary" and "archaic."

No Supreme Court justice, starting with John Marshall, has wholly avoided "result-minded" decision making. It is in the nature of the human mind to imagine where it wants to go and to contrive ways of getting there. But if the Constitution is to mean anything, a judge must enact a self-denying ordinance, excluding his own social preferences from the process of his judicial thinking. "Judicial restraint" is obviously hard to come by, yet Bickel and Bork both ended by embracing it as their judicial philosophy. Bickel found a model in Frankfurter, who in turn had found it in Holmes. Bork owed little to Frankfurter, but found a model of sorts in Justice Hugo Black, whose prevailing passion was fidelity to the language of the Constitution and to its historical intent.

Black went at both with a literalness that gave him the quality of an American primitive. But he too could not refrain from result-mindedness. He interpreted Fifth Amendment freedoms with far more defensive strictness than he accorded to Fourth Amendment "searches and seizures." His version of the historical intent of the Fourteenth Amendment has been called into question by recent scholarship, yet Bork was right to attempt a close reading of the language and to make his own forays into historical intent. Whatever lapses judges are guilty of, and whatever rationalizations they use to conceal them, it is the effort to cleave to the restraint doctrine that counts.

The fear that Bork will unleash a landslide to engulf the "social issues" (gender, sexual privacies, abortion, affirmative action, church-state relations, capital punishment) is strained on several counts. The first is his place within historical perspective. Court majorities come with presidential ones. A conservative-activist Court ruled imperially to freeze the status quo under Republican presidents from the Civil War to the New Deal. FDR's personal plan and his electoral strength, even after he failed to "pack" the Court, enabled him to populate it with a full roster of his own liberal activists. Bork comes at the end of Reagan's sway. His lone vote won't count for much when weighed against the huddle of appointments the next president will make to replace an aging Court. That president may well be a Democrat — unless the party throws away its present advantage with an obstreperous battle against the alternating rhythms of judicial selection. If that happens the Democrats will lose in 1988, and a new wave of conservative activists may make Bork look like a model of moderation.

Second, Bork has reached a high clearing from which he can see where he has been and where he is going. He has a strong sense of history and is more likely to achieve his place in it by making independent decisions than by retreating to past positions that were too far afield. He may join in a few reversals, but that isn't what the historians will hail him for. The "social issues" have run their liberal course. Their expansion may have halted, but a steep rollback would be too divisive.

Some who have studied Bork's decisions in the D.C. appeals court predict that very different issues will engage him, mostly concerning current revolutions (information, communication, biotechnic, money market, and corporate takeover), the new questions of property and regulation that are being put to government and the courts by the administrative agencies, and those arenas in which public protection and entrepreneurial freedom clash. The earlier free-market and libertarian Bork can move in boldly and make new law rather than reverse tired old law. Add to these the foreign policy arena, with its questions about competing presidential and congressional claims to war powers, covert operations, and special prosecutors, and you have some of the issues that await a new Supreme Court, with Bork or without.

If the Democratic Senate is prudent, it will not politicize and polarize the process of confirming judges. This would imperil the judicial choices of their own future presidents and rub away some of the great symbolic power of the Constitution, which has been a force for social cohesion. If they are wise, they will also temper the result-minded activist thrust that has all but erased the lines between the judicial and political cultures of liberalism. The liberals can best regain credibility by mixing more judicial restraint with their activism.

As for Bork, I suspect that he has long had in mind a role in remaking the reigning judicial culture and fashioning a counterculture at the law school and law clerk level. Justice Holmes told Harvard undergraduates a century ago, in 1886, that "a man may live greatly" in the law. "There as well as elsewhere," he added, "he may wreak himself upon life . . . and may wear his heart out after the unattainable."

This was the source of the phrase that Bork got from Frankfurter via Bickel. There are many of the young today with the same intellectual hunger that Bork had, waiting for the chance to make constitutional law a grand enterprise without making it an imperialist one.

1987

Everyone expected the Bork hearings to be extraordinary for the intensity of the political feelings involved. What we didn't expect was the completeness and candor with which Bork opened himself to the judgment of the nation, and not always to his tactical advantage.

This is not a seedy, slippery opportunist seeking to appease hostile senators or win over marginal ones. This is an embattled veteran of constitutional rule who is not result-minded but process-minded. He believes that the process of reasoning — by which decisions are reached — is the nub of being a judge, not the pros and cons of any social result.

This is also a man who appears before the nation after a long intellectual journey, which — unlike many judges — he is willing to talk about. He admits that he took some unproductive paths, including his effort to apply free-market and libertarian values to the Constitution. It didn't work for him. I like his honesty.

Listening to him in the intense give-and-take with the senators, it is hard to recognize the "extremist" scholar and judge who is outside the "judicial mainstream."

Is it outside the mainstream to take the Constitution's language seriously? Is it also outside the mainstream to take the history and intent of the critical clauses seriously?

At times Bork strikes me as defining "historical intent" too rigidly in cases where time has transformed society. Yet I recognize and respect his belief that judges have no divine right to read their own values into the Constitution, however worthy and humane. Too many Supreme Court majorities, both conservative and liberal, have done exactly that. It is refreshing to watch a judge trying to cleave to his principles in the sustained grilling of the hearings.

The great test of Bork's thinking comes in the cases involving an overriding social urgency. It has also, historically, been the great test of the Constitution itself.

OCTOBER 11, 1987

It is now fairly clear that the Judiciary Committee sitting in judgment on Robert Bork reached the wrong decision, for the wrong reasons, in the wrong climate, obeying the wrong political passion, and targeting the wrong man in its deliberate fury. In response, Judge Bork made a gutsy and principled decision. The easy one would have been to cut his losses, stanch his wounds, and retire from the battlefield. He chose instead to endure continuing punishment on the Senate floor.

In a sense the opening shot in the war against him was the victory of the Democrats in gaining control of the Senate in 1986. The decisive gains were made in the South, where the new demographics of the black vote operated in favor of the Democrats. The Reagan administration blundered badly in not understanding this. Senators Edward Kennedy and Joseph Biden *did* understand it and based their strategy on the critical role blacks and other voting groups would play in all the great industrial and urban states — including the South. Thus Bork's fate was decided even before the nomination went to the Senate committee.

I hear my friends say that Bork lost because of his ineffectual TV performance. Whether he did well or badly on TV is clearly the wrong question to ask. Yet a public that can't master the intricacies of constitutional law falls back on a candidate's TV performance as if they were watching a political campaign.

The fact is that if the fate of future judicial nominees is decided by pressure groups, on TV, this will have a devastating effect on the available talent for the federal courts. Constitutional scholars and sitting judges will begin to tailor their public views or decisions to the interest groups sitting in judgment on them.

OCTOBER 15, 1987

COURTING RITUALS

I wouldn't be as quick as some editorial writers to hail the change from the stormy Robert Bork hearings to the love-fest at the Anthony Kennedy hearings. The difference in decibels is welcome, as is the seemliness — almost courtliness — of the exchanges between the committee senators and their target. But peace has never been merely the absence of war, and I raise the question of the cost at which this change has been achieved.

I don't want to hark back excessively to the dark days of the Bork hearings and the trauma they brought. The Democrats worked hard for their triumph and relished it. The Reagan administration came to understand the impact of its blundering tactics. Both camps learned something from the experience — that there are limits they must observe both in the public image of the nominee to the Court and in the opposition to him. We must, I suppose, be grateful for such small gains.

I add that Judge Kennedy was a good choice, given his particular place in the campaign of history. He had no reeking paper trail, no disconcertingly strong judicial opinions, no injurious lapses of the behavior code in his youthful years. His spotless life — as attested by his college mates and his Sacramento colleagues — makes him the Galahad of all present and future judicial nominees. His 400 court opinions ruffled no one when they were first handed down, and the gaggle of lawyers who researched them for the Judiciary Committee must have found them soporifically satisfying, like the murmur a vacation boat's prow makes as it cleaves the halcyon waters.

I too enjoyed listening to Judge Kennedy, and I relished his adroit answers (doubtless meditated on over the weeks since his name was offered) to the inevitable questions. It was the culminating episode of a life spent avoiding confrontation, ever since his lobbying days in Sacramento. He managed to say satisfying things, where Bork always managed to say the disturbing ones.

There was an inspired doggedness of purpose in his replies, and a deftness of phrase to match it. When Senator Joseph Biden questioned his conversation with Senator Jesse Helms about abortion, Judge Kennedy gave an answer that quieted Biden without rousing Helms, who must have been characteristically crouched to leap at any liberal offense. Also, Kennedy's answer on his elite club membership made it clear he was "sensitive to the subtle barriers" of racism.

It was in his response on the "right of privacy" that he shone brightest, suggesting a "zone of liberty . . . where the individual can tell the government, 'Beyond this line you may not go.' " No wonder Professor Laurence Tribe of Harvard Law School, the custodian of liberal vigilance, knighted the nominee with the blunt tip of his sword.

In addition to making certain that Judge Kennedy will not challenge the activist Brennan group on the Court too abrasively, Tribe and the Senate liberals whom he counsels have achieved their overarching objective. They have established the precedent for all future confirmation hearings: no longer will a nominee of whatever political stripe be able to parry direct questions about where he stands on concrete constitutional doctrines, whether questions concern the right of privacy, the limits to First Amendment freedoms, the tests of affirmative action safeguards, or the reach of the "equal protection of the laws" clause.

Since the Bork hearings, there has been a subtle but important "battle of the legacy" being waged to determine what will be the lasting impact of the hearings. Their impact is clearer now. The redoubt that has up to now protected the judicial independence of the nominee on his future decisions has finally been breached. Which is why, even as I listened with admiration to the new nominee, I felt sadness about what has happened to the constitutional process.

DECEMBER 24, 1987

The wheel has come full turn for Robert Bork. The embattled scholar who wanted to reshape the profile of constitutional thinking, and who went through a fiery ordeal in his bid for the Supreme Court, has put aside his judicial robes on the District of Columbia Circuit Court of Appeals and resumed his old role as embattled constitutional scholar.

Curiously, after all the clamor about him, Bork's decision to resign has been greeted with a thunderous silence. The major papers quoted from his resignation letter, but the commentators and professors who had depicted him as the Genghis Khan of jurisprudence seem to regard him now as a closed chapter in a book they don't wish reopened. They mean to thrust him and the story of his confirmation back into the past.

I don't think they will succeed. Bork defeated turns out to be something other than Bork silenced. I, for one, welcome him back into the fray.

I don't go as far as he does — or as far as some of his supporters — in his concern about "original intent" in interpreting the Constitution and its amendments. It should be a factor, yes, but there are other ways to hold judges to "judicial restraint" and to keep them from translating their own social agenda into public policy. Where Bork can help best now is in his struggle against that activism.

"Those who want political judges," Bork writes in his resignation letter, "should reflect that the political and social preferences of judges have changed greatly over our history and will no doubt do so again. We have known judicial activism of the right and of the left; neither is legitimate."

Bork's challenge deserves a response in the "public discourse" he is asking for.

JANUARY 20, 1988

The process of getting a Supreme Court judge confirmed has turned into a political beauty contest. For that matter, it is also being turned into a virtue contest — a search for the lawyer or judge with a spotless past, who has never committed a youthful indiscretion and never taken a vulnerable public position that will hurt the feelings of single-issue voting groups.

Note also the role of the investigative press in the confirmation revolution. Who would be the first constitutional reporter to track down Ginsburg's pot smoking at Harvard Law School? The prize for the scoop fell to Nina Totenberg, a first-rate reporter for National Public Radio, and she returned to Washington from Cambridge a heroine to her media peers. Thus was history made. Yet, as the young judicial nominee asked somewhat wryly, what in the world does it have to do with his judicial philosophy, or the kind of justice he would have dispensed? We shall never know.

Note the role the law school faculties have played. In the 1930s they were regarded as a recruiting ground for Supreme Court members. Chief Justice Stone came from the Columbia law faculty, Justice Frankfurter from Harvard, Justice Douglas from Yale. Today, law professors have a new, primary role, that of consultants and advisers to the judicial committees — the role that Laurence Tribe of Harvard filled for Senators Biden and Kennedy as they prepared for battle against Bork.

The law school is no longer an ivory tower. It has become a prime player in the passions and actions of our time. Future judicial nominees will be compelled to answer questions proposed by law school faculties, and thereby hem themselves in from any real judicial independence. The constitutional culture is rapidly becoming indistinguishable from the political culture.

The media have taken considerable flak for their role in the confirmation process. Tocqueville noted in the 1840s that nothing gets finally decided in the American democracy until the courts have passed on it. Now, nothing gets decided until the courts and the media have passed on it.

NOVEMBER 15, 1987

Even in the context of the Supreme Court tussles that have provided political entertainment since at least the 1930s, the saga of Robert Bork, Douglas Ginsburg, and Anthony Kennedy broke new ground. What made the play rougher this time was the heightened consciousness of the stakes involved, a more aggressive deployment of interest groups, and a greater sophistication in media manipulation.

If the overworked term *watershed* still conveys some meaning, it applies here to the future direction of confirmation politics. It is now evident that the crisis in the confirmation of judges will turn on the question of how much they will reveal about their future positions under questioning, and thus how much of their judicial independence they will surrender.

In considering nominees for the seat of Justice Lewis Powell,

Attorney General Ed Meese — guided by Assistant Attorney General William Bradford Reynolds — made the prime blunder of imagining that a strict constructionist and "original intent" champion such as Robert Bork could survive the confirmation process. It was a rash decision made by a man who thought he could nail down an "original intent" Court majority until the century's end and beyond. Meese was especially blind to the intensity of feeling in the liberal law school culture about making a growing number of rights (including privacy) the centerpiece of constitutional concern, as against the Madisonian "balance" of freedom and limits. And he was unprepared for the almost metaphysical passion that gave unity of purpose to a loose gaggle of interest groups concerned about the balance of power on the Court.

One can now see ironies in the whole performance. There was the irony of a liberal Senate and law school elite committed to change and growth in constitutional interpretation, but rigidly hostile to any similar change and growth in the constitutional thinking of a legal scholar, denying evidence of it in his five years of decision making on a high federal court. There was also the irony of Bork, eager to win the suffrage of marginal senators, earnestly answering their intrusive queries about his thinking — past and future — on case after case, doctrine after doctrine, thus giving legitimacy to a line of questioning that concentrated on his intellectual rather than on his legal record. Traditionally, the Senate's role has been to deal with the nominee's character, possible conflict of interest, and flagrant bias. The questions to Bork went beyond this to his intellectual journey and future decision making.

In retrospect, one need not mourn Bork overmuch. He lived by the constitutional sword in his grandly polemical articles, and in a sense he died by it. He answered questions no nominee has any business answering if he means to be an independent judge.

But if the Bork story had saving ironies, the Ginsburg story had only absurdities. The Meese strategists, misinterpreting the Bork disaster as having been caused by his "paper trail" alone, too cleverly proposed Douglas Ginsburg, a young judge with no constitutional journey behind him, which left the Democratic committee majority opposing him with only the traditional "fitness to serve" strategy — the "character issue."

Enter the investigative reporters. Ginsburg's life yielded some trifles (a conflict-of-interest cloud, a second wife who had worked at a hospital that performed legal abortions), and then — the final blow — an obscure episode of marijuana smoking while on the law school faculty. Coming of age in the exploratory early 1970s, Ginsburg had violated the "just say no" prime directive. Exit Ginsburg, an innocent too rashly chosen to start with.

Anthony Kennedy came at just the right point in the drama — when both camps, exhausted by their wars in the first two acts, wanted to give the third a happy ending. He has proved to be a "safe" candidate for both sides to support — the very model of a modern judicial nominee. There were no behavioral lapses in his youth or early manhood, no ethical cloud over his lobbying years in Sacramento, no turbulent adventures in constitutional interpretation in some 400 judicial opinions. The Republicans are willing to settle for a "true conservative." The Democrats, including Laurence Tribe, are fearful of their image of excessive nominee bashing and welcome the chance to show themselves as "moderates."

At what cost to the judicial culture and the nation? Where Robert Bork was eager to answer questions the committee had no right to put to a nominee, Anthony Kennedy was deftly evasive. Bork often gave involved and unsatisfying answers; Kennedy — more adroit in avoiding confrontation — managed to give soothing ones. Asked about his restricted-membership club, he assured the senators he was "sensitive to the subtle barriers" of racism — a commitment that is bound to crop up in responses to his future decisions on affirmative action cases.

Harried by Senator Dennis DeConcini on the right of privacy, Kennedy tried to skirt it by positing a line beyond which "the government may not go." But DeConcini would not be put off: "But it's there? No question about it?" Kennedy's defenses collapsed. "Yes, sir," he said. He thus gave away the treasure of a judge's own right of privacy and independence, and his future freedom of deliberative choice, all of which are central to the maintenance of a sturdy, knowledgeable, and independent judiciary.

Questioned about his views on the meaning of the Fourteenth Amendment, Kennedy simultaneously embraced historical intent (what the legislators "thought they were doing and intended and said when they ratified the Amendment") and added sweepingly that "*Plessy v. Ferguson* was wrong on the day it was decided" and that "a people can rise above its own injustice." His candy box has bonbons for every doctrinal taste.

What is going on in these questions and responses? As I read it, nothing less than movement toward plebiscitary control of the "advise and consent" process of judicial confirmation. The fact that it is enacted in a public hearing room and transmitted on a TV screen instantaneously around the world doesn't make it any less a form of political hostage taking, under threat of an adverse senatorial vote.

This was not the way the historic judicial greats were chosen or confirmed. Whether they adhered to judicial restraint or activism, they would have met such questions and questioners with magisterial rebuffs. In their independence, Holmes, Frankfurter, and Jackson, Black, Douglas, and Brennan, were models for those considering legal and judicial vocations. Under far less provocation than greeted Bork or Kennedy, Felix Frankfurter, pushed by a hostile senator about his associations and beliefs, responded more sharply than either of them. Bork slipped dangerously away from Frankfurter's example when he let Senator Arlen Specter pin him down on how he would interpret Justice Oliver Wendell Holmes's "clear and present danger" doctrine in future freedom-of-speech First Amendment cases.

The confirmation hearings of 1987 are bound to serve as precedents for future hearings on future nominees, perhaps irreversibly. This may haunt the Democrats when they come to power. It is one thing to examine the life, character, and "fitness" of a nominee. It is quite another for senators to extort commitments on a nominee's doctrinal positions and legal philosophy, which are either on public record for them to read or are in a zone of integrity and independence that no nominee should be asked to barter away to save his skin.

FEBRUARY 8, 1988

Amid the clash of judicial doctrines, we have all but forgotten the intellectual zone that the justices of stature after Holmes and Brandeis inhabited. Their greatness lay less in championing restraint or activism than in interweaving precedent and change, in a play of statesmanship that focused always on the competition of doctrines and the balance it could achieve. The judges of stature, once on the Court, followed a judicial rhythm of their own that kept American civilization in a rough equilibrium for at least a century.

It will be harder now to achieve a similar balance. Sitting judges and constitutional scholars who aim at the Supreme Court will write less, more cautiously, and will dare less in their thinking and their decisions. They will be vulnerable to the tyranny of interest and pressure groups that has become as much a peril as the tyranny of the majority ever was.

There is a danger that a generation or more of judges will need a backbone transplant, because of the self-censorship they will have exerted on themselves from the time they were law review editors or law clerks onward. If this happens, it will deprive young men and women of any models of judicial independence — judges who grapple innovatively but rigorously with what the social revolutions of their time demand of them, as distinguished from what they demand of legislators and presidents. The young want nothing better than to wrestle with their heroes and rivals in an agon of intellectual and moral struggle.

The role that the Constitution assigned to the judiciary was meant neither to rigidify the past nor to invent the future. It was meant to mediate between them, with independence and reflectiveness. Hence the life tenure of federal judges, to protect them from the pressures of the immediate. Hence the appointment power given to the president, as expressing the will of the whole people more closely than any other agent of the government. Hence, finally, the "advise and consent" provision, to make certain of getting input from senior legislators without giving them the control of the process of choice that was intended for the president. Who can doubt that the intent was to achieve an equilibrating effect, in terms of past and future, on the entire process of government?

Fed by the currents of "participatory democracy" that the 1960s generated, by the interest pressures and entitlements of succeeding decades, by demographics and instant TV replay, the deep structure of group tyranny over judicial selection was already there, waiting to be recognized and set in place. The nomination of Robert Bork and the battles that ensued furnished the opportunity. Historically, that and that alone gave those battles their importance.

To recognize what happened is not to accept it as either desirable or inevitable. It is, after all, as John Marshall said, a *Constitution* we are interpreting — a charter for governing a whole nation over time. The selection process has been derailed, but it can be set back on track.

There are scholars wedded to liberal judicial activism who defend it on the fundamental grounds that judicial restraint is a never-never land, because all judicial interpretation — to a greater or lesser degree — is at base a "higher" lawmaking. There is a sense in which that is true, since every judge has his tacit postulates and moves toward his conception of what is best for the nation. But it is the "greater or lesser degree" that counts. I suggest that a lesser concession to the lawmaking impulse is healthier and less harmful than a greater concession.

When Justice Holmes, in a great case, was confronted by a similarly sweeping argument, that "the power to tax is the power to destroy," his answer was sharp: "Not while this Court sits." One may make the same response to the general proposition that all judicial interpretation is lawmaking. Not while the Constitution is still there to assign to judges their true role, not of legislating but of equilibrating.

1990

EPILOGUE

Oliver Wendell Holmes Revisited

1

An author is lucky to have the chance to revisit a book as early as this one, and to get his licks in once again.[1] I gathered these utterances by Justice Holmes and wrote prefaces for them half a lifetime ago, when I was instructing the young in constitutional history at Williams College. At forty, in 1943, I was already a veteran of the passions and actions of the New Deal's constitutional wars. Whatever impulse incited me to these labors, I recall the excitement that sustained me in grappling with the character and thinking of so enigmatic a figure.

The original version of one's work — if it amounts to anything — is always a hard act to follow. As I reread the book, the thing of wonder to me was my youthful brashness in daring to plan a venture in which a third of the pages consisted of my comments on the two-thirds that were Holmes's. Given his magisterial brevity, my prefaces to his opinions were often longer than what they prefaced. It was, I fear, a case of the context swallowing the text. What saw me through it was the effort to present a total rather than a specialized view of Holmes — to integrate the personal journey with the professional and intellectual, the mind and character with the style, the strengths and vulnerabilities of a thinker with his impact on history.

Happily the book had a sturdy life over the years, enduring the constitutional tumults that tested its viability. The occasion for re-publishing it is also an occasion for reviewing the scholarship of the intervening years, taking the measure of Holmes again, charting afresh the stages of his constitutional journey and the trajectory of his reputation, rethinking his relevance for an America almost a half-century after his death.

A federal judge's constitutional journey starts well before any actual decisions, with the early history and the turning points in the ideas that bear directly on them. Slow, step-by-step growth may be part of the story, but so are creative leaps — mutations, as it were — which are at times all but inexplicable.

The seminal period for Holmes was formed by the triad of the Civil War, his law school years, and the long days and nights he spent writing his formative essays for the *American Law Review*. For him, they were the source from which the river of legal history began its strong flow. Holmes was twenty-one when he was wounded at Ball's Bluff. He was in his late thirties when he began to write *The Common Law* — unillusioned, skeptical, stoic, yet with a deep fire of insight and purpose.

During his years of intense study, he shaped the leading ideas he put together in the *Common Law* lectures — the anthropology, history, economics, psychology, the deep experiential and pragmatic thrust, the epigrammatic style, the shying away from certitudes and absolutes, the legal philosophy that he saw (in Voltaire's phrase) as "history teaching by example."

We have the sense in reading his letters to Sir Frederick Pollock and Harold Laski that Holmes did everything with an easy grace. Yet his years of early labor suggest that it was a hard-won grace. He spoke later of the "icy night" that enveloped him in the harsh law school years, which must have seemed a continuance of the Civil War traumas, but on other battlefields, with other enemies. Holmes had in those years something like Yeats's knotty "fascination with what's difficult." He later gave the impression of a conjurer's capacity to untie the knots, presto, or to cut through them with a swift deci-siveness. But he had prepared the ground in his years of ordeal. Compared with the disciplined mastery he had to achieve early, every-thing after that was made to seem easy.

The Common Law, which he completed at age forty, was thus the deftly prepared turning point that made everyone take him se-riously as a comer. It forked off into two roads that were swiftly opened to him — as legal scholar and professor and as state supreme court judge. Like Robert Frost, another Yankee of ribbed words, Holmes could not take both. He chose the second, I suspect because it enabled him "to think for action upon which great interests depend." It is tantalizing to speculate about where the road not taken might have led.

Holmes never wrote another book. Yet in his two court tenures, of twenty and thirty years, he wrote a sheaf of opinions that led to his becoming in time a kind of judicial philosopher-king, somewhat disdainful of the crown he wore with an amused tilt — but he nonetheless wore it.

2

In my commentary on the state supreme court opinions, I drew a distinction between the Holmes of private and of public law. I might have made it sharper. His public law opinions formed a transition to his U.S. Supreme Court views, especially in his deference as a judge to majoritarian decisions of legislative bodies. But the reputation he achieved on both courts thrust his earlier importance for private law into the shadow. We all worked and wrote in that shadow.

What we missed was the shift in Holmes's private-law thinking under the nitty-gritty testing of his state court duties. As a scholar he had been an intellectual radical, like his friends in the Metaphysical Club, and was influenced by the positivist science of the time. It added a strong conceptual strain to his pragmatic inclinations. It didn't negate his recoil from formalism and from the heavy constrictions of philosophical idealism. But it made him willing to apply standards and strike principled approximations to resolve the hardest problems of legal thinking.

If the conceptual Holmes survived the state court experience, it was in a considerably altered state. He still aimed at clear principles and an "external standard," whether in torts, contracts, or property law. But the dividing line between the clashing sets of social desires was more blurred in action than it had been in the scholarly cloister. He couldn't fall back on the "not unreasonable" legislative bodies, as he did in public law. Nor was he willing to rely on the judgment of juries beyond their findings of fact. He saw no certainties in the competing social interests that clustered around every case. He saw instead a shadowy continuum that led to something like an "uncertainty" principle. He had to draw a line somewhere, however, to make a choice between "irreconcilable desires" — and thereby play something of an activist role in "making law."

It must have been a chastening experience for him, but also a growth experience. It was in these years that he moved decisively from the law as a set of rules linked with "rights" or "duties" or moral imperatives to the law as a prediction of what the courts will operatively do. This led him inevitably into the depths where certainties as well as logics dissolved, and where at times arbitrary choices had to be made. A half-century later (as G. Edward White notes) the efforts to dig into Holmes's importance as a private law thinker led to "a larger rediscovery of the history of private law."

Meanwhile, Holmes led a relaxed life, took vacations in Europe, read French novels, corresponded widely — and waited for the Godot of the coveted prize. We tend to see a kind of inevitability in his progression to the summit. Yet it was a near thing, hanging on the hairbreadth of Henry Cabot Lodge's reassuring response to Theodore Roosevelt's anxiety. Holmes had become chief justice of the Massachusetts court by the 1900 term and was attracting national attention. But he was already sixty-one when the choice was made, and he wouldn't have been *papabile* much longer. A lot of history would have come out differently if TR had insisted on a "safer" man.

3

This emphasis on law as what the courts will actually do led ineluctably to a focus on the judge himself and the workings of his mind — articulate or not, conscious or unconscious. There are hints of this in Holmes's state court opinions — this journey into the interior of a judge's mind — but the flowering came soon after he reached the Supreme Court.

It is clearest in his *Lochner v. N.Y.* dissent (1905), which created a new jurisprudence — one of awareness of a judge's unstated philosophical premises and his social priorities. It led to the recognition of the need to come to terms with this underlying set of personal premises, at the peril of "playing God" with judicial lawmaking.

It was a turning point in Holmes's intellectual journey and also in that of successive generations of students. I read the dissent as a graduate student in the mid-1920s, as did others of my generation.

It created a school of "legal realism" in the law school culture later, in the 1930s. Yet little note has been taken of its strategic aspect, from 1905 to the New Deal attacks on the Court in the mid-1930s.

Holmes was on polite terms with his Court brethren, but their succession of rigid decisions furnished the laboratory in which he developed his strategy for meeting and overcoming them. He was a solitary fighter, and had no one to talk with until Brandeis came to the Court in 1917. Brandeis brought a sociological jurisprudence with him from his Populist progressive years, and he documented the new "felt necessities" of the time. But Holmes dug deeper, into the hidden logic of the "unarticulated major premise" that underlay the conservative lawmaking, and also into the fears and commitments that shaped the priorities of judges like the formidable Justice Peckham who wrote the Court opinion in *Lochner*.

This led Holmes to his doctrine of "judicial deference." The important fact about it was that it brought all of Holmes's insights together and served as a strategic weapon in the doctrinal wars for generations. I don't say it was all calculated. I do say that without Holmes's shrewd conceptualizing capacity, it would not have happened that way or that soon.

In his address on John Marshall, with its guarded praise, Holmes asserted that Marshall's influence lay in being *there* at a strategic point in the campaign of history. We can turn his remark about, and see that it was true of Holmes as well. He was *there,* exactly when a Court of resourceful conservatives was creating a set of doctrines — notably "liberty of contract" and "due process of law" — to protect an archaic property system against its challengers.

We all declaimed and wrung our hands over these indignities. Yet it devolved on Holmes to bear the burden of contriving an equally resourceful doctrinal strategy to counter them. He achieved it with the concept of judicial deference to reasonable legislative majorities. By the mid-1930s and their constitutional battles, we were calling it "judicial restraint" and using it against the "judicial supremacy" of the conservative Court majority.

In Holmes's relations with the liberal law school professors, the ardor was all on their side, and it increased with his decisions and dissents on free trade in ideas. He saw these opinions of his as meditations on how to reconcile the clashing imperatives of speech — of a nation seeking to guard its very existence and of that same nation striving to retain its soul by refusing to quench the fires of competing ideas.

Holmes was not one of the "First Amendment voluptuaries" (as Alexander Bickel has dubbed them), drunk with an absolutism that sees only one of the imperatives. Holmes saw both and picked his way warily between them. To have moved in a brief period from the majority "clear and present danger" test of *Schenck v. U.S.*, to the majority opinion upholding the *Debs v. U.S.* conviction, to the ringing *Abrams v. U.S.* dissent was in itself a daring and scrupulous journey. Holmes performed his conceptual differentiations between them with a scalpel-like precision and couched them in quicksilver phrases that still dance and live in the memory of every constitutional scholar. The final product was his own, yet this was one phase of his journey in which a notable dialogue took place, involving exchanges with (among others) Brandeis, Laski, and especially Learned Hand.

4

Much has been written on the "apotheosis" of Holmes by the "legal realists" of the 1930s and more generally by the New Deal liberals. As an unchartered member of both groups, I can bear witness that the charge of our "hero worship" and "mythmaking" is overdone. I had few illusions, either in the book or the *Nation* and law review articles that preceded it, about Holmes as a liberal. We knew that he was an economic, social, and neo-Darwinian conservative and that his judicial doctrine — however powerful a strategic weapon it proved — was based on an intellectual austerity that few of us as combatants in the liberal wars could muster. Holmes never walked on water for us. There was no liberal canonizing of him as there was of Brandeis and supremely of Franklin Roosevelt.

One of the principal "realists," Karl Llewellyn, was poetic about Holmes because that was his style, but he was also sophisticated in his insights; Walton Hamilton saw his importance, but he was astringent about "dating Holmes"; and Thurman Arnold was caustic about everyone, not excluding Holmes. Only Jerome Frank was a bit excessive in his often quoted final chapter (in *Law and the Modern Mind*), about Holmes as a paradigm of a "mature man."

For a time the realists were fascinated by Holmes. They needed him more than he needed them. He was the symbol that gave cohesion to them as a "school." It was a passing phase. They have regrouped since, found other symbols, rallied behind more exotic causes, under other banners. Even when they marched to the same drum, neither Holmes nor they allowed themselves to be diverted from their own campaign of history.

Holmes left the Supreme Court just as the New Deal entered history. They barely bowed to each other in passing, although the White House and many of the new agencies were staffed by Holmesians. It was well that Holmes was no longer on the Court during FDR's attacks on the "nine old men": had he stayed he would have been the oldest — and the wisest. The court-packing plan would doubtless have been anathema to him, as it was to Brandeis and Hughes. Yet Holmes's opinions not only laid a base for attacking judicial supremacy, they also furnished a rationale for accepting legislative social experiments like the New Deal and validating an executive power adequate to the nation's survival.

Holmes could not have known — nor could I — that the Roosevelt constitutional revolution of the 1930s would first enshrine and then undermine his reputation. The trajectory of the rise and fall — and rise again — of the Holmes heritage is a richly theatrical chapter in the history of ideas. It has had echoes in the legal scholarship and is worth tracing for its ironies and paradoxes.

Broadly put, the Holmes legacy flourished in the 1930s, tottered in the 1940s and 1950s, collapsed in the 1960s and early 1970s, and revived in the later 1970s and 1980s. These vagaries of his reputation, curiously, had less to do with his constitutional doctrines than with his larger philosophy and indeed with the perceptions of his character. Most of all they were governed by what was happening in the law school culture as it watched the Roosevelt Court and its successors and responded to the pressures of the larger political culture. Holmes became part of history, and the story of his reputation is a story of the ways in which a dominant legal elite deploys the uses of history.

5

In retrospect the most radical thing about my book was its title and therefore its central theme — that Holmes possessed not only a striking mind but also a unique faith. This was heresy at the time and became even greater heresy during the decades when he was under attack. Is it possible (his critics asked) that this agnostic, skeptic

Darwinian had a faith? Yet the faith informs his thinking, which cannot be studied without it.

We must not forget that his core experience was the near encounter with death in the Civil War, when brother fought and killed brother, each convinced of the rightness of his cause — a conviction that Holmes came to call a "fighting faith." He knew that time withers every faith, but he also knew that we need it as a symbolic mode of giving meaning to life in an uncaring universe. His "can't helps" represented a way of coming to terms with the urgency of ultimate and absolute truths. It was as far as he was willing to go toward universal as well as unique patterns, and he made them personal, not general.

The liberals came to see Holmes as a disembodied mind, lacking compassion for the welfare of his fellows, unwilling to use his judicial gifts to elevate their condition. Yet to see him thus is to miss the point of the Holmes enigma. Compassion was not one of his prime values, but neither was force — certainly not the force of the state. Competition and struggle were the essence of life, death was its sanction, and faith transcended both.

Hence the "dark" quality that many have seen in Holmes. The attack was only in part on doctrinal grounds. It was largely characterological. Paradoxically it united the liberal Left, which dominated the legal culture, with the catholic and traditionalist Right, which had its own agenda of opposition to Holmes — the doctrine of "natural rights." For a time both Left and Right found common ground in seeing Holmes as a strange creature — the Left depicting him as a cold, uncaring spectator, the Right as a savage pre-Hitler totalitarian.

There is little question that there was in fact a side of Holmes that was extraordinarily detached from the everyday pressures and urgencies of life. Only a warrior who had been through the battles and had experienced death as closely as Holmes had could be so consistently "above the battle." There was an archetypal Jungian "shadow" in Holmes that not only furnished his dark side, but also gave him his rocklike strength of character and his steadiness of vision.

True, his death experiences also left a scar on his perception of life, making him less open to humanist thinking, so that he made short shrift of any liberalisms other than free trade in ideas, and wrote too much off as "uplift." Edmund Wilson, writing in the early 1960s, spoke of "the carapace of impregnable indifference to current pressures and public opinion" that marked Holmes. G. Edward White, in 1971, wrote of his "articulated refusal to take pride in being human," which made him "the least heroic of America's heroes."

Had Holmes lived longer, all this would have thoroughly disqualified him from membership in the Warren Court. It kept Holmes from being proudly and generously accepted, even during the recent decades of his "revival." But to ask for a Holmes with these added "enlightened" and "progressive" qualities would miss the point of the total Holmes, and how his critical life experiences had made him what he was. They account for the flaws in his thinking but account also in part for the strength of both his mind and faith.

One gets in Holmes the sense of life and death entangled with each other in an agon without end. He didn't use Eros and Thanatos as his symbols for it as Freud did, who wrote after another war, as he came to recognize the role of death. Both men, strikingly, went through a similar experience: they started with a positivist belief in the science of their day, they became fascinated by the hidden agenda of the mind, and they moved ever closer to the dark imperatives of the instinctual drives expressed in life and death.

6

If Holmes fell from grace as an idol of the liberal Left, he was anything but a darling of the conservative, traditionalist, and moralist Right. How could they not oppose him? His positivism and realism enabled him to define law operatively, without recourse to the dimension of "ought" that conservative as well as liberal moralists have found indispensable. In bringing the "bad man" into his theory of law, Holmes used the adjective almost wryly to mean, matter-of-factly, whatever had gotten him entangled with the law's sanctions. As a young editor he read all the Continental theorists on "natural law" and "natural rights," including the windy ones — and rejected them. Natural law was too static and absolute for an evolutionary thinker who knew how the conception of "nature" had changed over the ages. The breezy authority with which Holmes dismissed a whole phalanx of weighty scholars made him all the more exasperating.

I had to confess myself somewhat troubled, in my original prefaces, by the gap I found in Holmes's thinking: "Holmes did not adequately bridge the gap between [his] two worlds. There was in him a deep conflict between scepticism and belief, between mind and faith, between a recognition that men act in terms of a cold calculation of interests, and a recognition also that they are moved by symbols. . . ." I added that his effort "to take account of both strains . . . was not wholly successful," but that it stretched him into becoming "a full-statured person," more than he would have been if he had restricted his energies "to the narrow confines of one or the other partial view."

I still hold this to be a viable view, although I shall add some further reflections below on the "natural rights" (rather than "natural law") philosophy of both Left and Right.

When Holmes left the bench, in 1932, it was not yet clear how any coalition war effort against Hitler might fare. There were premonitory scholarly articles, from 1941 to 1943, mostly written by Jesuit legal thinkers, on Holmes as forerunner to the ideas of Hitler, Göring, Goebbels, and Himmler, but it was left to Ben Palmer, in the year the war ended (1945), to put the same thesis in a popularized form, yielding to the alliterative seduction of his title, *Hobbes, Holmes and Hitler*. Admitting that Holmes "did not go around like a storm trooper, knocking people down," he nevertheless saw Holmes as a source of "totalitarian" philosophy.

The controversy raged through the rest of the 1940s and the 1950s, engaging more time and verbiage than it deserved. It also evoked some necessary reassessments of Holmes's evolutionary approach to legal philosophy, which he had always put more nakedly — almost perversely — than he had to. What happened to Holmes's legacy, starting a decade after his death, came with a fantastic irrelevance out of the full revelation of the Holocaust, which would have been as alien to him as he to it.

We see the roots of Nazism more clearly now. They had nothing to do with the Hobbesian doctrine of sovereignty nor with Holmes's legal pragmatism. They shed a cruel light on the German intellectual tradition and a Europe in which Nazism emerged and flourished. One has to ask what good the centuries of French Enlightenment and German natural-law thinking did when it came to confronting the radical evil of Hitler. Holmes never had a love affair with either of them. Nor has Hannah Arendt's foray into the Enlightenment thinkers in the intellectual origins of totalitarianism tempered the continuing criticism of Holmes. The critics have not taken adequate account of the role of "social engineering" strategies and fantasies, both Right and Left, in the genocides of Hitler and Stalin.

There is a key passage in Holmes in which he concludes that he is "in the universe," not the universe in him — that he is therefore not God in it and disdains to "play God" in shaping the destinies of others in the same universe. In a deep sense, his working theory of judging was grounded on this metaphysic.

The liberals who found Holmes and his gnomic language so engaging in the 1920s and 1930s did so not because they liked all his judicial outcomes and his philosophy, and certainly not because of his metaphysic. They were willing to overlook his departures from their liberal ideal in his *Schenck* and *Debs* opinions because they fixed on *Abrams, Gitlow,* and *Schwimmer.* They too lived by symbols, and Holmes was for them a symbol of resistance to the reactionary Court majority, a symbol also of enlightenment on the Bill of Rights, and — in the case of the Realists — a symbol of a down-to-earth willingness to reckon with the here and now that they equated with a kind of liberal modernism. As with love and marriage, their disillusionment with him came out of their initial illusions. When they looked more closely and found that this wasn't the love object that had once enchanted them, they recoiled more strongly.

As it happened, their recoil (like that of the natural-law conservatives) came at the war's end, in the mid-1940s. It lasted for some thirty years, mounting during the Warren Court 1960s. The dynamics of the recoil are not analyzed clearly in the accounts of it in the legal literature. In the 1940s and after, a series of generations came into the law schools sharply different from the constitutional generation I knew in the 1920s and 1930s. The true key to their change was the succession of activist Supreme Courts, starting with a Court appointed almost entirely by Franklin Roosevelt. Behind this, in turn, is the story of the political cultures that we call the New Deal, the Fair Deal, the New Frontier, and the Great Society, and their impact at once on the Supreme Court members and on the law school culture that served as their support system.

Despite Holmes's half-century of judging, including thirty years on the Supreme Court, his impact on constitutional law proved narrower than seemed likely in the early 1940s. The "Holmesian moment" — if we may call it that — was his burst of creative fire between *Lochner* in 1905 and the free-speech cases in the early 1920s. The fact that many of his great opinions in this period were dissents is witness to Holmes's fate of having to spend his best years on a Court whose majority saw him as marginal to the judicial culture of the time. In fact, this brief spell saw the mature harvest of the great sowings in his hungry young years and the years of his manhood on the state supreme court.

Aside from the force of his basic decisional philosophy, Holmes's doctrinal resourcefulness in sheer constitutional terms was not great. On that score it didn't match Justice Hugo Black's on the Roosevelt Court or the doctrinal fertility of the later Warren group. The reason is clear enough. The burden of Holmesian thinking was to define the judicial power narrowly and set limits to it. The burden of the later activist thinking of the Roosevelt and Warren Courts was to expand the judicial power, and to that end a doctrinal fertility was imperative.

After Holmes's retirement in 1932 the Holmesian moment continued its brief triumph, in "a little finishing canter before coming to a standstill" — the horse race metaphor he used on his ninetieth birthday. It lasted as long as his strategic legacy was useful in helping to fight the anti–New Deal decisions and, later, to validate the New Deal legislation. But with the first Roosevelt appointments to the Supreme Court in the closing 1930s, the new masters of the Court no longer needed the Holmesian doctrine. After that it stayed alive until the Warren Court, but only as an element of contention in the great feud between two Court factions. The impetus of the new Zeitgeist succeeded in ending the Holmesian moment.

7

The nature of this Zeitgeist is worth some probing for the light it sheds on what happened to the Holmes legacy and why. The episode of Holmes's meeting with Franklin Roosevelt has a symbolic importance. Flanked by FDR's intimate, Felix Frankfurter, and Holmes's former law clerk, Tom Corcoran, the president-elect visited the ancient justice. Asked later what he thought of his visitor, Holmes replied, "A first-rate temperament, a second-rate mind." Whether Holmes was right or not, the episode was premonitory of the collision between the Holmes legacy and the New Deal. Holmes was wide of the mark in one respect. This "second-rate mind" was resourceful enough to use Holmes's judicial strategy, and then became impatient of it and exploded in the militancy of the court-packing plan. Roosevelt ended by appointing a Supreme Court that fused the expanded executive power with a new liberal judicial activism.

There were powerful minds and personalities on the Roosevelt Court, clearly the ablest in American constitutional history. No one's *epigoni,* they were masterful men in their own right. The most talented of them came out of the assertive New Deal political culture. They were *novi homines,* a new, aggressive breed of political men: an Alabama redneck from Clay County who became a brilliant lawyer and Senate militant; a Jewish immigrant from Austria who worked with FDR in World War I and whose law students planned and staffed half the New Deal administrative agencies; a farm boy from Yakima, Washington, who became a law professor and ran the Securities and Exchange Commission; a Buffalo lawyer who skipped law school and became FDR's creative attorney general.

These four men, forming as vivid a core for a Court as any we have seen, became involved in a doctrinal feud that continued into the Warren Court. Hugo L. Black and William O. Douglas found the Holmes legacy both irrelevant and obstructive to their aims, while Felix Frankfurter and Robert H. Jackson used it as a strong, shaping, decisional force.

They all strove to be resourceful tacticians in their doctrinal maneuvers. Of the first pair, Douglas had the less original mind, distracted by sprawling interests that went beyond law to a liberated philosophy of life, both private and public. He tended to follow Black's doctrinal leads, combining them with an adherence to Brandeisian concepts, including, notably, the right of privacy, which was to prove expansive in later Courts.

Hugo Black may prove to have been the strongest, most original judicial mind since Holmes. His aim was to translate the New Deal revolution into constitutional law, and he succeeded. Largely an autodidact, he used historical excursions (not always accurate) to discover the original intent of the Fourteenth Amendment, in order to enlarge its impact. He built a bridge between a literalist absolutism on civil liberties and an expansionism on social protections, using historicism, the "incorporation" doctrine, equal protection, and the Establishment clause. His writing had a crude power in place of style, but he was a constitutional warrior in the Roosevelt, Vinson, and Warren Courts, with an unmatched doctrinal creativeness.

Felix Frankfurter had a richer, more intricate, more complex mind than Black or any justice since, and his style reflected it. His problem was that he was overprepared for his Court role. He had lived too many lives when Roosevelt named him to the Court — as reformer and professor at Cambridge, as Brandeis's alter ego, as Holmes's most fervent adherent, as FDR's close friend and adviser on every issue of state. He was Faustian, reaching out to all his competing hungers, while Holmes was Lucretian, with a long view of how the evolutionary gods play with human destinies.

In terms of internal mental struggle, Frankfurter was the central dramatic figure of the Court's history — a neo-Holmesian at heart, striving to reconcile the Holmes legacy of a constrained judicial doctrine with his commitment to a strange mixture of Brandeisian and New Deal social progressivism. It made for great intellectual theater and resulted in some remarkable (if unpopular) opinions in which he balanced the conflicting pulls on a perilous edge of decision. Yet this couldn't overcome the thrust of social forces that sustained Black's views. In the end, in his historic meeting of minds with Chief Justice Warren in *Brown v. Board of Education,* Frankfurter achieved his ultimate ideal of judicial statesmanship, moving beyond the Holmes doctrine in a time and arena so fraught with the clear and present danger of ethnic divisiveness that Holmes might well have reached the same result. For Holmes didn't like a vacuum of action, and *Brown* filled a great one.

Robert H. Jackson went along with Frankfurter and Warren on *Brown,* although more reluctantly than any of the others. He had an asperity of thought and word that made him the best stylist of the group. He wrote eloquently against judicial supremacy in any form and was quick to note the twistings and turnings of his liberal brethren in trying to avoid the charge. But he too suffered, as Frankfurter did, from the constraints of a decisional method that left most of the juicy doctrinal inventiveness to the opposing camp.

From FDR's appointments through Truman's and Eisenhower's, the constitutional wars raged, with varying results. But the long trend in the political and legal cultures was liberal-activist, and the Holmes heritage seemed distasteful, even repugnant, to generations of the young. The impact of this era on Holmes's reputation can scarcely have come as much of a surprise. The dominant liberal group didn't like either the austerities of Holmes or his doctrine of judicial deference. Quite naturally they homed in on their own philosophy of judicial activism, social engineering, and doctrinal inventiveness — all of which had been alien to Holmes. The Eisenhower appointees, Warren and Brennan (paradoxically liberals), fed the fires of the Court generation that went by Warren's name, while the Johnson appointees renewed and sustained them. It was the apogee of constitutional activism, which makes some sense of the fact that the Holmes legacy reached its nadir during the Warren 1960s.

The perceptions of Holmes by the law school culture were too narrow. While Holmes was the source and father of judicial deference, it was only one of the principles he judged by. Since he was wary of "general propositions" and shied from making an absolute of any, he made no absolute of this doctrine either. It was a star to steer by, but no chart for rough waters. He saw it as useful for a time in keeping the reactionary activism of his brothers from seizing the new America that was coming to birth and holding it unconstitutional. He also saw his deference doctrine as a way of keeping the contending powers of a democracy in balance, giving leeway to the majoritarian principle in legislative bodies — except when the threatened rights were basic to the competition of ideas and value systems that underlies all social change.

Yet Holmes never turned his doctrine rigid, never carried it into historical excursions in search of "original intent," never read the Constitution with a literalism that would leach out its meaning, any more than he read it with an expansionism that would bloat it beyond coherence. He recognized that the Constitution is a changing organism, as the nation is. Yet he also saw that both Constitution and nation need power to make them effective.

He refused to turn any of the three powers — executive, legislative, judicial — into an eidolon. Each had its functions. But when confronted by an aggressive expansion from either of the others, the deepest power of the judiciary was to establish a principle and draw a line of separation. "A line there must be" was Holmes's constant imperative, from the time of his early state court decisions to his great national organismic ones on the executive and taxing powers.

8

Two current schools of constitutional thought present the strongest challenge to the Holmes legacy. One from the Left, the other from the Right, both strike at the vulnerable point the Holmes legacy presents in terms of finding firm criteria for confronting a constantly transforming world with a document two centuries old. Law is not like literature, art, and philosophy, which can be distanced from the daily immediacies. It is caught in their whorl. When the immediacies change, in the form of instant media, "artificial intelligence," global money markets, missile systems in space, biotechnics, born-again faiths, drug addictions, terrorisms, and AIDS, we spot the archaisms in the document and demand new judgments and constitutional relationships that will meet the current discontents.

The Holmes answer was that there is a plenitude of power in the total constitutional system, and the Courts must draw a line between its claimants, but not to the enhancement of the judicial power when others have acted or can act. This didn't satisfy the challengers from the Left, from Black and Douglas through Warren, Fortas, and Brennan.

If I call them the "Warrenites" for convenience, I refer to the Warren Court as symbol. I mean also to include its philosophical support system in the universities and law schools, those who felt that too many "rights," of individuals and groups, will slip through the crevices of the Holmesian doctrine, leaving them unprotected unless the Courts act to do the protecting — whence the need for their activism. Ronald Dworkin's phrase, "taking rights seriously," summed up their concern.

The Holmes legacy was vulnerable to this concern. It failed to meet the fear that in the absence of judicial action — given prejudiced, fearful, or apathetic legislatures and executives — the cases on voting reapportionment, desegregated schools, the right to counsel, the *Miranda* warnings, affirmative action, access to abortions, and protections against sexual harassment would all have failed to be taken seriously enough to fill the social void or meet the social injustice. More than anything, it was this fear and the failure to meet it that turned the courts and the law school culture away from Holmes for so long. His "felt necessities" applied to the shaping of the common law, but failed to still the social urgencies that besieged constitutional law.

The trouble was, of course, that the expanding universe of liberal activism had no moral philosophy of its own to set limits on its rising entitlements and the interest-group incitements they provoked. The embrace of an unlimited rights dynamic within such a society heightens the centrifugal forces in it, diminishes the centripetal ones, and makes it all but impossible to govern from a center that will hold. It was the growing awareness of this, from the early 1970s, that reached the electorates and courts, undercut the liberal legal culture, and sent Holmes's reputation into an upward arc.

While the liberal aversion to Holmes came from his deflating of all utopianisms, the conservative attack focuses on his pragmatism and his relativism regarding values. Unlike the liberals who read selective "rights" into the Constitution through the "penumbra" around them, the traditionalists make the stronger case against Holmes from their "natural right" base, with a firm belief that the essential nature of man can be used to ground a good society and keep it from the ravages of both a grandiose activism and a laissez-faire particularism.

It is an insight that has given the Straussians (if I may use them as a counter to the Warrenites) a considerable entrance into constitutional history and law. If they have a strong case to make against Holmes, it is not because they are right about their version of "natural right" and Holmes wrong in his skepticism of all such philosophies. It is rather because the fault line between his pragmatism and his evolutionism kept him from offering a principle of cohesion to keep a postmodern society from disintegrating under its centrifugal pressures.

The problem of the Warrenites was their failure to set limits. The problem of the Straussians is that their flight from relativism and their quest for the single "truth" expose them to the enticement of absolute thinking. No movement of thought has yet succeeded in finding the common ground of truths and values in the history of human experience on which an absolute "natural right" can be based. Yet the anthropological approach, which the young Holmes used in his researches for *The Common Law,* might still yield a cluster of intersecting values that would be useful for constitutional thinkers as well. This might give judges a direction for meeting the strong social urgencies of the time, and for adding a measure of statesmanship to the Holmes legacy of judicial deference.

9

A word about the Holmes style. Almost every attack on him pays tribute to it, but only as a kind of adornment, even an excrescence, which obscures the "savagery" or "bleakness" of his doctrine. It makes no sense, however, to garland Holmes for being an artificer of beautiful passages while dismissing him for being wrongheaded. There are in fact some flowery passages in Holmes, especially in his perorations, and over the years he repeated favorite expressions in his speeches and correspondence. Yet in the judicial opinions themselves there is hardly ever a surplus word, a self-indulgent adjective, an unnecessary phrase. It is a style that cuts to the marrow of the issue at hand.

"A word is the skin of a thought," he wrote. This is more than an epigram; it is a thought that sheds light on his style. Holmes became a jurist but never ceased to be what he had all along dreamed of being, long before his law school years — a philosophical writer. There is no separation in him between style and substance; they are one. The word encloses and illumines the thought, which gives content and meaning to the word. Both his word and thought have the same crispness, economy, cutting edge, the same sparkling sense of playfulness, the same perversity in the face of fashions, the same unerring aim at the jugular — the same essence and permanence.

I add a personal note about my own perception of Holmes. Several years before the book's publication, Walton Hamilton, then at Yale Law School, wrote an influential *Yale Law Review* article, "On Dating Mr. Justice Holmes." It said, in effect, that Holmes had come to seem both timeless and dateless, yet he was in fact a creature of his time and needed to be dated. As it happens, Hamilton was my teacher at the Robert Brookings Graduate School, where I learned some constitutional law in 1925 and first encountered the great Holmes decisions. One thing Hamilton taught us was to "place" a thinker in time and in social and personal circumstances. I sought to do it in this book, especially in the introductory essay on Holmes's "personal history."

Where the critics of Holmes (including Hamilton) had it wrong was in their belief that the act of placing a thinker or artist in time strips him of what timelessness he has achieved. This has not proved true of Emerson, Whitman, O'Neill, and Faulkner, nor of either William or Henry James, who were of Holmes's generation and social circle. Like them all, Holmes was a creature of his time and circumstance, but — also like them — he reached beyond it to universals. In his case the universals involved the process of judging, including the complex and intrusive role of being the judge himself.

Because judicial review is the greatest American achievement in the arts of the polity, we have needed thinkers with insights that start with particulars and reach to the universal. It cannot be said of Holmes that he was free of the judgment of successive generations. Yet, however savaged, he has survived and somehow prevailed. Of all the American judges in time and circumstance, there is a quality of *gravitas* in Holmes that gives him a measure of this timelessness.

There have been a number of attempts to write Holmes's life, but all have been partial or truncated. He is a hard subject to seize. Grant Gilmore, the custodian of the Holmes papers after the death of his biographer, Mark DeWolfe Howe, saw more "darkness" in Holmes than he could handle, and gave up. Yet he stated: "To the extent that I can follow the dark outlines of his thought Holmes was both a greater man and a more profound thinker than the mythical Holmes ever was."

I never took either of the Holmes myths as final — the mythologizing of the 1920s and 1930s or the countermythologizing of the mid-1940s to the mid-1970s. Holmes is indeed a mythic figure, but in a different sense than myth seen as unreality. He has become mythic in the sense that his constitutional journey has become part of the journey taken in each generation — including the journey of those who resisted and attacked him.

Nor do I take the Holmes "revival" of the past decade as decisive or final. His critics made law school reputations by him, only to be dismayed by the refusal of his reputation to lie down and die. The faithful on the Burger and Rehnquist Courts in the 1980s picked only a single strand of Holmes for their fealty — judicial restraint — and they turned it into a historicism of "original intent" that attenuated what he meant and missed the richness of his range.

There will be other dips and rises in his reputation. A figure like Holmes becomes a way of looking into the mirror of ourselves and our time. He will rise and fall with the "felt necessities" of time and self-hood, with attitudes toward civilizational change and continuity, with perceptions of the life and death principles, and with the imperatives of the most difficult of all arts of governing — the art of adjudication.

This is especially true in an America that has suffered convulsive changes since Holmes's death, becoming not only a nation of competing pluralisms but also a kingpin of the Western imperium, in a world of terrorism but also of an emerging community of law. Holmes couldn't have foreseen it, yet it is wholly compatible with his long perspectives. In such an America of changes and chances there is — more than anything else — a need for cohesion through permanences. I say permanences, not absolutes. "Continuity with the past," Holmes noted, "is not a duty. It is only a necessity."

Holmes didn't think much of engineered changes in which

politically minded judges decide what is good for others. He did very much believe in broad evolutionary change and wanted judges to be part of it and to help set its channels and limits. With such a philosophy, he defined the judicial tasks of his own age — and of ours — more trenchantly than any of his assailers or followers. This is his relevance for today and tomorrow.

1989

EDITOR'S NOTE

MAX LERNER BEGAN HIS INTELLECTUAL JOURNEY STUDYING THE DECISION-making processes of the Supreme Court, so it is fitting that his final contribution should be this volume. Working with him on it was a considerable privilege, and over a two-year period we discussed not only the contents of the book but also related matters pertaining to the body politic. As a man whose career spanned more than half a century, it would have been natural for Lerner to have a great deal to say in these conversations, but he contained his opinions, asking me instead what I thought. He never made me feel uncomfortable, but rather instilled in me the confidence to articulate positions that I thought might not be in accord with his own.

On one occasion, he and I discussed the ambiguity of the Supreme Court's authority, given the fact that a critical decision might be decided by one vote. By such a slim majority, a vital constitutional right might be preserved or lost. This was, he explained, the crux of the battle Roosevelt had with the Court when it overturned important New Deal legislation. I had covered this important matter of constitutional history countless times in my classes, but never had I discussed it with someone who had been in the center of the fight. The sense of immediacy he conveyed was startling, the history pouring from him in wonderful, rounded sentences.

Each time I sent a portion of this manuscript back to him, he would make further revisions and return it to me with his remarks written in the margins or at the very end. Invariably there would be a letter explaining why he had made the corrections. Gradually, as he became weaker physically, a sense of greater urgency prevailed. Several weeks before his death, we met at his apartment on East End Avenue in Manhattan, overlooking the East River. He had just returned from the hospital, where he had completed his last chemotherapy treatment, ever optimistic that he had yet again wrestled with the angel of death and defeated him. His wife, Edna, showed us to the dining table, where the manuscript was spread out, and left us to finish the project. Several hours later, she helped us put everything into boxes that I carried to the elevator and then put in my car. I said good-bye to Max Lerner knowing that I would probably never see him again. He died June 5, 1992.

R.C.
Bridgehampton, New York

MAX LERNER ON
LAW AND JUSTICE IN AMERICA

MAX LERNER'S FIRST BRUSH WITH THE WORLD OF LAW RESULTED IN HIS pleading, in effect, nolo contendere. After graduating from Yale University in 1923, he spent a semester at Yale Law School, but one semester was enough to convince him that he didn't want to contend in the pursuit leading to the legal profession. In a memoir of his early years, Lerner recalled: "I found law dreary going. The thought of spending my life scrambling for clients and fighting over someone's negligence suit didn't inspire me. The prospect of court work was more inviting but not enough. Was it for this that I had given up a literary career, only to move into a grubby jungle-like pursuit where any means was accepted if you could get away with it?"

Lerner's newfound desire for (in his words) "a career of teaching, writing and reform" propelled him to study economics and government in graduate school. Yet history and philosophy of law, as well as constitutional and Supreme Court concerns, repeatedly absorbed his attention as he completed his doctoral work and began to make his name as a writer and thinker. Less than a decade after leaving law school, Lerner was contributing influential and widely discussed essays to the *Yale Law Journal*. A devoted generalist committed to studying and expressing his opinions about a multitude of aspects of life and thought, he kept returning to matters of law in his books, scholarly essays, magazine articles, book reviews, and approximately 8,000 newspaper columns (published from 1938 until his death in 1992).

In remarks delivered at a memorial tribute for Lerner in New York, Irving Louis Horowitz, Hannah Arendt Distinguished Professor of Sociology and Political Science at Rutgers University and president of Transaction Publishers, singled out "Max's enduring faith in the law" as a hallmark of his intellectual life. Horowitz went on to note that "it was Lerner's special talent to appreciate the limits of power as defining the American civilization.

/ 315

Those limits were located in the law, in the delicate web of rights and obligations that our people are dedicated to preserve. But it is not simply the legal or juridical edifice that Max uniquely understood, it is the special compassion of a people capable of transforming law into justice. For without justice, the law is a punitive tool externally imposed. With justice, the law is the internal expression of a tradition, and of a people."

Max Lerner's legacy for understanding the law and justice in the United States — and for seeing the meaning of the law and justice for America as a civilization — can be found in the following works.

BOOKS

It Is Later Than You Think: The Need for a Militant Democracy. New York: Viking Press, 1938; rev. ed., 1943. Reprint, New Brunswick, N.J.: Transaction Publishers, 1989.
   The chapter entitled "Majorities and Minorities" has sections on "The Majority Principle" and "Civil Liberties for All."
Ideas Are Weapons: The History and Uses of Ideas. New York: Viking Press, 1939. Reprint, New Brunswick, N.J.: Transaction Publishers, 1991.
   This collection of essays has several about the Supreme Court and particular justices, and includes "The Jungle of Legal Thought."
Ideas for the Ice Age: Studies in a Revolutionary Age. New York: Viking Press, 1941. Reprint, New Brunswick, N.J.: Transaction Publishers, 1992.
   This collection of essays includes the earliest version of "The Mind and Faith of Justice Holmes" as well as seven articles under the heading "The Supreme Court Crisis" and the essay "Constitutional Crisis and the Crisis State."
The Mind and Faith of Justice Holmes: His Speeches, Essays, Letters, and Judicial Opinions. Edited and with an introduction by Max Lerner. Boston: Little, Brown, 1943; rev. ed., New York: Modern Library, 1954. Reprint, New Brunswick, N.J.: Transaction Publishers, 1989.
   A book that combines the classic works of Holmes and lengthy analytical commentary by Lerner.
Public Journal: Marginal Notes on Wartime America. New York: Viking Press, 1945.
   A collection of columns that were written for the New York newspaper *PM* from February 4, 1943, to November 15, 1944. Several discuss rights and justice while war is raging.

Actions and Passions: Notes on the Multiple Revolution of Our Time. New
York: Simon and Schuster, 1949.
A collection of newspaper columns — for *PM* and the *New York Star* —
that appeared between November 1944 and August 1948. Noteworthy
judicial cases and legal concerns receive consideration.
America as a Civilization: Life and Thought in the United States Today.
New York: Simon and Schuster, 1957. Reprint, New York: Henry Holt
and Company, 1987.
The sections "Law and Justice," "Keepers of the Covenant," and "The
Struggle for Civil Liberties" are particularly relevant. In the 1987
thirtieth-anniversary edition, the new postscript chapter, "Governing,
Belonging, Law," offers commentary on more contemporary concerns
and issues.
The Unfinished Country: A Book of American Symbols. New York: Simon
and Schuster, 1959.
A collection of columns, originally written for the *New York Post*
between 1949 and 1959, many of which focus on cases and legal
controversies occurring in the 1950s.
Tocqueville and American Civilization. New York: Harper Colophon Books,
1969. Reprint, New Brunswick, N.J.: Transaction Publishers, 1994.
The chapters "The Polity: Power, Law and the Elite" and "Freedom in
a Mass Society" offer close analysis of *Democracy in America* and an
assessment of Alexis de Tocqueville's interpretation of the American
legal system.
Magisterial Imagination: Six Masters of the Human Sciences. Edited and
with an introduction by Robert Schmuhl. New Brunswick, N.J.: Transaction Publishers, 1994.
Lerner's studies of Alexis de Tocqueville and Oliver Wendell Holmes,
Jr., deal extensively with the law in America and its civilizational
context.

ARTICLES

"The Social Thought of Mr. Justice Brandeis." *Yale Law Journal* 41 (No-
vember 1931): 1–32.
"The Supreme Court and American Capitalism." *Yale Law Journal* 42
(March 1933): 668–701.
"John Marshall's Long Shadow." *New Republic* 84 (September 18, 1935):
148–52.
"The Riddle of the Supreme Court." "I: The Divine Right of Judges"; "II:
The Lawless Supreme Court"; "III: Where Does the Supreme Court
Stand?"; "IV: The Fate of the Supreme Court." *Nation* 142 (January

29, 1936): 121–23; (February 19, 1936): 213–15; (March 4, 1936): 273–75; (March 25, 1936): 379–81.

"Justice Holmes: Flowering and Defeat." *Nation* 142 (June 10, 1936): 746–47.

"Brandeis at Eighty." *Nation* 143 (November 14, 1936): 565–66.

"Lippmann and the Court." *Nation* 144 (February 27, 1937): 230.

"Constitution and Court as Symbols." *Yale Law Journal* 46 (June 1937): 1290–1319.

"Hugo Black: A Personal History." *Nation* 145 (October 9, 1937): 367–69; (November 6, 1937): 515.

"Minority Rule and the Constitutional Tradition." *University of Pennsylvania Law Review* 86 (March 1938): 457–70.

"Justice Black, Dissenting." *Nation* 146 (March 5, 1938): 264–66.

"The Supreme Court Revolution." *Nation* 146 (June 11, 1938): 660–61.

"Homage to Brandeis." *Nation* 148 (February 25, 1939): 222.

"John Marshall and the Campaign of History." *Columbia Law Review* 39 (March 1939): 396–431.

"The Supreme Court and Labor." *New Republic* 104 (February 24, 1941): 262–64.

"Constitutional Crisis and the Crisis State." *William and Mary Bulletin*, November 1941.

"The Great Constitutional War." *Virginia Quarterly Review* 18 (Autumn 1942): 530–45.

"The Supreme Court." *Holiday* 7 (February 1950): 72–73ff.

"William O. Douglas." In *Encyclopedia of American Biography*, edited by John A. Garraty, 289–90. New York: Harper and Row, 1974.

"Robert H. Jackson." In *Encyclopedia of American Biography*, edited by John A. Garraty, 571–73. New York: Harper and Row, 1974.

"Walton H. Hamilton." In *Dictionary of American Biography*, supplement 6, 1956–1960, edited by John A. Garraty, 271–72. New York: Charles Scribner's Sons, 1980.

"Four Ways of Looking at the Court — And a Fifth." In *Costitutional Government in America*, edited by Ronald K. L. Collins, 457–466. Durham, N. C.: Carolina Academic Press, 1980.

"Judicial Review in America: Some Reflection. In *Constitutional Government in America*, edited by Ronald K. L. Collins, 494–497. Durham, N. C.: Carolina Academic Press, 1980.

"Bork's Progress." *New Republic* 197 (September 14–21, 1987): 18–20.

"Courting Rituals." *New Republic* 198 (February 1, 1988): 16–18.

"Some Reflections on the First Amendment in an Age of Paratroopers." *Texas Law Review* 68 (May 1990): 1127–36.

REVIEWS AND REVIEW ESSAYS

Review of *The Heavenly City of Eighteenth Century Philosophers,* by Carl Becker. *Yale Law Journal* 42 (May 1933): 1143–48.

Review of *The New Jurisprudence,* by Edward Jenks. *Columbia Law Review* 33 (December 1933): 1464–65.

Review of *Law and the Social Order,* by Morris R. Cohen. *Harvard Law Review* 47 (December 1933): 380–86.

Review of *Modern Theories of Law* (no editor given). *Yale Law Journal* 43 (March 1934): 854–58.

Review of *The Curse of Bigness,* by Louis D. Brandeis, edited by Osmond K. Fraenkel. *New York Herald-Tribune,* March 17, 1935, p. 6.

Review of *The Curse of Bigness,* by Louis D. Brandeis, edited by Osmond K. Fraenkel. *New Republic* 83 (May 22, 1935): 53.

Review of *Mr. Justice Cardozo,* by Joseph P. Pollard. *New Republic* 83 (July 17, 1935): 283–84.

Review of *Historic Opinions of the United States Supreme Court,* edited by Ambrose Doskow. *New Republic* 84 (September 11, 1935): 136–37.

Review of *Law and the Social Sciences,* by Huntington Cairns. *New Republic* 85 (November 20, 1935): 53–54.

Review of *Institutional Economics,* by John R. Commons. *Harvard Law Review* 49 (December 1935): 360–65.

Review of *Justice Oliver Wendell Holmes: His Book Notices and Uncollected Letters and Papers,* edited by Harry C. Shriver. *Yale Law Journal* 46 (March 1937): 904–8.

Review of *Selected Supreme Court Decisions,* edited by Myer Cohen. *Nation* 145 (August 14, 1937): 176–77.

Review of *Roger B. Taney,* by Carl B. Swisher. *American Historical Review* 43, no. 2 (January 1938): 415–18.

Review of *The Folklore of Capitalism,* by Thurman Arnold. *Yale Law Journal* 47 (March 1938): 687–703.

Review of *Mr. Justice Holmes and the Supreme Court,* by Felix Frankfurter. *Nation* 147 (November 19, 1938): 537–39.

Review of *Our Eleven Chief Justices,* by Kenneth B. Umbreit. *New Republic* 98 (March 1, 1939): 109–10.

Review of *Court Over Constitution,* by Edward S. Corwin. *Harvard Law Review* 52 (April 1939): 1033–35.

Review of *Our Eleven Chief Justices,* by Kenneth B. Umbreit, and *Judges of the Supreme Court,* by Cortez A. M. Ewing. *National Lawyer's Guild Quarterly* 2 (April 1939): 9–16.

Review of *The Contract Clause of the Constitution,* by Benjamin F. Wright, Jr. *Yale Law Journal* 49 (December 1939): 362–64.

Review of *Woe Unto You, Lawyers!* by Fred Rodell. *Journal of Politics* 2 (August 1940): 336–42.

Review of *The Holmes-Pollock Letters*, edited by Mark DeWolfe Howe, *Harvard Law Review* 55 (April 1942): 1069–73.

Review of *Yankee from Olympus*, by Catherine Drinker Bowen. *New Republic* 110 (May 29, 1944): 742–43.

Review of *Free Speech and Its Relation to Self-Government*, by Alexander Meiklejohn. *New Republic* 119 (September 13, 1948): 21–22.

Review of *My Father: A Remembrance*, by Hugo Black, Jr. *New Republic* 173 (October 18, 1975): 25–26.

Review of *Honorable Justice: The Life of Oliver Wendell Holmes*, by Sheldon Novick. *New Republic* 202 (April 2, 1990): 34–36.

Robert Schmuhl
University of Notre Dame

NOTES

CHAPTER 1 THE SUPREME COURT AND AMERICAN CAPITALISM

1. There have perhaps been states in the past more completely under the judicial sway than America. But the idea that the rule of judges through their veto power over legislation is the unique American contribution to the science of government has become a truism of political thought.
2. The phrase is that of Felix Frankfurter, "Mr. Justice Brandeis and Constitution," in Frankfurter, ed., *Mr. Justice Brandeis* (1932), 125; but the appraisal represented is a good one.
3. Albert Beveridge, *The Life of John Marshall* (1916–1920). This was due, to some extent, to the general bitterness of party polemics in a period of political realities. See also Charles Warren, *The Supreme Court in United States History* (1922), for a vivid depiction of a similar effect. Both Beveridge and Warren drew copiously from newspaper material.
4. Dall. 419 (U.S. 1793).
5. Oliver Wendell Holmes, *Collected Legal Papers* (1920), 295.
6. Thorstein Veblen, *Theory of Business Enterprise,* chapter 6, "Business Principles in Law and Politics."
7. Felix Frankfurter and James M. Landis, *The Business of the Supreme Court* (1927), chapter 8.

CHAPTER 2 CONSTITUTION AND COURT AS SYMBOLS

1. See Laura Kalman's brilliantly researched study, *Legal Realism at Yale 1927–1960* (1986), which focuses on a somewhat later period.
2. It will be readily apparent in this essay how much I owe to other writers: to Edward S. Corwin, "The Constitution as Instrument and as Symbol,"

Harvard Tercentenary address, *American Political Science Review* 30 (1936); to Schechter, "The Early History of the Tradition of the Constitution," *American Political Science Review* 9 (1915): 707; to Walton Hamilton "Constitutionalism," *Encyclopaedia of the Social Sciences,* vol. 4 (1931), 255; to Thurman Arnold, *The Symbols of Government* (1935); to Jerome Frank, *Law and the Modern Mind* (1930). I have, incidentally, used rather freely sentences from my series of articles, "The Riddle of the Supreme Court," *Nation* 142 (1936): 121, 213, 273, 379.

3. See Sapir's suggestive article, "Symbolism," *Encyclopaedia of the Social Sciences,* vol. 14 (1931), 492, 493.

4. Walton Hamilton, "Constitutionalism," *Encyclopaedia of the Social Sciences,* vol. 3 (1934), 255. See also Friedrich, *Constitutional Government and Politics* (1937), especially pp. 8−10, for a view of constitutionalism that differs from Hamilton's.

5. The phrase is that of Oliver Wendell Holmes, who was more canny in seeing through the judicial symbols than any other incumbent on the Court. It comes from his opinion in *Northern Pacific v. Jensen,* 244 U.S. 205 (1917), and refers to the mystical conception of the common law.

6. *Standard Oil Co. v. United States,* 221 U.S. 1 (1910).

7. Brooks Adams, *The Theory of Social Revolutions* (1913), 119−31.

8. "I love judges, and I love courts. They are my ideals, that typify on earth what we shall meet hereafter in heaven under a just God."

9. For a good analysis of this devotion, see Felix Frankfurter, *The Commerce Clause under Marshall, Taney and Waite* (1937), which, although a small book, is crowded with insights into the psychological and historical character of the judicial process in the Supreme Court.

10. 297 U.S. 1 (1936).

11. *National Labor Relations Board v. Jones & Laughlin Steel Corp.,* 57 Sup. Ct. 615 (1937).

12. The theory of judicial decision as resting on the "odd man" owes more, I think, to Thomas Reed Powell than to anyone else in American legal thought. See, for example, his remarkable articles, "Commerce, Pensions and Codes," *Harvard Law Review* 49, no. 1 (1935): 193.

13. The philosopher who made fear the classic psychological basis of state power was Thomas Hobbes. I agree with Harold Laski, however, that the motive to obedience in the state is by no means solely fear: "It may be doubted whether, save in times of passionate crisis, the vast majority of people ever think of fear in the context of obedience to the law." Laski, *The State in Theory and Practice* (1935).

14. Adams, *The Theory of Social Revolutions,* 232.

15. Friedrich Nietzsche speaks, in *Beyond Good and Evil* (trans. Zimmern, 4th ed., [1923], pp. 109−110), of "the moral hypocrisy of the commanding class," which "knows no other way of protecting themselves from their bad conscience than by playing the role of executors of older and higher orders,

of predecessors, of the constitution, of justice, of the law, of God himself."
16. Brooks Adams's comment in 1895 seems relevant today: "The only question which preoccupies the ruling class is whether it is cheaper to coerce or bribe." Adams, *The Law of Civilization and Decay* (1st ed., 1895), 292.

CHAPTER 3 THE EARLY CAREER OF JUDICIAL ACTIVISM

1. *Appalachian Coal, Inc. v. U.S.,* 288 U.S. 344 (1933).
2. *Home Building and Loan Assn. v. Blaisdell,* 290 U.S. 398 (1934).
3. *Nebbia v. N.Y.,* 291 U.S. 502 (1934).
4. *Rickert Rice Mills v. Fontenot,* 297 U.S. 110 (1936).
5. Eventually Congress provided that taxes be refunded only to the extent that the processors could show they had not passed the tax on. This was upheld in *Anniston Mfg. Co. v. Davis,* U.S. 337 (1937). And later still, the second AAA was upheld in *Mulford v. Smith,* 307 U.S. 38 (1930), which turned on the commerce power.

CHAPTER 4 MINORITY RULE AND THE CONSTITUTIONAL TRADITION

1. This essay was first read at the meeting of the American Historical Association in Philadelphia, December 30, 1937. It was first published in the *University of Pennsylvania Law Review,* March 1938, and was reprinted in Conyers Read, ed., *The Constitution Reconsidered* (1938).
2. Quoted in Nelles and King, "Contempt by Publication in the United States," *Columbia Law Review* 28 (1928): 401, 428.
3. The theme of usurpation, either in assertion or denial, is the grand underlying theme of most of the recent literature on the Supreme Court. Thus also has the theme of exploitation been used as the grand theme of much of the recent literature on capitalism. But the abstract question of legalism would seem to have as little to do with political power realities as the abstract question of social justice with economic power realities. In both cases, they are usable primarily as evocative myths.
4. Paraphrasing Lord Justice Buckley in *Hanau v. Ehrlich,* 2 K.B. 1056, 1069 (1911), one may say that it is a century and a quarter too late to apply our own minds independently to the task of determining whether judicial review was intended by the Constitution.
5. Elliott, "The Constitution as a Social Myth," in Read, *The Constitution Reconsidered;* Arnold, *Symbols of Government* (1935) and *Folklore of Capitalism* (1937).
6. *United States v. Butler,* 297 U.S. 1, 79 (1936), dissenting opinion.
7. I am referring, of course, to his famous distinction between status and contract. See Henry Maine, *Ancient Law* (6th ed., 1876), 170.

8. The case referred to involved the Agricultural Adjustment Administration. *United States v. Butler,* 297 U.S. 1 (1936).

9. During the public controversy in 1937 over President Roosevelt's plan to reorganize the Court, many liberals who had earlier been critical of the Court's decisions came to its defense, motivated largely by the fear that "packing" the Court or weakening its prestige would remove the principal guarantee of civil liberties.

10. Charles Beard, *Economic Interpretation of the Constitution* (2nd ed., 1935). I do not mean that Mr. Beard has himself fallen into the error of posing an antithesis between the Constitution and the democratic impulse, but that the emphasis in his early work lent credence to that error.

11. Hamilton and Adair, *The Power to Govern* (1937).

12. Edwin S. Corwin, "The Constitution as Instrument and Symbol," *American Political Science Review* 30 (1936): 1071.

13. *Fletcher v. Peck,* 6 Cranch 87 (U.S. 1810).

14. *Lochner v. New York,* 198 U.S. 45 (1905).

15. *New State Ice Co. v. Liebmann,* 285 U.S. 262 (1932).

16. Henry Adams, *History of the United States during the Administration of Jefferson* (1930), 85.

17. Ames's writings are the classic repository of antidemocratic comment. "Our country," he wrote in 1803, "is too big for union, too sordid for patriotism, too democratic for liberty." See Adams, *History of the United States during the Administration of Jefferson,* 83. And George Cabot, another high Federalist, wrote in 1804: "We are democratic altogether; and I hold democracy in its natural operation to be the government of the worst." Ibid., 165.

18. Dorothy Thompson, "The President's Political Philosophy," *New York Herald-Tribune,* Aug. 23, 1937, p. 15, col. 7; Aug. 25, 1937, p. 17, col. 7; Aug. 27, p. 15, col. 7.

19. This conception of the common man is embodied in the antidemocratic philosophy of Nietzsche and other German romantics; it deeply influenced the thought of Carlyle, Ruskin, and other English writers of the nineteenth century. See Brinton, *English Political Thought in the Nineteenth Century* (1933); Lippincott, *Victorian Critics of Democracy* (1938). It has also found expression in such contemporary writers as Wyndham Lewis, *The Act of Being Ruled* (1926); H. L. Mencken, *Notes on Democracy* (1926).

20. See Konopczynski, "Minority Rights," *Encyclopaedia of the Social Sciences,* vol. 10 (1937), 525.

CHAPTER 6 SOME PERSPECTIVES ON THE COURT

1. See Max Lerner, "The Social Thought of Mr. Justice Brandeis," in *Ideas Are Weapons* (1939).
2. See Max Lerner, *The Mind and Faith of Justice Holmes* (1943), 90 passim.
3. See Max Lerner, "John Marshall and the Campaign of History," *Columbia Law Review* 39 (1939): 386.
4. Originally used in an article in *Fortune*. See also Daniel Bell, *The Cultural Contradictions of Capitalism* (1976).
5. See Reich, "The New Property," *Yale Law Journal* 73 (1964): 733.
6. See Max Lerner, *Tocqueville and American Civilization* (1966).
7. On this theme see Arthur Schlesinger, Jr., "American Experiment or Destiny?" *American Historical Review* 82 (1977): 505.
8. See, generally, Max Lerner, "American Agonistes," *Foreign Affairs* 52 (Jan. 1974): 287.
9. For the typology of which "active-positive" is part, see J. Barber, *Presidential Character* (2nd ed., 1977).

CHAPTER 7 JOHN MARSHALL AND THE CAMPAIGN OF HISTORY

1. Oliver Wendell Holmes, *Collected Legal Papers* (1920), 268–70.
2. "It will be difficult to find a character of firmness enough to preserve his independence on the same Bench with Marshall." Jefferson to Madison, May 25, 1810. *Jefferson's Writings*, vol. 9, ed. Ford (1892), 275. And Attorney General Rodney, referring to the defection of Justice Johnson, thought to be a staunch Republican, wrote in a letter to Jefferson, "You can scarcely elevate a man to a seat in the Court of Justice before he catches the leprosy of the Bench." Letter of Oct. 31, 1808.
3. Albert Beveridge, *Life of John Marshall* (1916), 3–19.
4. Joseph Story, *Life and Letters*, ed. William Story (1851), 505–506; Marshall to Story, Nov. 26, 1826.
5. Edward S. Corwin, "John Marshall," in *Dictionary of American Biography*, vol. 12, 316.
6. " 'Millions for Defense but not a cent for Tribute' is one of the few historic expressions in which Federalism spoke in the voice of America. Thus the Marshall banquet in Philadelphia June 18, 1798, produced that slogan of defiant patriotism which is one of the slowly accumulating American maxims that have lived." Beveridge, *Life of John Marshall*, vol. 2, 348–49.
7. As early as 1800 Marshall wrote to Otis, "There is a tide in the affairs of nations, of parties, of individuals . . . I fear that of real Americanism is on the ebb." Beveridge, *Life of John Marshall*, vol. 2, 515. And as late as

1833, "Marshall could not free his mind of the despondency that had now settled upon him. . . . He was sure to refer to the woeful state of the country and the black future it portended." Ibid., vol. 4, 575. See also Story, *Life and Letters,* 172–73.

8. *The Works of Thomas Jefferson,* ed. H. A. Washington (1884), 424–25; letter to John Dickinson, Dec. 19, 1801.

9. It had for some time been believed that Marshall did not know of President Adams's intention to appoint him until he received formal notice. This was Beveridge's view. But a recently discovered letter of Marshall's to Story in 1827 gives a different picture. Adams first asked John Jay, whose Federalism could be trusted. On Jay's refusal, William Paterson was considered. But Marshall relates that Adams said: "I shall not nominate him." Then, after a moment's hesitation, "I believe I must nominate you [Marshall]." "I was pleased as well as surprized," Marshall writes, "and bowed in silence." *An Autobiographical Sketch by John Marshall,* written at the request of Joseph Story, ed. John Stokes Adams (1937).

10. Holmes, *Collected Legal Papers,* 267–68.

11. Charles Beard, *Economic Origins of Jeffersonian Democracy* (1915), 454–55.

12. Edward S. Corwin has called this the "political" or "departmental" doctrine of judicial review, as against Marshall's "juristic" doctrine. See his *Court over Constitution* (1938), 5–7.

13. Marbury, a small-time Federalist politician, was one of John Adams's "midnight appointments," as justice of the peace for the District of Columbia. The appointment had been ratified by the Senate, the commission had been signed and sealed; everything had been done to give William Marbury his petty office and eternal obscurity except one thing — the commission had not been delivered. It had been left on the desk of Secretary of State John Marshall, who had been too busy to follow the affairs of William Marbury. Now Marbury was seeking from the Supreme Court a writ of mandamus commanding Secretary of State James Madison to give up the commission.

14. Whether President Jackson actually said this is now extremely doubtful. See Beveridge, *Life of John Marshall,* vol. 4, 551. It was Horace Greeley, in his *American Conflict* (1864–66; vol. 1, 106), who attributed the remark to him. See Marquis James, *Andrew Jackson, Portrait of a President* (1937), 304–305.

15. J. A. C. Grant, "*Marbury v. Madison,*" *American Political Science Review* 23 (1929): 673, 681.

16. Louis B. Boudin, *Government by Judiciary,* vol. 2 (1932), 230–31. See also Corwin, *Court over Constitution,* 65–68.

17. "The morals of the author of the letter to Mazzei," wrote Marshall, "cannot be pure." *Works of Alexander Hamilton,* ed. J. C. Hamilton, vol. 6 (1850), 501–503; Marshall to Hamilton, Jan. 1, 1801.

18. Judge Pickering of New Hampshire was a known drunkard, and his eccentricities bordered on insanity. Justice Samuel Chase of Maryland delivered from the bench tirades against Republican principles and practices that would have graced the speeches of President Timothy Dwight of Yale, who had brooded so deeply on what the Republicans might do in the future that he had convinced himself they had done so in the present.

19. "No state shall . . . pass any . . . law impairing the obligation of contracts." Art. I, 10, paragraph 1. For a full discussion of the history of the clause and its constitutional interpretation, see Wright, *The Contract Clause of the Constitution* (1938).

20. Henry Maine, *Ancient Law* (1906 ed.), 165. Maine valued Marshall's work highly and was deeply influenced by it. In his *Popular Government* (1885), 248, he calls the Marshall contract decisions "the bulwark of American individualism against democratic impatience and socialistic fantasy."

21. Edward Corwin was more responsible than anyone else before Wright for tracing the history of this doctrine. See his "A Basic Doctrine of American Law," *Michigan State Law Review* 12 (1913): 247–76, and "The Doctrine of Due Process of Law before the Civil War," *Harvard Law Review* 24 (1911): 366–85, 460–79. See also Haines, *The Revival of Natural Law Concepts* (1930), chap. 4, and my own article, "Vested Interests," *Encyclopedia of the Social Sciences*, vol. 15 (1934), 240–43. Wright, *The Contract Clause of the Constitution*, n. 40, includes the vested rights doctrine in its discussion of the history of the contract clause.

22. The first important one, *Calder v. Bull*, 3 Dall. 386 (U.S. 1798), involved the interpretation of the ex post facto clause.

23. *Fletcher v. Peck*, 6 Cranch 87 (U.S. 1810). Quotation is from Morgan, "New England and the Yazoo Land Frauds, 1795–1814," *Americana* 9 (1914): 324, 325. This is easily the best discussion of the political and social context of the case, and a brilliant piece of writing. See also Haskins, *The Yazoo Land Companies* (1891); Edward S. Corwin, *John Marshall and the Constitution* (1919); Wright, *The Contract Clause of the Constitution*, 29–34.

24. This opinion will be found reprinted in Wright, *The Contract Clause of the Constitution*, 22.

25. Story's brief is summarized in 6 Cranch 115–125, Martin's in 6 Cranch 115 (U.S. 1810). Justice William Johnson raised the question of collusion in his concurring opinion, but Marshall did not. Beveridge guesses that the reason that Johnson, a Jefferson appointee, did not press the matter more strongly was that Madison wanted the ruling that Marshall favored.

26. Cranch 603 (U.S. 1813).

27. Nine months after Story handed down the decision in 1813, Spencer Roane and the other judges of the Virginia Court of Appeals unanimously refused to obey the Supreme Court's ruling. Jefferson, in a letter to Roane (Oct. 12, 1815), approved of Roane's action. *Jefferson's Writings*, vol. 9,

ed. Ford (1892), 530–532. The case reappeared in the Supreme Court as *Martin v. Hunter's Lessee,* 1 Wheat. 304 (U.S. 1816). Again Story reiterated his first decision.

28. 6 Pet. 691 (U.S. 1832).

29. 9 Pet. 137 (U.S. 1835).

30. 10 Pet. 100 (U.S. 1836).

31. *Trustee of Dartmouth College v. Woodward,* 4 Wheat. 517 (U.S. 1819).

32. Letter to Governor William Plumer, July 1, 1816, in *Writings of William Plumer,* ed. A. Peabody (1857), 440–41.

33. This is apocryphal. Professor Goodrich of Yale, who attended the trial, told the story to Rufus Choate, in whose biography it appears. See also Fuess, *Daniel Webster* (1930). Although Webster's speech was a great example of forensic art, Hopkinson seems to have delivered the better argument.

34. Marshall wrote the court opinion upholding the charter as a contract: 4 Wheat. 518 (U.S. 1819); Justices Washington and Story wrote concurring opinions: 4 Wheat. 518, 654, 666, mostly supplying the legal learning Marshall's opinion lacked. Justice Johnson concurred with Marshall. Justice Livingston acquiesced in all the opinions. Justice Duval dissented without opinion.

35. This of course excludes business corporations that have the direct character of public utilities, which might be argued to come within the scope of public contract.

36. For an earlier case involving tax exemption specifically, see *New Jersey v. Wilson,* 7 Cranch 164 (U.S. 1812). See also *Providence Bank v. Billings,* 4 Pet. 514 (U.S. 1830), where Marshall limited his own doctrine of tax immunity, along much the same lines of strict construction of a charter that Taney was to follow in the *Charles River Bridge* case.

37. *Proprietors of Charles River Bridge v. Proprietors of Warren Bridge,* 11 Pet. 420 (U.S. 1837).

CHAPTER 8 THE GREAT GANGLION THAT WAS HOLMES

1. Roosevelt wrote Lodge a similar letter in 1906, on the appointment of Justice Horace Lurton. See *Selections from the Correspondence of Theodore Roosevelt and Henry Cabot Lodge* (1925), vol. 1, 517–591 for Holmes, and vol. 2, 228–229 for the striking letter on Lurton.

CHAPTER 9 FRANKFURTER ON HOLMES AND THE AUSTERITY THEORY

1. This was written before Professor Frankfurter's appointment as associate justice of the Supreme Court.

CHAPTER 10 JUSTICE LOUIS D. BRANDEIS AND JUDICIAL ACTIVISM

1. The most valuable source material is to be found in the records of the Senate Judiciary Committee that held hearings on the appointment of Mr. Justice Brandeis in 1916.

2. Brandeis's work on the money trust originally appeared as a series of articles in *Harper's Weekly* (1913–14). The articles, especially those on the size of the corporate unit and on the failure of bank management, are brilliant economic analyses that have scarcely been surpassed on the literature. The title under which Brandeis published them in book form, *Other People's Money* (1914), became a catchphrase in economics and journalism.

3. See the reprint of Norman Hapgood's introduction to *Other People's Money* in Hapgood's editorial for *Harper's Weekly* entitled "Arithmetic."

4. "We are sure to have for the next generation an ever-increasing contest between those who have and those who have not." Louis D. Brandeis, *Business — A Profession*. This book is a collection of articles and occasional speeches by Mr. Brandeis.

5. The phrase was first used in *Muller v. Oregon,* 208 U.S. 412 (1908).

6. 280 U.S. 234, 266 (1930).

7. 208 U.S. 412 (1908).

8. 244 U.S. 590, 615 (1916).

9. 173 U.S. 34, 37 (1926)

10. 277 U.S. 389, 403, 410 (1928).

11. 254 U.S. 443, 479 (1920).

12. 264 U.S. 504, 517 (1923).

13. 257 U.S. 377, 413 (1921).

14. 257 U.S. 312, 357 (1921).

15. 278 U.S. 515, 528 (1928).

16. 257 U.S. 312, 357 (1921).

17. See, for example, *Gilbert v. Minnesota,* 254 U.S. 325, 338, 41 Sup. Ct. 125, 129 (1920); *Whitney v. California,* 274 U.S. 357, 373, 47 Sup. Ct. 641, 647 (1926); *Schaefer v. United States,* 251 U.S. 466, 40 Sup. Ct. 259, 264 (1919); *Pierce v. United States,* 252 U.S. 239, 273, 40 Sup. Ct. 205, 217 (1919).

18. The setting of the Sherman, Clayton, and Federal Trade Commission Acts in the history of American economic opinion is well presented in *Federal Trade Commission v. Gratz,* 253 U.S. 421, 429 (1919).

CHAPTER 12 FELIX FRANKFURTER AND THE ESSENTIAL TENSION

1. Thomas Kuhn, *The Essential Tension* (1979).

CHAPTER 13 THE MIND AND STYLE OF ROBERT H. JACKSON

1. Robert H. Jackson, *The Struggle for Judicial Supremacy* (1941).
2. 295 U.S. 555 (1935).
3. 295 U.S. 602 (1935).
4. 298 U.S. 1 (1936).
5. 298 U.S. 238 (1936). For an extended discussion, see Hamilton and Adair, *The Power to Govern* (1937).
6. 298 U.S. 587 (1936).
7. 300 U.S. 379 (1937).
8. 301 U.S. 1 (1937).
9. 301 U.S. 49 (1937).
10. 301 U.S. 58 (1937).
11. 301 U.S. 103 (1937).

CHAPTER 14 WILLIAM O. DOUGLAS: TRUE MILITANT

1. First published in 1937; reprinted in Max Lerner's *Ideas for the Ice Age* (1939), 267–274.
2. 381 U.S. 479 (1965).

CHAPTER 15 THE VINSON REGIME, CAUGHT IN MIDPASSAGE

1. 341 U.S. 494 (1951).
2. "The question in every case is whether the words used are used in such circumstances and are of such a nature as to create a clear and present danger that they will bring about the substantive evils that [the state] has a right to prevent." *Schenck v. United States*, 249 U.S. 47 (1919). In *Gitlow v. New York*, 268 U.S. 652 (1925) — Holmes and Brandeis dissenting — and in *Whitney v. California*, 274 U.S. 357 (1927) — Brandeis concurring — the doctrine was clarified.
3. 330 U.S. 1. Decided February 10, 1947.
4. 268 U.S. 510 (1925).
5. In the next important case involving education and the separation of church and state — *McCollum v. Illinois*, 92 L. Ed. 451 (decided on March 8, 1948) — the Court majority (including Justice Black) dealt a blow to the "released time" program when it is an integral part of the school program.
6. "Released time" refers to programs in which students were released for a period of time so that they could receive religious instruction away from school property.

CHAPTER 16 THE CAREER OF THE WARREN COURT

1. *Brown v. Board of Education,* 347 U.S. 483 (1954); "Brown I."
2. *Brown v. Board of Education of Topeka,* 349 U.S. 294 (1955); "Brown II."
3. 212 U.S. 78 (1909).
4. 287 U.S. 378 (1932).
5. *Colgrove v. Green,* 328 U.S. 549 (1946).

EPILOGUE: OLIVER WENDELL HOLMES REVISITED

1. Max Lerner, *The Mind and Faith of Justice Holmes* (1943). This essay was written as a preface to the edition published in 1989.